EUROPE TRANSFORMED

Norman Stone

EUROPE
TRANSFORMED
1878–1919

Harvard University Press
Cambridge, Massachusetts
1984

Library of Congress Cataloging in Publication Data

Stone, Norman.
    Europe transformed, 1878–1919.

    Bibliography: p.
    Includes index.
    1. Europe—History—1871–1918. I. Title.
D395.S77 1984   940.2′8   83-22830
ISBN 0-674-26922-5
ISBN 0-674-26923-3 (pbk.)

In memory of Jack Gallagher

CONTENTS

INTRODUCTION

'The lamps are going out all over Europe; we shall not see them lit again in our lifetime.' This, one of the most famous comments in European history, was said by the British foreign secretary, Sir Edward Grey, as he watched the lights of Whitehall gradually being extinguished on the evening when, in 1914, Great Britain and Germany went to war. At the time, not many people shared Grey's opinion of what was happening. They thought that it was war 'for civilization'; throughout Europe, men rushed to the barracks, and cities exploded in patriotic euphoria. It was only after four years of slaughter, after Bolshevism in Russia, after the rise of Fascism, after the disintegration of the European economy in the Slump, that people appreciated what Grey had meant. The pre-war world became invested with a golden glow: 'The Proud Tower', as Barbara Tuchman called her book on it.

The forty years before 1914 were a period of extraordinary peace and prosperity. By 1914, although the population had risen very considerably, most people were fed, housed and generally looked after far better than before. Education progressed, to the point of virtually universal literacy in most countries – indeed, it may even be the case that there was less illiteracy in England in 1914 than there is nowadays. People were brought up on the Bible and the national classics; they expressed themselves with vigour; standards of parliamentary debate were so high that in Berlin in the 1890s there was even a black market for tickets to the public galleries of the *Reichstag*. In Europe, outside the Balkans, there were no wars after 1871; and European civilization swept over the globe. This world came to a dramatic end in 1914, when the lights went out.

In 1934, George Dangerfield wrote a classic book, *The Strange Death of Liberal England*. In it, he argued that British liberalism, though it had many fine qualities, was under mortal threat from several quarters – especially socialism: its days were over, whether war had broken out or not. This thesis has not been very popular among British historians. One point of my book is to show that what Dangerfield said of Great Britain can be applied, almost without qualification, to the countries of the continent. Before the First World War, parliamentary government was in crisis almost everywhere. It had been closed down in Austria; it barely functioned in Russia and Hungary; in the Third Republic there was a dizzying turnover of governments after 1910; Germany and Italy displayed the precursors of Fascism.

The era from 1878 to 1914 is one of great complication. Parliamentary government had been established almost everywhere, so that the political record becomes complex – endless elections, parties, political manoeuvres. Economic and social changes came thick and fast; populations doubled and trebled; there were deep alterations in the family, in education and in attitudes to religion. With six European Great Powers laying down the law in the world at large, international affairs also became extremely complex; and the war in which it all ended was so vast that the French official history justifiably contained over fifty large volumes, while the Powers' publications about their diplomatic dealings before the war ran to well over a thousand.

Still, though the period is very complicated, the political record in European countries can be simplified quite easily. Very often, political manoeuvres which held national audiences' attentions were being paralleled in other countries. The years of political confusion in London after 1911 are an obvious case in point. Equally, around the year 1905, there were upheavals virtually everywhere which allow me to describe it all as 'the ghost of 1848'. In the 1890s, there were confusedly left-inclined governments in most places in the early part of the decade, and forthrightly imperialist ones in the later part.

In the 1880s, the political record in most countries is
extremely difficult to follow. Socialists were emerging; a new
mass-conservatism appeared; and liberalism divided between radical and classical varieties, each of which, in turn,
also divided. This process was sometimes complicated by the
emergence of political Catholicism or minority nationalism.
For the continental historian, English politics in the 1880s
are bewildering, because of the splits and reversals of alliance
that occurred. But confusions in London had counterparts
elsewhere – in the France of Boulanger, or in Bismarck's
Germany where the *Reichstag* twisted and turned in its
attitudes to colonies or the army, and where electoral changes
were quite dramatic. An Italian prime minister, Agostino
Depretis, put his finger on this process when he remarked,
early in the decade, that 'enemies will be transformed into
friends'. *Trasformismo* – the desertion of liberals to the right
– became a dirty word in Italian affairs. But it applies quite
well to other European countries, and so can serve as the title
of this book.

To display the common European dimension, I have used
the first two sections of this book to explore common
European themes and to establish a political and international chronology. However, this does not do justice to the
individual character of European countries, and in the third
(and longest) section, I have discussed the five Great Powers
– in essay, rather than narrative, form. A further section
discusses 'war and revolution', and a final one the cultural
developments of the period.

In writing this book, I have incurred many debts of
gratitude: to Mr Richard Ollard, my editor, for his endless
patience and helpfulness; to Sir J.H. Plumb, for his
encouragement; to Mr Toby Abse, Professor Richard Cobb,
Dr Harold James, Mr Daniel Johnson, Dr Dominic Lieven,
Mr Andrew MacDonald and Dr Ian McPherson for reading
all or parts of the manuscript; to Mr Steven Beller, Mr
Orlando Figes and Dr Alistair Reid for applying a brake on
matters of technology and of cultural history; to Mr Jonathan

Hill, for help with the bibliography; to Dr Anil Seal, for teaching me the principles of Christian democracy; to Lord Russell of Liverpool, for helping me through bad patches; to my mother, Mary Stone, for her generous hospitality while an early version of the manuscript was being composed; and to Christine Stone, for being. Finally, in the context of a book the origins of which go back so far into my past, I remember with gratitude my own teachers – especially Mr B.G. Aston, Mr Colin Bayne-Jardine and Mr George Preston, who encouraged what must have been a tiresome obsession with the Habsburgs, and Mr Christopher Varley, who gave me, and many others, a capacity to approach languages that has stood me in good stead ever since.

Norman Stone
Trinity College, Cambridge
December 1982

I

THE END OF 'MORAL ORDER'

1. Metropolis

From 1870 to 1900, Europe changed at a faster rate than ever before or, arguably, since. In 1870, most Europeans lived in the countryside, obeying their pastors, priests or land-owners. Most of them did not bother with politics. Most were illiterate. Most could look forward only to a life of extreme harshness, which could easily end in an early death from disease or famine. In the cities, the death-rate exceeded the birth-rate and towns kept up their populations only by importing people. In Berlin of the 1860s, or St Petersburg of the 1880s, two-thirds of the adult male population had been born outside the city.

There was a huge gulf between the west-end world of the well-off, and the east-end world of the poor: the uncounted armies of unemployed casual labour, of servants-of-servants, of seamstresses crammed seven to a room. In the St Petersburg of Dostoyevsky's *Crime and Punishment*, cholera was a regular visitor. It was brought in the city's canals, which were filled with sewage and rubbish of all kinds. Large notices were put up warning people not to drink the water, but they were often ignored by illiterate working men, who would dip greasy caps into the water to slake their thirst. Even in the central, government districts of St Petersburg the death-rate was higher than elsewhere in Europe. In the better-off countries there was some provision for the welfare of the people, whether through the Church or through institutions such as the English Poor Law which, although it condemned recipients of charity to wear pauper dress or to be buried in pauper graves, at least kept body and soul together. Elsewhere, people relied on their families or on the priests. As cities grew, the resources of both became swamped.

But by 1900 this Europe had been transformed. There was a great flight from the land: millions of people emigrated or went to the towns. Twenty-five million Europeans reached the United States in the last quarter of the century, and millions went to other countries overseas. The countryside rapidly became more modern. Lack of labour forced wages up, and everywhere peasant cottages became better constructed, equipped with furniture similar to that of the towns – wooden chests and benches being replaced with cupboards and chairs. But it was the cities that were most transformed.

By 1900 horse-drawn traffic, the rule almost everywhere in 1870, had been supplemented by city railways and subways – the Berlin *Stadtbahn*, the London 'tube' or the Paris *métro* (1901) which, being rather late by British standards, could benefit from more modern technologies that allowed the tunnels to be shallower. Elsewhere, electric traction permitted trams and trolleys to proliferate in the 1890s. This easy and cheap transport allowed the more modern cities – London above all – to develop suburbs.

There was an explosion of printed matter. New printing techniques, cheap timber and a huge new reading public caused the four *journaux d'information* of Paris in the 1860s to develop into seventy daily newspapers a generation later. Proud provincial cities, like Manchester, Glasgow or Lyons, could count on selling their chief newspaper quite easily in the capital city. Education developed as fast as the press. Books and libraries proliferated, and working-class organizations took a pride in building up their own learned collections, to show that they were as good as their 'betters'.

One spectacular discovery or invention succeeded another. Medicine improved almost beyond recognition. In earlier times, most people died if they underwent an operation – not, usually, from a cause any more complicated than the simple shock of the pain. Now, hospitals became hygienic; people survived, rather than died, in them; and death-rates were cut in half in most countries. There seemed to be no end to this process of improvement. In 1895 the novelist Henry James acquired electric lighting; in 1896 he rode a bicycle; in 1897 he wrote on a typewriter; in 1898 he saw a cinematograph. Within very few years, he could have had a Freudian analysis, travelled in an aircraft, understood the principles of the jet-engine or even of space-travel. The great cities had already embarked on clearances of their own worst areas, the 'slums' – an English word which, like many others (strike, meeting, weekend, football) passed into almost every other language because the British had been first off the mark when it came to discovering the new age. The years from 1870 to 1900 were the classic age of Progress, a time when the history of the world appeared to be as H.G.Wells was later to see it in his *History*: a matter of enlightened people using science to promote the cause of 'Up and Up and Up and On and On and On' (in the expression of Ramsay MacDonald, a characteristic pre-war progress-ive).

2.　The Liberal Revolution

The prosperity of the later nineteenth century owed its origin to liberalism. In the later 1850s and in the 1860s, all countries in Europe had taken up reform of their institutions. In many places, these reforms added up to a destruction of the old order. Of course, liberalism had precursors in the eighteenth century, and Great Britain had clearly become a liberal country in the first half of the nineteenth century. It was the success of Great Britain, in contrast to the poverty and unruliness of the continent, that inspired many continental

Europeans to want to imitate the British example. In the 1860s, liberalism came into its own.

On the ground, it varied from place to place, since concessions had to be made to the old order. But its essentials were clear enough. Liberalism meant Reason. It believed in centrally run nation states, and created them in Belgium, Germany and Italy. Education was a key factor. Liberalism, a descendant partly of the ideas of Natural Law, and partly of utilitarianism, had to do with the morally responsible individual. In the *ancien régime*, status and privilege had reigned. Liberals objected; they felt that it was best for the whole of society if people of energy and competence could be allowed to rise to their proper level. Education was therefore a paramount consideration, and in all countries there were battles to improve the school system. Often, that meant a struggle with the Church, which controlled most of education in Europe.

In economic affairs, liberals had a clear-cut attitude. The *ancien régime* had often imposed barriers to trade, because inefficient producers in one region could be protected from more efficient ones elsewhere. The State also took money in the form of tariffs to raise the prices of imported – and often, better or cheaper – goods. The institution of serfdom, which still existed in Russia until 1861, and – in effect, though not in law – elsewhere until 1848, was particularly repugnant to the liberal mind, whereas in the *ancien-régime* view it was a precondition of civilization, since it forced peasants to stay and cultivate land. Liberals wished labour to be free to be bought or sold according to circumstances, not pinned to a particular place. They were sometimes bitterly opposed to State legislation that interfered between master and man. The British Factory Acts, for instance, were promoted by Tories, not Liberals; although in practice many liberals had a large share in the promotion of private charity.

In the 1860s, the old order, everywhere, mended its ways. Education was promoted. Trade was made much easier. Central banks were established to govern the currency on lines of probity, different from the days of paper-printing and coin-clipping of the *ancien régime*. Tariffs were abolished, where possible, and otherwise were greatly reduced: Napoleon III's France and tsarist Russia, the two most protectionist states in Europe, promised to abolish their tariffs some day soon. Bureaucracies everywhere were made more rational. In England, for instance, under the first Gladstone government (1868) the civil service was opened to competitive examination, and the purchasing of officers' commissions was ended. Military reform came about in most countries. To the liberal mind, armies were not desirable. But, since they existed, they might as well be used for educational functions. The principle of universal liability to military conscription was asserted in Austria in 1868, and in Russia in 1874: now, men were taken into the army for five years and then released, to be called back only in wartime. In the old days, a very limited number of men would have served for twenty-five years. Now, far greater numbers of men could be taken in, trained and educated, and given some idea of the national community of which they formed a part. Ukrainian soldiers in Russia were taught Russian in the army. In southern Italy, conscription was a device by which southerners, who frequently did not feel themselves to be at all Italian, would gain national consciousness. In France, the army was strictly used as an agent of 'Jacobin centralism', to eliminate the *patois*, such as Breton or Provençal, which were still widely spoken. Often, generals were consciously liberal: Dmitri Milyutin, the reforming war minister of Tsar Alexander II in the 1860s and 1870s; the Spanish general Prim, son of a chemist; Kameke, of the Prussian war ministry. They believed in centralization, efficiency, education: not in class privilege and clericalism.

The impetus towards these reforms had been the success of Great Britain and the failure of most of the continental countries in the middle of the century. In 1856, Russia had been humiliated in the Crimean War's outcome. Austria had been defeated in 1859 by the French and the Piedmontese, who established the kingdom of Italy in 1861. Prussia had been humiliated in 1850 by the Austrians. In the 1850s, most countries experienced financial confusion, and needed serious reforms and considerable loans to make good. But the financiers would not give money unless there were reforms. One of these was that the running of the State should be entrusted, not to a court and its hangers-on, but to experts, with the backing of law. The liberals everywhere believed that there must be proper constitutions, parliaments elected by men of economic weight and of education. They would pass laws, binding equally upon all members of the community: no privilege. In general, the liberals were not in favour of granting the vote to the mass of the people. The masses, ignorant, prejudiced and selfish, would use their vote either for revolutionaries who wanted to take away the money of the rich, or for landowners and priests who knew how to corrupt and lead the masses. The liberals had their way in most countries in the 1860s: parliaments came into existence in Austria, Hungary, Italy and, in 1871, the new Germany. In Russia, Alexander II instituted liberal reforms – abolition of serfdom (1861), a State Bank (1859), elected county councils (1864), universal conscription (1874) etc. – but he felt that Russia was so vast and backward that an elected central parliament would simply be a chaotic affair; he resisted all appeals for the creation of one.

Russia lacked the liberal element that was responsible, elsewhere, for pushing through the reforms: a large, educated, energetic middle class with enough money for its support to be essential to any state that wished to develop. In Great Britain, that class existed so strongly, even in the eighteenth century, that liberal reforms were introduced piecemeal there, and often without formal involvement of parliament. Existing *ancien-régime* institutions, such as the old guilds or corporations, would be gradually adapted to suit a changing era. Thus, in form, England (more than Scotland) is the last of the *anciens régimes*; she did not even have a formal law to abolish serfdom. Religious institutions, such as the colleges of Oxford and Cambridge, were simply turned into secular places of education, together with their ancient constitutions and bizarrely named officers, whereas on the continent religious colleges had been formally abolished either by the Enlightenment or by the French revolution. The colleges of the old Catholic University at Louvain were used as stables by the French occupants, and when the University was reconstituted, it was the central body which ran things, not the colleges, which became simple halls of residence. In France, to some degree, local liberalism also made headway, but in most of the other countries, the degree of development had not permitted this, and, in the 1860s, states, short of money, had to follow the British example by formal legislation.

The liberals – Cavour in Italy, Delbrück in Germany, Schmerling in Austria, Valuyev in Russia – were confident that they held the formula for future prosperity. They could not understand the vehemence of the opposition to them. But liberalism had many enemies. In the 1860s and, generally, the early 1870s, there was a great boom in Europe. Liberalism was widely accepted, and the opposition to it was muffled – except in the case of the Pope's decree of Infallibility. But in 1873, and in later years, the prosperity which liberalism promised was interrupted for many people in Europe, and the enemies of liberalism came into their own. In 1870 the Belgian classical liberals lost office. In 1873–4 the first Gladstone ministry collapsed, and Gladstone resigned his party leadership (to resume it later on). In 1876 the Italian classical liberals, the *Destra*, fell. In 1878, the Austrian liberals, of the Auersperg ministry, lost power; in that year, too, Bismarck in Germany abandoned his alliance with the liberals; and then, too, Tsar Alexander II began to dismantle some of his earlier legislation, to turn Russia towards a police-state with tariffs. In France, the classical liberals who – for reasons peculiar to France, though not lacking parallels in Spain – had been unable to discover a suitable constitutional monarchy, and were therefore unwillingly republican, lost control in 1876, and especially in 1879. These classical liberal régimes were followed by various groups: in Great Britain, Disraelian conservatism; in France, first by clerical exponents of 'moral order' and then by radical republicans;

in Belgium by clericals; in Italy by 'transformist' radicals; in Russia and Prussia by reactionary conservatives; in Austria by clericals who, for all their conservatism, also had a tinge of radicalism. It was a sign of how varied the opposition to liberalism could be.

3.   The 'Great Depression'

In the last third of the nineteenth century, Europeans became much richer than ever before: the liberal, or capitalist, revolution had done its work. It is curious that this era should be known to historians as the 'Great Depression' – an expression that was of British origin, since a Royal Commission was established in 1882 to examine the causes of the decline ('depression') of prices, profits, exports which also brought about unemployment. In reality, apart from a few bad moments (1879–83, 1891–5), these years were ones of remarkable development in the towns. The 'Depression' affected some quite distinct social groups, who became loud in complaint at the economic liberalism that had caused such troubles.

In the 1880s, aristocracies everywhere were in decline. By the early 1890s, they were often hysterical in their complaints. Agriculture had ceased to supply an income on which they could satisfactorily survive. In the two decades up to 1896, the middling and lesser aristocracy sold up more and more, although great estates did survive quite well. After 1896, as costs rose, even the large estates declined in size and relative weight. Where possible, noble families made more of their urban property (here the English aristocracy supply spectacular instances, as with the Grosvenor Estate in Westminster, or the Stanleys [Derby] in Lancashire). Many aristocrats married into new urban money, often American: the French Marquis Boni de Castellane married Anna Gould who had a dowry of £3,000,000 from her family's heavy-industrial and railway money; the Duke of Marlborough married Consuelo Vanderbilt; the Hungarian Count Széchenyi married her cousin; Gladstone's ally, Rosebery, married a Rothschild and acquired the extraordinary house and collections of Mentmore. But in most cases, the nobility were going gradually, and not so gradually, to the wall at this time. The background to Chekhov's plays is an erosion of noble landowning in Russia. By the early 1890s, over 14,000 estates had been mortgaged; only in 2800 were there no arrears in payment; and from 1891 to 1895, on annual average, the creditors moved in to effect a forced sale (foreclosure) in $7\frac{1}{2}$ per cent of the nobles' estates. Some of the greatest families in Europe abandoned their town palaces. The Lieven Palace on Morskaya in St Petersburg, close to the Winter Palace itself, was rented out to the Italian government; the Hôtel de Talleyrand in the rue Saint Florentin was taken over by the Rothschilds; the Stolberg Palace in Berlin, which belonged to the only family of imperial counts with the right to be addressed with the sovereign title *Durchlaucht* (inaccurately translated as 'Serene Highness'), was sold up to pay gambling debts, and became the Hotel Adlon, the grandest in Berlin. In France, by 1900, thirty *départements* lost virtually all of their noble landowners; and in most countries men of gentry origin found that they needed to make money somehow or other to compensate.

Not surprisingly, there was an expansion of the gentry element in armies. In this, there was a clash between old liberal war ministries and class-minded gentry conservatives. Quarrels over appointments to important and not-so-important posts caused trouble within the Prussian military establishment in 1883–4, and again in 1896–7 as the reactionary chiefs of the emperor's military office (which ran appointments) clashed with the liberals of the war ministry. In Russia, the liberal General Milyutin experienced strong opposition from conservatives like Vannovski, who succeeded him in 1881. In France, a conspiracy of aristocratic officers against the Jewish outsider, Captain Alfred Dreyfus, brought the most famous scandal in French history in the

later 1890s. In most European Great Powers in the early
1880s, and still more in the later 1890s, there was a great
burst of imperialism and conquest. How much did this have
to do with gentry officers' search for ways to make up abroad
for what they were losing at home?

But it was not only the landed nobility which complained.
In the comfortably-off middle class, there were also
grumbles. It was common for many people in that class to
invest in government bonds – the French *rente*, the British
'funds' – or in safe 'blue-chip' company shares. Now, for
reasons that no one understood, rates of profit seemed to be
falling, and rates of interest with them. Rentiers, who, as the
bonne bourgeoisie of French provincial towns, had achieved
a life's ambition to do nothing, fell under pressure. In the
1880s and, still more, the 1890s, they deserted the small
country towns for larger places, and they declined in
numbers. Dividends of the Austrian metal and textile
companies did not exceed three per cent in the years of the
'Great Depression'. In 1887 the Poet Laureate, Alfred Lord
Tennyson, spelt, in his *Locksley Hall Sixty Years After*, an
elegy for the rentier world, of Hierarchy, Religion, Progress,
as it was displaced by the new world of the 'democratic' age
in the 1880s.

The chief reason for these social shifts was that the agrarian
base of Europe was being eroded. Before 1870, Europe was
overwhelmingly agricultural, although she had also a few
historic centres of manufacturing – northern Italy, Flanders,
Bohemia, Franconia – and although there were some quite
highly industrialized countries, especially Great Britain,
Belgium and Prussia. Until 1870, broadly speaking, the
advantage in economic life lay with agriculture. The 'terms
of trade', that is, the quantity of manufactured goods needed
to buy a given number of agricultural commodities, tended
to favour the farmer. In the 1840s there had been a great
crisis. Artisans had competed with each other and driven
down the prices of their goods; that had coincided with a
financial crisis and some bad harvests; and the result had
been misery in the towns, which eventually produced the

European revolutions of 1848. Matters had improved in the 1850s and 1860s with the 'liberal revolution', although food prices had tended to rise rather faster than industrial ones.

In the 1870s, this picture changed dramatically, more or less as Marx had foretold. Usually, farmers had done better than manufacturers. But now, after 1873, the terms of trade shifted for several decades against agriculture and against commodities in general. Now, it was raw material and food prices that fell relative to manufacturing prices; and, with some interruptions and exceptions (such as oil), that process has been going on until the present day. The 'Great Depression' was a (rather misleading) name for the first part of this process.

Grain supplies the best and most important instance. In the 1860s and 1870s, the great plains of North America, the Argentine, Australia, Russia and, later, Romania and Hungary were opened up to exploitation and large-scale export of grain. The amount of grain marketed in western Europe doubled in the 1850s and quintupled up to the end of the century. Railways accounted for much of this, for they linked the American centre with the east-coast ports; and, with the proliferation of railways, costs fell – from 33 cents per bushel from Chicago to New York in 1874, to 14 cents in 1881. Then again, shipping made progress, especially when the Parsons steam turbine was introduced, to make better use of coal. In the old days, sailing ships had needed large crews; shipping firms would sometimes try to cut their costs by overloading ships (a murderous practice which led to the introduction of the 'Plimsoll Line' in the 1870s). Now, ships needed smaller crews and less coal, and costs declined accordingly. In 1874, it cost 20 cents per bushel of grain from New York to Liverpool, but in 1881, only 2 cents. Finally, the introduction of refrigeration ships (a process invented by a Frenchman but developed by an American, Birdseye) allowed similar exports of meat. It cost 200 francs to ship a ton of goods from Marseilles to Hong Kong in 1875, but only 70 francs in 1906: i.e., seven months of a skilled artisan's salary in 1875, but only two months' salary in 1906. Into all

European countries, grain came from overseas. Even in Italy, which was poor, grain imports amounted to 1,500,000 quintals in 1880 and 10,000,000 in 1887. In turn, grain prices fell, and fodder for horses thus also cost less. That process further assisted the fall of transport costs within cities. In St Petersburg, the transport authorities were able to reduce the cost of a journey by horse-tram from 10 kopecks in the 1860s to 4 in the early 1880s.

Food prices everywhere fell. European producers of grain, meat and vegetables were competing with each other, and doubled their output in the middle decades of the century. The presence of overseas competition in meat and grain was such that the producers had to reduce their prices still more. In London, a standard loaf of bread (4lbs 5¼oz) cost 1/5½d in 1873, but only 4½d in 1905. In Italy, maize, which was part of the standard peasant diet, *polenta*, fell from 22.41 lire to 13.41 between 1876 and 1880. Spelt, the main winter crop of Württemberg, cost 20.68 marks per 100 kg in 1854, but that figure was last attained in 1872, and after 1882 it was only in two years that the price rose above 15 marks; in 1894, the price was 11 marks. Romanian wheat, bought at Brăila, cost 305 lei per ton in the early 1870s, but only 175 in the early 1890s; in Russia the average price of all grain moved down from 80 kopecks per pood (just over 16 kg) in 1881 to 67 in 1885, 53 in 1887 and 42 in 1894.

Such figures could be reproduced for virtually every other commodity – Brazilian coffee, Malayan rubber, Peruvian guano, Chilean copper, Swedish iron-ore, dairy-produce and wine. One reason for the extensive campaign against drink which went on in most European countries at this time was that spirits (from grain or malt) and wine were costing less. In the 1880s, Italy trebled her output of wine, but the return on it actually declined, from 28,300,000 lire to 25,900,000 from 1879 to 1886. In Russia, vodka-drinking became something of an epidemic; spirit was turned into a State monopoly. As transport improved, cheap coal could reach areas where it had not been known before, undercutting the price of local coal. By the end of the 1880s, coalminers, who in earlier times had counted among the best paid workers (and who were often conservative in their political attitudes), began to form unions and to revolt. There were miners' strikes in Great Britain, the Ruhr and northern France at the turn of the 1880s and 1890s. With the decline of agricultural prices, small peasant proprietors and wage-labourers sometimes also revolted – a factor that underlay the agrarian troubles of Ireland and Russia in the later 1870s and early 1880s, and in central Italy in the middle of the decade.

The villages began to empty, partly because the younger peasants abandoned agriculture, partly because the village artisans – wheelwrights, leather-workers (tanners), brewers, coopers, smiths, who have left their trace in the commonest surnames throughout Europe – could not or would not compete with cheaper goods coming from towns, and suffered from the decline of agricultural prices which had guaranteed them a market. In the Austrian province of Oberösterreich, the number of nailsmiths fell from 299 to 67 in the years 1870–90. The brewers of Württemberg complained because 'vending machines' were installed at station platforms so that travellers could get cheap beer instead of going to the nearest inn. In Münster, the number of brewers fell by almost a quarter in these years. In Germany, especially, these independent artisans – the *Mittelstand*, situated between aristocracy and peasantry in *ancien-régime* days – produced a litany of grievances that lent decisive shape to German politics right up to the 1930s, when many of its members were enthusiastic Nazis.

It was of course possible for an agile man to survive in these conditions, provided that he worked out a suitable balance of labour, machinery, interest-rates and marketing. But it meant – as the liberal economists had expected – very hard work. The bulk of the European gentry could not respond accordingly. Their expectations were too high. Truly large estates could have the benefit of capital reserves and skilled advice, but smaller ones had neither and their owners sold up, usually to townspeople who could afford to subsidize the land and who wished to own a manor house: people such as the Berlin Oppenheims who bought a Pomeranian estate and became 'Oppenheim zu Rheinfeld' in the 1880s. In France, the value of land fell by one quarter between 1880 and 1890; in Loir-et-Cher, rents fell by fifty-five per cent between 1875 and 1902. Sometimes, gentry land would be taken over by hopeful peasants, such as the Scottish (Fife) families who invaded East Anglia in the 1880s and 1890s. But the process of agrarian decline affected peasants as well, because the price-fall went on with only brief interruptions between 1873 and 1895. Liberal economists had wished farmers to take an enlightened view of credit, to stop their barbarous habit of putting money in a sock, to invest it in a co-operative or rural savings bank (such as the Raiffeisen credit associations which were a success story in Germany). But that was not always successful. In Austria, mortgaging in agriculture did rise by sixty per cent between 1867 and 1892, but there were 73,777 foreclosures in Bohemia, 34,118 in Moravia, and 28,742 in the province of Niederösterreich merely in the years 1888–94. In such conditions, millions and millions of people left the land, whether for the United States or for the nearest large city. Ireland's population fell to little more than half between 1830 and the end of the century. The rural population of England and Scotland was eight per cent of the whole by 1900. German conservatives were loud in complaint at the 'flight from the land' in the 1890s. The French agrarian statesman, Jacques Méline, referred to *le désert français*.

But emigration from the land was not simply, or even mainly, a matter of compulsion. The fact was that the towns were becoming hugely prosperous in comparison with the past. The fall of food prices affected the countryside badly. But, as liberal economists had foretold, it greatly benefited anyone who bought, rather than sold, food – i.e., townspeople. Given that food prices fell by forty-five per cent in the last third of the century, townspeople were that much better off; and, since raw materials fell generally in price, manufacturers could also reduce their prices, so that townspeople benefited there, too.

There are important qualifications to be made. In the first

place, in some countries the share of agriculture was so great in the economy generally that a decline in its prosperity would mean that it bought less from the towns, and so dragged them down. This was by and large the case in Italy, much of France, Russia, Austria-Hungary and, especially, Spain in the 1880s. Their economies tended to stagnate: 1881 was the leanest year in the Italian kingdom's history, when income per capita was at its lowest point. These countries found that the only way ahead was for the State to take action, to build up an economic base in transport or heavy industry, and not simply to rely on industrial entrepreneurs who, without State help, would be unable to move because of the country's poverty, or, in France, industrial backwardness. French radical liberals produced the *Plan Freycinet*; Alexander III's finance ministers, Bunge and Vyshnegradski, and the Italian finance minister Magliani promoted tariffs to protect State-led heavy industries, the bulk of whose market lay in railways or shipping or armaments. In stagnating agrarian regions, such as Ireland or Croatia, there were often nationalists who could see their way out of stagnation only in an independent government that would take a similar view of economic problems. In Italy, this showering of State money in the era of Agostino Depretis produced both a spate of hideously ornate buildings and a continual financial difficulty. Paris was spared both because the plan was cut back by an austere finance minister, Léon Say, in 1883. This had immediately adverse consequences, although it left the French economy healthy enough to make considerable progress after 1895.

In countries which had already developed industry – Great Britain, Germany, Belgium and parts of several other countries – and which could take great imports of food and raw materials, the 'Great Depression' was a time of continuing prosperity. Townspeople simply bought more and more as they became better off and as they benefited from price-falls. In the first place, population could expand. Even although there were many Malthusian complaints, the fact was that increased numbers of people could now be fed, and in all countries except France the period from 1870 to 1914 was a time of vastly expanding populations. Germany rose from 35,000,000 to over 60,000,000, Great Britain from 25,000,000 to 40,000,000, Austria-Hungary from 35,000,000 to 55,000,000, Italy from 26,000,000 to 40,000,000, Russia from 60,000,000 to 140,000,000 (in Europe). Birth-rates ran at around 40 per 1000 in the 1870s; death-rates, with medical improvements, fell from 30 per 1000 to under 20 per 1000 in the better-off countries. It was not until the 1920s that population figures became stable once more, or even declined.

It was, as the cliché has it, an age of the masses, of which the 1880s marked the inauguration. In 1800, no city had contained more than a million people, and very few had even contained 100,000. A century later, there were nine cities with over a million inhabitants, and soon afterwards Barcelona, Madrid, Warsaw, Brussels, Birmingham and Budapest joined the list. Cities like Sheffield and Düsseldorf shot ahead from being small places to cities with over 500,000 inhabitants. The agricultural share of the population declined in most countries, though numbers often did not: Germany, which had been three-quarters agrarian in 1870, was only two-fifths agrarian in 1914, and it was commonly thought that Metropolis was being erected on the deserted village.

The better-off parts of these cities were sometimes very grand indeed: Leeds, Manchester and especially the west-end district of Glasgow, which was planned and executed with distinction – and which, happily, has mainly survived the grotesqueries of urban destruction that marked the 1960s – had their counterparts in Europe, although usually on a much less imposing scale, except perhaps in Berlin where the architecture was, however, only distinguished by its bulk. Cheap transport also allowed some cities to develop their suburbs as middle-class ghettos, an art-form in which the English, with their demand for a sturdily independent home, reigned unchallenged. The 1880s were marked in England by 'villas' – stoutly built structures in a variety of historical styles, which gave place, later on, to 'bungalows' which were more like boxes, with space uselessly taken up by a 'hall' that whispered the last enchantments of the Middle Ages. In other countries, the middle classes were less independently minded. The French bourgeoisie, for instance, did not mind living in a city flat, so long as they could escape to a property in the country (*villégiature*); indeed, all over the continent, the country-house-and-town-flat existence was preferred to the English suburban home combined with holidays in hotels or boarding houses.

The expanding cities also had their poor, and middle-class consciences were increasingly stirred by this as the 1880s progressed. The armies of immigrants from the countryside had to be housed somewhere, and in all cities vast tenements arose which could house, sometimes, seven people to a room. The housing statistics of the 1880s are unimaginable. In Glasgow, it was quite common for letters to be addressed to 'Bridgegate, No. 29 back land, stair first left, three up, right lobby, door facing'. In Budapest or St Petersburg, even letter-addressing might not have been possible, for people shifted from one dreadful cellar to the next, often chased out by the winter thaws that flooded these cellars. No one really knows what such cities' populations were. The floods of migrants from the countryside supplied endless quantities of building-labour in the great cities: Irish in Liverpool or Glasgow, where they made up a third of the population; Poles in Bochum, in the Ruhr; Slovak peasants in Budapest; Bohemian or Slovene peasants in Vienna; peasants from Pskov or Vologda in St Petersburg; peasants from everywhere and anywhere in New York. The children of these immigrants, as distinct from their parents, were not likely to submit to it all.

Still, the 1880s were a wonderful decade for anyone who could describe himself as professional-middle-class. A twenty-year-old journalist, W.T. Stead, working on a small provincial newspaper, the *Northern Echo*, could earn £150 per annum or double the rate for a skilled artisan, in 1870. In two years, he was earning £250. A headmaster in Scotland could earn £700, slightly more than a university professor; an assistant teacher, with £81, earned more than the upper sections of the working class. Middle-class people could easily buy property, at a time when a six-bedroom house in Darlington cost £600, a bottle of whisky 2/-, a term's school fees a guinea, the grandest house in Oxford £1500, a year's study in the highest form (*rhéto*) of the best Paris *lycée*, 450 francs (£18). In 1897, the architect Edward Lutyens designed and built 'Fulbrook' in Surrey, which was sold for £6840: not seven years of decent middle-class income in that time. The professional middle class, especially in Great Britain, but also on the continent generally, could afford large houses with half a dozen servants, private schools for the children, lavish holidays in the pompous hotels of the era, because labour was very cheap.

Underneath this *belle-époque* middle class there was a burgeoning lower middle class, purveyors of goods and services who were more and more in demand as the towns and industry and commerce grew. There was a great expansion of retailing everywhere. Cheap transport made it possible for huge shops to import masses of different goods, and refrigeration helped the storage of food, while the cost of shop-assistants remained low because of the continual migration from the land. In the 1880s, there were gigantic department stores in every capital city: a Bon Marché or Galeries Lafayette in Paris, a Harrods or Whiteleys in London, a Herzmansky or Gerngross on the Mariahilfer-strasse in Vienna, a Tietz or a Kaufhaus des Westens in Berlin; even, in Moscow, the large Muir and Merrilees, set up by two emigrant Scotsmen and now the State's *GUM* (*Gosudarstvenny universalny magazin*). These shops were built on a magnificent scale, with interiors like film-sets (as was the case with the hotels); it was from them that Samuel Butler, writing *Erewhon* towards the end of the century, drew his notion of 'musical banks' in which commercial transactions would be carried out to the strains of palm-court orchestras. At the heart of the calculations behind these huge shops was the reflection that profits might be lessened provided that turnover was expanded. But even without these huge shops, retailing was advancing as the towns grew and became more prosperous. The French began to develop their mania for chemists' shops. In Germany, from 1882 to 1895, the number of tobacconists grew by 53.7 per cent as tobacco fell in price and smoking became a more widespread habit. In Rostock, there were only three pharmacies in 1875, but there were seventeen twenty years later, for idle continental middle-class women often suffered from hypochondria, and in France the liver was a conversational topic almost as frequently used as the weather in England.

The decade also saw a vast expansion of the printed word. Timber fell in price. There were improvements in printing techniques. There was an expanding market as education affected more and more people. Able marketers began to appreciate the value of advertisement. In the old days, the press had been pompous, given over to lengthy discussion of parliamentary debates and, very frequently, to learned consideration of religious matters. The Americans showed the way towards a more vulgar, easily comprehensible press, and the British, with other Europeans, soon followed. By 1896, the *Daily Mail*, the best-known English newspaper of this kind, could cut its price in half, to ½d. Paris had seventy daily newspapers in 1914, including *Le Petit Journal*, a 'tabloid' (of forty-four centimetres by thirty) which could be read by a clerk sitting in a row of other clerks in a jostling carriage or trolley. It serialized Jules Verne, and the journalists were often rich men. In Austria in 1873 there had been 866 newspapers and periodicals of which 590 were in German and of which 35 covered mathematical and scientific subjects, and 22 literary or historical matter. By 1891, there were 1801 such publications of which 1171 were in German and of which 103 covered scientific, and 90 literary questions. By 1914, the figure had reached 3000.

As education went ahead, people wrote more letters, and the standardization of postage turned any country's ministry of posts and telegraphs into big business – especially in appointments, which became the target of political 'machines'. Cheaper posts also fostered the press, which in turn gave the post offices considerable revenue. In Austria, in 1877, there were 4006 *Postanstalten* handling 263,000,000 pieces; in 1897, 5754 handling 920,000,000.

Liberalism had always concerned itself with education. With cheap building-labour, low interest-rates and low-cost textbooks, it was possible to build schools in the 1880s in a way unmatched before or since. By 1890, Scotland had acquired 8000 schools, France 150,000, and northern Italy 100,000 – schools which were often built to quite lavish specifications, with a classical exterior and, often enough, elaborate devices for keeping the sexes apart except at the earliest school-age, for which there would be a single staircase marked 'Mixed Infants'. Behind the pressure to secularize education in many countries, there often stood building firms and lenders of money who could look forward to considerable activity once the State determined to replace Church schools with institutions devoted to 'secular and moral instruction', of the kind proposed by the French radical liberals in the early 1880s, by the British radical liberals during the first Gladstone government, and by the liberal supporters of Bismarck's *Kulturkampf* against the Catholics in the 1870s. The outcome of this expansion was a great rise in literacy which reached near-universality in most countries, and even two-thirds in tsarist Russia by 1914. The schools were usually run in a highly formal and disciplined way; boys would be addressed by their surnames, girls as 'Miss' or sometimes also simply by their surnames; clothing was drab and severe; instruction was austerely practical; certain Protestant regions of Europe – especially Scotland and Prussia – stood out for their success-rates in producing technical graduates, both in schools and in technical colleges.

The standards of education were extremely high, and the era was strong on polymaths – men like the Moravian Ernst Mach, who moved from one scientific subject to another, and eventually to the philosophy of language, revolutionizing everything he touched. There was life even in the memoirs of statesmen. A French politician like Edouard Herriot, long-time mayor and deputy for Lyons, could speak excellent German and hold his own on Wagner and Kant; the British Liberal statesman, R.B. Haldane, was a distinguished amateur philosopher who had studied with the neo-Kantians in south-western Germany; Bismarck's memoirs belong in German literature. This was an age which read, in which a pamphlet of Gladstone's on the Papal Decrees could sell 100,000 copies in a month, and in which a book-sale of 4000 copies – a figure that, nowadays, might put a work into bestseller lists in England – would have been thought trivial. There was a great appetite for serious literature of all kinds, and this age produced scholars who could write, without condescension, for a general public, and a general public which could read learned works without mystification. Universities were conscious of being at the centre of civilization, and the years before 1914 saw them flourish – frequently on a financial shoestring. A Carnoy at the Catholic University in Louvain, in biology, or a Rutherford at Cambridge, in physics, let alone private scholars like the great French historians Albert Sorel and Louis Eisenmann, did not have much in the way of material resources; and most universities were places that displayed an often picturesque meanness, as at Louvain, where the Abbé Jansen, domestic bursar, was also employed as designing architect and building contractor for some particularly unfortunate buildings, over the construction-sites of which he would leap, in his cassock, excitedly giving out contradictory orders. The universities and the higher forms of the schools were closely linked, to the benefit of both sides. The link gave aspiring graduate academics a meaningful job, taught them something about communicating their work, and made them put it in a wider context. In France, where this system was most worked out, the country's best feature was an intellectual class that was honest, hard-working, and vertically, though not horizontally, puritanical.

After 1870, Europe acquired her armies of schoolteachers, clerks, small shopkeepers, purveyors of goods and services of all kinds: the 'tertiary sector' (as distinct from the primary, agrarian, one and the secondary, manufacturing, one) which grew in all countries in this era. By the 1880s, this huge mass was beginning to take holidays away from home. Cheap labour and food meant that hotels could flourish: in England, Blackpool was the fastest growing town, but Scarborough in Yorkshire, the holiday place for the Yorkshire bourgeoisie (especially the textile owners of Leeds or Bradford) and Troon on the Ayrshire coast, with its huge hotels and elaborate golf-courses for the bourgeoisie of Glasgow, were not far behind. In Austria, spas flourished. Karlsbad (Karlovy Vary) was an extremely smart place, attended by the Prince of Wales, by German and Austro-Hungarian generals, by the European aristocracy as a matter of course. It took 26,450 visitors in 1880 and 34,296 in 1890. Marienbad was not far behind. The presence of Emperor Franz Joseph also made the little town of Bad Ischl popular. It took in 6431 visitors in 1886 and 13,599 in 1896. There were 215 such spas (*Kurorte*) in 1886 and 248 in 1896: partly because, in multinational Austria, the development of a spa in one area had to be matched by development of another spa in its rival area. There were also great restaurants in every city to match the new demand: London's Café Royal, Romano's (in Piccadilly) or the Trocadéro had their counterparts everywhere else, especially in Paris; and a restaurant dinner could be an elaborate and not necessarily very expensive affair.

In the towns, this was a decade of *arrivistes*, of new money. The old aristocracy – and especially its poorer members – often resented this. In return, the new bourgeoisie sought, often with lamentable results, to display its power in pseudo-aristocratic ways. The 1880s were generally not a good time for architecture. A variety of historical styling developed, and buildings lurched uneasily from late Gothic to Italian Renaissance or 'Pont Street Dutch'. Skilled labour was still cheap, and architects could still indulge their clients' expectations of endless ornament – not usually with happy results, as can be seen from the Fine Arts Academies both of Vienna and Berlin. Berlin, the centre of a rapidly expanding country, was 'new' almost from top to bottom: a dynasty that, for most of the time, had been inconceivably dowdy and provincial, knocked down the best classical parts of its capital to build the *Reichstag*, the State Library, an unspeakable cathedral, and a *Siegesallee* through the town's centre which was lined with statues of tedious ancestors; a show-off bourgeoisie, putting up bombastic residences; unscrupulous speculative builders, uncontrolled in Berlin – though not elsewhere in Prussia – who themselves boasted that the only good thing about the tenements which they built was the acoustics. Brussels, hideously disfigured by pompous structures built out of loot from the Congo, was not dissimilar, although enough of the old Burgundian and Habsburg structures did survive. Paris alone escaped the building boom of the 1880s because of a regulation that prevented buildings from being too high. In this era, the regulation was slightly relaxed to allow inhabitants to add an extra mansard storey, but the city was not extensively built up. The buildings which it did acquire in this era – the Grand Palais, the Gare de Lyon etc. – were often quite distinguished by contemporary standards; and the Eiffel Tower, put up for the exhibition of 1889 as a monument to the Engineer, deserved its place in history. The French, who were more settled than any other European people, and whose population was barely expanding at all, might look forward with equanimity. In other countries, where people were wrenched from their old roots, the need was for some stability, some sense of history. This appears to have given European capital cities their extraordinary fake-medieval statuary, their ornate public buildings and, towards the end of the decade, the odd fashion for rediscovered olde worlde Christian names such as 'Cedric', 'Deirdre', 'Roswita', 'Udo' or 'Szabolcs' and other such Hungarian extravaganzas.

For aristocracies with property in towns or with coal-mines; for the bourgeoisie generally, provided it did not live from interest on bonds; for the growing army of the lower middle class in the towns; for a growing part of the better-off working class – the 'Great Depression' was an excellent time.

For most of the peasantry, most of the gentry and a good part of the high aristocracy, it was a time of increasing difficulty, since the heart of the Depression lay in food prices. Townspeople bought more because they had more to spend. The result was a huge proliferation of goods and services and technical advances. A vital element here was that the shift from agriculture to industry and the towns could be managed because the later nineteenth century was an era of monetary stability. The gold standard reigned.

It is perhaps worth considering why the two chief troughs of the Depression, in the early 1880s and especially in the early 1890s, did not produce conditions resembling the Great Slump of 1929–33: i.e., a dramatic fall in employment, of commodity prices and of manufacturing prices generally, as well as a collapse (by 1932, of two-thirds) in world trade. The most obvious difference between the earlier and later Depressions was that in the earlier ones the international monetary system held up. Money supply was a vital element.

Nineteenth-century economists were not surprised by Depression, and did not regard it as a wholly bad thing. If labour and business priced themselves out of the market, then both would collapse. If, say, farmers did not respond to overseas competition, then they too would go out of business – as so many of them did in the later nineteenth century. But for anyone not directly or indirectly involved with these bankrupt elements the results would be beneficial: they would be able to buy the same goods more cheaply and probably in the expectation of better quality. Again, this was the case in the later nineteenth century when the towns prospered. The process would be uncomfortable for a time; but then people would mend their ways. In time, the spare capital and labour would be taken up again. The bulk of the population would have more money to spend because of declining prices in the goods and services they ordinarily bought: what was known to economists as a 'margin of consumption' would come into existence, and it would be filled by new goods and services. This, again, did happen in the later nineteenth century. Food prices (and other prices) fell; people were therefore better off; and the gap was filled with a whole range of new goods and services. To put it at its crudest, people who paid only a shilling, not 1/5d, for a loaf of bread would have an extra fivepence to spend. The decline in basic prices therefore did much to stimulate bicycling, travel, hotels and the rest.

It was always possible – in theory – for the producers of basic commodities to combine, reduce their output, and thereby force prices up again. Nowadays, such restrictive practices exist to a large extent. American farmers are paid thousands of millions of dollars not to produce. The Common Market exists in order to stock commodities until prices improve: the 'wine lakes' and 'butter mountains'. In the 1930s, efforts were made to cut back production. In Great Britain there was a Milk Marketing Board which came into existence precisely to avoid marketing milk – indeed, to pour it down mineshafts. But even in well-organized countries the producers were too fragmented and disunited for such things to work, and they did not work at all at international level: in 1931/2, for instance, the Soviet Union dumped 6,000,000 tons of grain on to an already declining grain market. The grain was taken, almost literally, from the mouths of peasants, and this caused famine. The deal was done in order for Stalin to pay for foreign machinery that would launch his industrial plan. It caused havoc in the world's grain market. In the later nineteenth century, producers of commodities were even less equipped to organize a stocking or a decrease of output than they were to be in the 1930s. There were too many small producers, who went on competing with each other – producing more and more, cutting their costs to the bone and responding with venom (in Germany in the 1890s there was a rash of proto-Nazi parties). Commodity prices in these circumstances went on falling, and there was a flood of cheap labour in the towns. Commodity producers simply had to put up with this; an effort to organize world sugar production (with a conference at Brussels in 1902) was not very successful; similarly, efforts by industrial producers –

especially of steel – to organize international cartels were only partly successful. The only possible response in these conditions was for producers with political strength at home to demand tariffs, to keep the cheap goods out. This caused a great deal of political trouble in the 1880s, dividing liberals everywhere. Tariffs could do nothing about the problems of internal competition, nor were they especially effective even against foreign competition.

However, for the fall of commodity prices to benefit the consumer, it was vital that the consumer's own purchasing power should be maintained. If the money which he had to spend declined at the same rate as commodity prices, then he would have no 'margin of consumption'. His purchasing power depended ultimately on the money supply.

In the later nineteenth century, the money supply consisted to some extent of banknotes and coinage (very broadly, the 'fiduciary issue' of the Bank of England). But actual cash was only a very small part of the total money supply, i.e., the financial resources of people and businesses. Their bank accounts, only a small part of which would, at any moment, be turned into cash, were the heart of the money supply; and these accounts amounted to a set of figures in a ledger. Besides, the banks could create credit: they could, with another set of figures in a ledger, advance money to people as a loan and thereby create money or spending power. If the 'margin of consumption' were to be maintained, then bank-lending must not decline faster than prices did.

In the 1930s, money supplies virtually everywhere went into terrible confusion. Banks collapsed; in the United States, in 1932, 5000 of them closed their doors; in Germany, in 1931, 3000 were closed down by government decree. Then again, interest-rates went up – in Germany, in summer 1931, to over twenty per cent – which strongly deterred people from borrowing at all. It appears that in Germany the money supply actually fell faster than commodity prices had done. There was no 'margin of consumption'. Accordingly, the German Slump went on getting worse and worse, to the point where Hitler came to power. World trade fell by two-thirds, and employment fell accordingly. In many European countries, especially in the east – and the Soviet Union, here, is not to be excepted – the uneasy stability of the 1920s degenerated into political nightmare.

Yet, in the later nineteenth century, the 'margin of consumption' not only pulled countries out of depression; it made them richer than ever before. Money supplies held up everywhere, although there were troughs of serious decline at certain stages in the process. Interest-rates remained low: often, not above $3\frac{1}{2}$ per cent; bank-lending went ahead, and although there were some spectacular bank crashes – the City of Glasgow Bank in 1878, the *Union Générale* in 1881, the *Banca di Roma* in 1890, the Baring Bank (almost) in 1890, and the French Panama Company in 1892 – on the whole the banks survived, learnt from the Depression and, by 1895, had very greatly improved their ways throughout Europe. The British, in particular, took an enlightened long view: lending more when times were bad, and using prosperity at home to lend money to countries where there was trouble ('counter-cyclical lending'). The (almost) £4,000,000,000 of British investment, and the £2,000,000,000 of French investment in the world kept foreign countries going in the international market; they guaranteed 'international liquidity'. In these circumstances, the 'Great Depression' did not, for most countries, result in a collapse of trade. On the contrary, international trade expanded faster than anything else in the later nineteenth century. Both internally and internationally, the 'margin of consumption' functioned to most countries' greatly increased prosperity.

Why? The short answer is that there were no crises of foreign exchange: the value of the leading currencies did not have to be defended by high interest-rates; and confidence in the banking system generally remained high enough for depositors only very rarely to respond with panic and cause bankruptcies within it. Contemporaries assumed that both features reflected the gold standard. Since the main currencies of Europe were interchangeable into gold, on demand, they kept their value and inspired confidence. The Pound Sterling and the *franc germinal* had gold equivalents that went back several generations. There were complications in other currencies because of difficulties in the relationship of gold and silver, but in effect there was a European-wide gold standard, and formally all of Europe was 'on gold' by 1897.

Not only were currencies therefore 'solid' in terms of some tangible item – gold was durable, and there was not much of it: the sum total of the world's mined gold, up to 1890, would not have filled a small house – but the countries' balances of trade, and monetary policies generally, were subjected to a discipline. In theory, and, at least in the early years of the gold standard, in practice, if a country sold less abroad than it bought, the purchases would have to be paid by outflows of gold. That would cause interest-rates to rise to get the gold back, so that business would face more difficult credit, would have to release labour, and 'rationalize', i.e. cut their costs. Hence, through interest-rates (the central one of which was the Bank of England's) a country could be made to mend its ways.

It does not appear that theory matched practice very far. Gold inflows and outflows seem not to have followed the rules; nor did interest-rates. Again, although in theory the money supply, i.e. the volume of lending, should have followed gold-standard rules, in practice the amount of lending in most countries was not held back by outflows of gold from the central bank. Gold was, in fact, merely a name for the willingness of western European countries – Great Britain and France in the lead – to lend money abroad, which in turn fuelled the purchases of these countries in Europe. It all required, from the bourgeoisie of western Europe, a high degree of saving. It also required a willingness on the part of the labouring classes to put up with occasional wage-reductions and unemployment. More generally, it needed relative freedom of trade. Such were the creeds of nineteenth-century liberalism, and when they came under pressure the days of the gold standard were over.

In the later nineteenth century, it looked as if this world would go on for ever. Money not only kept its value; it increased in value as prices gently fell. People signed contracts leasing out their property for almost a century at sums such as £25 per annum and looked foolish when they were still picking up such sums a generation later. Churchmen would agree to give visiting sermons in perpetuity for four guineas, a sum that, within fifty years, would not pay their train fares. Above all, the stability of money meant that, in all of Europe, people could have a wonderful time in being thrifty. Everywhere, there were savings associations, co-operatives: in France a newspaper, *L'Avenir de l'Épargne*; in Germany, many *Sparvereine*; in Italy, *Casse di Risparmio*. Co-operatives came into existence. There was much picturesque meanness. Emile Combes, French prime minister in 1902, gave his salary to his wife and reserved only twenty-five francs (£1) to himself each month, which he spent mainly on books that he would investigate on the *quais*, along the Seine. A schoolboy in Glasgow would find that his headmaster would snoop around turning off electricity and heating: the headmaster was paid a total sum for running the school, including his own salary.

The later nineteenth century was an era of absolutes. Governments and people were aware of rules in most things. Paternal authority in the family was virtually unchallenged. Religion reigned. In schools, the supremacy of classics and mathematics was nearly total. The State, and its ceremonies, amounted to a Mystery. The dominant model, even for Italian politicians, was Gladstonean, austere. Agostino Depretis dyed his beard white in order to gain authority. Students, in college photographs, clearly make an effort to appear much older than they are: whiskers and *gravitas*, like government ministers. Ricasoli put his Annunciata collar into a box, never wore it, and refused to use the free railway-pass which, as a deputy, he had been allotted. Zanardelli, like Garibaldi, lived sparely and, when he became prime minister, lived in a little box and gave interviews from a deck-chair. English politicians often behaved as if they had the mandate of a very Protestant God. At the centre of it all was the bourgeois family, with its elaborate Sunday lunch, issuing forth for an almost ceremonial Sunday walk, in Sunday best, to the family tomb or to visit another family. It was a world of resplendent confidence, often priggishness and smugness; very low on humour, though high in rectitude.

4. *'Transformism': the Politics of the 1880s*

Politically, the 1880s were very confused: an odd mixture of old and new. In most countries, the expression 'the decline of the notables' fits the decade well enough. Politics ceased to be a matter for a few local big men; instead, parties began to organize seriously and to appeal for the votes of masses that were too large to be controlled in the old way. Many countries, for instance, widened their franchise quite considerably in the first half of the decade. At the same time, in ways that are often quite mysterious, organized religion began to lose control of its flocks, at least in the Protestant world. Church attendances in England ran down from 1882, anti-clericalism flourished in France, and Nietzsche echoed Dostoyevsky in pronouncing the Death of God. New political forces began to emerge in strength – socialism and trade unions; political Catholicism; anti-Semitism; populist conservatism; minority nationalism. Liberalism itself underwent a change of character, and radical, rather than classical, liberals made the running. The background to all of this was the extraordinary pace of urbanization. But even in the more backward countries, such as Ireland or Russia, the social changes of the 'Great Depression' had their impact, in that the social control exercised by churches and by noblemen was weakened.

By the end of the 1870s, classical liberalism everywhere had lost its commanding position. Usually, it did so because of financial troubles which were related to the effects of Depression on government revenues. Classical liberals believed in free trade and in minimal state interference with the economy. When government demands went up – as, in matters of defence, they were bound to do – there were wrangles as to how these costs should be met. Liberals disliked direct taxes because they penalized enterprise. The same objection applied to tariffs. They disliked proposals for State monopolies in drink, or for State lotteries – both of them were thought to be immoral. Yet indirect taxes – such as these on salt in Russia or on grain-grinding in Italy (the *macinato*) – were regarded as injurious to the poor. Proposals to make ends meet by the State's taking over all or part of the railway lines (another great issue of the 1880s) were equally divisive. Many liberals felt that the State would be wasteful and inefficient in anything it took over. In these circumstances, classical liberalism came to grief everywhere by the end of the 1870s. Liberals could not present a common front over financial matters, which, in this era, took up most parliamentary time.

Increasingly, too, the classical liberals were challenged from within by radical liberalism. Where classical liberals had been free-traders, men of religion, believers in a strong centralized state (though one run economically), supporters of a national, educative army and upholders of a very limited franchise that would exclude the 'irresponsible' masses from the vote, there were also middle-class liberals who took a quite different view. They were quite violently anti-aristocratic and they regarded religion as mumbo-jumbo. They advocated divorce, and wholly secular education; sometimes, they supported the emancipation of women; they believed in business efficiency, whatever the cost: they wanted the franchise to be extended. They were, on the whole, contemptuous of the past and confident of a progressive future, for which the lumber of past centuries should unhesitatingly be swept aside. In many cases, these radicals sympathized with the grievances of the socialists and expected that these grievances could be contained by a more forward-looking liberalism. Joseph Chamberlain in England, Francesco Crispi in Italy (himself a bigamist), Eduard

Lasker in Germany, Jules Ferry and Léon Gambetta in France spoke much the same language.

These radical liberals were challenged. Their own power-base was usually in the towns, and they could quite easily capture the popular press. But in the villages, the countryside and some of the towns they faced a challenge from conservatives who wished to use their social prestige to build up a mass party. The British were first off the mark in this: Disraeli, in the 1870s, put together a party that, in continental perspective, was an alliance of right-wing liberal and clerical conservative (a combination that had its own strains). Increasingly, too, Catholics became anxious to organize a mass following from the lower middle class and the peasantry. In the 1880s, political Catholicism changed character, and by the end of the decade it had become a mass movement, led, in the main, by middle-class figures. The politics of Europe, although very confused and bewildering, began to follow a recognizably parallel course.

On the whole, most countries produced parallel patterns. In the more advanced, urbanized countries, there was, in the early 1880s, a period of radical, liberal government. Lord Salisbury – who rightly regarded the 1880s as the decade of greatest change that he had ever known – felt that the election of 1880, which returned the second Gladstone government, marked the start of 'a serious war of the classes'. The dominant Frenchmen of this time, Jules Ferry, Léon Gambetta and Charles de Freycinet, spoke the language of the left: for instance, they relaxed the censorship, permitted publicans to open drinking places without a licence, allowed divorce and, in effect, made trade unions legal (1884). Belgian liberals did much the same, under Frère-Orban. In the middle of the decade, the reigning liberals split: the moment when Joseph Chamberlain seceded from the party and joined Salisbury, when most German liberals moved towards direct support of Bismarck, despite his contemptuous attitude towards parliamentary government, when Italian liberals became overtly 'transformist' and, having arrived by banging the drum against the Establishment, ended up by joining its ranks – the era of Francesco Crispi, an anti-clerical republican who had been Garibaldi's secretary and who, by 1890, was having his portrait made, kneeling before a statue of the Madonna, in the company of the king and queen. It is not too much to say that the arrival of 'mass politics' in the 1880s quite rapidly pushed many liberals into alliance with a right which, earlier, they had fought. The later 1880s were a period of right-wing régimes almost everywhere: Salisbury and Chamberlain in Great Britain, Bismarck's *Kartell* in Germany (an alliance of national liberals and conservatives). In France, characteristically of the politics of the Third Republic, there were governments which talked left and acted right.

In the more advanced countries, this decade was the start of 'the age of the masses': politicians had to organize their parties, to talk popular language, because electorates were quite substantial. In Great Britain half of adult males had the vote since 1868; in France there was universal male suffrage; for Bismarck's *Reichstag*, though not for the (more important) Prussian parliament, there was also universal male suffrage. Local managers, the *notables* of France, the *Honoratioren* of Germany, the 'eminent citizens' of Great Britain, could not simply line up their supporters as in the days of a very limited suffrage. They needed organization, and a press. In the later 1870s, many parties behaved accordingly. The French nationalist demagogue, General Boulanger, who made a stir in the mid-1880s as he tried to break the system, had an agent, Dillon, who learnt his craft from the elections he had seen in America. By the end of the decade, Catholic politicians in many places were using the priests as a (very effective) political machine. Karl Lueger, mayor of Vienna, was ahead in this; but Irish politicians were frequently not far behind.

In less advanced countries, the process of urbanization had not gone far enough for the masses to be an active factor. But the undermining of social structures in the 'Great Depression' was still such that landowners were losing their grip. It was 'the end of the notables', whether in Italy or even, towards the end of the decade, in Spain, where politics became too complex for the earlier method known as *caciquismo*, in which local bosses, the *caciques*, sometimes declared the results of an election before polling had taken place. In Russia, the response of Alexander III (1881–94) was simply to tighten up the autocracy which his father, the liberal Alexander II, had relaxed. But tsarist Russia was too poor for a thoroughgoing reaction to take place. The State could not afford to conscript very widely. Not more than a quarter of the young adult males were taken in for military service, and even then the cost of supply (*intendantstvo*) was 100,000,000 roubles out of a total army budget of 119,000,000. There was not much room, here, for the militarist reaction which the new tsar trumpeted abroad.

Political changes in the West – the radical phase of the early 1880s, the confusions of mid-decade, and the right-wing phase of the later 1880s – coincided, roughly, with economic movements. The turn of the 1870s and 1880s, and the early 1880s generally, were a bad time. In mid-decade, the Depression lifted. There was an odd moment when continuing unemployment, a hang-over from the 'trough', coincided with rising prices. There were riots in most countries in 1886: in Great Britain, a crowd moved along Pall Mall, smashing the windows of the clubs, and there was a famous riot in Trafalgar Square. In Amsterdam, the 'Eel Riot' (*Palingoproer*) occurred, when the police tried to put down a revolting dock-district game in which eels were pulled to bits: it resulted in several dozen deaths and hundreds of casualties and arrests. In Belgium, strikes and lock-outs in the industrial east – Liège and Charleroi – came to an end only with intervention of the army. By 1887, in most countries, there was a boom; it lasted until 1890–1, after which came a severe down-turn.

It was, then, the division of liberalism in the middle of the decade which marked political patterns in the more advanced countries. These divisions occurred in response to the rivals which 'the age of the masses' created for a liberalism that was, essentially, individualistic. Up to the later 1870s, parliamentary systems had been matters for 'the notables', rather than the masses. By far the most obvious case of this was in Great Britain, where the parliament of the 1860s was heavily dominated by men from large landowning families, but in France, too, a third of the Chamber in the early 1870s was aristocratic, and in Germany, a quarter of the *Reichstag* had noble origins. Parliaments behaved accordingly: they did not meet very often, and spent two-thirds of their time discussing budgets. In the 1870s, the masses accepted leadership of this kind. In most countries, the vote was restricted: in Italy, to a twentieth of the population, since the liberals of the 1860s feared, probably rightly, that the masses would vote for priests or radical democrats if they were given a vote. But elsewhere, there was a great deal of apathy. In universal-male-suffrage France, a third of the electorate did not bother to vote. In Bologna, only ten per cent of it voted; in Prussian elections, only twenty-five per cent; for the St Petersburg city council, only eight per cent of the 21,000 potential electors. But such abstention became much less common in the 1880s, and, as 'the masses' voted, they brought defeat to liberal notables. In Stettin-Uckermünde, in 1877, thirty-one per cent of the electorate voted, and returned a national liberal. In 1879, forty-nine per cent voted, and returned a conservative; and the same result again in 1884, when seventy per cent voted. It signified a revolt of many of the masses against the reigning liberal creeds of the 1870s.

Liberalism bred up its own enemies. The chief of these was socialism – a product of the economic progress which liberalism promoted. As the towns filled with a new proletariat, and flourishing heavy industries, there were demands for trade-union rights; eventually, too, for political parties that could express the direct interest of labour. Especially on the continent, there were also many intellectuals who sympathized with the grievances of the working class and who foresaw a shining future in which the evils of capitalism would be eradicated. Unemployment, slums, malnutrition, poor health would be swept aside; education, equality of the sexes, State welfare, taxation of the rich, nationalization of businesses would create a new world. It was to be the City of God – but without God, since most people who called themselves socialists were violently anti-clerical. 'Scientific materialism' – the philosophical outlook which Marx had propagated and which gave socialists their hopes for the future – had no place for God or Original Sin: it foresaw infinite Progress and, in a sense, turned Man into a demi-god, a viewpoint memorably satirized by Dostoyevsky in the pages of *The Possessed.*

The 1880s were a decade of dramatic change: opening with discussions of 'moral order' between liberals and conservatives, and closing with the obvious inauguration of class-war, with strikes affecting docks and mines in France, Germany, Belgium and Great Britain, and with a 'new unionism' in all of these countries. It was not until the early 1890s that the political effects of this – the formal creation of mass socialist parties – were felt in full. But it was in the course of the 1880s that socialist consciousness became developed. An immediate problem was that the socialists quite soon became divided.

The advanced countries, particularly Great Britain, had inherited trade unions from the past decades when groups of craftsmen would combine to govern rules of apprenticeship, standards of output, rates of pay, or to establish 'Friendly' societies which could operate insurance funds against sickness, old age, infirmity and unemployment. In all countries, printers were well to the fore in such organization. They were threatened, often enough, by new technology, and they were usually paid sufficient and had sufficiently permanent employment to afford the costs of a union. The London Society of Compositors, or the *Fédération du Livre* in France, flourished. In the later 1870s, an effort was made to establish rather broader unions. Dockers at Le Havre saw business expanding, profits increasing, and an army of migrant would-be dockers at the gates; in Marseilles or Barcelona or Genoa or London it was much the same. These unions were small, and not 'representative'; very often, they recruited one set of workers at the expense of another set. In

conditions of depression, in the early 1880s, their numbers
fell away because their union dues could not be afforded. One
response to this was political: to establish groups that called
themselves 'Workers' Party'. A *Parti ouvrier français* emerged in 1879–82; a *Partito operaio italiano* in 1883; a *Parti
ouvrier belge* in 1885; a *Partido socialista obrera española* at the
same time, promoted chiefly by a printer, Pablo Iglesias, who
was the son of a washerwoman and who had seen how, in
1880, a third of the 900 Madrid printers had been casually
thrown out of their highly skilled employment because of the
vagaries of international capitalism.

The largest of these parties was the German Social
Democratic Party, which had been created (from a fusion of
earlier groups) in the preceding decade. It had won a dozen
seats in the *Reichstag* even then, and by the end of the 1880s
was well on the way to dominating German politics. It
flourished earlier than other such groups – and especially
earlier than British Labour – because German liberals and
conservatives could not capture the working-class vote in the
way their British counterparts did. The German proletariat
could well see politics as a conspiracy, in which nobles,
industrialists, professors and farmers found common cause
in tariffs: making the working class pay more for its food in
order to subsidize the landed classes. Besides, Prussia was
operated with a class franchise which effectively did working
men out of voting, even when they were decently off.
Bismarck completed this picture by promoting anti-socialist
laws which forbade formal socialist activity, harassed socialists and prevented them from meeting. These laws were
prolonged until 1890. They did not prevent men from
standing as *Reichstag* candidates, and the socialist vote rose
during this decade as the liberal one declined (from just
under half in 1871 to hardly over a third in 1890). The
German socialists had good organization, and a strong link
with the trade unions. No other party could claim the
same.

In Great Britain, cheap food prevailed, with the highest
wages in Europe; both parties wished for free trade; and the

Liberals, with whom most working men identified, were reasonably adept at promoting working-class or trade-unionist candidates for constituencies. Efforts to create socialist parties in these circumstances were not very successful – an anti-Semitic intellectual or two in the early 1880s, the Scottish saint, Keir Hardie, a decade later. It was not until the later 1890s that changed circumstances made a Labour Party seem desirable to more than a few people.

On the continent, outside Germany, the socialists of the 1880s were very divided. Anarchism was still a powerful cause in Italy, Spain and, to some degree, in France; and anarchists usually got on badly with socialists. The socialists were, on the whole, opposed to violence: why make things difficult, in finance and in legal matters, for the sake of some spectacular but futile piece of 'propaganda by the Deed'? Socialists preferred to educate, to use resources for libraries and organization, not for 'revolutionary gymnastics'. Anarchists disliked this 'attentism'; in Spain, they openly objected to 'doing the goose-step in some Prussian regiment'. Then again, there were differences between intellectuals and trade unionists, who wanted their parties to be strictly proletarian, i.e. with trade unionists looking after the money, not fanciful intellectuals like the French Marxist, Jules Guesde. The preference was for parties that called themselves 'Labour' (*ouvrier, operaio* etc.) not 'socialist', which repelled anarchists (as well as Catholics in Belgium and, later, Ireland). These parties divided, especially in France, between anarchists, socialists, intellectuals, trade unionists and would-be participators in the parliamentary process. It was not until the 1890s that the discipline of success began to operate there, as it had earlier done in Germany. In the 1880s, people became widely aware of a class crisis. At the end of the decade, it showed itself in widespread trade-union activity. In the latter part of the decade, it became associated with the fifty or so socialist deputies in any of the universal-suffrage parliaments. It also became clear in a spate of anarchist outrages.

Still, the threat of 'socialism' did not acquire much

shape in the 1880s. The question: what to do about the non-propertied classes? did, to some degree, unite the parties of property in the later 1890s (the era, in Prussia, of *Sammlungspolitik*, 'the politics of concentration'). But in the 1880s, it divided them. Some were for force; others were for appeasement. In the early 1880s, the left-leaning governments of a Jules Ferry or a Gladstone or a Depretis or, in Austria, a Count Taaffe would practise appeasement: recognition of trade-union rights; support (in Austria and France) for the independent artisan; relaxation of censorship; above all, extension of the vote to the lower middle class or the upper end of the working class and peasantry. Great Britain, Italy and Austria (with some other countries) had a widening of the franchise in the early 1880s; in France, the substitution of a form of proportional representation, the *scrutin de liste*, for the earlier single-member constituency, the *scrutin d'arrondissement*, was similarly intended to weaken the mainly conservative local notables.

This extension of the franchise in itself eroded the position of classical liberals, and in the 1880s parliaments became much less a preserve of the nobility and the upper middle class. The Whigs in London deserted the Liberal fold and joined up with the right in the early 1880s; by 1885, MPs from large landowning families no longer constituted even the largest single group in the House of Commons, where they had been in a majority a few years before. The Irish MPs became a pronouncedly lower-middle-class group. Two-thirds of them had been landowners in 1863; only 23 of their 109 in 1873; in 1880, only 8 of the 59 Home Rule MPs. By 1888, a quarter of the party came from the lower middle class. In the German National Liberal Party, businessmen made up thirteen per cent of the deputies in 1878, but almost a third of them in 1887. In France, the nobility, who had made up half of the assembly in 1871, made up only a fifth of it in 1889, and less than a tenth in 1902. In the middle of the decade, some of the more right-wing republicans, known as the *Opportunistes*, were looking to alliance with the right:

if only to scare their left-wing colleagues back into the fold of republicanism.

The extension of politics to a mass constituency greatly strengthened the hand of the radical liberals. The classical liberals, a Cavour or a Gladstone or, in France, a duc de Broglie had been men of 'moral order': in favour of religion, hierarchy, constitutional free trade, and balanced budgets. Liberalism of this kind tended to be against extension of the franchise, to favour guidance by a centralizing state: in France and Italy, and much of Germany, many communes and even large towns were not allowed to elect their own mayors, but had them selected by the prefect or (in Germany) by the royal authority. The argument, here, was a characteristic mid-nineteenth-century one: that those who *knew* should rule. If communes chose their own mayors, the result might well be financial confusion and corruption. In all European countries at this time, there was concern to prevent the development, for instance, of municipal housing, transport or public utilities such as tramways. They were left in private hands, as a guarantee of competent management and of public probity.

But the classical liberals lost their battle in the 1870s. They were challenged, from within the liberal fold, by radicals: in the latter part of the decade, and increasingly into the 1880s, they were also challenged by a phenomenon that struck far greater fear into liberals than, at the time, even socialism did: mass clericalism, the rise of which did more to shape the politics of any parliamentary country with a mixed population than any other factor in the 1880s. Both radical liberalism and clericalism were products of the enfranchisement of the lower middle class.

Classical liberals had, on the whole, been religious, but tolerantly so. They had had Catholic allies. In France, the Third Republic was established by a predominantly conservative assembly, of which the anti-clerical, liberal Catholic element found a tolerable alliance to the left, and not to the Bourbon-minded, high-clerical right. In Great Britain, Gladstone found an alliance with the Irish MPs, who were liberal, though Catholic. In Austria, liberal Catholics themselves wished to see the extensive powers of the Church cut back, for they resented the bigoted interference, the economic clumsiness and the educational inferiority which high clericalism often entailed, with all of its obscurantism and snobbery. In Italy, the liberal *Destra* was supported in power by the votes of independent liberal-Catholic deputies who – in defiance of Papal instructions – had 'compromised'. In Belgium, the liberals, again, owed their power to Catholic support against the Triumphalist and Ultramontane claims of the Church. A man like Cardinal Cullen in Dublin, a lad of the village who co-operated with Gladstone, might formally say 'amen' to Pius IX's fulminations, the Syllabus of Errors, Infallibility and non-recognition of the Italian state because of its seizure of Papal lands. In practice, he despised the upper-class English Catholics and knew he would never have been anywhere in the old Church, in which an archbishop of Paris could blithely claim that 'Jesus Christ was not only the Son of God; he was also of good family.' An Ultramontane figure like the long-term professor of philosophy at the Catholic University of Louvain, Charles Périn, terrified his allies more than he terrified his liberal enemies, so great was his hatred of the liberal state, though not of liberal economics.

The social changes of the 1880s made for a different Catholic attitude: in which the liberal Catholics, in the main, deserted liberalism while the Church became markedly less Ultramontane. Of course, political Catholicism stood for morality. But there was more to it. Extension of the franchise gave a vote to lower-middle-class Catholics, including peasants. Many of these had grounds for complaint against liberalism. Education, for instance, did not suit everyone. A farming family had to keep its labour on the land (and a shopkeeping one at the counter) since a father depended on his sons and daughters (and sometimes also his brothers and sisters and cousins and aunts). Farmers quite often did not want their children to be taken away from home for schooling. In the Austrian province of Oberösterreich, the liberals' *fiat* of 1868, that education must be universal, was modified and abolished in the 1870s because farmers would not part with their offspring. In Bavaria it was much the same. The Church hierarchy became markedly more 'populist' in many countries. Of the Hungarian cardinals from 1878 to 1918, three were sons of provincial artisans, one was of Slovak peasant origin, and one was son of a village teacher.

It was part of liberal economics that the comfortable world of the artisan, shopkeeper and farmer should be disrupted by competition. But as the 'Great Depression' went ahead, these groups became more and more discontented. Railways and roads brought hardship in the form of imported goods and services. Farmers in Württemberg found, for instance, that they were competing with each other and with farmers outside, and that the prices they were being offered for their meat or vegetables declined. The dealers who appeared were, often, Jews. The men from whom they had to borrow were often Jews as well – forty-five per cent of Germany's banks were said to be under their control. The chain-stores in the towns – Kaufhaus des Westens, Wertheim, Tietz etc. – were also, often, in Jewish ownership. A great number of the liberal deputies in the *Reichstag* and the Prussian parliament were also Jews, including the National Liberals' leader, Lasker. In Vienna, Jewish predominance in banking, dealing, business, journalism and industry was almost overwhelming.

Vienna and Budapest attracted thousands of Jewish immigrants from the east, especially from the Polish province of Galicia. Austrian liberalism – and, still more, Hungarian liberalism – had removed the restrictions from Jewish immigration which had existed in more heavily religious days. The Jewish population of Vienna went up to 250,000 by 1914 (over one-tenth of the city) and in Budapest Jews made up a quarter of the city. Their preponderance in Hungary was such that Karl Lueger talked of 'Judapest'. Official Austria-Hungary was extremely tolerant of Jews. When, in Linz, a Jewish school was opened in 1886, the ceremony was attended by the imperial governor of Oberösterreich. Jews became army officers just as did other middle-class young men, by virtue of their education: in 1894, of 26,897 officers, 3179 were Jews. The senior medical officer became ennobled as 'Michael Waldstein Edler von Heilwehr'. Intermarriage, at one level, was such that several of the leading figures in the monarchy were partly Jewish, or had married into Jewish families. These included the German liberal Giskra, and the founder of Austrian liberalism, Anton von Schmerling; they also included the prominent Hungarian figures Fejérváry, who governed the country in 1905–6, and István Burián, who became foreign minister in 1915; while many members of the Hungarian cabinet in 1914 had 'Magyarized' their names from a Jewish original – thus Samu Házay, minister of defence, who had been born 'Kohn', or Teleszky, the finance minister, who had been born 'Theikles'.

Such families were highly assimilated. But they were only a very small proportion of the Jewish population in Austria-Hungary. In Cracow, from 1891 to 1914, there were only 444 converts away from Judaism in a population of 30,000, concentrated in the ghetto of Kazimierz. Only 0.5 per cent of the Prague Jews who married that year married 'out' in 1881, and 11.8 per cent of the Vienna Jews (though by 1900 the percentages had risen, respectively, to 7.6 and 14.9). Many of the remaining Jews were content to live in their own communities, and to live, as they had done in the past, from highly intensive artisan labouring (the name 'Portnoy', or its Yiddish equivalent, 'Sznajder', means 'tailor'). Some developed finance, at any level from stockbroking to peddling; in the villages of upper Hungary, in what is now Slovakia, Jews managed local credit, usually in collaboration with the chief nobleman of the region. With the development of capitalism at all levels, Jews became strongly identified.

In France, the Jewish presence was reinforced, in Catholic eyes, by a Protestant one. The Third Republic found Protestants in high places in far greater proportion than their numbers – half a million – warranted. Léon Say at finance,

Monod in education, Freycinet and Casimir-Périer as prime ministers, Jauréguiberry as minister of marine (and hence, colonies) were only the tip of an iceberg, composed, lower down, also of Jews. To right-thinking French Catholics, this Protestant-Jewish presence amounted to a conspiracy, the more so when the Chamber passed laws to take education out of Catholic hands (1879–80). A Catholic bank, the *Union Générale*, was established to channel right-thinking savings; it crashed in 1882. By 1885, the right, which had done disastrously badly in the early 1880s, established a single list of candidates and won two-fifths of the seats.

The Catholic press, throughout Europe, denounced the works of Protestants and Jews. In Württemberg, names of Jews who were caught in some compromising position would be printed in heavy type, or with an exclamation mark attached. In France, towards the end of the decade, the speculative Panama Company came under pressure; its supporters included Reinach, Hertz and many deputies, whether radical-socialist or Protestant, and there was an orgy of complaint which, in many ways, anticipated the language of the more celebrated anti-Semitic orgy of the 1890s, the Dreyfus affair. In 1882, the Austrian government – under the clerical, Taaffe – produced a law to suppress usury (*Wucher*) in Galicia, where there were many tiny peasant plots. It was a clearly anti-Semitic gesture, as was the foundation in Germany of the Raiffeisen credit and co-operatives. In Austria, Karl Lueger became mayor of Vienna with a programme of opposition to large capital and Jews. He founded the 'Christian Social party', which took the vote of the Viennese lower middle class away from the reigning liberals in the later 1880s. Lueger's language and programme were symptomatic of what was to come. His demagoguery was violently anti-Semitic. His practices included discriminating against Jewish firms in buying goods and services for his municipality. He also sought to buttress the small artisan against large capital. Small shops, for instance, paid a smaller proportion in tax than large ones. In time, under the name of 'municipal socialism', he took over public utilities from private firms. That gave his political 'machine' a wonderful chance to appoint its clients to municipal jobs, the numbers of which rose considerably. Artisans and peasants, victims of the 'Great Depression', could thus find alternative employment through the priests and the 'machine'. In Munich, Liège and many of the North Italian cities, 'Christian Socialism' developed as a radical challenge to the liberals. In Liverpool, there was a bitter fight between Irish Catholic migrants or their descendants and the Presbyterian locals, with the Anglican Derby interest trying, not always effectively, to hold the balance. Matters became so bad that in the truant school, the Catholic inmates had to be separated in the playground by a wall. There was a common bath-house which had two doors, one of which would be kept unlocked on alternate days.

This was tantamount to a revolution in the Catholic world. The old Catholic notables were pre-empted by lower-middle-class elements who wished to turn Catholicism in a 'social' direction, opposed to liberalism. Enlightened landowners – in the stricken Basilicata, Jacini and Fortunato; in Hungary, Count Zíchy; in Austria, Vogelsang; in Ireland, Sir H. Plunkett – assembled statistics and promoted peasant co-operatives, with the priests' help. There were Catholic congresses in Austria and Germany and Belgium (Liège, in 1890). The Pope eventually became interested in the new method of combating socialism and liberalism. By 1890, the new, lower-middle-class, clerical element was felt everywhere, from Lublin to Galway. The fall of the Protestant landowner, Charles Stewart Parnell, as leader of the Irish Home Rule Party was symptomatic, not only of changes in Ireland, but of changes all over Europe. 'Christian democracy' had been born. It offered bureaucracy, social reform, and 'peasantism'.

The emergence of this movement, with its anti-liberal economic connotations and its wasteful political machines, irked the liberals beyond all measure – especially their radical element. The radical liberals differed from their classical colleagues in many things: it was shirt-sleeve against frock-coat. The radicals were often successful capitalists, of humble social origin – Joseph Chamberlain, the boss of Birmingham, had his counterparts in the Frenchmen Magnin, an iron-master from the Côte d'Or, or Dubochet, an engineer who had been a *carbonaro* republican in the 1830s, and the Italians Bastogi and Di Ferrari of Livorno or Orlando and Ansaldo of Genoa, all of them former *Garibaldini*, detesters of monarchy and Church. Radical liberalism really came directly from positivism, the (supposedly) scientific attitude so well expressed by Bazarov in Turgenev's *Fathers and Sons*, in which anything metaphysical is condemned, along with anything not of practical utility. It was characteristic that the left-wing liberals in France, who called themselves – misleadingly – 'radical-socialist', were very frequently doctors or engineers. These 'new men' chafed under the leadership of the old liberals and, in England, the Whigs.

On the whole, radicals were people who did well out of liberal economics, whereas clericals did badly out of it. The radicals were violently against Establishments; they wanted a wholly secular education, *la foi laïque* in France, the ills of which radicals ascribed to a stupefying religion. Inside many towns, Catholics would patronize one set of shops and schools, and radicals another set. In politics, that same rivalry soon came to affect local government as well, since Catholics proved to be good – better, usually, than radicals – at promoting 'machines', which were prepared to work for less money. In the early 1880s, the left-leaning French governments, anxious to control their radical allies, unleashed some anti-clerical legislation, which caused a great fuss. In the 1870s Bismarck appealed to liberals of all kinds in Prussia with his anti-Catholic campaign, the *Kulturkampf*, or 'battle for civilization', as the Progressive surgeon, Virchow, called it. Joseph Chamberlain's radicalism turned him against the Irish Home Rulers and, for a time, broke the Liberal Party over this issue. Catholics committed a further sin in liberal eyes; one that damned them in some respects more than any other. The Church was a powerful patron of national minorities: in Ireland, clerical patronage of the nationalists appeared, to Englishmen, anomalous. But it was part of a large European theme.

Classical liberals, and radical ones still more so, usually regarded minority peoples with disfavour. J.S. Mill spoke for many liberals when he said: 'Nobody can suppose that it is not more beneficial to a Breton, or a Basque ... to be [French] than to sulk on his rocks, the half-savage relic of past times, revolving in his own little mental orbit... The same remark applies to the Welshman or the Scottish Highlander.' Karl Marx himself had supposed that, with the onward march of civilization, people would abandon 'useless' languages that were spoken by no one of serious pretensions to education. By mid-century, Czech or Flemish appeared to come into this category. The done thing was to speak German in Bohemia, or French in Belgium. Even after Czech and Flemish had been well launched, with educational institutions to match, many Czech and Flemish parents, in the search for respectability, wanted their children to be educated in German or French. The 'Charles University' in Prague was divided between German and Czech after 1882, but even twenty years later a third of the students at the German university were in fact Czech. Similarly, Flemish nationalists in Belgium discovered that so many even of the Flemish bourgeoisie in Ghent, the Flemish heartland, wished their children to be educated in French that the only answer to this must be legal compulsion. In Scotland or Wales, children were beaten for speaking Gaelic in the playground; characteristically it was a Conservative home secretary, R.A. Cross, who did something to promote the Gaelic languages in both countries. In France, Jacobin centralism was the republicans' greatest cause: the eradication of *patois* such as Breton or Provençal which had no role in modernity. In liberal Spain of the 1860s, the Catalan language was condemned: it was to be used, in the theatre, only for 'minor characters in comic roles'. In Austria, radical liberals of German origin – or Germanized liberals of different, Slavonic origin such as the Czech, Giskra, in the

1860s – regarded Czech as an obstacle to Progress. That same attitude was widespread in Hungary, where Slovak, Serb, Romanian and the various mountain dialects of the 'sub-Carpathian Ukraine' – i.e. north-eastern Hungary – were written off as 'jargon'. Later on, a Hungarian prime minister could dismiss 'the idea of a Romanian university' as 'an absurdity'.

All of this linked up with another radical-liberal theme: dislike of the peasantry, who were often dismissed as 'quadrupeds'. The peasants did not easily fit in with liberal economics or with education; they tended to follow the Church. In many European countries, Church and peasants had a close link. In Italy before unification, the Church had had 2,500,000 acres of land; in Austria, 4,000,000. These lands were held in 'mortmain', i.e. could not be sold. Therefore they attracted no credit and were badly developed. Liberals regarded all of this as wasteful, and executed land reforms. These reforms often meant the eviction of small peasants who had done reasonably well in Church days. In Spain in the 1860s, the Church lands around Seville supported 6000 people until secularization, when they supported only 400. In Italy, suppression of the Church lands brought widespread hardship in the south; the more so as the lands had once supported charities and education, both of which, inevitably, suffered. Now, in the 1880s, radical liberals contemplated revived clericalism as an enemy worse than socialism: it offered political machines, obscurantism, the end of education, economic wrong-doing, 'peasantism', provinciality and 'jargons'. It also collected many votes: practically the whole of Catholic Ireland; virtually all of Catholic Germany; half of the Italian parliamentary deputies (although without much formal organization); in 1885, two-fifths of the French Chamber; and, after 1884, the Belgian government in perpetuity.

The Church was also well to the fore in protecting the national minorities. The Catalans' chief figure of the 1860s and 1870s, Mañe y Flaquer, was a Catholic traditionalist who lived in Madrid and derived sustenance from Catholics in the government. The Flemish language in Belgium was kept going by priests, one of them a Frenchman. The Irish cause gained much organization from the clergy. It was a priest (of the O'Neill O'Malley) who coined the word 'boycott' in 1881. His flock could not pronounce the word 'ostracize' when such measures were proposed for a harsh land-agent, Captain Boycott. In Bohemia, but especially in Moravia, Czech was promoted by priests; the chief Czech nationalist, František Palacký, though himself (like Tomáš Masaryk later) a Protestant, exploited alliance with the clergy and the Bohemian nobility, particularly the Kinský and Thun-Hohenstein families. In partitioned Poland, the national cause was kept alive largely by the Church. Bismarck imprisoned the archbishop of Gniezno, Count Ledóchowski, and Prussian education was harshly discriminatory both to the religion and to the language of Polish pupils. Indeed, it was characteristic that the first king of Prussia to forbid his son to learn Polish – a habit that had gone on for centuries, since the Hohenzollerns owed fealty to the kings of Poland for the lands of the Teutonic Order – was not the reactionary Wilhelm I, but the Gladstone-admiring Friedrich III, father of Wilhelm II. In the mixed German-Slav areas of Austria, there were always proportionately more Slav than German priests – for instance in partly Slovene Carinthia in 1918, 215 Germans to 148 Slovene. In Moravia or even German parts of Bohemia, it was the same. In Austria a radical liberal, Georg von Schönerer, made a great noise in the mid-1880s when he attacked Jews, Rome, Slavs and Habsburgs all at once in the Austrian parliament.

In Italy, with the help of a limited franchise, the liberals, classical and radical, endeavoured to rule 'above' the emerging Black (Catholic) and Red (socialist) challenges. In Austria, the emperor sought to profit from his peoples' divisions, to obtain shifting majorities in his parliament, the *Reichsrat*. His chief minister, Count Taaffe, had the price of most men. He could appeal to Czechs by letting them have their own 'Charles University'; to the lower middle class by giving small shops exemption from company taxation while also allowing them the expenses that incorporation permitted; to the clergy by exempting syphilis from illness that qualified for State assistance. Taaffe went on until his régime was blown up by the social explosions of the early 1890s.

Elsewhere, the political battles of the 1880s were equally complex. The older groups were conservatives (the party of noblemen and pastors), classical liberals and radical liberals. They were now confronted with the 'mass-parties' of the future. But they had quarrels of their own which prevented them from making common cause.

The first of these quarrels came over free trade. The rise of cheap imports in the 1870s made many farmers and manufacturers demand protection. Classical liberals were almost always free-traders, as was Delbrück, Bismarck's economic manager. The *Zollverein*, in which most German states had been included, had been a free-trade zone, and had done wonders for the Prussian economy in the 1850s and 1860s. But, now, cheaper American steel and grain caused many farmers and industrialists to want protection, even though it meant 'the masses' would pay more for food and goods. In Germany, by 1879, 'an alliance of iron and rye' came about. In France, tariffs were also a cause of the Ferry republicans; in Italy, the free-trade men of the Cavourian *Destra* were replaced, after 1876, by protectionists associated with the parliamentary *Sinistra* ('left') of Cairoli, Agostino Depretis and Baron Nicotera. Grain was an important theme. But in countries such as Italy, shipping and steel interests also wanted protection from cheaply made and more efficient foreign competition. In the 1880s, tariff wars resulted between France and Italy, and between Germany and Russia over such issues – exactly the kind of battle that free-traders had been anxious to avoid.

But the tariff issue concealed much more than it revealed. The governments, everywhere, were now confronted with an inexorable rise in their costs. As towns expanded and armaments progressed, as post offices and railways went ahead, as populations expanded, there was increasing demand on government. In Germany, towards the end of the

1870s, there was virtually a second 'Foundation of the *Reich*'. The empire established in 1871 was a federation, in which the parts – the various separate states – had most of the power. The central authority was very thin: a *Reichstag* with power only over the central budget, which concerned only the armed forces; a *Reich* chancellor, Bismarck, who alone could address the *Reichstag*; the vice-chancellor (Delbrück) who helped him. Otherwise Prussian ministers sometimes did *Reich* work. It was a system that could not respond to the changing circumstances of the later 1870s. In 1878–9, a 'deputizing law' gave secretaries of state – for railways, posts, justice etc. – the right to address the *Reichstag*, since they too needed *Reich* money.

In Russia, a not dissimilar problem was presented. Tsar Alexander II had been consciously liberal in many respects. But by the later 1870s there was a wave of agrarian and urban disturbances in which the terrorist organization *Zemlya i volya* ('Land and Liberty') took the lead. The tsar was assassinated in 1881 by an anarchist. But, before then, the problem of unrest was such that the tsar's ministers had been driven to create a stronger police organization. In 1878, true to liberal form, tsarist Russia had contained only 5000 policemen in all; 2000 policed St Petersburg. Huge provinces, such as Penza, contained only twenty-five policemen and five officers. The province of Kiev was operated by a governor, Prince Vasilshchikov, with a staff of sixteen, who reckoned that their labours were heroic in that they managed to receive, answer and copy 222 missives per day. The tsar had even formally abolished the death penalty. He had brought in trial by jury in 1863. The trouble was that unrest rose because of foot-loose students (the 'intelligentsia' – a Slavonic adaptation of the German words *Intelligenz* and *Intelligenzler*) and land-hungry peasants. Some of Alexander's ministers, especially the liberal General Loris-Melikov, wished to answer this by greater liberalism. Others, such as the minister of finance, preferred force. 'Governors-general' with wide powers were appointed to control groups of provinces. The police force was expanded.

In Russia – and it was rather symptomatic of the difficulties which liberalism met in countries of that kind – trial by jury did not work well. Many Russians took the Dostoyevskyan view that it was not up to them to find a miserable fellow-sinner guilty. On principle, they would not convict. In the towns, many of them sympathized with political grievances. A would-be assassin, Vera Zasulich, was in fact acquitted. In the countryside, Russian officials could well echo the remark of a judge in contemporary Ireland: 'You have been acquitted by a jury of the county of Limerick, and leave this court with no other stain upon your character.' In time, the spate of outrages led to a roundabout reintroduction of the death penalty. Martial law was proclaimed in 1881, as a temporary measure. Under it, army courts could sentence people to death. They did so, though not often. These 'temporary' rules went on until 1917. The unrest of the later 1870s, rather than the accession of Alexander III, a reactionary tsar, in 1881 put paid to Alexander II's liberal experiment. In tsarist eyes, Russia could not be ripe for liberalism.

In other countries, the tasks of government, both for enlightenment and repression, were also greatly extended. In France, Jules Ferry's educational laws of 1879–81 ('the triple star of free, lay and compulsory education') required 100,000 teachers and, in the event, a great many new schools. In Italy, the liberals, anxious to destroy the power of the Church, also built schools on lavishly classical lines. Most countries became involved in foreign enterprises, which, in the middle of the decade, resulted in the partition of Africa. It was all very expensive. Yet, at this time, no one could imagine having it paid for by direct taxation. Liberals generally disliked income tax, because it penalized the efficient. They shrank from putting up indirect taxes on items of mass consumption because they provoked popular unrest. Indeed, radicals came to power in Italy with a promise to abolish the tax on grain-grinding, the *macinato*, which southern peasants disliked; in 1881, the tsarist government similarly abolished the salt tax. Revenue could come from the imposition of a government monopoly on items of mass consumption, such as tobacco (in Germany) or spirits (in Russia). There were proposals for State lotteries. These proposals – whether as an interference in the market or as an encouragement to immorality – revolted liberals and classical economists.

A further way, which proved popular in most countries, was to nationalize the railway system and gain State revenue from that. Railways had, in most places, been a matter for private companies. This had resulted in confusion. Speculators had burnt their fingers in 1873. Lines would overcompete. In Austria, the *Kaiserin-Elisabeth Westbahn* failed to pay its dividend in gold to German creditors in the depressed circumstances of 1881. Trains belonging to it were seized as soon as they crossed the German border. For some time, the competing chaos of railway lines had prompted demands for rationalization, if need be by State control. Ministries of railways were set up. On the continent, though not in Great Britain, the lines were gradually taken over by the State, with, often, a mixture of nationalization and private enterprise. Lines would be nationalized, and then leased out to private companies. It was not the happiest of compromises, since the private companies did not have much incentive to invest and they often overworked the rolling-stock, the lines, and, latterly, the railwaymen. This issue caused much political confusion, since classical liberals and radical liberals disagreed profoundly as to questions of nationalization. On the whole, classical liberals favoured it; radical liberals, the capitalists, opposed it. They opposed it still more when the Catholic challenge arose in the 1880s. The appointment of station personnel (as of postal staff) was to turn railway ministries into client systems on a vast scale. In southern Italy and southern France they were a prime target for 'machines'. Even the Czech radical-liberal nationalist, Karel Kramář , voted against the establishment of an Austrian ministry of railways in 1896, although such a ministry, in the right hands, could have supplied innumerable jobs for the clients of the Czech nationalists.

However, nationalization of the railways, although it came

about in stages throughout the later 1870s and the 1880s, could not answer the immediate problem of revenue. Governments looked to tariffs, and they were imposed, or increased, in France, Italy, Germany, Russia and elsewhere in the years 1878–81. They were continued, or increased, at regular intervals thereafter, as trade treaties fell due for renewal; the only exception being in the early 1890s. They had less effect on the economy than their opponents (or their supporters) had imagined. Even a tariff of twenty-eight per cent on foreign grain (the French figure) did not add a very significant part to retailing costs, for the handling of grain inside a country was the particularly costly part of the process. In Germany, the food tariff may have added a tenth to the German working man's food bill, and in the 1880s, less than that. But this was a breach of the free-trade principle.

It was a breach that divided the liberals very badly. Classical liberals were appalled to reflect that inefficient producers were being rewarded, in industry and agriculture, efficient ones penalized, food prices (and hence wages) artificially driven up, and all for the sake of armies, police, colonies. In Great Britain, where the agricultural population was not large enough to form a very significant pressure group, the principle of free trade was kept up, although Randolph Churchill, a populist Conservative, sometimes advocated 'fair trade', meaning tariffs. In Europe, outside the small countries dependent on foreign trade (especially Belgium and the Netherlands) the pressure from industrialists and farmers was too strong for tariffs to be resisted. In Germany, Bismarck got them through the *Reichstag* with the help of liberal votes; in Italy, the *Sinistra* politicians and, especially, Francesco Crispi after 1887, staged a regular tariff war against France; in France, the republicans of the later 1870s and early 1880s again put through a tariff. The figure for iron and grain dues was not high – it did not compare with the figures of 1902 (in Germany) or 1912 (in France and Russia), let alone with the burlesques of the 1930s when tariffs virtually killed off foreign trade. But it was a breach of principle. Radical liberals were seriously divided. Some

stood to profit; others were repelled at the thought of higher
food and raw-material prices. Classical liberals, similarly,
were divided. In Germany, the liberals divided between
radical anti-Bismarckians ('Progressives'), anti-tariff right-
wing liberals (the 'Secession') and pro-tariff liberals, the
National Liberals. Later, they split in a still more confused
way.

These debates preoccupied parliaments in the early 1880s.
It was possible for agile political managers, such as Bismarck
or Ferry or Depretis or Taaffe, to play off one group against
another. Alliances shifted and re-formed; political chronicles
in most countries make very confusing reading.

A final feature that divided the parties was the question of
empire. Classical liberals had regarded colonies with disfavour: they had been wasteful of public money, profitable
only to a few; they involved armaments and international
disorder; they were oppressive and gaudy. Yet from 1880
onwards, European Powers were engaged in almost frantic
colonization. A British protectorate was established over
Egypt, a French one over Tunisia, in 1881–2. The king of
the Belgians took over the Congo as a huge private estate.
The Germans seized parts of eastern and south-western
Africa. The French set up a huge central and western African
empire. The Italians launched into north-eastern Africa and
were worsted in Abyssinia in 1886 at Dogali, as was the
British General Gordon in the Sudan.

To account for this quite sudden burst of colonization is
not easy. Theories of economic determinism are not very
helpful for this period of European expansion (unlike the
case of the later 1890s): the colonies that were made in this
period did not pay, received little investment, and were not
attractive to immigrants. There was not much popular
demand for them, and the French colonial enthusiast Jules
Ferry remarked that the only thing that interested the
French in their new empire was the belly-dance. There were,
of course, apologists. The German liberal, Gustav Rümelin,
spoke for many other liberals when he argued, in 1882, that
the only answer to the increasing proletariat and the seething

cities was emigration. Ferry himself said that colonies would be a 'safety-valve' proper to an age of industrialization. But it is not easy to connect such theorizing with the activities of soldiers far away from the metropolis, who were usually responsible for the initial creation of colonies. It is perhaps safer to argue, as Joseph Schumpeter did, that the imperialist mind – a product, perhaps, of the declining gentry – coincided with a disintegration of 'native' civilizations. Egypt was in many respects the key to it all. The Khedive was unable to pay his debts, had his finances internationally supervised, faced an internal revolt against foreigners; the Gladstone government, rather than abandon Egypt, which held the key to the Suez Canal, was forced to intervene and to establish a protectorate. The French clumsily failed to take up the junior partnership they were offered. The resulting Anglo-French rivalry then rebounded on to other parts of Africa, and Bismarck, to exploit it, also took his share of Africa. In this way, Africa came to be partitioned, and 'gimcrack empires, spatch-cocked together' came about – a process later regretted. It is not accidental that this process of colonization occurred just as the classical liberal world was breaking down in other matters. But it was not until the later 1890s that the rival imperialisms were systematized into military-economic concerns.

Colonies badly divided liberals everywhere, and by the middle of the 1880s, French republicans, British liberals and the various German liberal groups had split into two, and sometimes more, elements. The right in all three cases stood to profit from this, and in the later 1880s in all three cases something of a 'new conservatism' emerged. In earlier times, conservatism had been a straightforward business of noblemen and Established clergymen – the Anglicans in England, the Lutherans in Prussia. Now, with the expansion of electorates, the conservatives went beyond their earlier parish-pump attitudes and created parties. They gained a quarter of the German vote in 1887; in France, governments were dependent upon them as the radical and classical republicans split in 1885. There were even some demagogic 'populists' – Lord Randolph Churchill, General Boulanger – who seemed to disrupt the parliamentary process altogether. The new conservatism developed beyond the narrow circle of noblemen and clergy, and recruited middle-class support. Very often, anti-Semitism was not far from the surface. To gain mass adherents, the conservatives in most countries consciously espoused the peasant cause: protection for agriculture was a cause that went together with a variety of new organizations which linked pastors, noblemen and peasantry. In Bavaria, the prince regent and his court took up wearing picturesque peasant dress. In Prussia, the military authorities deliberately attracted peasant recruits as NCOs – not proletarians, who were thought to be less deferential – by offering a long-service NCO a guaranteed place in the post office or the railways: by 1910, over 100,000 former NCOs enjoyed such small-scale privileges. On this basis, most countries had a period of right-wing government in the later 1880s. These governments spoke for Empire, Protection, Religion. They profited from a few years of prosperity. In Germany, Bismarck used his majority to push through State welfare schemes – the first in Europe – which compensated the working class for infirmity, sickness and old age.

The world of classical liberalism also disintegrated in international affairs: it is not accidental that it was in the later 1870s that the pattern which led to 1914 was laid down. Classical liberals abhorred armies and wars. But they were outflanked. In 1878, the Powers assembled to solve the Eastern Question at the Congress of Berlin; Russia and Austria-Hungary disagreed as to the Balkans, and everyone feared a possible Russian takeover of the Turkish empire. In the outcome, a compromise was established. But, to underpin the existing settlement, Bismarck agreed, in 1879, to make an alliance with Austria-Hungary which was implicitly anti-Russian. He tried to preserve his independence with a variety of interesting devices, and there was next to no military preparation for a possible war. He was very anxious to isolate France.

The international scene in the 1880s remained quite fluid, in that Powers co-operated now with one, now with another. But there were two constant factors. The first was Franco-German hostility. The Third Republic, as self-conscious heir of the revolution, was nationalistic; no French statesman could afford to forget the defeat of 1871 at Bismarck's hands, and the lost provinces of Alsace-Lorraine were a permanent grievance. Ferry's enemies threw him out for putting colonial gains above national ones in 1885. True, the revanchism of General Boulanger was contained by the French themselves, and the nationalist poet Déroulède was imprisoned and sent into exile. But it was easy enough for Bismarck to scare his own parliament with the likelihood of war with France.

The other constant was Anglo-Russian rivalry. In 1877–8 Russia had established a large, satellite Bulgarian state as the outcome of her war with Turkey. For Great Britain, and to a lesser extent the Habsburg Monarchy, this had aroused fears that Russia would take over the Straits that led between the Mediterranean and the Black Sea. The Russian Black Sea fleet would therefore be free to move in and out of the Mediterranean, which would cause nightmares in London: Russia would, in these circumstances, disrupt the British position at Suez. Austria-Hungary feared Russian promotion of satellite Slav states in the Balkans. In 1878, the Powers had combined to force a compromise, at the Congress of Berlin: a smaller Bulgaria, an Austro-Hungarian occupation of the two Turkish provinces of Bosnia and Herzegovina, and a British seizure of the island of Cyprus. But the Balkan position remained unstable. In the middle 1880s, there was unrest in Bulgaria, and the supposed satellite, Prince Alexander of Battenberg, tried to assert his independence of Russia. He was removed; eventually, his successor, Ferdinand of Saxe-Coburg, did rather better than his predecessor in prising his country loose from Russian control, and appealing for Habsburg patronage. There were also Anglo-Russian quarrels in Afghanistan, which Russian troops could menace once their railway had advanced in Central Asia. At the Pendjeh Incident (1885) there was much rumour of war.

Anglo-Russian rivalry was complicated by the further Anglo-French quarrel over Egypt (since 1882); French governments felt hard-done-by, since the British had preponderance in Egypt, with a military presence. The French constantly appealed for German help in this, and sometimes got it, since Bismarck's aim was to deflect French concerns from Europe. France and Italy, too, were at odds over Tunisia where the French had won a position not unlike Great Britain's in Egypt. Towards the end of the decade, Franco-Italian rivalry was further complicated by a tariff war.

In these circumstances, Bismarck could play one side off against the other, and he used colonial disputes to further his own mediating position. The British arrived, in 1887, at Mediterranean agreements with Italy and Austria-Hungary which were designed to block Russian expansion (with French help). Bismarck had his own agreements with Austria-Hungary and Italy (the Triple Alliance) but also made a pact of friendship with Russia. But this situation of uneasy stability changed quite dramatically in 1890.

Germany, in the two earlier decades, had not appeared to be overwhelmingly superior to France. But by 1890 industry had been so strongly built up, and the population had moved so rapidly upward, that Germany clearly became by some head the strongest power on the continent. Then again, the tariff wrangling inside Germany had worked out strongly to the advantage of the agrarian interest; and that could only affect Russia, an exporter of agricultural goods, in a disadvantageous way. The Russians, who built up their own industry with protection in the 1880s, also brought in a tariff to discriminate against German machinery. Bismarck himself had imposed a prohibition on German acceptance of Russian loans. There were also highly placed Germans who wished to collaborate with Great Britain in establishing a German overseas empire; and they were prepared to jettison

Russian friendship if that was the cost. Finally, armies and navies began to complicate foreign affairs in a novel way.

In the old days, technological progress had been slow, and the nature of military forces did not alter very rapidly. But in the 1880s there was a whole set of complicated technical changes – smokeless powder or cordite, which improved gunners' sighting beyond comparison; the Parsons turbine, which allowed navies to move further from their bases and to operate with less coal, smaller crews and more guns; a little later, the quick-firing revolution in artillery, which, by the development of a sprung recoil mechanism, made reloading a much simpler matter than before. Improvements in explosives and in metal shell-casings completed this picture. By the later 1880s, armies everywhere were coming to terms with these changes: there were military laws in most countries in the years 1888–93, as Powers tightened their systems of conscription. German military spending rose from 93,000,000 marks in 1874 to 376,000,000 in 1890, with corresponding increases in 'non-recurrent' ('extraordinary') expenditure (from 10,000,000 to 244,000,000); the British doubled their naval expenditure in the 1880s; the Russians, who had spent 119,000,000 roubles on their army in 1875, spent 285,000,000 in 1894. Something of an arms race was developing, although it did not reach the proportions of 1912. In Germany, there were alarms at the increases in Russian strength.

Out of all this, a Franco-Russian rapprochement emerged. The tsar looked to France for loans, and for co-operation against the British and their 'Mediterranean agreements'. No doubt Alexander III would have preferred to co-operate with Germany, and his diplomats often courted France only with a view to prodding the Germans. The rapprochement was a very long-drawn-out affair, its first steps being taken in 1890, and the formal Franco-Russian alliance not finally ratified until January 1894. The position was dependent on Germany; and there the fall of Bismarck in March 1890 was decisive. Bismarck's successors looked to Great Britain, and allowed the 'reinsurance treaty' with Russia to lapse, so as to appeal to the British. In 1892, a Franco-Russian military convention was concluded; it became a full-scale alliance rather later.

By the early 1890s, the shape of international politics had become plain. True, the immediate effects of the Franco-Russian alliance were anti-British. There were many reservations, particularly on the Russian side, about the anti-German implications: if Germany went back to support of Russia, the alliance would probably count for little, and its military terms were certainly a matter of fantasy on the Russians' part. A great deal would still depend on how the Germans used their new status as a Great Power.

II

STRANGE DEATH, 1890–1914

1. *The New Course*

In 1888, Kaiser Wilhelm II came to the German throne. He was young and aggressive; he had his portrait painted in a martial pose, with *Pickelhaube* glittering, moustache sprouting and eyes glaring. He was impatient with the restraint of the aged Bismarck, and in March 1890 he 'dropped the pilot'. He expressed the enormous energies of the new Germany, and his chancellor, Caprivi, proclaimed 'a new course'. At the same time Francesco Crispi, the dominant figure in Italian politics, proclaimed 'a new life'. In Great Britain, the Liberals solemnly framed their Newcastle Programme along radical lines. In all three cases, and not there alone, national greatness was to go in parallel with better integration of the nation at home. In practice, this did not work out. The first half of the 1890s saw the final trough of the 'Great Depression'; not until 1895–6 were graphs moving up again. Far from creating 'a new life', the hopeful statesmen of the early 1890s presided over a very marked extension of class-war. In most countries, there were bad strikes; in most, in the 1890s, socialists entered politics in force. The confusing picture of the 1880s gave way to new pattern in the 1890s, and from then until 1914 the atmosphere was of class tension and, at the international level, of war scares.

The themes of this era were twentieth-century ones: armaments; inflation; bureaucracy; levels of direct taxation; trade-union rights; local government; town planning; rationalization of secondary education; 'modernism' in the Roman Catholic Church; protectionism; 'social legislation', in the form of insurance, by the State, against unemployment or old age. In this era, too, a process was inaugurated that has continued well into the twentieth century: a rise of much of the working class and a decline of the middle class.

The 'Great Depression' had already done damage to the landed nobility and some of the peasantry. In the middle of the 1890s, it lifted. Agriculture became quite prosperous once more; in England, there was even a movement back to the countryside, which contained more people in 1914 than in 1892. Grain prices, which had fallen by forty-five per cent between 1873 and 1896, rose by twenty-five: in 1898 a quarter of grain cost £1.6s.0d, in 1914 £1.18s.0d. This was true of other commodities. The price of Peruvian guano had run down partly because of excess supply and partly because the Germans discovered that its fertilizing qualities could be more cheaply reproduced synthetically (through the Haber-Bosch process and its antecedents, nitrates could be extracted, literally, from the nitrogen of the air). But the synthetics' qualities proved to be inadequate; they exhausted soil. The guano also turned out to have other applications, and it rose in price accordingly. With sisal, it was much the same story. Artificial fibres were introduced to make the rope for which, earlier, sisal had been needed. But, then, sisal turned out to have an application in pharmaceuticals that no one had suspected: it supplied (and supplies) an important ingredient of cortisone. Prices rose, as they did with virtually every other commodity, and land prices rose in parallel.

But it was not just a diversity of uses that caused such commodity prices to rise. There was also increasing demand. That demand came, partly, from the very expansion of industry and towns which the earlier decline of prices had encouraged. Populations, almost everywhere, had gone up. Industry had expanded vastly, and its requirements in raw materials had increased equally vastly. The industrialization of countries like Italy, Russia and Hungary created a new demand altogether, and, by 1896, it was commodities, not manufactures, that were becoming scarcer. Finally, the countries that produced the commodities had themselves entered the market for them. The United States, for instance, consumed more of their own grain, and exported at a decreasing rate: 117,000,000 bushels in 1881, 171,000,000 in 1891, 161,000,000 on average from 1891 to 1907 and 117,000,000 from then until 1914. Cotton exports had grown by 6.4 per cent between 1878 and 1882, then by 2.8 per cent from 1888 to 1892.

A drought in Australia killed half of the country's sheep in the early 1890s. The British used more and more of their own coal, and so the Italians and French found it profitable to use hydro-electricity to offset high coal prices. High prices for steel prompted the French to apply the Gilchrist-Thomas process, and then the Martin process, to exploit their own iron-ore in Lorraine, and later in Normandy, although its high phosphorus content, earlier, had ruled out its use. Search for new fuels led to the development of petroleum. The Russian and Persian wells were developed. In 1890, little had been produced. By 1900, 21,000,000 metric tons were produced, and by 1910, 42,000,000. After the turn of the century, ships could use diesel oil, and the development of aircraft depended on cheap fuel. This made for vast fortunes in Russia, Persia, Indonesia. The oil-wells of Walachia in Romania attracted international attention, and the *Steauă Romînă* became big business. With Bolivian tin, or world sugar (later), or rubber, or coffee it was the same. Fortunes were made in 'the colonies' and by Latin Americans, whose offspring would be packed off to Europe for an education. Buenos Aires sported its golf-clubs, its 'Harrods', its 'Mappin and Webb' for family silver. Other Latin Americans reforged, in 'Hispanism', their old links with Spain. In Haiti, a former French colony in the West Indies, the mulatto bourgeoisie found that it was not much more expensive to send their children to France for an education than to send them by ship to the capital, Port-au-Prince; Canadian timber-millionaires like Max Aitken (Lord Beaverbrook) in London, or American fortunes like that of Waldorf Astor, also in London, could be transferred to the European metropolis, together with South African diamond-chiefs or

Australian wool-chiefs, without difficulty. It was, in a phrase invented by the Italians, 'plutocracy': a time when the old European aristocracy coincided with very new overseas money. This accounted for Edwardian plushness.

Contemporaries associated the rise in commodity prices, and prices generally, with a factor much simpler than the combination of cost-push and demand-pull. They assumed that it had to do with the rise in gold output. Historians at this time assumed, almost as a matter of course, that the sixteenth-century inflation had been 'caused' by an influx of gold into Spain from the New World. According to orthodox gold-standard economics, it was certainly the case that prices would move upwards if there were more money in circulation; and since money, whether credit or coinage, was equivalent to gold, an increase in the world's mined gold ought to have that effect. It happened that, from new sources, new techniques and better working of old sources, the amount of gold in the world rose very sharply. New mines in America and Australia, and especially in South Africa, produced, in the 1890s, a flood of new gold. The eighteen years from 1890 to 1908 produced £1,000,000,000 of it: as much as had been produced in the years 1848–90, and four times the amount mined in the first half of the century. It was, even, twice the quantity mined in the three centuries from 1550 to 1850.

Contemporaries usually assumed that this new gold underlay extensions of credit; and that the greater volume of credit produced an inflation. Certainly, after 1895, and especially after 1906, in most countries, prices rose. In Great Britain, the cost-of-living index rose from a base of 100 in the 1890s to 118 in 1914; in France from 94 to 111; in Germany from 104 to 127. It was claimed in Russia that prices rose by one-third or more from 1907 to 1914. Stock-exchange indices everywhere rose – indeed, in the United States, in 1907, there was an anticipation of 1929, when 500 banks failed, and the Bank of England came to the rescue. In all European countries, the volume of bank deposits rose very fast, to double or, in the case of Russia and Italy, to treble between

1900 and 1914. Government revenues also rose. In Russia, they doubled, because the spirit monopoly and the railways brought in higher returns.

The explanation of all this in terms of gold is far from proven. Goldstone has shown, for Russia, that the development of credit in the banking system had no link with the amount of gold held by the Central Bank: Russia's 'money supply' simply reflected demand for money. Shepperd has shown that the British 'money supply' rose quite regardless of gold movements: it rose by 2.7 per cent from 1880 onwards as an average; by 0.8 per cent in the years 1899–1905; by 2.8 per cent from 1905 to 1913. The price-rise after 1895 cannot, it seems, be ascribed only to gold.

One new factor that supervened was a modern one: 'velocity of circulation'. In the old days, when commercial transactions were paid in coin or by banker's draft, when banks were few and transport was difficult, money would change hands only slowly. A banking transaction in, say, 1860 was a cumbersome business. Institutions guarded themselves against fraud by having everything in triplicate, signed and countersigned. There were very few countries where the element of trust, which underlay all banking, extended much beyond close acquaintances or members of the same religious community. The element of mistrust can still be seen in any continental bank, where there is a sharp (and, for the customer, tedious) distinction between the teller who handles the transaction and the cashier who handles the money. Banking was almost a closed order, which conveyed respectability on its lowliest acolytes; the Bank of England's strongest card was its reputation for probity. Personal cheques could be handled like constitutional documents, and in every continental country transactions tended to be in cash. Even the professors of Louvain were in the habit of queuing up every Friday at the bursar's office to collect their salaries in cash. In the Vienna Opera, before a performance, a little old woman would come round the performers with a bag of cash, and would solemnly count out their fees into their outstretched hands – a practice which continues to this day, though no doubt for different reasons. All of this began to change quite rapidly after 1895. The cheque, and other 'instruments of credit', became more frequently used; the number of banks in all countries rose as railways and roads allowed rapid transport of money. Money changed hands faster; there were many more transactions with the same stock of money; in these circumstances, the ascription of price-rises to inflows of gold could only make for a partial explanation. Even, it could be argued that the mining of gold was itself a response to price movements.

The Austrian economist, Schumpeter, felt that the price-rise had much to do with a novel factor: the growth of technology in the 1890s and 1900s. Firms kept back a higher proportion of their profits for investment; banks, supporting the firms, had to use more and more of their funds for this purpose; interest-rates rose; businesses merged, and so reduced competition, in order to afford the technology; and prices rose. The twentieth-century configuration of inflation, cartel-monopoly-'multinational', and strong trade unions was coming into existence.

There is no doubt at all that the two decades before the First World War were a period of the machine. Bicycles, telephones and typewriters (which in themselves must have contributed significantly to the velocity of circulation of money, in that banking transactions became infinitely simpler) had been invented before, but it was in the 1890s that they came into general use. They only expressed principles that were being given much more important use in industry: precision tooling, usually by some automatic process; electro-magnetism and electrical engineering, themselves dovetailing with advances in chemistry which allowed endless invention with by-products of coal. Electricity had been adapted to domestic and industrial use in the 1880s – Lord Kelvin lit Peterhouse in Cambridge with electricity even in 1882, and Lord Salisbury conducted dinner parties at Hatfield House under arc-lights – but the processes were cheapened enough for mass use only in the 1890s. Milan, early on in that decade, found that electricity was a substitute for coal, and Italians (and French) were early off the mark, with the great network based on Paderno sull'Adda and a comparative electrical giant, *La Edison*. Hydro-electricity took off from there, and reached the Rhône valley in France, around Grenoble, with dramatic effect for the industrialization of that region by 1900. Cheap energy made possible processes that otherwise would have been too expensive – for instance, the exploitation of by-products of coal. These were used to make synthetic materials of all kinds; and by 1903 a Belgian, L.H. Baekeland, took over from German research and produced the first plastic – a brittle material, used for radio cases and bodywork of motor cars, called 'Bakelite'. Like his fellow-countryman, the chemist Ernest Solvay, Baekeland became very rich: for some reason, chemists were better at making money than engineers or physicists, both of whom were often gulled when it came to exploiting their patents.

Technology revolutionized the last decade of the nineteenth century and the first decade of the twentieth, so much so that it is not a platitude to say the twentieth century started in 1900. The automobile had been invented in the early 1880s, but by 1900 it was well launched in European cities. By 1906, Paris had nearly 7000 motor vehicles. The first lorry in Europe was sold by the firm Daimler to the *Böhmisches Brauhaus* in 1897, and the first motor car registered with the Prussian police in 1892 (characteristically it received the number 'IA'); in 1901 there were 845. By 1903, a motor-bus route was laid along the Friedrichstrasse. In Italy, the *Fabbrica Italiana Automobili* (*FIAT*) company started in 1900, together with other famous names, Lancia for one, in Turin; French Panhards and Hispano-Suizas came slightly later. With aircraft, there was similar development, and again France and Italy became very efficient at making them, even if the principles of aeronautics had been worked out elsewhere. In both cases, it was a question of ingenious improvisation in backyards, rather than expensive technology, which came later. What was needed, in the first instance, was a market. By 1910, motor cars had been well

developed, and France before the First World War had
90,000 of them; even Russia had 25,000. There were motor
rallies, including a famous one from Paris to Peking (won by
Prince Scipione Borghese) in 1909, and a lorry test from
Rome to Riga (won by a Russian model, produced in St
Petersburg in the *Russki Renault* factory). It was part of the
strangely modern atmosphere of this era before the First
World War that, even in 1905, there were many magazines
of rather manic content, with names like *Autocar*; even in
1903, these magazines were calling for what they agreeably
described as a 'pedestrian code', since pedestrians had an
alarming way of interfering with the progress of the motor
car. 'Safety First' was in fact imported from the United
States, though General Baden-Powell, of Boy Scout fame
(founded in 1908), regarded it as un-British, since pedestrians should have the right to be knocked down while
defending their right to the road.

New technology was sometimes thought to have a
revolutionary effect on labour, particularly skilled labour.
Machines like the electro-magnetic riveter used by Denny's
on the Clyde could obviously replace existing manual skills;
they could be handled by semi-skilled labour, apprentices,
and even women, whose wages were considerably lower than
a skilled man's. In printing and engineering this factor
clearly counted; it could also count in textiles as far as
spinners were concerned. In France, in 1906, the printers
struck over issues of this kind; in England, the boiler-makers
of the Tyne struck in 1910 over trade unions' right to
determine whether a machine should be worked by one man
or two. In Germany, wages in metal-working rose by 13 per
cent and profit by 37.6 per cent in the decade before 1914.
In most countries, engineers and metal-workers (*métallos* in
France, *Metallarbeiterverband* in Germany, *metallisty* in
Russia) supplied a great amount of the labour militancy of
pre-1914. In all these cases, official unions – where they
existed – would often be challenged by a shop-floor revolt
against agreements negotiated at union level. In Great
Britain, manufacturers were beginning to respond weakly,

even before 1914. They switched to easier markets in their own empire, and abandoned other competition to Germans and Americans, who took the lead in new technology, whether in electrical, chemical or machine-tool industries. This supine attitude did not prevent Great Britain from having the worst record of industrial trouble in any of the European states before 1914.

The great strength of western Europe had been the individual craftsman. The origins of technology lay far back in the medieval past; the Byzantines had been taken aback by the strength of the Franks in that respect even during the Third Crusade. Even in the seventeenth century, the Scots had been known to be good engineers, the Germans to be good chemists; the Italian skill in electricity similarly had remote origins. But, now, technology went far beyond the inspired imaginings of an individual craftsman. It could be adapted to labour that was far less skilled. By the later 1890s, tales of the 'mass-production' methods of America were amazing Europe. A Henry Ford, turning out motor cars by 'flow-methods', i.e., with semi-skilled workers at a moving belt performing the same operation, mindlessly, and then passing on the piece to the next worker for a different operation, was a portent; so too was the American engineer Charles Taylor, whose doctrine, 'Taylorism', was designed to achieve maximum efficiency in factories by replacing skilled artisans, each with a finished product, by cost-benefit-analysed semi-skilled workmen (or women) each performing part of the operation. Efficient lay-out of factories could do much to improve production, quite regardless of the qualities of the labour-force. It was a formula for extraordinary tedium, which managers and unions in the older established industrial centres regarded with horror. Ship-builders on the Clyde went on turning out high-quality products without very much of the new technology. But these products became very expensive.

Still, after 1895, Europeans saw an extraordinary growth of large-scale technology and large-scale business, which were often planted, quite suddenly, in a peasant landscape.

Italy and, especially, Russia showed a strange mixture of old and new: in Russia, factories employing sometimes 40,000 people would grow up in the middle of the countryside because, thereby, they could be sure of a constant labour-force. In St Petersburg, there were, by 1914, over 900 very large factories working well within the city's perimeter, using the most advanced German technology with a recalcitrant labour-force, an inefficient factory lay-out and elements of very backward technology, to the bewilderment of foreign observers. This technology, though stemming from a very long tradition (and not only in western Europe), flourished so greatly in this era because it gained the backing of large-scale capital and of some famous entrepreneurs.

For the first time in history, economists (and economic historians) became preoccupied with the question of growth. The first article in a learned journal that was devoted to this subject appeared in 1904. It was around 1910 that the expression 'the industrial revolution' was first used widely to describe what had happened in eighteenth-century Great Britain: hitherto, the adaptation of technology to industry had been known, from a French phrase, as 'the machine-system', and no decisive breach in the mid-eighteenth century had been recognized. Now, economists and historians read back their own experience to the eighteenth century, and we have suffered ever since from a meaningless concept, 'the industrial revolution', alleged to have occurred in that century. Economists like Werner Sombart wrote classic works on the history of capital; Max Weber, the great sociologist, discussed the entrepreneurial mind and its links – which in the 1890s and 1900s were, in Germany, obvious – with the Calvinist outlook.

Economists became aware of a 'business cycle' to an extent that the era deserved. They appreciated that up-swings and down-swings were somehow not to be dissociated; that, together, they were an engine of growth. The Russian economist, Kondratiev, read the circumstances of the 'Great Depression' backwards (and he could have done so forwards as well) to identify 'long waves' of roughly fifty years during which prices would tend upwards or downwards. Certainly, it was not wrong to ascribe the great burst of technological growth in the 1890s to the circumstances of the preceding price-fall. Agrarian resources and commodities had been mobilized by the agrarian depression. Millions of Europeans had been propelled towards new employment, whether in the towns or overseas. In many cases, they brought skills from their villages which could be adapted to industry, but, even where they had nothing to offer but brute force, as with the general labourers or 'navvies' in construction, they were contributing far more to economic growth than if they had stayed in their villages. The 'Depression' had, in effect, mobilized labour, just as it had created an expanding urban market and just as it mobilized capital.

Capital illustrates how the new flourished on the wreckage of the old. In the 1890s, it was created, to some extent, from a more energetic and intelligent attitude to credit on the bankers' part. This new attitude came about because the bankers were doing badly. In most European countries, they were highly conservative. They took respectable savers' money and invested it, for a small profit, in government bonds. Land took a large proportion of the available funds: even in Lombardy, the most advanced part of 'transformist' Italy, it took eighty per cent of savings, because it was 'safe'. The banks in France became a by-word for conservatism; they would not easily advance money to industry long-term. In Russia, there were very few banks, and entrepreneurs, themselves often foreign, looked to foreign banks for their capital. In most agrarian countries, it was much the same. True, as governments borrowed and spent in the 1880s, some banks did become highly speculative. There was a building boom in Rome, financed by speculative banks which, in the odd circumstances of Italy, were allowed to print their own banknotes. In the early 1890s, as commodity prices, on which an economy like the heavily agrarian Italian one depended, went into a new decline, these banks came under pressure, and there were famous scandals in Rome (as in Paris, with the Panama affair) at this time. In Russia, the agrarian disasters of the early 1890s – which included a famine – equally put banks under pressure. They were driven towards something new.

The example before them was the 'mixed' bank in Germany. These banks had emerged in the outcome of the 'crash' of 1873. They took ordinary savers' money, which could be called back at short notice, and lent it long-term to industry; thereby they laid the foundation of the German industrial advance of the 1880s, or at least a substantial part of it. Many reputable economists regarded these banks as fraudulent. But they profited from the circumstances of the 1880s: new demand, fresh, adaptable labour. In Germany, they flourished, and promoted industry in turn. If they came under pressure, they merged. Four great banks – the *D-Banken* (because they all began with 'D') – dominated the business. In the early 1890s, the gradual erosion of earlier banks' positions caused their more forward-looking directors to adopt different attitudes. In 1895 three German Jews, Joel, Goldschmidt and Teplitz, bought up almost bankrupt Italian banking stocks and set up two new banks, the *Credito Italiano* and the *Banca Commerciale*, which borrowed German money and began to develop the electrical network of northern Italy. They also took an interest in Italian heavy industry. From 1900 to 1914, Italian steel, which had started from almost nothing, amounted to 1,000,000 tons per annum. In Russia or Austria-Hungary it was much the same story: a quite sudden flourishing of progressive banks, which mobilized capital that had become available because of the agrarian decline and the collapse of banks that were too heavily involved in things that were directly or indirectly agrarian. In France, the *Crédit Lyonnais* similarly found a go-ahead director in the mid-1890s, and he did much to foster the French chemical industries of the Rhône valley, using German examples as his starting-point. It was not accidental that France, in the First World War, proved to be considerably superior to Germany in her invention of explosives and in her output of shell.

The freeing of capital for new technology was a direct

outcome of the 'Great Depression'. Economists of this generation – such as Schumpeter – well understood that the hardship of Depression had been a necessary part of such progress. Provided that money supplies were kept in some kind of parity with price movements, and provided that impediments to internal and international trade were kept to a minimum, the harshness of Slump would not be lasting. Economists disagreed about the uses of gold. An Austrian school, which produced Schumpeter (and also von Mises and F.A. Hayek) probed means of adapting gold-standard orthodoxies. Austria was the weakest of the gold-standard countries. Adaptations of silver and paper money had been the stock-in-trade of Austrian economists for some time past. Now, they updated their past freedom from gold-standard rigidities to investigate new ways of dealing with money, using it not as a recorder of economic events, but as a stimulator of them. The Austrian socialist, Rudolf Hilferding, anticipated the discoveries of Maynard Keynes; the Swede, Wicksell, moved in parallel. Other economists, although they maintained the wisdom of their age, that nothing serious is created without trouble, also looked for ways of mitigating Slumps. Alfred Marshall in Great Britain tried to adapt considerations of 'welfare legislation' to economics. He examined the possibilities of decentralizing industry and of reducing pollution without the heavy-handed State interference that almost all economists regarded as harmful. Still, economics, too, moved away from classical liberalism after 1890. A considerable number of British economists, and an alarming number of continental ones, had been converted to protectionism and empire. It is tempting to conclude that their prejudices had got the better of their sense.

As prices moved upwards after 1895 or, in the preceding decade, as agrarian countries were able to afford less and less, there were strong impulses towards new industry. In Germany or Great Britain, costs had to be cut; and machines were stimulated. In Italy or Russia, agrarian depression prompted industrialization, even if only its baby-steps, textiles and railways. In the 1890s, and especially in the 1900s, new technology was passed, through foreign invest-ment, from the advanced countries to these weaker ones, which, accordingly, experienced dramatic economic change in very few years. Proletarian (and peasant) armies appeared in the factories. In the 1880s, in other countries, they had found prices that were gently declining, and real wages had risen quite substantially. In the later 1890s and again after 1906, they found prices that were going up quite fast. The result, everywhere, was a degree of labour militancy that led some observers to conclude that revolution was just round the corner. After 1900, there was a steady growth of trade unionism, only marginally affected by temporary down-turns in economic advance. In Great Britain, membership went up from 2,500,000 to 4,000,000; in Germany from under 2,000,000 to over 3,000,000; in France from 100,000 to 1,000,000.

This militancy occurred in response to inflation, which caused real wages to rise far less fast than in the 1880s (and, according to some writers, caused real wages even to fall in the pre-war years). It also came about because profits were rising quite substantially after 1895. Great Britain, for instance, experienced a boom in some of her most old-fashioned industries, the staples of shipping, coal and textiles. As commodity prices recovered, traditional British clients came back for British goods. Once more, the British staples did well – for the last time, as it turned out, if we except the odd circumstances of the short-lived post-war boom. Statistics vary, but British foreign trade clearly rose from its stagnant level (according to Clapham, of around £650,000,000) in the early 1890s to £870,000,000 in 1901, £975,000,000 in 1905, over £1,000,000,000 in 1907, £1,201,000,000 in 1910 and £1,405,000,000 in 1913. In 1908 British shipping was a million tons greater than in 1904. Everywhere in Europe by 1909, profits were rising, and were often used to promote new technology rather than to raise wages.

Firms found that it made sense for them to merge or to

co-operate. In the early 1900s, a depression occurred that was particularly severe in the rapidly developing agrarian countries, Italy and Russia; stock-exchange imprudence, an international financial crisis, a temporary glut of grain combined to check growth. In Russia, two-thirds of the businesses quoted on the stock exchange threatened to go bankrupt. In response, businesses combined so as to pool their resources. Cartels came about. They had already appeared in Germany in the 1880s, to make scarce capital go round further: concerns like AEG (electricity) or the Westphalian coal syndicates set a model for Europe, particularly Russia. These mergers and alliances took various forms, but by the turn of the century 'big business' had become a common concept as cartels strove for a monopoly position. Since, now, tariffs were put up, it made sense for these concerns to transcend national borders. AEG became established in Russia, and long before 1914 German business was buying up important parts of the French economy. It was the start of the 'multinational', with a huge pile of capital that was not based in any one country. These cartels were used, to start with, for aggressively anti-union purposes; trade unions faced 'lock-outs' of a whole range of employers who wished to discipline their men, and who co-operated in establishing black-lists of trouble-makers. In time, trade unions found, especially in Germany, that large businesses were quite easy to deal with: they could afford high wages because their monopoly position enabled them to pass the costs on to their clients.

However, in the later 1890s and the early 1900s, employers tended to adopt a combative stance. They did so in response to the wave of industrial trouble which affected most countries in the early 1890s. The beginnings of a down-turn – which lasted until 1895 – caused employers to demand wage-reductions in the old way. Coal was particularly vulnerable to fluctuations in industrial demand, and the average mining wage at Bochum in the Ruhr went up and down – 941 marks in 1889, 1120 in 1892, 946 in 1893, 1208 in 1904. In 1889 the coalmines erupted in Great Britain and

Germany. In France, in 1893, they also erupted, after a great disaster at the Carmaux colliery. In all three cases, miners rapidly formed trade unions to defend their positions. Docks, too, were vulnerable to fluctuations; there, too, most countries experienced trouble in the early 1890s, and in Amsterdam the dock-strike produced serious rioting and some fatal casualties. In France, Italy and Great Britain the railwaymen, too, became more militant. In the old days, railways were among the best places to be: uniforms, pensions, decent wages, perhaps a small plot of land to cultivate. But the confusions of competition, and the unsatisfactory compromises between nationalizers and private enterprise resulted in countries' avoiding capital investment. The railways became quite dangerous: in the French *Nord* there was one major accident a day. Managers of the lines over-used the rolling-stock and the personnel, and wages were kept low (and bewilderingly complex in their combinations of piece-rates and local allowances and overtime). In the inflationary period after 1896, and especially after 1905, there was trouble in most countries over this. In Great Britain, before 1914, a 'triple alliance' of miners, railwaymen and dockers threatened to suspend economic life altogether; but in Italy, France or Germany that triple alliance was never very far from realization, while Sweden and Belgium experienced some intense industrial strife in the years 1902–14.

Employers responded, at first, with force. They denied that unions were representative (and, in the 1890s, they had a good point) and would not recognize them. This produced troubles such as the engineers' lock-out in 1897 in Great Britain, and the gigantic textile-factory strikes of Crimmitschau in Saxony or Ivanovo-Voznesensk in Russia, in 1903. German heavy industrialists, especially, were violently against the unions: they adopted a '*Herr-im-Haus*' attitude (roughly, 'what is mine is mine'). They organized company unions and 'yellow' (as it was called in most countries) or 'black' (the British expression) labour, to defeat strikers. These company unions were sometimes more successful than the socialist unions, especially if they were combined with enlightened paternalism on the employers' part – as, for instance, with company housing, education, and subsidies for spare-time activity (such as the workers' tennis-courts installed in a Lancashire cotton factory in 1900). But firms which operated on low profit-margins – and they included most of the cartels, including those in Russia – could seldom afford such paternalism.

Throughout the 1890s, employers usually met the emerging trade unions with force, and they wished the State to help the cause of unrestricted capitalism. In the later 1890s, the State obliged: there were laws to allow the imprisonment of pickets in Sweden. To employers, the pickets were an interference with the right of labour to find its own market. Trade unions often included only a part of the work-force. By using bully-boys, and by threatening reprisals, the unions could exert pressure on a work-force that would work perfectly well if left to itself, or would at least refrain from striking. Pickets made an, often violent, appearance in most strikes, and the employers wished the police to be used. In Sweden, such a law was enacted. It led to the importation of 'black' (British) labour at the port of Malmö, a riot with some deaths, imprisonments, and in the event a general strike. In Germany, the Kaiser demanded a law to imprison pickets (the *Zuchthausvorlage*) and was rebuffed by a *Reichstag* that had learned from the failure of Bismarck's anti-socialist laws. In Great Britain, the courts were used, in the Taff Vale Judgement of 1901–2, to allow trade unions to be sued for damages by an employer who had been struck against. In France, at the same time, the Loichot case similarly made trade-union funds liable for damages, even though the funds in question might be of the 'friendly' variety, to pay for pensions and insurance.

In response to the changed economic circumstances and to the employers' reaction to trade unions, socialist parties began to adopt a different attitude in the early 1890s. In 1889, in the context of the Paris Exhibition which marked the centenary of 1789, the Second International of socialist parties was established, the First International having split into warring fragments fifteen years before. From 1889 to 1893, socialist parties were formed in most countries, though in Russia only in 1897. Earlier rivals – anarchists, orthodox Marxists, intellectuals, trade unions, 'Possibilists' (as the French exponents of collaboration with middle-class radicalism were called) – came together. The Italian party emerged in 1892 from the Columbus centenary: Genoa offered cheap railway travel, and the left used it to stage a conference which founded the Italian Socialist Party, although the word *operaio* – labour – was dropped from its official title only later, in deference to the anarchists and trade-union elements to whom 'labour' meant a good deal more than the intellectuals' 'socialism'. By 1900, in most countries, these parties were in flourishing condition, although in Great Britain it was not until then that trade unions and a few intellectuals combined to set up what was to become (in 1906) the Labour Party. In Great Britain, it was not until just before the war that most trade unions shifted their support away from the Liberals.

After 1890, class-war made the basis of politics in Europe. Its intensity varied from place to place: indeed, there is hardly a country in Europe which did not, and does not, regard its own class system as worse than any other country's. Class-war flared up in different ways and at different times; people disagreed as to how it should be fought, and sometimes they forgot to fight it at all. The whole concept lends itself to endless relativization. Still, its main lines were clear enough. In all countries before 1914, the political struggle was fought on class lines. There were parties who believed that money should be transferred from rich to poor by means of the tax-screw, and there were parties who would fight this. The increasing integration of the European economy meant that economic ups and downs now tended to affect all countries alike, at roughly the same time. Since these ups and downs clearly influenced voting behaviour more than anything else, the politics of Europe moved in parallel: in the early 1890s, a period of liberal apologia; in the later 1890s, an orgy of nationalism and imperialism; around

1905, left-wing upheavals; around 1906, liberal or left-leaning governments that were too divided to achieve much; after 1909, an era of political chaos in almost all countries as internal politics became confused with the threat of international crisis and the arms race.

In the early 1890s, the arrival of socialism, trade unions and class-war had become plain enough. Elections in Germany and Great Britain showed swings to the left; and the clerical-democratic element – whether in the German Catholic Centre Party or the Irish Home Rulers – had also grown in strength. Its managers were perplexed. They had to appeal to a wide variety of supporters. Catholic workers in the cities counted more and more, and the Church set up its own trade unions in Italy and Germany; priests were usually well to the fore in the paternalist enterprises in France. Peasants and small-town artisans supplied the Catholics' chief support in Germany and parts of every other Catholic country. They responded to the promotion, by the clergy, of savings associations and co-operatives (the first of which was established by a priest in the Veneto in 1886). But there was also a liberal-Catholic element, a reactionary-Catholic one, and a clerical Establishment that could sometimes sacrifice the immediate interests of a Catholic party in one country for the sake of the international concerns of the Papacy. Windthorst, the German Catholics' leader in the 1880s, once remarked that he had been 'shot in the back' when the Pope dealt with Bismarck over his head: the Pope, needing Bismarck's support against the anti-clericals of France and Italy, forced German Catholic leaders to co-operate with the chancellor instead of pursuing the opposition that came naturally to them in this Protestant-dominated state.

In these circumstances, it was almost as difficult to hold Catholic parties together as to hold socialist ones together; to some extent, the two acted as wall and flying buttress, for they were deadly rivals for the votes of the masses. The Catholics organized in the early 1890s just as the socialists did. In the later 1880s, they (largely) jettisoned their equivalent of the 'Whigs' who had supported British liberalism until that decade: the Lichnowskys and Hatzfelds who had promoted political Catholicism in the 1870s now joined the conservatives. In many cases, democratic language could now be used; the Catholics' leaders tended to be middle-class or even lower-middle-class, men like the German Matthias Erzberger, illegitimate son of a postman, or Josef Wirth, a schoolteacher, or the countless middle-class lawyers of Italian political Catholicism. Sometimes, 'social Catholicism' made an impact. In Belgium, Carton de Wiart with *L'Avenir social* at Liège, appealed to the rebellious mining communities. At Hazebrouck, in the French *Nord*, Abbé Lemire spoke for 'Workers' Circles'. In Spain, the Jesuits' *Razón y Fe* promoted the cause of Father Vicent among the working classes of Barcelona. In Italy, the 'Red Priest', Father Murri, spoke for the proletariat of Milan; and it is significant of the atmosphere of liberal Italy at this time that in 1898 a general ordered the bombardment of a monastery in Milan because he had grounds for supposing that anarchists were being hidden in it. In the years 1890–3, political Catholicism was officially launched in France with the *Ralliement*, in Germany with the *Volksverein für das katholische Deutschland*, in Austria with the *Christlich-soziale Partei*; and in other countries Catholics began consciously to appeal to the masses. In 1891 a Papal encyclical, *Rerum Novarum*, showed that Leo XIII himself was prepared to bless the new social concerns. An Italian professor, Toniolo, worked out plans for a State-run economic system that would iron out class differences. It was called 'the corporate State', in honour of the medieval guilds.

'Social Catholicism' was seen by liberals and conservatives as a great threat. It could mean land reform, recognition of trade unions, nationalization of business concerns, taxation of the rich. True, these issues divided Catholics as they divided everyone else, but in a country like Italy the alliance of Catholic and socialist, of Black and Red, was not unthinkable. In any case, as local government developed, the Catholics were often good at putting in their own candidates and turning the local bureaucracy into a machine, in which municipal contracts and appointments went to the favoured Catholics and not their liberal rivals. Karl Lueger, who took over Vienna in the 1890s, behaved in this way. He would, for instance, appoint as chief surgeon of the city a relatively junior Catholic, and not the obvious candidate, the experienced and highly competent Dr Ludwig Klaar, who was a Jew. In Munich, in the same era, an alliance of liberal Catholics and Protestants came under severe strain from the radical Catholics who worked city machines and spoke the language of the peasantry. In the countryside, priests swept all before them, whether in Ireland, Catholic Bavaria or Belgium.

Holding these Catholic parties together was not easy. The working-class element had to be appeased, for it might move over to socialism (in England, the Catholic vote tended overwhelmingly towards the left). On the other hand, Catholicism needed its rich supporters; and in the 1890s a gap between worker and peasant was becoming clear in most countries, since the two sides disagreed over food tariffs and much else. In Germany and Belgium, political Catholicism was therefore exposed to strain; in France it never quite took off; the Irish Home Rulers hardly dared to advance any cause other than Home Rule and religion, because it would have divided them. Their political behaviour was therefore, in Joseph Lee's words, a pattern of 'major missed opportunities'.

By the end of the 1880s, it had become clear that repression of the new mass parties had not worked. In Germany, socialists and Catholics gained a majority in the *Reichstag* in 1890; elsewhere, Red and Black ate into the liberals' position. Liberals divided over the question of alliances: some preferred the left, others the Catholics. Conservatives everywhere spoke firmly for an alliance with the Catholics – the 'Blue-Black Block' as it became known in Germany. In the early 1890s, the left-inclined liberals won their case. In Germany, Bismarck was dismissed. His successor, a liberal general, Caprivi, wished to appeal to the left. He cancelled the law against socialism, and he allowed trade unions. He would reduce food tariffs (and other tariffs as well); he would combine this with a decrease in the amount of time a man spent as a conscript; he made conditions for Catholics easier, and relaxed the anti-Polish methods of the Prussian ministry of education. In England, Gladstone came to power with a programme of Home Rule and extension of democracy in local government. In Austria, the long-term prime minister, Count Taaffe, encouraged his lieutenant, Dr Emil Steinbach, to produce a plan for universal suffrage. In Belgium and the Netherlands universal suffrage was introduced in 1893–4, though it was hedged around with qualifications to such an extent that it became almost meaningless. In Spain, the liberal Sagasta government introduced it in 1890. In Italy, in 1892, Giovanni Giolitti came in, as a man of the left. In France, a whole set of governments appealed now to the right, now to the left. By 1895, there was a brief anticipation of the Popular Front, in the form of Léon Bourgeois's radical-dominated government. It promoted State-led co-operation, '*Mutualité*', in place of socialism; in England at the same time Gladstone's home secretary, H.H. Asquith, took up the same cause, which he called 'fraternalism'. All of these governments were essentially concerned to contain the left, and to stop the working classes from voting socialist by showing what enlightened capitalism could achieve.

The effort to kill socialism by kindness was, everywhere, a failure. The years 1890–5 were not prosperous ones, and governments were blamed. The right was intransigent. The liberals themselves became very divided over matters such as tariffs and armaments. It was characteristic that in Italy, Germany and Great Britain, these governments collapsed over naval questions. The Catholics, too, became divided. These left-leaning governments therefore abandoned positive programmes, and their rhetoric became tired. The resignation of Gladstone in 1894 marked the end of paternalist classical liberalism everywhere. The right, however, had a programme of increasing coherence: the cause of empire.

2. 'National Efficiency' and Sammlungspolitik, 1896–1904

After 1896, there was an orgy of imperialism which for the first time became a popular cause. The Italians launched it, invading Abyssinia (and suffering defeat at Adowa). In Germany, in 1897, Tirpitz began his great battle-fleet. In 1898, the United States and Spain went to war, and Spain lost her possessions in the Pacific and the Caribbean. In 1899 the British went to war with the Boers. France extended her central African empire, and there was a war scare in 1897–8 when she collided with British forces on the upper Nile, at Fashoda. The Franco-Russian alliance was tightened up in 1898. Russia and Japan went to war in 1904–5. This imperialism was not the rather haphazard affair it had been in the early 1880s, when at least the pretence could be maintained that Africa had been partitioned 'in a fit of absence of mind'. It was part of a coherent programme, which involved tariffs, a streamlining of government, the pursuit of more practical education, and, in the English expression, 'National Efficiency'. The proponents of this programme sought to link the political right and centre in the imperialist cause; there would be an alignment of the parties of Property against the now formidable left; the sting would be removed from class-war by the export of proletarians to a new empire, or by the help given by imperial loot to native industry. That was what the German political manager, Johannes von Miquel, meant by the word *Sammlungspolitik*. He would 'collect' (*sammeln*) Catholics, conservatives and liberals as a *Reichstag* majority.

Everywhere in Europe, there were governments of the right. The strikes and the economic troubles of the early 1890s scared many liberals and Catholics into alliance with the conservatives; for a time, economic recovery gave the new alliance a strong support. In internal affairs, there were attacks on the trade unions by the courts in England, France, Sweden and Prussia. In Italy a general, Pelloux, was appointed in 1898 to deal with the social question by force, if need be by upsetting the constitution. The king remarked, 'this time let us have a big bang'. In Milan, in May, the army was used to suppress the left (and the Catholics) in the *fatti di maggio*, during which there were hundreds of arrests and casualties. In Spain, the 'regenerationist Christian general', Polavieja, was moved in for similar purposes. In France, Jacques Méline led a right-wing nationalist coalition which, from 1896 to 1899, denied justice to the victimized Jew, Alfred Dreyfus, who had been imprisoned for supposed espionage. That affair dominated French politics; although it soon became embarrassingly clear that there had been a miscarriage of justice, the clerical and nationalist right kept up the anti-Dreyfus cause because it appealed to popular anti-Semitism. In Great Britain and Germany, imperialism did indeed link the parties of Property; Joseph Chamberlain, advocating a British tariff, gained many adherents on the conservative side, because it would turn the British empire into an economic bloc, isolated from foreign competition. It was not accidental that he took a leading role in the making of the Boer War of 1899–1902: through it, Great Britain came to control the gold and diamond mines of southern Africa.

In the 1890s imperialists looked hopefully towards Turkey and China. These empires were disintegrating: their finances in a mess, their internal government breaking down, their outlying regions open to all manner of adventurers. Turkey's Balkan possessions and the island of Crete (which revolted and caused a Greek-Turkish war in 1897–8) were scenes of nationalist turmoil; Morocco, which was formally a Turkish possession, and Persia had been penetrated by agents of European Powers; Manchuria, the northern part of China, was the scene of rivalry among the Powers. In most of these cases, the battles concerned railway concessions: if these were given to a single European Power, then it would dominate the local economy. There were wrangles as Powers established extraterritorial settlements in various ports on the Chinese coast. Russia and Great Britain quarrelled over these matters; increasingly, the Japanese, who had 'Western-ized' very rapidly, took an interest in northern China; they too clashed with Russians who built a Far Eastern railway that ran through Chinese territory, in Manchuria.

In response to all of this, the German government decided to create a great battle-fleet, for which laws were passed in 1897 and 1900. Germany had clearly become the greatest Power in Europe; the merchants of *Sammlungspolitik* wished to make her a true world Power. But Germany could not gain colonies unless she could gain the partnership of Great Britain, whose navy was by far the largest in the world. Admiral Tirpitz, the architect of Germany's navy, argued that the British could be forced into concession. A German navy might be smaller than the British, but if it came to a battle between them, so many British ships would be sunk even in the event of a British victory that the victors would risk becoming inferior to the next strongest naval Powers, France and Russia. That risk, the British would not take. They would be compelled to take Germany's side in world affairs.

This coincided with a complicated battle over China. Russian adventurers and soldiers wished to seize Manchuria, and eventually Korea as well. They collided with Japanese interests in both cases, and, on the whole, the British supported Japan. France, Russia's ally, could therefore be dragged into a Far Eastern quarrel in which she had little interest. There were, therefore, two separate and in a way contradictory diplomatic problems: an Anglo-Russian quarrel, which set Great Britain apart from the Franco-Russian alliance; and an increasing fear in London that the German navy was meant to threaten the British position in the world. By 1900, both quarrels dominated British thinking. For the moment, these problems were not acute. The British navy was so large that it could contain both problems. The Boer War was fought in 'splendid isolation', despite gestures by the Germans on behalf of the Boers. The French threat to the upper Nile was easily contained at Fashoda. In the Far East, the British position was made much easier, in naval terms, because in 1902 an Anglo-Japanese alliance was concluded.

The dominant motive, here, was naval: the British, who had controlled Far Eastern waters without difficulty a generation before, were now outnumbered there by the warships of other Powers.

From time to time, one or other of the continental Powers would suggest a continental league against the British. But these ideas lacked reality. The French were far more worried about German strength than about British imperialism. The tsar did look favourably on a link with Germany, and, in 1897, agreed to put Balkan questions 'on ice' (the Mürzsteg agreement) so as to avoid tiresome quarrelling over the Near East. But the Russian foreign ministry could not abandon its French alliance; and in 1898 that alliance was subtly altered to become, in effect, an offensive one. Another often-discussed idea at this time was an Anglo-German alliance. It was proposed by Chamberlain in 1898 and again in 1901; there was frothy talk about 'the Teutonic and Anglo-Saxon races'. But such schemes foundered for obvious reasons. The British would not go to war with France in order to make Germany even more clearly the leading continental Power. The Germans would not make war on Russia for the sake of British investments in Shanghai.

Still, by 1903 Anglo-German rivalry in naval matters was causing a considerable change in the climate. In the Far East, Russian blundering brought about a very tense situation. Troops were sent into Manchuria, promises were made to withdraw them, and the promises were not kept. In the event, Japanese forces attacked the Russian concession at Port Arthur early in 1904, and a war broke out, which lasted until summer 1905. It ended with Russian humiliation, especially in the spectacular affair of Tsushima, when the Russian Baltic fleet, having carried out an odyssey lasting for several months, was sunk almost without trace in the straits between Japan and Korea.

The quarrelling between Japan and Russia greatly alarmed Paris and London; in 1903, the British and French began to discuss ways of improving their own relationship. On one level, it was simply an imperial bargain. The French gave up their claim to Egypt; the British agreed to support French claims to Morocco. It was a sensible enough bargain, and could easily be justified in its own terms. But it also had anti-German implications, which were largely brought about by Tirpitz's ambitions. On 4 April 1904, the bargain was concluded, and described as 'Entente cordiale'. In this way, the imperialist wave of the turn of the century created an international tension which made everyone conscious of war.

Still, nationalism and imperialism were popular causes at this time. A considerable literature, on all levels, propagated them. Schoolboys in England read G.A. Henty, and in Germany, Karl May. Crowds gathered, almost hysterically, to celebrate the relief of Mafeking in the Boer War, or the launching of Tirpitz's great ships. Historians made fortunes as they celebrated their nation's past as a procession of great men and great events; a Holland Rose could smugly close his life of Napoleon with the sentiment that the whole story displayed, not the martial vigour of Latin peoples, but the sturdiness of 'the Teutonic Races'. In Great Britain, empire was a cause that suited the millions of people who had relatives abroad; everywhere, the thrills of imperialism seem to have taken people, in imagination, away from the humdrum world of the suburbs and back-streets.

On another level, empire generated a quantity of theorizing, both for and against. The arguments for it were simple enough, though they were often stated at great length – never more so than in the pages of Hitler's *Mein Kampf*, although it, written in the early 1920s, was much further away from nineteenth-century morality than its precursors. Theorists such as Gustave Le Bon in France or Heinrich Class in Germany contemplated the proletariat, the strikes, and the vicissitudes of the economy. If there were colonies, then the surplus proletariat could be exported. There would also be a captured market and cheap raw materials. A tariff wall around the empire would keep out cheap foreign competition; metropolitan industry would complement imperial agriculture to the benefit of all parties; in that way, industrial strife would be diminished, since prosperity would be guaranteed. The alternative was endless class-war. 'Who will avoid civil war must be an Imperialist,' said Cecil Rhodes, architect of the British empire in southern Africa. 'To keep the masses from revolt,' remarked the Kaiser's friend, Prince Eulenburg, 'we must have a forward policy.' The navy, said Tirpitz in his arguments of 1897, would be the answer 'both to educated and uneducated social democracy'. 'Colonial policy is the daughter of industrialization,' thought Jules Ferry. 'Social Darwinism' was often brought into imperial matters, as into discussions of class, to demonstrate that racial and social hierarchies had a biological foundation, i.e. that Might was Right. This went down well, especially in Protestant countries, and especially in Prussia.

It also mattered that imperialists could present themselves as doing good. The British saw themselves as bringing good government, Roman-fashion; the French justified their empire in terms of a 'civilizing mission' (agreeably parodied as *'la syphilisation française'*). In the colonies, nationalist opposition was usually driven on to the defensive, arguing merely for greater autonomy, or for the colonists to live up to their own precepts. On the whole, German imperialism was much harsher. In 1904, a revolt in south-west Africa was crushed by methods of extermination: a whole Herrero population was deprived of access to water. The régime of the Belgian king's private estate in the Congo was so cruel that it was condemned even by an international commission which the king himself had chosen after the régime had been memorably denounced by an Irish investigator, Roger Casement. In western Europe, there were always many metropolitan consciences that could be stirred at imperialist misdeeds. To some extent this was responsible for the growing habit, in the few years before 1914, of not calling spades, spades. By 1905, colonies were coming to be known as 'protectorates', an anticipation of the later 'mandate'.

The opposition to imperialism came, in the first place, from radical liberals who detested the gaudy pretence and the piracy of empires. In the 1880s, such radical-liberal opposition was very strong, both in Great Britain and France; in Germany the anti-clerical (*Freisinn*) leader Eugen Richter was loud in denunciation of imperialism and profiteers, and the clerical radical Matthias Erzberger took over his anti-colonial role in 1905. The chief text of such radicals was J.A. Hobson's book on empire. To Hobson, a British radical, empire was a fraud – it syphoned off money that ought to be left at home to develop the national economy. But there was also a socialist concern with empire. As mob-imperialism took over in many countries, socialists sometimes feared that they would be defeated by it. The masses would go over to nationalism; more importantly, the economic fruits of imperial exploitation would stave off the social crisis which Marxists expected. However, both Rudolf Hilferding and Rosa Luxemburg were able to offer a convenient (and often convincing) explanation of it all, which Lenin subsequently adapted in his *Imperialism*. The worldwide competition for empire would create more economic problems than it solved; the primary producers would be impoverished; their impoverishment might bring down native peasantries and turn them into proletarians; empires, by exploiting the conquered peoples, would also be impoverishing their own markets; and in any case imperial rivalries would, in the end, bring about a European war which would wreck everything. These arguments did not cut much ice in France or Great Britain, where socialists, for most of the time, wanted only to make the empires work more fairly. But they meant a great deal to the German left and to the Bolsheviks, Lenin's followers, who regarded Russia as a semi-colony of the more developed West.

The new imperialism also involved an internal programme: indeed, ideas of national planning really date from the later 1890s. In Great Britain, there was widespread alarm at the progress of German and American competition, which had already destroyed the preponderance of British trade in the world. There, and elsewhere, the growth of class-war alarmed anyone who thought about it. Liberals who looked at the cities were shocked at the slums, and felt that the State could act; many economists were now prepared to allow the State a greater economic role than in the past, so that the ups and downs of the business cycle could be smoothed out. In the era of conservative imperialism, around 1900, there was a very clear choice as to how such improvements would be carried out. Either there would be a much greater tax on income, with the rich paying proportionately more, to pay for a bureaucracy that would do more efficiently what, in the past, had been done by Churches, families, private charity and private enterprise; or governments would gain money from imperialism and a tariff on foreign goods.

In most cases, governments became concerned with 'national efficiency', i.e. simply with making the existing system work better. In Great Britain, there was widespread imitation of the Germans' technical colleges; Imperial College, London, was set up; the new University of Birmingham and the London School of Economics were supposed to turn out 'technocrats' of various sorts. An Education Act in 1902 followed. It was supposed to clear up some of the muddle of conflicting local authorities and religious bodies, and to bring order to secondary education. In Italy, the Bocconi Institute of Economics was set up in 1902 by the father of the later economist, Piero Sraffa. The Leipzig Business School began in 1898. In France, in 1902, the classical *baccalauréat* was reformed to allow study of modern languages and science. In Prussia, compulsory secondary education was introduced in 1906. In all cases, there were wrangles over religion, as there had been over the institution of primary education in the 1870s. But the Churches had become victims of the economic decline which so many established bodies experienced in the later nineteenth century. They could not afford schools as they had done in the past; in England, the unaided Anglican schools were often financed by Church bazaars, and in France the Church schools usually depended on hand-outs and fees from the rich. On the continent (including Austria-Hungary and Russia) the State's ministry of education could act according to the principles of the eighteenth-century Enlightenment, as transmitted by the Despots or by Napoleon. School-students took a final examination, whether *baccalauréat* or *Matura*, which required them to know a great deal about many demanding subjects. In England (though to a lesser extent in Scotland) the survival of a semi-*ancien-régime* system meant that specialization in classics was still very much the order of the day; and that specialization was carried over, at the older universities' behest, to other subjects as well.

'National efficiency' meant strong government, combined with measures of social welfare to silence the socialists – an old-age pension, insurance against sickness, insurance against unemployment. The ruling conservatives around 1900 feared that these things would be paid for by a direct tax. In Great Britain, the principle of graduated taxation, by which the better-off paid a higher proportion of their income or property (e.g. death duties or, as they were called in the bureaucratic euphemism that became more frequent later on, 'inheritance taxes'), had been launched by the last Liberal government in 1893. The Prussian government levied an income tax of this kind in 1891. But in agrarian countries, where farmers either did not keep books or could easily 'cook' them, levying an income tax was difficult. Even in England, when a million income-tax forms were sent out, 600,000 were not returned. The Italian and French parliaments refused it again and again in the 1890s and 1900s; the imperialists of 1900 in Great Britain and Germany sought to avoid it through the fruits of empire. They also wanted to use tariffs to augment revenue and thereby increase 'social expenditure'.

Great Britain was the classic country of free trade. But by 1900 many of her manufacturers complained at more efficient foreign competition from Germans or even Japanese (who were rumoured, for instance, to be taking over the Australian market for hair-brushes). Joseph Chamberlain, the dominant spirit of the government at this time, stumped the country in 1903 to explain that full employment and social welfare would follow from a tariff. Industrial goods from outside the empire would be taxed throughout the empire, and British goods would therefore have a near-monopoly. In return, the agricultural produce of the empire would have a near-monopoly in Great Britain herself, since there would be a tax on non-imperial foods. This programme did not suit Great Britain since a very small part of her population lived from the land, and Chamberlain could simply be accused of making the working classes pay higher prices for their food. The young Winston Churchill broke with the conservatives on this issue, and Chamberlain nearly broke his own party.

Elsewhere, arguments over tariffs also raged, and, when it came to food tariffs, the presence of large agricultural populations made a considerable difference to their acceptability. In Germany, in 1902, the new chancellor, Bülow, managed to put through a considerable increase in the tariff, both on food and on iron and steel: agrarian deputies made up two-fifths of the *Reichstag*, and the National Liberal party had, by this stage, become little more than a gramophone-record to be played by heavy industrialists in western Germany. France and Italy were already high-tariff countries, at least by the standards of the day. It was in vain that liberal economists such as Pantaleone or Einaudi in Italy, or Charles-Roux in France, or Lujo von Brentano in Germany complained. They were probably right in arguing that free trade, for all of its temporary problems, would be superior to tariffs in the long run; in the high-tariff circumstances of the 1930s, world trade was indeed ruined, and did not recover its level of 1913 until 1951. The whole issue was very complex, and went above most people's heads. In 1909 the Italian government sent out questionnaires to thousands of businesses about their view of tariffs; 291 replies were received. Still, too many people, in too many countries, had a direct interest in tariffs, and, once a great country like Germany introduced them, other countries could hardly do other than follow. By 1912, Russia and France threatened to impose a greater tariff than ever before, and Chamberlain's cause had converted the Conservatives by 1910.

In many respects, the imperialist régimes at the turn of the century had been trying to find external solutions for internal problems. The trouble was that they all ran into contradictions. Empire was supposed to bring profit. In practice, it brought substantial loss, even in day-to-day administration. By now, armies and navies were becoming exceedingly expensive. There had been technological revolutions in military matters, just as there had been in civilian affairs. Better steel allowed artillery to develop in a revolutionary way in the 1890s, making guns lighter and faster firing. By 1905, the British were able to plan an all-big-gun ship which made all others obsolete. The longer range of artillery also made most fortifications obsolete; and the rise in commodity prices made the supplying of conscripts so expensive that armies were driven, more and more, to exempt possible candidates – the Habsburg Monarchy faced serious difficulty in financing its army, and although its population doubled between 1868, when conscription was introduced, and 1914, when war broke out, the army that took the field in 1914 actually contained fewer military units than the army of 1866. The British found that the Boer War, from 1899 to 1902, was very expensive indeed: £222,000,000. The tsarist government spent 2,000,000,000 roubles in the Japanese war of 1904–5, which was more than a whole year's ordinary budget. The German navy's costs rose from 90,000,000 marks per annum in the mid-1890s to almost 400,000,000. 'Defence' was in fact costing more than all of the then imaginable social reforms rolled into one. Budgets, everywhere, came under strain. The first British government borrowing from the United States occurred in 1901; the German government, in the depressed circumstances of 1900, also borrowed from the American firm, Kuhn, Loeb and Co., and in 1902 made its first use of the short-term *Schatzwechsel* (treasury bonds) that were to become the main tool of the new century's inflationary finance.

The opponents of direct taxes were, therefore, themselves responsible for a situation in which these were becoming unavoidable. But this expensive imperialism also coincided with an economic down-turn in the years 1900–3, which affected all countries, though especially Russia. Government spending, especially in Great Britain, did something to smooth out this depression, but it also brought about another twentieth-century phenomenon, a combination of unemployment and inflation. By 1904, there were very widespread troubles throughout Europe. In France and Italy, the imperialist class-warriors had been wrecked by their own folly in 1899; left-leaning liberal governments had already made their appearance. Elsewhere, there was an upsurge of discontent which resulted, almost everywhere in Europe, in governments that could claim to be 'Popular Fronts'.

3.   1905: the Ghost of 1848

Around the year 1905, there were upheavals all over Europe. Many discontents became fused into a detestation of the status quo. Working men struck; peasants rioted; women rebelled; national minorities erupted; 'revolutionary syndicalists' threatened, or rather, promised, anarchy; young middle-class radicals demonstrated, and swung liberal parties towards the left.

These eruptions varied from place to place. They were at their mildest in Great Britain where, in January 1906, a landslide brought the Liberals, once more, to power, this time with a huge majority. Still, the outgoing Conservative prime minister, Arthur Balfour, was quite correct when he remarked, to the king's secretary, that 'We are face to face (no doubt in milder form) with the socialistic difficulties that loom so large on the continent.' In Russia, these 'difficulties' took the form of a revolution which began in January 1905, continued through general strikes, and almost cost the tsar his throne. He kept it only by agreeing to parliamentary government in October. In Belgium, the Netherlands, Luxemburg, Sweden and Italy there were general strikes between 1902 and 1904. In Austria, huge working-class demonstrations in October 1905 compelled the emperor to introduce universal suffrage. There were conditions almost of civil war in Hungary in 1905; Sweden and Norway split apart. 1904 and 1905 were the worst years for strikes that Germany experienced at any time before the revolutionary upheavals of 1918–19, and a strange régime (the *Bülow-Block*) came to power. In Munich, huge demonstrations brought about universal suffrage. In France, the left-inclined Combes government separated Church and State in 1905, to widespread rioting; and in the following year, in May, France was disrupted by a set of strikes, collectively known as '*les espérances de mai*', when the bourgeoisie stocked their stables with chickens and rabbits, and, in some cases, moved over the Swiss border with their cash in suitcases. In Romania, in the spring of 1907, there was a huge peasant revolt which was crushed only after the killing of 20,000 people. In Spain, the 'tragic week' of Barcelona in 1909 involved an epidemic of violence, in which twenty-one churches and forty convents were sacked and burned; in 1910, a revolt in Portugal put an end to the monarchy there.

The common factors in all of these upheavals were the bankruptcy of the right, and the challenge from the left. The first of these was displayed in loss of parliamentary control, in budgetary confusion, and, often, in the failure of imperialist enterprises. Right-wing parties everywhere were divided as to what should be done, and these divisions resulted in the British Conservatives' simply resigning late in 1905 – calculating (wrongly) that the Liberals would themselves split, and that some would opt for a Conservative alliance. In Germany, the 'Blue-Black Block' of conservatives and Catholics, which had forced through a high grain tariff in 1902, broke apart when the Catholics' leader, Erzberger, denounced the follies of colonialism in 1905. In France, some years before, the Méline alliance of agrarians and right-wing republican liberals also broke apart, largely because of the tensions of the Dreyfus affair; most right-wing liberals, with Waldeck-Rousseau and Raymond Poincaré at their head, preferred to make an alliance with the left-wing groups (the *Bloc des Gauches*), and by 1902 there was a solid alliance of left and centre, presided over by the radical, Emile Combes. In Italy, too, the follies of the right, in the era of General Pelloux, had prompted the king to establish a government under the radical, Zanardelli, who gave place, in 1902, to Giovanni Giolitti, a man who could talk common language with the emerging left.

The challenge from the left, which was at the centre of the European upheavals at this time, varied very greatly from place to place, and, within countries, from region to region. At its heart was a combination of circumstances not incomparable with those of the revolutions of 1848. As Eric Hobsbawm has remarked, the political instability of a depression appears, not at the depth of the trough, but just as the economy is recovering.

Concentration of industry in Berlin, 1895–1907

	Metal-working	
	1895	1907
Small works	2991	2582
Employees	6804	6291
Medium works	1011	1169
Employees	14,217	17,462
Large works	97	154
Employees	10,164	20,121

	Engineering	
	1895	1907
Small works	1874	1842
Employees	3618	3849
Medium works	738	1119
Employees	12,000	19,240
Large works	133	256
Employees	20,000	71,918

After the boom of the later 1890s, the European economy had encountered trouble, especially in countries which had only just 'taken off' in industrial terms, i.e. Russia and Italy. Building, iron and steel declined sharply in 1900–1. Prices fell, as producers off-loaded stocks which they could not afford to maintain; and in Germany, for instance, sheet-steel prices fell from 139.90 marks per ton to 103.40 in 1901–3. There was an impulse for cartels to be formed, for businesses to rationalize. In Berlin, there was a marked concentration of the metal-working industry (see the table on page 109). Unemployment rose sharply in Germany, which depended to a large extent on the Russian market, and, after the end of the Boer War, in Great Britain. By 1903, most countries were recovering. As had occurred in the past, the fall in prices made some people better off, if they were in steady employment. Latin America, for instance, bought more European goods, and business moved upwards again. Prices rose accordingly, as demand increased, and so too did employment. But there were still pools of unemployed in the industrial countries; and the workers who had been newly taken in found that their wages were not keeping pace with inflation. In Berlin metals, wages rose by 13 per cent but profits by 37.6 per cent in the decade before 1914, and prices by roughly one-third. Workers faced businessmen who had formed price-rings – the effect of cartels – and who, especially in Germany, co-operated with each other to avoid recognizing trade unions and to keep wages low. Continental Europe experienced labour-unrest as never before in the years 1903–6; Great Britain experienced a similar, and much greater, wave of it after 1909, although she had largely avoided industrial trouble in mid-decade. In Russia, Italy and, later, in Spain, industrial discontents became fused with riots of the unemployed and peasant upheavals to such an extent that the movement rapidly took on a political character. In Germany, the trade-union leadership was nearly brought to endorse the 'revolutionary general strike', i.e. strikes by all workers which would be pursued to the destruction of capitalist society.

In practice, the labour movements of Europe presented a very incoherent picture. Strikes broke out for many and various reasons: here because of 'luddism', or rather, trade-union efforts to dictate the manpower levels for new machines; there, because of trade-union attempts to wrest recognition; here, because of inflation, and the bosses' profits; there, because of a desire to involve the State. It would be tempting to argue that new technology was undercutting the skilled labourer; that machines, worked by apprentices or women who were paid less than a skilled man, were making the skilled worker a revolutionary rather than, as before, an aristocrat of labour. The difficulty here is that, apart from some branches of engineering, the high-technology industries were not especially militant. In Germany, chemicals, electrical works and even shipping were among the least troubled industries, whereas, everywhere, textiles produced most trouble, although they were not centres of rapid technological change. On the whole, it was those industries that had least investment and the most unstable markets that produced industrial trouble. Besides, the truly revolutionary socialist consciousness came, not from trade-union activity in established industries, but, rather, from almost unorganized mass-protests in a context of casual, unskilled or semi-skilled labour.

Still, 1905 was the first moment in European history when strikes, breaking out for some ostensibly absurd cause, hit people who could not answer back. There was, for instance, a four-day railway strike on Tyneside in 1910 over nothing in particular; in the same year, boiler-makers struck over whether a machine was to be minded by one man or two; in 1906, the electricians turned out the lights of the Paris Opera at the start of a gala performance for the king of the Belgians; in 1911, it became common for French and Italian postal workers and primary schoolteachers to threaten to strike. There were railway strikes in both countries, and in Great Britain, where the question of 'differentials' between ordinary railwaymen and skilled locomotive-drivers was an increasing preoccupation.

These strikes sometimes caused a wave of alarm among the propertied elements of society. German industrialists, such as H.A. Bueck, the long-serving secretary of their *Zentralverband*, often responded with hysteria, and described the 'crushing of socialism' as 'a blow for civilization, without parallel in the annals of history' (1912). The monster-demonstrations of 1905, when a quarter of a million working men and their wives marched round the Ringstrasse of Vienna to demand universal (male) suffrage, terrorized many members of the middle classes. But the strikes themselves were not overtly revolutionary: they were meant only to settle a grievance against a private owner, and did not – ostensibly – involve any threat to the State. In January 1905 a huge concourse of working people of St Petersburg converged on the Winter Palace to petition the tsar for improvements in their lot. Under the leadership of a priest, they held up portraits of the tsar and sang patriotic songs. In Sicily, in the bloody affair of the *Fasci* in 1892–3, the crowds held up portraits of the king and queen, and of the Virgin (though they also held up portraits of Marx). During the First World War, English strikers sometimes demonstrated with 'God Save the King' to the bewilderment of International Socialists. Indeed, sensible bureaucrats – and each ministry of labour contained many – well understood that, the stronger the trade-union movement, the weaker the revolutionary potential of the industrial proletariat. The more strikes, the less revolution. The United States, Great Britain, Belgium, Germany and France headed the strike table for the decade before 1914. There, trade unions were relatively strong, and it was quite clear to most people, including revolutionary socialists, that their aim was to improve conditions, not to change the system.

Strikes might turn into a revolutionary force if the system itself proved to be too rigid (as was certainly true of Russia). After 1900, there was certainly a widespread feeling in most places that the class structure and the prevailing economic system were unjust. Intellectuals like Rudolf Hilferding might try to grasp the whole phenomenon, to demonstrate

its contradictory and unsatisfactory nature. Most people
voted socialist simply because of some harsh manifestation
of the system – for instance, the French peasants who voted
left because they disliked their creditors, or thought their
rent was too high. As the towns grew, and education reached
the working classes, discrimination became only too obvious.
The Russian war minister, Kuropatkin, would not conscript
proletarians 'on moral and physical grounds'. The Prussian
war ministry conscripted a far higher proportion of peasant
than of proletarian youth on the grounds that peasants were
more deferential and in better health – although in reality the
conditions of the great cities improved greatly after 1895. In
public parks, people with a proletarian appearance would be
turned out by aggressive park-keepers; in Berlin, and
elsewhere in Europe, house entrances would have a notice on
them, 'This staircase to be used only by persons of quality'
(the German has an insulting succinctness: *'Nur für Herr-
schaften'*). In the old days, such things might have seemed to
be part of the natural order. Towards the turn of the century,
there was a change in atmosphere of quite a dramatic kind.
The Russian socialist revolutionary, Yekaterina Breshko-
Breshkovskaya, returned from two decades' Siberian exile to
her native town, Tambov, and was astonished to see how the
churches contained only old women and children, whereas
in the past they had been full, and the spaces for candles had
been so overwhelmingly taken up that the sacristan would
have to remove candles before they had fully burned.

Socialism (and, in France, self-consciously secular radical
liberalism) offered a counter-culture. Working-class organizations were designed to offer not only 'economic struggle'
but also self-respect for the despised proletarian. The
German socialists built up large libraries; the miners of the
Rhondda, in South Wales, had a vast collection of closely
argued pamphlets on 'scientific socialism'; the Spanish
socialist leader, Pablo Iglesias, lived an austere existence in
which he studied, dressed neatly, kept himself clean and –
like a great many other socialists in Europe – avoided drink:
all of it a conscious campaign against the bourgeois opinion

that proletarians were inevitably scruffy, drunken, improvident and unfaithful, as in G.B. Shaw's contemporary dustman, Alfred Doolittle. True, there were cynics around, who discovered that, of books taken out of the Favoriten district headquarters of Vienna socialism, eighty-three per cent came under the heading *Belletristik* – i.e., 'penny dreadfuls' – and that the pages of the heavier academic works in German socialist libraries were usually uncut after the first few, for it required real dedication for a man to get through works such as Karl Kautsky's *Peasant Question*. Did this mean that the working classes were not as class-conscious as their leaders expected them to be; or did it mean only that Kautsky was a crashing bore? Opinions divided. Even so, socialists of this era were self-consciously progressive, believers in education, callisthenics and uplift. In Great Britain the Workmen's Educational Association and in France the *universités populaires*, both of them started up around the turn of the century, brought middle-class educational missionaries to complement, in a self-consciously secular way, what organizations like the Salvation Army or the *Cercles ouvriers* aimed to achieve for religion. 1905 was a time of hope for Progressives everywhere: they could look forward to a hygienic, problem-free, educated future, regulated by rational principles. It was not accidental that the first exercises in 'Brave New World' literature were produced before the First World War, as with E.M. Forster's *The Machine*, in which featureless zombies press buttons to satisfy their narrow range of wants and then blow themselves up.

Socialism emerged in strength in any parliamentary country with a wide franchise because it offered immediate social reforms by State action. In the 1880s, people had relied for welfare on their own efforts or their families or the churches or private charity. Insurance companies and 'friendly' societies offered insurance against old age or sickness. The more enlightened businesses offered pensions (as in the railways) or sick-beds. Since money kept its value until 1895, savings were promoted, and post offices could be used to that effect: in the 1880s, clerical-dominated régimes in Austria and Belgium had deliberately used the post offices to complement the campaign against village usury (which in Austria was thought to be a Jewish-Protestant plot), and in the later 1890s Karl Lueger subsidized the construction of a spectacular piece of modernist architecture, Otto Wagner's *Postsparkassenverein*, on the Cochplatz in Vienna. But, after 1895, these private arrangements, even with modest State encouragement, were breaking down.

Modest inflation after 1896 did not affect the volume of savings – on the contrary, they doubled or trebled in all countries before 1914 – but the cities had grown to such an extent that welfare could not be left to families alone, which, themselves, were under pressure. The churches had, generally, collapsed as agents of charity, and even as agents of education. In Italy and Spain, their lands had been secularized, and in most other countries, the churches, whose property was generally in land, had been victims of the 'Great Depression'. Fellows of King's College, Cambridge, an ecclesiastical foundation with its endowments in land, were paid £270 per annum in the 1870s, but they had to accept only £80 twenty years later. In Russia, church schools were so dilapidated that tsarist educational statistics are largely fictitious. In France, when Church and State were separated in 1905–6, there was a great row over the supposed *milliard* of clerical property. It turned out to be much less; indeed, the State made a considerable loss on the deal, and, as well, lost its influence over Church appointments.

The 'Welfare State' appeared to be the only possible alternative: a system designed by the State to insure people against the ills of the age. The expression itself, though now best known in its English form, came from a German original – *Wohlfahrtsstaat*, which referred to 'prosperity' rather than 'welfare'. Classical liberals had not been heartless about welfare; but their priority had always been the prosperity of the economy, which depended on flourishing businesses, which in turn must not be burdened with 'social' costs – such as the provision of hospital beds, paid holidays and the like.

The harsher economists of the neo-classical school were, in principle, against the 'feather-bedding' of labour, on the grounds that labour would become lazy and expensive. In all European countries, the industrialists were usually opposed to provision of welfare, since it would add to their costs and would maybe price them out of the market. Indeed, they would contemplate such measures only if there were an agreement among the European Powers to make social legislation similar throughout the continent. In 1906, there was, for instance, a conference at Rome to discuss such measures as the equalization of unemployment insurance. Nothing came of these well-meant initiatives.

Bismarck had been the first politician in a major country to undertake large-scale provision for welfare. In 1883, 1884 and 1889 his *Reichstag* had passed measures for insurance against sickness, old age and infirmity. The State underwrote funds for these purposes, to which employers and employees contributed. The German liberals, in the main, voted against this, and their equivalents everywhere else acted similarly, though with more success, on the grounds that the State had no business to be interfering. But the Prussian State had a long paternalist tradition; it also had a long history of interfering with capitalism; and in any case Bismarck, and a great many *Reichstag* members, were terrified of the young socialist movement. By 1900, many liberals in the West were anxious to defeat the socialists by measures of social reform. In all countries, there was extensive discussion of a State-organized, universal old-age pension by 1900, and in most there already had been provisions for insurance against accidents and sickness. These provisions were not compulsory, and the State contributed very little. Governments shrank from saddling the tax-payer with such costs; and in any case, there were many technical problems. In Great Britain, the existing insurance companies were doing, they thought, a decent job. An old-age pension was not a simple matter: in Ireland, registration of births had been quite recent, and there was nothing to prevent people from claiming their pensions although they had not reached the pensionable age – a fear that was by no means groundless, as the rapid rise of pension costs after 1912 was to show. In the later 1890s and early 1900s, wrangling went on inside governments, and within parliaments; but nothing much was changed. In England, the Poor Law continued to operate, with its provisions for 'aged paupers', its convict dress and its workhouses for the children of the poor. The principle of the 'New Poor Law' of 1834 continued to operate, that charitable provisions should be so appalling that any form of employment, however ill-paid, would be preferable. It was on such grounds that insurance against unemployment was resisted by employers generally.

In the more advanced countries, there was always a substantial part of the working class and the peasantry who could 'stand on their own two feet', i.e., pay school-fees and the various kinds of insurance. But for the bulk of the lower classes, secondary schooling, medical attention and security in old age were hardly conceivable. By 1900, socialist parties, which offered an alternative, were already well to the fore; and by 1914 they usually became the dominant party in any universal-suffrage parliament. In France, they rose from an eighth to a fifth of the Chamber; in Germany, from a fifth to a third; by 1914, there was even serious question of socialist official participation in the Dutch government; an independent socialist, René Viviani, was French prime minister; local government in most of Europe already had socialist mayors and councillors in great number.

Socialists at first presented a united front. In the early 1890s they had absorbed the anarchists, and by 1904 even the squabbling French left-wing groups had fused into one party, the grandly named *Section française de l'Internationale ouvrière* (SFIO). The International met every two years, in cities such as Copenhagen or Stuttgart or Amsterdam, where local laws would not be used to harass respectable socialists. Its executive body, the Bureau, met more frequently, with the Belgian, Emile Vandevelde, as its long-service secretary. Socialist delegations from all over Europe vowed to fight capitalism and war, although they often disagreed as to methods.

These disagreements between European parties were, if anything, less violent than disagreements within parties and unions. In countries where there was universal suffrage, and where there were sympathetic radical liberals, socialists could easily foresee the day when they would come to power. They would be able, if not to create socialism overnight, at least to introduce reforms that would bring benefits to the ordinary working man: provision for health, education, old age, the eight-hour day, progressive taxation of the rich, land reform and a running-down of the war machine. True, these reforms would make no sense if capitalism were going to collapse in the way Marx had foretold. But in the later 1890s, capitalism was thriving as never before, and the proletarians themselves were clearly better off as a result. Eduard Bernstein, a German socialist who had spent years of exile in England, wrote a series of articles and then a famous book, *The Preconditions for Socialism* (1899), in which he set out an argument for 'revision' of the original socialist programme: instead of waiting for the collapse of capitalism and the revolution to come, German socialists would do better to forget much of their anti-liberal stance, co-operate with the democratic liberals, and gradually introduce reforms that would benefit their voters. In France, Alexandre Millerand, a young lawyer who had made a name for himself by defending socialists in the courts, made a speech in his constituency, Saint-Mandé, in which he argued much the same. In 1899 Millerand went further and accepted a post in the cabinet of Waldeck-Rousseau. Orthodox socialists were shocked to see one of their number sitting in the same cabinet as General Galliffet, who had crushed the Paris Commune in 1871. But Millerand used his post to bring in social reforms of a sort – greater trade-union presence in the councils to adjudicate wage-questions, for instance. He could argue that more would have been achieved if more socialists had followed him. 'Revisionists' and 'Reformists' (not quite, though nearly, the same thing) echoed Millerand's arguments all over Europe, especially where they found a wide suffrage and radical-liberal allies, as was most obviously the case in Great Britain.

Millerand was expelled by his own party, and the International not only voted him down, but formally forbade any of its member-parties to take part in a government of the capitalist order. The bulk of socialists might have sympathized with Millerand and Bernstein. There was every case for Millerand to support the Third Republic in the face of its nationalist and Catholic enemies. In southern Germany, where universal suffrage prevailed, socialists occupied prominent places in parliaments; in Baden, they encountered a sympathetic ministry, and voted for its budget when otherwise its proposals for graduated income tax would have been voted down. In Austria, in 1905, the ministry looked to social democrats to save the Habsburg Monarchy from the endless, dreary nationality disputes: the social democrats would talk money, not nonsense, and the prime minister, Baron Gautsch, regarded them as 'a wholly tractable party'. In Great Britain, the Labour Party was *Millerandiste* from its inception. The unions and most members of Parliament were happy enough with their solid Liberal alliance, the 'Lib-Lab' arrangements concluded in 1903.

In countries with harsher political systems, social democrats responded with much more strongly revolutionary talk. In Prussia, the legacy of Bismarck's anti-socialist laws was large, even after 1890. The mass electorate was effectively disenfranchised, through the workings of the 'Three-Class Franchise' which gave weight to the votes of the better-off. The police and the courts were extremely hostile to social democrats, and the bosses usually disliked trade unions. In Russia, socialists were exiled. In Italy and Spain, they faced discriminatory legislation.

Besides, even in universal-suffrage countries, there was a vociferous socialist left. Its officers were frequently intellectuals, such as the French journalist Fernand Pelloutier, or the Polish-Jewish Rosa Luxemburg or the Neapolitan professor of economics, Arturo Labriola. The left tended to recruit men and women who felt out of even the established organizations, such as trade unions. Often, very young people were involved, people whose parents had migrated to the towns, and who tried to find casual work in a hostile economic climate. The orthodox socialists did not believe in immediate, violent revolution. 'Scientific socialism', endorsed by at least the middle-period Marx, was about patient organization, the building up of adherents and funds for the great day when the final collapse of capitalism would occur. If there were premature action, then the bourgeoisie would only have an excuse for using the police, and setting the socialist movement back. The anarchists had disliked such 'attentism' – i.e., a policy of waiting – and had broken with Marx. Later, a fusion did occur of anarchists and socialists, but it was an uneasy partnership.

Anarchic impulses were still very strong within the official socialist movement. In France and Italy they came from an institution which anarchists captured: the *Bourses du travail*, or *Camere del lavoro*. These bodies had been set up at the suggestion of a Belgian economist, Gustave de Mollinari, in 1887; they had been quite widely instituted in France and Italy (and even had an equivalent, though of different subsequent development, in the British Trades Councils or the German Trade Federations). They were buildings that could be used as employment exchanges, and they contained 'cultural facilities'; working people could meet in them. In Italy and France, they were infiltrated by anarchists, and a federation of them appeared in both countries. The federations were not liked by ordinary trade unions, but fusions occurred in the 1890s. The result was that at every socialist conference there would be a battle between the orthodox, the 'reformists' or 'revisionists', and the left. Increasingly, the left used the term 'revolutionary syndicalist' to describe itself. The trade unions (in French, *syndicat*, in Italian *sindacato*) should proclaim a general strike. Then, capitalism would collapse. Trade unions would take power, and would organize the economy as a huge producers' co-operative: no churches, no repressive legislation, promotion of technology, leisure, etc. Anarchists were given to reading science fiction. Orthodox socialists would point out that these general strikes would, very likely, not succeed: workers themselves would report for work, and the police would crush the strikers. To this, revolutionary syndicalists answered that, the more the police crushed strikers, the worse the mood of the proletariat would become, and the more class-conscious the working classes would be. The worse, in other words, the better – an expression used by the Russian social democrat, V.I. Lenin.

Revolutionary syndicalists occupied headlines. In September 1904 they organized a general strike in northern and central Italy, although it collapsed after a few days. They made a name for themselves in Great Britain in 1909–10, and again with James Larkin's Dublin dock strike of 1913. The Italian party was captured, for a time, by the left in 1912–13. In Germany, the trade unions were on the verge of adopting Rosa Luxemburg's resolution for the political general strike both in 1905 and in 1910.

However, in political terms, revolutionary syndicalism never broke through orthodox socialist positions. It suffered, as did the 'revisionist' right of the party, from a fatal flaw: it would divide the party. Socialism had been built up painfully and, usually, successfully, almost as a missionary creed. Its established leaders were proud of their creation; they were all optimistic; they wanted to keep together. 'Provocateurs' on the left, or secessionists on the right, were equally a danger, however appealing, for the moment, the arguments of one or other might appear to be. It was safer for the orthodox, the 'Centrists' – as they were called in Germany – to do nothing. Kautsky expressed this well when he said, 'We are a revolutionary party, but not one that makes revolutions.' Filippo Turati, the Italian party's leader, dismissed the general strike of 1904 as 'revolutionary gymnastics'; a colleague, Leonida Bissolati, called it 'a purely choreographic pose'; and for the next few years, the party was 'centrist' in its line – no participation in a bourgeois government, but equally no revolutionary antics. In these circumstances, the general strikes of the years 1902–6 came to nothing, at least in political terms. Even in Russia, where the upheaval was easily the greatest in Europe, the divisions of socialists (in this case, between Socialist Revolutionaries and Bolsheviks) did much to leave the tsar in power.

The Austrian socialist leader, Viktor Adler, reproved Bernstein for making public demands for a formal revision of the German party's programme so as to turn it into a radical-democratic one similar to the British Labour Party: 'You don't say these things, you just do them.' The fact was that, in 1905, the 'revisionists' could legitimately hope for considerable help from middle-class sympathizers. Was it not worth dropping the old class-war slogans in order to attract them? After 1890, there was a shift in middle-class opinion away from the old courses. The radicalism took many forms: radical-democratic; radical-clerical; radical-nationalist; sometimes, too, crypto-fascist. The old bourgeois world of self-help, pacifism and individualism was disappearing quite fast.

The bourgeois world was partly undermined by its own success. Education and technology had raced ahead in the previous generation: they supplied new middle-class or lower-middle-class jobs, and endless candidates for them. In 1896, there were 40,000 bank clerks in France; by 1914, there were 126,000. In the electrical firm of Siemens in Berlin, there had been 605 *Angestellte* (or clerks) in 1895 and there were 12,501 in 1902 as the volume of correspondence shot up. There were more and more government employees – 100,000 teachers in France, for instance. Five per cent of the London population now consisted of clerks, those armies marching over Waterloo Bridge in the morning rush-hour. In Germany, from 1880 to 1905, the numbers of the 'new *Mittelstand*' went up from 500,000 to 2,000,000.

The greatly increased production of educated men and women meant that, crudely, their ability to command the relatively high salaries of the past would not survive. In the 1870s, teachers, for instance, had been quite well paid: their £81 in Great Britain put even those teachers who were starting out above the level of a skilled artisan. That same sum, thirty years later, put them substantially below the artisan. In the church, the army and even the law in most countries, a similar process was at work. There are plenty of signs of it. After 1890, in England, domestic service for the first time declined, though in other countries there was still a flood of cheap labour from the land for some time to come. Houses were rationalized: the architects in vogue in the later 1890s and especially in the 1900s were men who built with as few complications as possible – a far cry from the cornices and 'features' of the 1880s. Windows, for instance, were much more common than before, and the light, geometric architecture so common in the 1920s was already present some years before 1914. In England, middle-class incomes (judged from tax returns) grew by forty-eight per cent in the 1870s, but only by eleven per cent in the 1900s. One obvious result of this was that middle-class birth-rates declined, because children could not be afforded as before. The decline affected France, the most bourgeois country of all, so severely that her population hardly grew in this period; by 1899, government fears, and suggestions of family allowances, had become plain enough. In Prague, two districts were compared: in working-class Žižkov, the birth-rate was 4.1 per cent in the 1880s, and 3.8 per cent in the 1890s; in lower-middle-class Vinohrady, the figures were 3.3 and 2.1 per cent respectively. It was quite common for middle-class spokesmen to complain at the 'eugenics' of this: society was reproducing its least worthy elements. Increasing costs of family holidays led to the first experiments in package tours (by Kuoni Tours) in 1906. Bridge and squash were invented, dinner-parties became simpler, and informality grew. The familiar *tu* and *Du* became more widely used on the continent; so did Christian names, rather than surnames, in England.

Women were very badly affected by these social changes, for the brunt of the effort to keep up appearances fell on them. It is not surprising to find a women's movement developing in most places at this time, for the younger women, especially, were finding that it was essential for them to find some job or other. It was still a very male world. Laws to grant women even the elementary rights over their property had only been passed in the 1880s; it was not until 1909 that grounds for divorce were made the same for men and women; many professions – especially the law – kept women out (a court case declared in 1909 that the word 'person', in an old statute, meant 'man'); in 1913 the main medical journal in Great Britain would not accept articles by women doctors. In England, quite a powerful women's movement started, with a view to obtaining the vote (which women already had in Australia and in much of America). It had its counterparts elsewhere. Oddly enough, the area where women had made the greatest advance in the professions was in Russia and Poland. There, gentry daughters had never had an easy time, and after 1861 it became more difficult because the supply of money from estates tended to dry up. Women had a far greater role in everything than they did in the West: even in the 1880s, women students made up a quarter of the Russian university population. The 'New Woman' – dressed much more simply than in the be-bodiced and be-flounced past, smoking cigarettes and earning her living – was a product of this Edwardian era. Together with this came an attack on Victorian morality. In England, Samuel Butler attacked it in *The Way of All Flesh*; in Berlin, before 1914, a raffish café-society anticipated the ways of the 1920s. Even the American habit of mixing drinks became known. Maxims in Berlin advertised 'Drinks' – a few years later, they would be 'Cocktails'. 'Femininism' became a startling enough matter, though many of its advocates retained considerable snob-bishness when it came to working-class women.

But for young middle-class males the world was also a harsher place. In many professions, you depended on 'contacts'. An apprenticeship in the law, for instance, meant unpaid work for long hours at the behest of some petty tyrant; it was the same in the Church of England, or in teaching. To obtain a university job was an extremely uphill struggle, especially in France, where there was no retirement age, and where some professors lived to an extraordinary age.

By 1900, the competition for middle-class professional jobs was such that the professions – themselves products of 'restrictive practices' for centuries past – were not required to adapt, and remained arthritic in their ways. Two generations before, it would have been easy for a graduate to obtain whatever job he wanted. Now, it was much more difficult, and families' spare resources were less. It was symptomatic that in 1906 the Cambridge University Appointments Board (i.e., Graduate Employment Exchange) was set up. The world in which a W.H. Auden or an Evelyn Waugh would have to find work in a preparatory school was not far off.

Middle-class discontents exploded most obviously where one nationality quarrelled with another. The educational system had expanded; and that meant, in Bohemia, Flanders, Catalonia, Norway, that lower-middle-class people were going through it more than ever before. In the old days, educated people in any of these countries would automatically have learned the language of the dominant culture, the 'people of State'. Indeed, Czech patriots and revivalists like František Palacký and Rieger wrote their works in German. But, now, a technical and lower-middle-class element was coming in; and it could not be bothered with learning in another language. That had already caused problems at the Charles University in Prague in the later 1870s, and in the 1880s it was divided between Czech and German parts. It caused problems that were quite severe at Ghent University, and even at the great Catholic centre of Louvain where, however, Cardinal Mercier denounced any idea of teaching in Dutch.

Radical nationalism was the upshot. A Basque nationalist party (PNV) emerged in 1894 out of dislike of the *maketas*, the immigrants to Basque industry from the south; a Catalan *Lliga* (and later *Solidaridád*) came in 1904. *Sinn Féin*, in Ireland, was founded in 1905, again as a lower-middle-class protest, of journalists and newsagents or publicans, against the respectable Home Rule people. Its chief, Arthur Griffith, had studied Hungary. In time, this radicalism became violent. After 1906, out of discontent at the slow pace of change, the radical nationalists took up where the anarchists had stopped, and began to throw bombs at dignitaries. This became frequent in Russia and in Croatia. In most cases, the bomb-throwers were men who had come from peasant families and were destined for ill-paid drudgery in a primary school: thus Gavrilo Princip, the assassin of Archduke Franz Ferdinand in 1914. It is easy simply to dismiss all of these people as the outcome of a struggle for jobs, particularly in the bureaucracy. If their languages were officially recognized, they would get the jobs; if the 'people of State' remained dominant, then not. Radical nationalism therefore tended to attract people with hard-luck stories. In 1897, the first great demonstrations for the extension of Dutch in Belgian affairs coincided with the riots between Czechs and Germans in Prague and Vienna, which followed the decree of the Badeni government that the two languages should have equal status in the civil service.

A vital part of this new middle-class radicalism was in the independent sector – farmers, small shopkeepers, artisans (cobblers, tailors etc.). That sector, which the Germans called the *Mittelstand*, had been exposed to an economic drubbing in the 1880s. Now, it faced inflation as well. Interest-rates, a factor of great importance to it, climbed and climbed in the decade before the First World War: generally, they fluctuated around six per cent, instead of the previous generation's two or three. In Great Britain, Bank Rate ran down to two and a half per cent in 1909, but it went rapidly back to five, and was not back to two and a half until twenty years later. Then again, the progress of transport meant that articles could be sold locally which had been made hundreds of miles away; and by 1910 both France and Germany, which supported a great many artisans and peasants, had many organizations set up to defend them, though in politics they went in quite different directions. Broadly speaking, the German *Mittelstand* (the Protestant section of which did most to bring Hitler to power) took up ideas of anti-Semitism and anti-socialism; in a sense, these people altered the German conservative party before the war; and perhaps a similar line can be argued for Belfast, or Nördlingen, or even Liverpool, for in all of these cases a radical conservative movement emerged which, in many respects, anticipated fascism.

By 1906, a movement that had nothing at all to do with traditional politics was under way: the mobilization of backward, peasant Europe. In much of the continent, and indeed in Ireland and parts of Scotland, politics passed far above the heads of that section of society whom the French called 'brutal rurals', or 'quadrupeds'. Life proceeded there as it had done for centuries past. Nowhere was this more the case than in tsarist Russia, where the vast steppe country had not been touched by railways or canals. Since 1890, change had come even to these backward parts. It became quite common for their inhabitants to shift back and forth to towns; the arrival of railways sometimes meant that agrarian capitalism could start, with a consequent loss of land to self-sufficient peasants. Quite often, 'agrarian capitalism' is too grand a term for a process that meant only the arrival of a pedlar, and perhaps rather more usury than in the past. Even so, that backward world was changing. In western Europe, the troubles remained relatively local and small-scale – a revolt of the fishermen of Hebridean islands because the government sent inspectors round on Saturday nights, when the men were in the pubs, to see whether their nets had illegally small openings, which would catch even the little fish which, for the sake of future fishing, the government wished to leave alone; 'cattle-driving' in south-eastern Ireland; a revolt of the wine-growers in Languedoc in 1907; the upheaval of Sicily, known as the *Fasci Siciliani*, in 1892–3.

It was in eastern Europe that the agrarian troubles really declared themselves. Southern Russia erupted in 1902, in a spate of manor-burning; it did so again in 1905, to be discussed below. Romania, in the spring of 1907, provided a symbol of it all. The prefect of Dorohoi, in northern Moldavia, Văsescu, declared prohibition of sales of alcohol, early in March. He did so knowing the temper of the countryside. In Moldavia, half of the land was in great estates; since 1861, they had been worked to provide grain-exports. Rents had trebled, the population also. Landlords would rent out land to peasants for a labour-rent, the *dijmă la tarla* or *clacă*; if the peasants got into arrears, then they were faced with very harsh penalties, although a law of 1900 did state that 'it is absolutely forbidden to take the peasants' clothes to settle such debts'. The peasants had their own communal arrangements, the *obştea sătească*, and – as in Russia – there were many complaints that the communal agriculture worked very inefficiently. The owners of the great estates tended, more and more, to leave things to their agents, the *arendaşi*, who acquired five-year leases. In a majority of cases, these men were foreigners – Greeks or Jews – and they appear to have driven the peasants very hard. At the estate of Prince Mihai Sturdza, at Flămînzi, the second-largest estate in the principality of Moldavia, the Fischer family competed with the peasants and with the Juster family for the lease. The peasants could not find the 62,000 lei. The Juster family dropped out, too, but successfully sued the Fischers for malpractice. The Fischers then had to make more money from the estate, and raised peasant rents from the promised twenty-five lei per *falce* (one and a half acres) to thirty-two. A great revolt then broke out, and peasant mobs entered the provincial towns of Botoşani, Dorohoi and Iaşi demanding vengeance – which tended to be against the Jews. After 20,000 people had been killed, the revolt was crushed. The Romanian government immediately began to consider land reform, and was to bring it in after the First World War.

Such were the discontents of 1905. In answer to them, came the State. After 1906, governments became much more technocratic and social-engineering in their attitudes, and the twentieth century began.

4. 'Technocracy', 1906–10

The upheavals of the period around 1905 brought in new governments everywhere. They were very consciously 'technocratic', for they intended to use the power of the State to eliminate social evils. In most countries, there was an alliance of centre and left in politics. Politically, it appealed to the masses in the name of reform. It did not shrink from a considerable creation of bureaucracy, and it talked the language of planning. In the war of the classes, the State would become arbiter.

The British Liberals, who took power with a huge majority in 1906, headed this movement. But in France, the *Bloc* governments of 1902 were continued, in effect if not in theory, by a long radical ministry under Clemenceau (1906–9). In Austria, Max Wladimir, Baron von Beck managed, in these years, to operate the *Reichsrat* on the basis of parliamentary majorities, and not, as in the early years of the century, by imperial decree, because he collaborated with the mass parties, socialists and Christian Socials, who had flourished after the declaration of universal suffrage. In Italy, Giovanni Giolitti had a 'long ministry' in this same period. In Germany, there was a peculiar alliance of radical liberals, national liberals and conservatives, known as the *Bülow-Block*. In Russia, the tsar had created a parliament, the *Duma*, and although its powers were limited, it did have a veto on the budget, and the tsar's ministers had to treat it with respect. The chief minister of this era (1906–11) was P.A. Stolypin. Even Spain, in this era, had a period of 'technocracy' under the 'regenerationist' Maura.

This era ended everywhere in 1909–10 when these left-inclined governments collapsed. The Liberals in Great Britain lost their parliamentary majority and needed Labour and Irish votes to keep going. Everywhere else, the centre-left alliances broke apart over questions of money. But the years 1906–9 created a government machine that was far stronger than it ever had been. Education, post office, health services, urban government, the police forces and, increasingly, social-welfare agencies expanded. There was greater pressure for the State to take over parts of the economy. Railways were an obvious and partly achieved target; but there were many others. On the continent, there was a long bureaucratic tradition: nowhere stronger than in Austria, where, by 1914, railways, hospitals, schools and even some factories had been taken over by the State. This was, in a sense, the inheritance of the Counter-Reformation: an era of glossy bureaucracies, high taxation, and lavish, baroque, public works which supplied labour at the expense of the individual entrepreneurs who often responded to it by going away. Protestants, then and later, looked on all of this with contempt (well expressed in the multi-volume *Dutch Republic* of Bismarck's austere Bostonian friend, John Motley). But now even the Protestant countries were having to come to terms with bureaucracy. In Great Britain, local government had been run on a shoe-string and the taxes were very low: indeed, local government usually consisted of an energetic man with a telephone and a part-time secretary. Now, in the era of technocratic liberalism, that changed. In the main countries of Europe, bureaucracy, and taxes, went up quite sharply:

Numbers of public servants (non-military)

	1881	1901	1911
Great Britain	81,000	153,000	644,000
France	379,000	451,000	699,000
Germany	452,000	907,000	1,159,000
(of which Prussia	–	152,000	542,000)

Everywhere else, it was much the same, although no country had a luxuriance of bureaucracy to compare with Austria-Hungary's four million.

In the Habsburg Monarchy, bureaucracy was deliberately used as a device for pre-empting minority nationalism. If

sufficient Slovenes, Czechs or Poles were given State jobs,
with a pension attached, they would have no incentive to
pursue minority causes. Roughly a third of all students in
Austrian universities therefore took law degrees and headed
for jobs in the bureaucracy, for which a training in law
(especially 'administrative law' or *Verwaltungsrecht*) was an
essential preliminary. In other countries, the imperialist
coalitions around 1900 had absorbed dissident young men in
a drive for empire. The Habsburgs could not do this, for they
were too weak. Instead, in the era of Ernst Körber (which
ended in 1904) they spent government money on building up
government concerns, such as canals and railway lines. It all
made for more bureaucracy and more law degrees.

In the more backward countries, such growing
bureaucracy could be dangerous. It amounted to a social
revolution of a sort. The old 'notables' – landowners, for the
greater part – began to lose their control of the countryside
in the 1890s. The days when *caciquismo* ruled Spain, when
a family of bosses (*caciques*) like the Pidáls in the Asturias
could run a locality, securing tax concessions, exemptions
from conscription, post-office jobs and even 'fixed' trials for
their clients, all in return for votes, were going: not least
because by 1900 even large estates were suffering from the
rise in costs, and everywhere, without exception, were
registering a perceptible fall in surface area. In Ireland,
Spain, Sicily or Russia, whether the government attempted
land reform or not, the great estates were in decline. In these
parts, there was usually not much industry or commerce to
revive the economy; more and more, government jobs were
the only way ahead. In Italy, it was said, 'in the south, the
only industry is power'. A government job, the prefect, the
various hired thugs of the *mafia* or, in Naples, the *camorra*,
were parasitical. In Russia, the police department was often
part of the underworld. Anti-Semitism was tolerated and
sometimes organized by the police, and it flared up in a
context of declining great estates, in the western Ukraine or
Bessarabia, the capital of which, Kishinyov, produced a
notorious pogrom in 1903. In the province of Tver, a

governor, Aklestyshev, actually did appoint men with criminal records to deal with the local representative council. The Irish Home Rulers became, in their enemies' eyes, a huge 'machine', especially when English forms of local government were extended to Ireland in 1898. The city administration of Naples was dismissed fourteen times by government decree because of its corruption. There was a startling illustration of the problem in 1908, when the Sicilian city of Messina was wrecked by an earthquake and a tidal wave. From all over Italy, and subsequently from all over Europe, money and volunteers arrived to restore the city and its stricken inhabitants. But the tons of goods and thousands of lire passed without difficulty into the hands of local 'bosses', and were sold off elsewhere.

In the West, the new bureaucracy also gained power, although that power could plausibly be represented as progressive. Senior civil servants could in effect dictate government policies, as was done by Morant at education, Llewellyn Smith or Askwith in matters of industry, or, in France, Arthur Fontaine at labour or Monod at education. In Great Britain, until shortly before this era, feudal institutions had survived: parish vestries, grand juries and quarter-sessions had been uneasily adapted to modern needs. The administrative reform, when it came, was too hasty and ill-thought-out, especially in its financing – the rating system, which was both oppressive and ineffectual. British towns did become healthier in this period, but the process really depended on their capacity to attract loans, which the City of Liverpool had pioneered in 1880, at a time of low interest-rates. In general, the expansion of bureaucracy in Great Britain compared badly with continental experience, since there was virtually no corpus of law to control the bureaucrats. In France (and, by extension, most other countries influenced by Napoleon) there was a *droit administratif*, over which the *Cour des comptes* presided. In England, the bureaucrats made it up as they went along, and could have gone much further than they did, only, in this era, they were held up by the extraordinary (in continental eyes) respect for property that English Common Law preserved. The local-government bureaucracy (in some ways it included local trade unions) could adopt widely different policies, for widely different rates, and with vastly different results in matters such as housing, policing and education. The transformation of England, the classic country of *laisser-faire*, of 'the night-watchman State', of the self-reliant moral individual, was clumsily under way.

Throughout Europe, statistical machines came into existence. Virtually for the first time, historical statistics became reliable, and the theory of statistics became a matter of practical importance, whether in the newly emerging area of 'sociology' or in economics, in which the term 'econometrics' first came into existence in 1909. It is only in this era that statistics of the Russian agrarian question became reliable. After 1904, we can at least make enlightened guesses as to how much the successive harvests were, although half of them continued to be eaten by rats. The Russian statisticians – A.V. Chayanov, an extraordinary polymath whose agrarian studies are still valuable; the painstaking agronomists, Khryashcheva and Shcherbina above all – led the way in Europe. Everywhere, too, factory inspectorates produced statistics that were much more reliable than the largely imaginary figures of previous exercises in the 1890s.

This State machine came about, to a large extent, to deal with the rising war of classes: the State was to arbitrate, to treat social problems as if they were mathematical exercises. The expansion of education was an obvious beginning, and one to a large extent anticipated, in the name of 'National Efficiency', by the preceding régimes. The 'technocrats' spent money quite lavishly on new schools and teacher-training colleges – in French, *écoles normales* – which produced a self-consciously crusading class of teachers. The Church, generally, now gave up efforts at mass education. The Church of England accepted State money for its 'maintained' schools, the only way for them to survive the collapse of the Church's income. In France, Church schools were virtually ended in the era of the separation of Church and State (1905–6). In Italy, Giovanni Giolitti had a lengthy row with the Catholics in 1908 which disrupted his coalition; in Austria, the universal-suffrage Beck government collapsed over a clerical issue (the Wahrmund affair, involving the University of Innsbruck) in the same year. Now, State schools became very strongly the rule, and their religious component was extremely limited. The expansion of education also did much for the 'emancipation' of women, who occupied low-paid teaching posts in profusion. The educational establishment everywhere became a powerful machine, and it developed its own corporate ethos and its own press. '*Nous, les maîtres d'école*' were self-consciously the backbone of the Third Republic. In England, the *Times Educational Supplement* first appeared in 1910. In central Europe, including Italy, upper-grade schoolmasters were addressed as 'Professor', and took themselves extremely seriously. In France, they were not even required to exercise discipline in the classroom: that task was entrusted to a *surveillant*.

In some countries, there was continual talk of land reform. The agrarian disturbances of the later 1890s and early 1900s had affected most grain-exporting countries, such as Romania, Hungary or Russia. Later on, agrarian disturbances hit Austrian Poland (Galicia). In all cases, governments responded, after 1900, by greater awareness of the need for reform. Tsarist ministers discussed it in 1902, and proceeded to a large-scale reform, associated with the technocratic constitutionalist, P.A. Stolypin. The Romanians took their first steps towards reform in 1910, and carried out a lengthy programme under General Averescu after the war. The Austro-Hungarian administration in Bosnia-Herzegovina tried – not very hard – to subsidize the semi-serf *kmety* who wished to buy their freedom from the Moslem landlords, who rented out land and tools to them in exchange for a varying share of the produce. The British governments, in 1903 and especially in 1909, produced schemes that eventually enabled Irish tenants to buy their land. In the later nineteenth century, these schemes had been anticipated, but the terms had not been generous, and in any case, at a time of agrarian depression it was often better for people to take land on lease than to own it outright. The Gladstone land Acts and the various other English schemes, though well-meant, and though endlessly wrangled-over, were generally ineffective. Up to 1887, their provisions were used by only 731 farmers in all. By the time of the Wyndham Act of 1903, and especially its Liberal supplementation in 1909, land prices were rising again, farmers bought, and, where there was opposition, the Liberals allowed compulsory purchase. These land reforms had a very varied rate of success. If urban markets and secondary employment were available, the countryside generally prospered, regardless of reform; where, as in most of Russia, the villages were quite isolated, the old ways would go on. In southern Italy or Spain, the great estate owners could always argue that they alone guaranteed some kind of cohesion, irrigation and investment in their backward regions; and if eighteenth-century schemes for land reform were anything to go by, great estates had a way of re-forming because of this need for cohesion.

In the towns, the 'technocrats' began to perceive great horizons. In the years before 1914, 'town planning' became a widespread concept. It originated in Germany, where the expression 'town-extension' (*Stadterweiterung*) struck a visiting councillor from Birmingham, Nettlefold, in 1905; it became *urbanisation* in France in imitation of a Spanish original, promoted two generations before by an engineer, Ildefonso de Cerda, in Barcelona. By 1906, there were conferences and exhibitions in many Western cities to discuss the reshaping of the chaos which had emerged during the expansion of the later nineteenth century (or, in England, since 1815). A new, municipal architecture made its appearance around this time. In 1906 there was even an International Association of Local Government, promoted – inevitably – by the Dutch and the Belgians. It held its first conference in Ghent. It would have talked Esperanto, but no one could understand the French accent in that language.

Town planners in Germany could have a field day almost

from the start. The German cities had lost much of their power in the later sixteenth and early seventeenth centuries, and princes had acquired a capacity to override the town magistrates. In law, therefore, German cities took over from their own states a system that gave greater public power over private property than elsewhere. Compulsory purchase, though in abeyance for the era of classical liberalism, was formally allowed in Saxony in 1891 and in Prussia in 1900. In England, such overturning of private property rights was still unthinkable. In Germany, the *Bürgermeister* or, in large cities, the *Oberbürgermeister*, was a government official with a salary and a large number of permanent local-government officers. They had much more power than the representative assembly of councillors in the *Magistrat*. This was not true in Great Britain, where elected mayors and councillors represented 'interests' (including, latterly, the trade unions).

The German cities grew very fast indeed in the generation after 1870. They were also very ugly. There would be a pompous official centre, studded with heavy structures like the *Reichstag*; around it were large, dull tenements; and beyond these, the vast 'rent-barracks' (*Mietskasernen*) which were speculatively constructed by 'terrain associations' to house the working class, which was thus consigned to the dreary streets of Wedding or Kaulsdorf in Berlin. Elsewhere in Europe there were similar problems. St Petersburg had almost no town-planning organization at all, and many of its inhabitants lived in cellars which were sometimes flooded in the spring thaw. The industrial towns of northern France were exercises in dreary, squat brick. The *extraradio* around Madrid started off almost as a shanty town for immigrants from the south. The western European city with the worst reputation for slums was heavy-industrial Glasgow. It attracted immigrants from the Highlands and from Ireland, and then it took in Jewish refugees from Russia. The migrants took over a lower-middle-class district just south of the River Clyde, the Gorbals, and the whole area became a by-word throughout Europe for gang-warfare and drink.

Maryhill, on the city's northern edges, followed. A fifth of Glasgow's families each lived in a single room, and in most of these families there were three or more persons. The 'Second City' (of the British empire) was an extraordinary combination of cultures; the industrial and shipping money generated there, as in Liverpool, could make parts of it very grand indeed; and yet its social problems were probably worse than anywhere in Europe. One feature, which it shared with some other Calvinist cities, was a feeling among the demonstrably non-Elect that there was nothing left but drink. Glasgow produced Europe's first football hooligans: in 1909 Ibrox stadium was burned down by ignited whisky after a match between the Catholic team, Celtic, and the Protestant one, Rangers. Even so, it was an oddly rich civilization, producing, before the First World War, a quarter of the world's shipping. In common with other Calvinist regions of Europe – south-western Germany and the French Protestants – it also produced, in this era, more than its due share of physicists, engineers, entrepreneurs and medical doctors. Graduates of the 'Glasgow Tech' (the Royal College of Technology) were to be found all over the world.

The Scots had a legal system that differed from the English one in many matters of substance. They were concerned to have the law predictable, a sort of machine, even if the application of hard-and-fast rules did, in some cases, cause injustice, whereas in England the concept of equity had more effect (sometimes to the confusion of the law). Scottish property law allowed greater public power than English law, and town planning, based on public powers, was quite an old concept in Scotland. The Edinburgh 'New Town' was constructed in the latter half of the eighteenth century on grandly rational lines, and was a model for many other European cities (and, later, American ones which also followed a 'grid' pattern). It was not altogether surprising that, in the first stages of modern town planning, the Puritan mind was well to the fore. In England, Scotsmen like Patrick Geddes and Patrick Abercrombie wrote and planned voluminously (Abercrombie occupied the first university Chair of Town Planning, at Liverpool, in 1910). They had continental counterparts – a surprising number of Swiss (who included Le Corbusier, the greatest exponent of 'Alphaville', or 'the City of Towers' which the twentieth century created), French Protestants like Eugène Hénard, who, as traffic-director of Paris, proposed the *carrefour à giration* and 'multi-level traffic intersections' (which a later generation knows as 'spaghetti junctions'), and a great number of North Germans, who planned what were in effect the first 'housing estates'.

Town planning arose in response to an undoubted need. By 1900, the roads of most large cities were chaotic. In the 'rush-hour' there were frequent traffic jams, in which horse-drawn and motor vehicles wrestled for hours. From 1906 to 1912, the number of motor vehicles in Paris rose from 4077 to 12,222; in the rush-hour at the intersection of the rue Royale and the rue du Faubourg St Honoré there was, from 1891 to 1906, an increase of forty-five per cent in the traffic; it took half an hour to cross the intersection at the Opera. This, together with the existence of slums (an English eighteenth-century slang word which was adapted all over Europe), caused planners to enthuse over what might be achieved. Otto Wagner, a Viennese architect (and, by origin, yet another Protestant), proposed 'the great city of the future', in which new building-techniques would be adapted to construct huge towers, separated by 'air centres'; people would live in 'zones', travelling to work in an 'industrial zone', and there would be gigantic motor-roads to exploit the possibilities of new transport. Patrick Geddes proposed the addition of 'parks, gardens and cultural institutes' (which the Bolsheviks, later, in their period of cultural progressivism, turned into 'parks of rest and culture'). By 1910, Wagner's 'Great City of the Future' (*Grossstadt der Zukunft*) dominated the thinking of progressive architects. In Germany, there were continual city-exhibitions, to which foreign observers were invited, to display municipal enterprise. In 1913, even the French – among whom traditions of individualism survived longer than elsewhere on the continent – were joining in. The long-term progressive mayors of Lyons, Augagneur and Edouard Herriot, promoted change in this city, which, as the chief place profiting from the industrial boom of the Rhône valley, was almost the French Birmingham. They employed Tony Garnier (another Calvinist) and René Mallet-Stevens to design tower blocks which they saw as a marriage of European aesthetics and American skyscrapers.

In architecture, the style that a later generation regarded as *Bauhaus* – the school associated with Walther Gropius and Mies van der Rohe in Weimar Germany – was thus well to the fore before 1914. It was severely functional, eschewing decoration. By 1909, the French architect, Auguste Perret, had put up his '25, rue Franklin' (a suitable location) and Otto Wagner had constructed his 'Neustiftgasse 40' in Vienna's VII district. They were shoeboxes. Wagner's construction comes as a special disappointment from the architect of his earlier churches and his block of flats on the linke Wienzeile (1899). But he was far from being alone in dreaming of severe, functional architecture. Maybe it was true that the nineteenth-century styles could not be prolonged. The much admired English architect, Edward Lutyens, made his reputation at the turn of the century with country houses built in an extraordinary range of styles; and although these houses did deserve their fame, there was something suspiciously film-set about them. It was not accidental that Lutyens went on to design New Delhi for the British Raj, on lines that were pure 'Bengal Lancers', suitable for middle-class, besuited viceroys who could get themselves up in fancy dress to patronize Maharajahs in an empire that, within a few years, was clearly moribund. It was also not accidental that Lutyens went on to design tower blocks and bland, pompous office buildings that do nothing for his reputation.

The 'modernist' architects (some of whose inspiration came from the contemporary cubist movement in painting) were very frustrated before 1914, since town councils were often quite retrograde, and in any case lacked resources for the destruction of old cities which the 'modernists' proposed. In Great Britain, the Local Government Board, under John Burns, was dismissive; in France, a conservationist movement, *Vieux Paris*, developed to quite vigorous effect after Eugène Hénard proposed knocking down much of the old Palais Royal, and even much of the Île de la Cité quarter, to build a road to extend the rue de Rivoli over the Seine. In England, Geddes, who hated 'conurbations' (a word that he coined), proposed the construction of smaller, light and healthy 'garden cities' (1904); he took up an idea proposed, in England, by Ebenezer Howard in 1898, when he produced a privately printed work on *To-morrow: a Peaceful Path to Real Reform*. These schemes owed something to the example of the American 'City Beautiful Movement', which had influenced both Chicago (home of the first skyscraper) and Washington. There were many Englishmen of the Anglican tradition who wished to solve city problems by creating model communities. T.C. Horsfall, heir to a fortune in the north, thought that drink and fornication would be 'the ruin of our race'. University chairs in eugenics were set up (they are now called sociology). Lady Betty Balfour worried about 'the State and motherhood'. The answer must be, Horsfall thought, 'pleasantness' – parks, gardens, public baths, callisthenics, decent, tidy little houses and, as it was grotesquely misnamed, 'temperance'. The upshot was the garden city – pioneered partly by the enlightened industrialist Lord Lever at Port Sunlight, and developed by Geddes at Letchworth, or by Dame Henrietta Barnett at Hampstead Garden Suburb. A French observer, Georges Benoît-Lévy, applauded all of this, 'given that the social question is mainly a matter of hygiene'. *Cités-Jardin*, *Gartenstädte* were demanded on the continent; in Hellerau, near Dresden, or Drancy, near Paris (the writer Céline called it 'Rancy') these dreams were partly realized. The German architect Bruno Taut put up a council housing estate near Milan, and called it 'Milanino'. By 1910, Paris had promoted council-built *Habitations à bon marché*, which a later generation turned, genteelly, into *Habitations à loyer modéré*, or, as they have now become, 'HLM'. But it was only a beginning. It needed money.

In most European countries, the years from 1906 to 1909 were self-consciously progressive; technocrats well to the fore. Still, these governments were strangely barren of achievement. In France, the radical Clemenceau had a long ministry. He promised eighteen reforms, and carried only one of them – the nationalization of the railways of the west. In Germany, the chancellor, Bernhard von Bülow, tried to govern in defiance of both Catholics and social democrats, and fell foul of budgetary problems. In Great Britain, the first years of the Liberal government were also barren, except for pieces of tidy-mind legislation. The single greatest legacy of that era was the trade-union law of 1906: it removed virtually all constraints from union activity, short of the criminal law, because the Liberals proclaimed their policy as 'no enemies to the left'.

In Great Britain, that policy did much to prolong the life of the Liberal government until 1914; and Lloyd George's credibility on the left was such that he could, in 1916, lead an enormously strong parliamentary coalition in the name of national unity. In 1910, the reigning Liberals held elections, and found their own position much eroded; but with the help of Labour votes (and the Home Rulers) the Liberal government continued in an atmosphere of mounting turmoil. It was able to push through financial measures which made social reform (and defence-costs) manageable; these financial measures included an increase of direct taxation to include a progressive income tax and a levy on the profits of land that rose in value without the owners' contributing anything beyond title deeds.

The income tax itself was quite small (1/7d in the £) and the land tax, although theoretically quite high, could easily be evaded. But it was an important assertion of principle. To pay for old-age pensions for other people, the better-off would have to contribute more in taxes. Later on, the State also undertook schemes of medical insurance and, in 1912, unemployment insurance which would have to be taken from the tax-payer. The socialist Philip Snowden thought income tax should rise to seven shillings in the pound: which was widely regarded as confiscatory and revolutionary. The British Conservatives therefore beheld a government that would concede power to trade unions, would tax inherited wealth, would levy large taxes on income, in order to pay for the subsidizing of people who had not provided for themselves. In 1909–10 there was a great wrangle, since the House of Lords, with its huge Conservative majority, resisted; two elections were needed to confirm the parliamentary power of the Liberals (1910); and the king, George V, had unwillingly to agree that he would create sufficient Liberal peers if need be to swamp the Conservatives in the Lords. In practice, the Lords gave way, after a battle between 'hedgers' and 'ditchers', as the compromisers and the extremists were respectively known, and agreed both to the budget and to the weakening of the Lords' power. This debate was conducted to widespread public indifference, and if England alone had been involved, the Liberals would not have kept power.

Elsewhere, the technocratic régimes of 1906–9 were unable to prolong the coalition of left and centre that permitted British liberalism to survive. The question of government finance wrecked other governments. Landowners and businessmen, and a large part of the professional middle class, would not allow direct taxes to pay for more than a small part of government outgoings. On the whole, government-dominated welfare schemes were hated; and since, everywhere on the continent, agriculture occupied a far greater share of the economy than in Great Britain, a direct income tax was completely impracticable. Farmers kept their own accounts, and there was no way of checking these, where, indeed, they existed. Even in Great Britain, income tax was not levied on Irish farmers at all, and only a crude rule-of-thumb operated in England.

In 1908–9 the rise of government expenditure, on arms, on bureaucracy, on State-led economic schemes (such as the Stolypin reforms in Russia), and, in France and Italy, on the small beginnings of social welfare, prompted budgetary confusions. Giolitti in Italy was driven to propose a direct income tax; in France, Clemenceau strove mightily to avoid putting that question, and was thrown out of office late in 1909 by discontented radicals; in Germany, the *Bülow-Block* did propose a direct Reich tax on inheritances, and its conservative component refused to support the scheme, so that Bülow, deprived of control in the *Reichstag* (and having lost the Kaiser's friendship in a characteristically absurd affair, the *Daily Telegraph* interview), was driven out in June 1909.

These matters of finance touched on the central question of this era: the role of government, and the share of government enterprise in economics. Liberal individualism was on the defensive, and, in a sense, had been since the days of railway nationalization and tariffs. Now, there were nightmares of the People's State, which would centralize the economy, and reduce its citizens to an ant-heap.

5. *The Ghost of Bonapartism:* Réveil National, *1910–14*

In his *Strange Death of Liberal England*, George Dangerfield called attention to the collapse of the Asquith government before 1914. That government prolonged its existence by an alliance with the left, in the name of social reform, and by a link with the Irish Home Rulers, whom it sought to satisfy by granting Irish Home Rule. On both counts, it ran into problems. Its own rich supporters by and large disliked the social measures and the taxation; Liberal constituencies began to reject working-class candidates, and Liberal voters often switched to the right. The proposal of Home Rule in Ireland drove the Protestant quarter of that country – mainly settled in the north-east, in Ulster – towards a more and more violent opposition. By 1913, there was a clear threat of civil war, which caused Asquith, the following year, to put the Home Rule proposal into abeyance.

Dangerfield's ideas have not been universally popular among English historians. But his *Strange Death* thesis applies with considerably greater force to the continent. After 1909, almost all European countries went into a period of political chaos. In France, the relative stability of the left-centre coalition (which supplied four governments after 1899) gave place to an era when *'les gouvernements valsent'*: there were ten, including a three-day Ribot ministry. In Italy, the relative stability of Giolitti gave place, in the same era, to parliamentary chaos: there were five governments in four years, and, although universal suffrage was introduced in 1912, Mussolini could plausibly call it 'the oxygen pump administered to a dying patient, parliamentary liberalism'. In Russia, the *Duma*, elected by a very restrictive franchise, had a nationalist, anti-Semitic majority that sometimes embarrassed the government. After 1909, it made no serious effort to extend its own power. In 1914, the tsar asked its speaker, M.V. Rodzyanko, if he wished the *Duma* to meet during the war; Rodzyanko himself answered that a meeting would not be necessary, but, if the tsar insisted, there might be a 'ceremonial session, lasting for an afternoon'. In Bohemia and Istria, in 1913, the provincial Diets were disbanded; these quarrels, transferred to the central Austrian parliament, provoked its dissolution in 1914. The Habsburgs went back to absolutism. Everywhere in Europe, much of the right now talked the language of fascism. After 1910, in most countries, industrial unrest resulted in many more strikes than before, and in some places – Barcelona in 1909, Ancona and St Petersburg in 1914 – general strikes almost resulted in a takeover of whole towns by 'the Reds'. It all occurred in the context of an international tension which makes issues of foreign and domestic politics extremely difficult to separate, both in the four years before the war, and in the war itself. In these circumstances, political alliances were often unstable and short-lived, and countries' internal affairs became accordingly confused.

The challenge from the left was plain enough in most countries. 'Revolutionary syndicalists' profited from inflation, high profits, and an influx of youthful labour. They were associated with vast, brawling dock-strikes in England and Ireland; they managed to dominate the Italian socialist party by 1912, when they expelled the 'revisionist' Leonida Bissolati for proposing to join a radical-dominated cabinet. In Germany, there was a movement of young metal-workers who, in Berlin, threatened to break away from their own trade union; their shop-stewards (*Obleute*) regarded the union officials as cowardly and conservative. In Great Britain, there was a similar movement, on a rather larger scale, when local workers refused to accept their national union's decisions; and the Board of Trade's arbitrators complained that there was an unaccountable 'new spirit' at large. In 1912, 40,000,000 working days were lost through 'stoppages', and a national rail strike, which was an almost permanent threat after 1908, was seemingly near to realization in 1914. In France, the railways suffered from similar problems; and rail strikes were broken, there, only when Clemenceau, and after him, Aristide Briand, formally served conscription notices on the strikers and thereby made them liable for military justice. In Italy, Giolitti used the same tactics. In Russia, the killing and wounding of hundreds of striking workmen on the Lena Gold Fields in 1912 provoked huge demonstrations in the large cities, and a wave of strikes, which culminated in the general strike of St Petersburg in July 1914. In most (though not all) European countries, strikes were more frequent after 1909 than ever before.

This picture can be, and has been, 'relativized' almost out of existence. In the first place, there was no doubt that in most of Europe conditions for the bulk of the working class were improving. The eight-hour day, for instance, was becoming general – partly because of legislation, but, more often, because of businesses' improved organization and technology, or because of the unions' greater power. The 'English weekend' was also becoming more widespread on the continent, and in most countries 'social legislation' had gone some way. The 'technocrats' also found that it was much easier to co-operate with trade unions than to fight them. In Germany, more and more workmen concluded collective wage-contracts through their union, and in all countries State arbitration schemes were becoming more effective. Even the 40,000,000 days lost in English strikes were a tiny fraction of possible days worked.

Besides, there was plenty of evidence that working people were vastly indifferent to the political causes that agitated their leaders. In 1909, one Osborne, of a British railway union, claimed in the courts that he ought not to be liable for a political levy demanded by the union. The courts supported him, and made it voluntary. There was a great fuss. The union then balloted its own people to find out whether they supported the compulsory levy, and discovered that, of 107,499 members, only 5610 agreed with that levy. In Greater Berlin, the socialists were balloted in 1910 to ascertain their willingness to contribute to a fund that would subsidize a monster campaign for universal suffrage in Prussia. Out of 116,889 questionnaires, 35,157 were returned. Of these, 25,138 replied negatively, and of the 9538 'yes' answers, 6288 offered only ten pfennigs per month ($1\frac{1}{2}$d). In Italy, Giolitti co-operated with the trade unions in distributing public works in the region of Emilia; in Germany, during the war, trade unions almost became a branch of the State; in Sweden, before 1914, they 'recognized' capitalism in return for a social-welfare, high-taxation State, which unions would have a powerful say in running. As the State developed into a machine, the socialists divided. In most countries, only a small minority of them persisted in the utopian nineteenth-century dreams; the rest got on with practical politics, in alliance with middle-class radicals. That was what the Italian philosopher Benedetto Croce meant when he wrote a work, at this time, on 'the death of socialism'.

Socialist parties, which occupied between a fifth and a third of most parliaments, were dragged into parliamentary politics. They could use their votes for measures of immediate reform, and they did so. It was a sign of their increasing integration that they became prepared to vote even for armaments. The original socialists had, of course, usually been pacifists, and had seen armies as agents of civil war. But the argument of national defence was difficult to refuse. German socialists, especially, felt that in a Russo-German war they could hardly refuse to take part. True, a general strike against it might succeed in Germany, where the unions were strong; it would fail in Russia, where they were weak or non-existent. All that would happen would be a Russian conquest of Germany. The International itself divided over this issue, and hypocrisy was such that, at the Copenhagen meeting in 1910, the German socialist speaker, Paul Ledebour, asked his interpreter to exclude from the French version of his speech a section that had been designed for German and English hearers. By 1913, socialist votes, both in France and Germany, allowed considerable increases in military strength.

Some Marxist contemporaries argued that, in Europe's march to war, a prime motive, in all countries, had been to defeat socialism by nationalism: in other words, national unity, and not the class-war, was to be stressed; and that foreign policies were really made for internal consumption. To German historians, these considerations are known as the 'primacy of internal politics' (*Primat der Innenpolitik*). Thus, when the German government launched international crisis over Morocco in 1911, it did so, in this view, because of impending elections and fear of a takeover by the left; and in the French case it has been argued that the wave of nationalism which broke in 1911 – the *réveil national*, associated with Poincaré – was meant to divert the nation's mind from social reform. It has also been suggested that, when the British Conservatives raised a scare in 1908–9 about the number of German battleships being illicitly constructed, they were trying to stop Lloyd George's social reforms by making him spend the money on battleships. Similar assertions can be made for Italy, Russia or Austria-Hungary.

It was unquestionably true that, in the orgy of imperialism (and tariffs) at the end of the 1890s, statesmen and generals quite often said that foreign expansion was needed to defeat socialism. Instead, expansion had provoked endless social trouble; and after 1905, conservatives everywhere perceived that war would probably bring social revolution. The Russian conservative, P.N. Durnovo, argued this in a famous memorandum of February 1914; and Lenin said much the same. In a sense, the war broke out, therefore, because conservatives had overcome that fear. It is the arrogance of statesmen in 1914, and not their fearfulness, that is striking.

The States had become very powerful machines. Already, huge armaments, monopolies, trade unions, bureaucracies, high taxation and inflationary public finance marked the social scene. There were many people who disliked it all; and after 1910, there was a radicalization of middle-class discontents which, to some extent, anticipated fascism.

One instance of this occurred in areas with a mixed Catholic and non-Catholic population. The most obvious case was that of Northern Ireland. Here, the prospect of rule from Dublin, in the context of the Liberals' schemes, caused open revolt. In Ulster, Protestant Volunteers threatened force; they drilled and marched openly; a section of the British officer corps sympathized with people who wished to retain their government from London. The Protestants' grievances, expressed in religious terms, seemed (and seem) to be wildly anachronistic. But they made sense on the ground, for the ways of people of the two different religions were often different to the point of incompatibility – differing views of the roles of the sexes, differing inheritance traditions, differing standards of hygiene, of family size, of education, of enterprise.

No doubt, at root, much of this was simply a reflection that Catholics had been a generation or two later than Protestants in joining 'the flight from the land' (although there was obviously more than that to it). In most places, Catholics had a faster rate of population growth than Protestants. In the

Protestant towns of Bavaria – Nördlingen, for instance – this was quite obvious, and such towns became islands in a Catholic sea. Protestant middle-class families remained limited in size, to save expense; Catholic families required the incomes of many children. In Latvia, the Catholic region, Lettgallia, was a source of navvies for the ports, especially Riga. Young men left their families behind, in villages which operated on the same communal principles as in Russia proper, and returned with some urban money (and, often, some socialist ideas). The Latvian Catholics, who had made up a fifth of the population in the 1860s, amounted to a quarter of it a generation later; and in much the same way the Netherlands, having been the heartland of dour Protestantism, were on the way to having a Catholic majority in 1914.

By then, Catholic backwardness, although still an obvious enough factor (in Ireland Protestant incomes were four times that of the average Catholic), was also becoming a thing of the past, in that the gap was now much less than before. As Catholics became educated and took urban employment, they were more adaptable than Protestants who were immured in their own skills: whether in heavy industry, or the professional middle class or the craftsman-artisan lower middle class. Catholics were also good at operating political machines, at taking over ministries of posts and railways, and appointing their own clients throughout such networks. On a municipal level, the expansion of bureaucracy enabled such client systems to develop, with local taxes to match. Events in Northern Ireland, far from being anomalous, were wholly ordinary in a European context. At almost exactly the same time (1911–13) there were great battles in Bavaria, Baden and Belgium as all of the non-Catholic groups, from socialists to conservatives, teamed up against Catholic domination of politics. In Belgium there was a general strike over this issue. In Bavaria and Baden, the non-Catholics constructed a 'Big Block' (*Grossblock*) to defeat the machines. These Blocks failed to defeat the priests, not least because of their own, inevitable, internal tensions. By 1911, the Church dominated

Belgium. A book by G. Barnich, *Le régime clérical en Belgique*, showed how it ran insurance, savings associations, sports clubs, appointments to jobs. In Vienna, the 'Christian Socials' amounted to a first-class machine, in which the city promoted the welfare of the small man – objecting, for instance, to military bands because they put street musicians out of business. It was a form of small shopkeeper conservatism, and, like the Irish Home Rule movement, could in many ways deserve the title 'reactionary' (Karl Lueger once remarked of advocates of women's suffrage that they were 'in general ... Jewesses'). But it was very powerful, and anyone involved in municipal government could not fail to come to terms. The socialists did so in much of Europe. In Munich, the bus service was divided up on the lines of 'proportion' (*Proporz*) – bus drivers to be socialist, bus conductors to be Catholic. The Irish Labour Party had its constitution written, in part, by the bishops. 'Red Clydeside' came into existence when the Catholic vote was shifted towards the left.

To much of this, Protestant establishments responded hysterically. In some countries, establishments were menaced by a further threat, from minority nationalism, which crisscrossed with clericalism. In Europe at this time, small nations, some of them unnoticed since the late Middle Ages, were flourishing; and lesser nationalities within great empires were becoming conscious of their own potential in a way that had not been true for several generations. Irish literature had a remarkable revival; architects in Finland, Poland, Bohemia and Catalonia strove for new forms which would supplant the neo-Byzantine or neo-Nuremberg or neo-baroque forms that, hitherto, had dominated their chief cities: the Ramblas in Barcelona, and the buildings of the Catalan architect, Gaudí, were almost a nationalist statement in itself. The same was true in Czech music, particularly in Dvořák; in Norway, writers like Ibsen and Hamsun rescued Norwegian, which, before, had been regarded as a kind of Danish Creole. In the 1890s, the forgotten languages of many minority peoples were being rapidly revived, often with clerical patronage, and often by 'transferred patriots'. An Englishman, Douglas Hyde, developed Irish Gaelic, or, according to his enemies, invented it. A Scotsman, John McLeod, developed Flemish in Belgium, and tried to make Dutch the literary form for a language that had divided and sub-divided into countless different accents and dialects. In many towns, statues and opera houses declared the historical worth of these lesser nationalities; and there was no lack of historians to demonstrate their pedigree, sometimes by outright forgery.

The established nationalities – or, to use the Austrian expression, 'the peoples of state' (*Staatsvölker*) – responded to this with hysteria. Germans in a Bohemia that was now two-thirds Czech resented the Czechs' insistence on the spread of their language; the diffusion of Czech bureaucrats and teachers, even in solidly German regions, provoked troubles; and the Diet in Prague was closed down because one side or the other obstructed its business. The Austrian social democrats split into different national groups in 1910, and even the Catholic parties ceased to have meetings of all the Austrian national groups. In the South Slav regions, a new nationalist radicalism challenged the Habsburg Establishment. In the Ukraine, a similar, rather inchoate, nationalist ferment gathered. The German consul in Lwów, in eastern Galicia, was told from Berlin to observe this movement and, if possible, to steer it towards Germany.

The background to the outbreak of war in 1914 was therefore a feeling, everywhere in Europe, that things were somehow splitting apart. That feeling was not confined to political matters; it affected virtually everything else. There was, for instance, a great row in the Théâtre des Champs-Élysées in 1913, when Igor Stravinsky's *Rite of Spring* was first performed. Its loud, bizarrely syncopated and percussive nature offended Parisian taste – although Vienna had been used to sounds even more bizarre for some years. In a way that the historian can only chronicle, and not explain, the mood changed around 1911. Dangerfield had it right when he observed how, in the cartoons of *Punch*, there was a sudden leap out of the Victorian world in 1912. Quite suddenly, different things became funny; and the figures in the cartoons were dressed differently. It is probably not too much to claim that, before 1914, a new irrationalism had gained currency.

Certainly, the politics of this epoch became quite strange. Confusion ruled; and in its midst there were voices that anticipated fascism. The North Irish issue made many British Conservatives respond with hysteria: marches, uniforms were the order of the day. In Germany, early in 1912, the social democrats won a third of the vote, and became the largest party in the *Reichstag*. Hysteria was the response in many industrial and *Mittelstand* circles. The industrialists' Central Association denounced the 'Reds'; and there was a profusion of 'leagues for the defence of the middle classes' or 'anti-socialist leagues' which talked anti-Semitism and totalitarianism. In Italy, *La Voce* in Florence talked of 'proletarian imperialism'; indeed, the expression 'the third world' came from an Italian original, in that Italian nationalists sometimes regarded themselves as neither capitalist nor socialist, but capable of forming a third kind of empire. English Conservatives, led now by a businessman, Andrew Bonar Law, were, if anything, much saner than their continental counterparts. But they too were afflicted with a mania that deprived them of sense when they contemplated Irish issues.

All over Europe, there was hardly a man of the right who would not echo the words of a pan-German leader, Heinrich Class: 'I long for the holy, redeeming war.' War was seen as a great restorer of sense; action itself, in whatever direction, would solve problems and restore the proper values. In all of the Great Powers, the Right began to patronize military and naval associations. In Great Britain, Lord Roberts put forward schemes for the conscription of young men. In France, Poincaré found an ideal way of uniting the Chamber around the slogan *réveil national*, and in France the nationalists, who had been discredited by the Dreyfus affair, now had a field day. In Germany, 'military leagues' –

promoted by a former general, Keim – had an equal run. After 1911, the atmosphere was of arms race. Oddly enough, this served, in most countries, to solve the problem of taxation which had bedevilled parliamentary affairs since the early 1890s. The right would vote for graduated income taxes, provided they were spent on arms; and the left would accept arms, provided they came with graduated income taxes. By 1912, that problem had been sorted out almost everywhere, and large armies went together with large taxes: although the details of this process caused endless trouble, and, in France and Italy, the upsetting of endless governments. By 1913, all of Europe was committed to an arms race; and after 1911, the war had already broken out in people's minds. The countries of Europe had become machines, and the machines now assailed each other. It was Germany that took the lead.

III

THE GREAT POWERS OF EUROPE

1. *International Relations, 1897–1914*

The origins of the First World War can be clearly seen from the early 1890s. In that period, the foreign policies of the imperialist age were taking shape. This responded to a changing international order, in which ancient states – China, the Ottoman empire – were disintegrating. But it also responded to a changing order at home.

The rise of the left at home caused some people in the political centre to attempt to kill it by kindness. Whether in the last Gladstone government (1892–4, with a brief and confused Liberal sequel to 1895) or in the régime of Bismarck's successor, Caprivi (1890–5), efforts were made to appeal to 'the people', whether with democratic improvements in government or with food-price reductions. But these measures were very far from being popular among all the supporters of these régimes, many of whom were either anti-democratic, in the sense that they feared 'the people', or overtly protectionist. Imperialism was quite a good cause for them to deck out their rather threadbare domestic policies.

Populations everywhere had shot up, and armies wanted to conscript more men in accordance with that. The existing laws made that difficult, for they fixed a number of men (and in Germany, a sum of money) over a long period. Generals also worried that, if they maintained a service of three years – the rule in most places, though in Russia it was five years – the armies would become unpopular. Besides, they themselves recognized that, with modern education for the men, a two-year period with the colours would suffice. After that the soldiers could serve for wartime purposes only, and would be liable for recall as reservists for a further eighteen or twenty years. Accordingly, in Austria, France, Germany, Italy and Russia, from 1889 to 1893, military bills were introduced which cut the length of service and put up the number of men taken in every year.

The passage of these bills, in all cases, was difficult, for the generals and the liberals found many things to quarrel about. But in a climate of internal and external tension, they went through: it was a timid beginning of the arms race, and the Gladstone government in Great Britain responded by expanding and improving the navy. The Russians responded to all of this by making an alliance with the French (1893–4). For Germany, since 1870, had become extremely powerful, and the British were taking an anti-Russian stance everywhere in the world. Russia needed a friend.

In practice, the arms race on land then became slower. This was not because international tension became less. It was because Germany concentrated her efforts on constructing a great battle-fleet and so had no money to spare for building up the army. The fleet, the creation of Admiral Tirpitz, was designed as an imperialist tool. It was clearly aimed at the British: indeed, its ships carried more armour than British ones precisely because they did not need the extra weight of coal, to carry them round the globe, which British ships needed. German ships could sail across the North Sea and back, and by 1900 the British woke up to the challenge. The Germans' main idea was simple enough. If the British went to war, they would no doubt sink the numerically inferior German fleet; but they would lose so many of their own ships in the process that they would be exposed to the attacks of other naval powers. Hence the British would act together with Germany, and share out the imperial spoils, such as had not happened before.

In practice, it did not work out that way. The British preferred to make a deal with France in 1904: for the French, under the energetic Théophile Delcassé's foreign ministry, had become depressed at the weakness of their Russian ally in the Far Eastern war, and feared a new isolation. They themselves wished to seize Morocco, which was in slow disintegration; they did not wish the Germans to take it; and they needed British help. In exchange for recognition of British control of Egypt, they gained British help for their own control of Morocco when the time came. This deal was known as the 'Entente cordiale'. It coincided with other problems in the vast Ottoman inheritance. Finance houses and businessmen from all of the industrial countries, and sometimes also from Russia (though generally with foreign money), wrestled to gain from the Turkish government's efforts to expand railways and mineral output. A German group gained a concession to build a railway across Turkey – a project known, grandiosely, as the Berlin-Baghdad railway. This railway, in German hands, might have given Germany a preponderant role, and the project was opposed by other Powers. It was not at all a simple matter, since the project was financed with money from countries other than Germany. The Russians, in particular, felt that a Turkish army would now be easy to shift against their own southern borders, in the Caucasus, and they were alarmed.

In 1905, Germans could reflect that the international position was quite favourable to them. Russia had been defeated in war with Japan, and so France could not rely on her. Indeed, in July 1905, the tsar came quite close to making an alliance with Germany after meeting the Kaiser at Björkö. It broke down largely because, in this highly troubled period, Russia was heavily dependent on French loans. The German foreign office and military chiefs felt that the moment had come to challenge France over Morocco – always hoping that the British would not support France. The Kaiser landed at Tangier in March; there was demonstrative support for the cause of Moroccan independence. German diplomats threatened France with war; Delcassé himself resigned when the cabinet would not support him. A conference of all Powers interested in Moroccan affairs was convened in January 1906 at Algeciras. In it, the British supported the French; French preponderance in a still-independent

Morocco was assured (e.g., with control of the police); Germany's representatives were outvoted. Their acceptance of this defeat showed partly a consciousness of the unpopularity of colonial issues as a cause for war, and partly the great fear of the German admiralty that, if it came to war with Great Britain, the navy would be pulverized and Germany's coasts laid wide open to invasion. Until the Kiel Canal had been enlarged to take vast naval traffic, and until Germany had built sufficient ships, Tirpitz felt, there must be no war with the British. The Moroccan crisis petered out, but it left the link between London and Paris stronger than it had been. In August 1907, a similar arrangement of spheres of interest in Persia, Afghanistan and the Far East led to an Anglo-Russian understanding – the Triple Entente. Germans felt aggrieved that they were being excluded from overseas expansion. Tirpitz increased his naval programme in 1907–8: four capital ships per annum. The British in 1909 responded by authorizing the production of eight capital ships.

By then, the 'constants' in international affairs were beginning to change. The Turkish empire, which still covered a large part of the Balkans, was splitting apart. The future of the ancient Habsburg Monarchy seemed to be very questionable. Germany and Russia, already at odds over Turkey, could hardly agree to a peaceable partition of the Habsburg Monarchy. In March 1909, when the Russians objected to a forward move on Austria's part – the annexation of the formally Turkish province of Bosnia – the German foreign office sent them an ultimatum. Within two years, international relations had become one crisis after another: a second Moroccan crisis, when the Germans sent a gunboat to protect their interests, in the summer of 1911; an Italian attack on Tripolitania, again part of Turkey, in October 1911; then, a few months later, a coalition of the Balkan states against Turkey which, by the end of 1912, had almost cleared the Turks from the Balkans, after 'the first Balkan war'. In the summer of 1913 came another Balkan war, which resulted in Bulgaria's losing territory to the others.

What counted, in this, was that the greatest of the Balkan

states, Serbia, acted as a focus for loyalty to the millions of Serbs who lived under Austro-Hungarian rule. The Austrians could see a solution only in the use of force to crush Serbia, for the South Slav provinces – and not only these – were becoming ungovernable. Dignitaries were continually assassinated, and it was the murder of one such, Archduke Franz Ferdinand, at Sarajevo on 28 June 1914, that provoked war. His murderer had been a Serb, though a Habsburg subject, Gavrilo Princip. He has gone down to history with the remark, made just before his death in a Bohemian prison in 1918, that 'If I had not done it, the Germans would have found another excuse.'

The chief difficulty was that a quarrel between Austria and Serbia threatened to invoke alliances on both sides: indeed, the situation in which the First World War actually did break out was foreseen, in diplomats' and generals' exchanges, for five years beforehand. By virtue of the alliances and their military consequences, an Austrian attack on Serbia would mean a Russian move against Austria; that would mean a German move against Russia; it would in turn provoke a French move against Germany. The British had been careful not to conclude a formal undertaking of such a kind, but in 1911 they had assured the French that they would defend the Atlantic coast, and British and French generals had agreed on co-operation in the event of war with Germany.

In the July crisis of 1914, which followed the archduke's murder, all of this came to a head. But it made no sense except in terms of a vast stepping-up of the arms race since 1911, and also in terms of a new, radical nationalism that had arisen in the same period. In the Great Powers, that process occurred, in an atmosphere of increasing hysteria since 1890, and the most advanced case of that was Germany's.

2. Germany

It has been aptly remarked that, in the century after 1870, there was one dominating question in British foreign policy: Germany or Russia? The British, in both world wars, ended up with alliance with Russia. But in these decades, there were a great many people in Great Britain who would much rather have had a partnership with Germany. Joseph Chamberlain, in 1898 and again in 1901, spoke for the partnership of the 'Anglo-Saxon' and 'Teutonic' races; even in the First World War, there were efforts to sort out the difficulties between the two countries, on the lines of what appeared to be an obvious partnership – Great Britain with her empire, Germany with her expansion at Russia's expense. In the 1930s, such ideas were quite common.

They broke down on a simple fact: that German ambitions did not appear to be confined to eastern Europe at all; that they extended to western Europe and the world beyond. They were, moreover, being pushed ahead with an increasing degree of aggressiveness after the fall of Bismarck in 1890. Germany boomed, became the strongest country by far on the continent. She already had a great army; after 1897 she was building a great navy as well, one clearly designed for use against the British. Besides, Germany was not a country like Great Britain, where parliamentary power ensured that most things of importance would be publicly debated and decided upon. She was a 'managed autocracy', in which parliamentary power was very limited. Her government was a cabal, and appeared to be unwilling or unable to make the elementary parliamentary reforms that would have made Germany a constitutional state of the British type. The power and the bad behaviour of the Prussian army were such that Germany was widely accused of army-worship, militarism. Civilians stepped off the pavements to let officers pass; officers had a monopoly of the first-class carriages to Potsdam. It was a militarist, authoritarian state; and yet, it had the most powerful industry in Europe.

Ostensibly, Germany broke various rules of political development. Liberals, and Marxists after them, assumed that, with industrial progress, a large middle class would come into existence which would secure bourgeois-liberal reforms – a strong parliament, an end to 'feudal' ways, a properly constitutional monarchy. In Germany, up to 1918, hysterical conservatives were prominent in political affairs; and yet the country's economy not only was not backward: it was the most flourishing economy in Europe.

By 1913, Germany was producing two-thirds of all European steel (16,200,000 tonnes) – double the British figure, and not far short of the American one. She produced almost as much coal as Great Britain, and took many European markets from her. With 8,000,000,000 kilowatt-hours of electricity, she had more than Great Britain, France and Italy put together, and in the electrical industry German firms like the *Allgemeine Elektrizitätswerke GmbH* (AEG) or Siemens-Schuckert and Siemens-Halske led the world. Her cotton industry used twice the raw material of the next largest cotton industry in Europe, the French one. The Prussian railways rose from 5000 kilometres in 1878 to 37,000 in 1914. The change was extraordinarily rapid. In 1880, well over half of Germany's population worked on the land, a third in industry and handicrafts, and the rest in various forms of service industry (the tertiary sector). By 1914, not much more than a third worked in agriculture (thirty-five per cent), almost two-fifths in industry. But, within industry, there was a great change-over from small firms employing a handful of workmen to middle-sized and, most spectacularly of all, very large, concentrated firms whose huge, ugly factories dominated the Ruhr, Silesia, Saxony. Their unlovely bosses dominated the National Liberal party, especially in the Prussian Chamber of Deputies.

Germany's industrialization proceeded partly from the great heavy industries that emerged in nineteenth-century Europe – iron and steel – and partly from new industries such as the chemical and electrical ones. The chemical industry emerged from the textile industry which Germany, like all industrializing countries, had acquired (largely, though not entirely, from the English example) in the earlier nineteenth century. A need to substitute chemical dyes in this industry for the imported, and expensive, indigo was the initial spark, although Prussian military needs for explosives also fostered the process. Germany had abundant coal and potash, the bases for chemicals, and after 1880 her chemists (who had been renowned in Europe in the eighteenth century, or even in the sixteenth) went ahead with almost endless inventions in by-products of coal. By the 1890s, Germany had almost a world monopoly in synthetic dye-stuffs, which produced artificial fibres (the ancestors of rayon), photographic materials, drugs, the first plastics, new explosives, celluloid and – through ingenious adaptation in the Zeiss factory at Jena – optical glass.

It has been suggested that, in matters of industrialization, what counts is the matching of new economic forms with the long-term character of a country. In the sixteenth century, the Dutch rose to greatness because they were uniquely well placed to act as middle men in the carrying trade of Baltic products, especially grain; in the seventeenth century, the English could profit from a worldwide version of the same process; in the eighteenth and the nineteenth, the northern English and Scottish habits of skilled engineering suited the industrial developments of the age, and were combined with banking, a relatively flexible stock exchange, entrepreneurs from the north, and agriculture that was efficient, at least by the standards of the day.

In Germany, chemistry corresponded with a national character that had always leaned towards theoretical research; mathematical approaches to scientific problems had a long history. Leibniz, at the turn of the seventeenth and eighteenth centuries, had approached chemistry almost in an anticipation of the statistical methods of the later century; in the middle of the nineteenth century August Kekulé, by adapting mathematical approaches to the subject, was able very greatly to simplify experimental processes for synthesis which otherwise would have been impossibly complex. Bunsen and Liebig, early in the century, had made a similarly inspired approach to soil-chemistry. In the 1880s, the existence of railways – of which Germany acquired 10,000 kilometres in every decade after 1870 – allowed a national market to be exploited. The circumstances of the 'Great Depression' expanded this market's urban element. A need to cut costs in supply from abroad prompted efforts to substitute one natural material for another (organic chemistry) or, later, to find a synthetic process that would enable the natural materials to be done away with altogether (inorganic chemistry). By 1883, even in pharmaceuticals, intelligent entrepreneurs appreciated a need for research. Carl Duisberg, owner of what became the *Badische Anilin-und Soda-Fabrik* (BASF – still one of the largest German concerns), had, in 1900, 6300 workers and 233 chemists; the *Farbwerke Hoechst* 3500 and 165 respectively. By 1914, the chemical industry had expanded very greatly indeed, since the price-rise in organic materials (commodities) prompted an even more intense search for substitutes. Employment rose to 300,000. It was a process of endless invention, especially when it was allied to electrical energy. By 1904, the three main chemical firms – the third being the Bayer works at Leverkusen in the Ruhr – had formed a trust to pool their resources and hence concentrate investment; in the Leuna works near Leipzig, before 1914, catalysts were discovered and applied in synthesis of ammonia, which led to the Haber-Bosch process for fixing nitrogen (hence to the bulk of Germany's explosives in the First World War, which came literally from the air) and later to synthetic petrol.

In heavy industry, Germany was also well placed to take advantage of nineteenth-century circumstances. Here again, although contemporaries could not fail to be impressed as giant iron and steel works came to dominate the Ruhr, Prussian Silesia and Saxony, the element of continuity is very strong. Indeed, the expression 'industrial revolution', at least in its modern sense, is an invention of the early part of the twentieth century. By then, it could properly be applied to the extraordinary urbanization of Europe in the generation since 1870; economic historians were coming to terms, more or less for the first time, with the problem of Growth (a subject that concerned the specialist periodicals only after 1900). Even in the eighteenth century, Prussia had been the second largest manufacturing country in Europe – some way behind Great Britain. Her annexation of Silesia, with its coalmines and textiles, and, in 1815, her annexation of Prussian Saxony and the kingdom of Westphalia (i.e., the Ruhr), gave her entrepreneurs an enormous field for expansion, which was well launched by 1840.

In the Ruhr, entrepreneurs who themselves had emerged, with a hard struggle upwards, from a harsh and almost always Protestant background could preside over the development of the abundant local coalfields. The onset of the 'Great Depression', the troughs of the early 1880s, the early 1890s and the early 1900s, each prompted a degree of rationalization: the firms merged, formed cartels first for joint selling, then for quotas of production, then for joint investment. They needed to export in order to escape the internal quota limits. They therefore needed tariffs, not only to offset foreign competition, but also to have high prices at home which could compensate for very low prices abroad – the *Kampfpreise*. Since the State accepted arguments for a tariff even in 1879, and went on accepting them in the main up to the First World War, these cartels flourished – scooping the pool in overseas markets, at the expense of the consumer and the small manufacturer inside Germany, who had to pay higher prices for his metal and coal than he otherwise would have needed to do. Industrialists divided into two blocs – the *Zentralverband der deutschen Industrie*, which had originated in the heavy industrialists of the Westphalian syndicate with a very long name, and the *Bund deutscher Industrieller*, which attempted, not very effectively, to unite medium and smaller concerns against the high-tariff men. Very broadly speaking, the tariff men were associated with the National Liberals after 1880, while the *Bund deutscher Industrieller* was linked with the Progressive liberals.

The world of German heavy industry was very ugly and very successful. Protestant entrepreneurs and administrative staff, Jewish financiers like Emil Rathenau or Carl Fürstenberg, and a frequently Catholic (and in Bochum or Gelsenkirchen largely Polish) work-force reproduced conditions almost ideal for the success of the very cruel heavy-industrial sweated trades of the later nineteenth century: conditions reproduced quite widely in the United States, and up to a point in Great Britain as well. In Krupp's Essen as in Pittsburgh or Cleveland – where an Andrew Carnegie could reign over a largely Polish work-force – hundreds of thousands of peasant sons, arriving by rail or ship from the collapse of peasant agriculture, turned the wheels of heavy industry. In the 1880s, the introduction of the Gilchrist-Thomas process allowed these firms to use the iron-ore of nearby Lorraine, and the German steel industry boomed accordingly.

Capital was not abundantly available. It was stretched a long way by a banking system that led Europe as far as investment banking was concerned. British banks advanced credit for particular transactions, and firms, for investment, ploughed back their profits or relied on the stock exchange. German banks conscripted savings and lent them out long-term. It was a fragile system, and, had there been a panic, the banks, unable to recover their debts, would have collapsed – as was to happen in 1931. Forty-five per cent of the German banking system, Werner Sombart discovered, was in Jewish hands, and it is tempting simply to write off the financial adaptability of German credit institutions to this factor: for 'out of the ghetto' was as important a part of German industrialization as any other. Jews in general became associated with finance and commerce; after 1880, there was a distinct Jewish issue in politics, since many of the victims of economic change blamed the Jews for their troubles.

However flourishing and modern the German economy

seemed to be, the Kaiser's Germany was not, in political terms, the classic prosperous western European state which hopeful liberals might have imagined in 1870. Despite its large middle class and the growing prosperity of its working class, it was not 'bourgeois-democratic' and liberally pacific in international affairs. It did not follow the 'English' rules.

Before and during the First World War, Germany's troubles were often ascribed to the constitution which Bismarck had set up in 1871 for the new Reich. In the first place, 'Germany' only barely came into existence. It consisted of twenty-six separate states, ranging from Prussia, which contained two-thirds of the population, to Schwarzburg-Rudolstadt, a few square miles of comic opera. These states had different constitutions: universal-male-suffrage parliamentary liberalism in some, restricted liberties in others, and, in the two Grand Duchies of Mecklenburg (Schwerin and Strelitz), absolutist systems of seventeenth-century style, including Estates, though, since the Reformation, without the Church. These particular states had considerable powers, especially in financial affairs. Their existence prevented any true centralization, although beyond the main states – Prussia, Saxony, Bavaria, Württemberg and Baden – they did not count for much, except as historical furniture of a kind much loved in the later nineteenth century.

The separate states dealt with internal affairs, leaving war and foreign affairs to the emperor in Berlin. He enjoyed large prerogatives; but there was also a central parliament, the *Reichstag*, which could debate as to the imperial budget. It was elected by universal male suffrage, with constituencies that, at least in the 1870s, were fairly arranged. But its powers were strictly limited. *Reichstag* members could not become government secretaries of state; they had first to resign their seats. This meant that the Western system, by which leading politicians took over the government, was ruled out. The chancellor was not dependent on *Reichstag* votes: he was appointed and dismissed only by the emperor.

He was not required even to answer *Reichstag* members' questions; and the *Reichstag* had no right to initiate legislation – all of it an offence to western European liberal orthodoxy. In military matters, the *Reichstag* was often powerless. In theory, the Prussian war minister was answerable, ultimately, to the parliaments which supplied the funds. But the emperor and Bismarck insisted on preserving much military business in imperial or royal hands; and in any case they overloaded the war ministry with endless administrative triviality, while passing serious matters to the chief of the General Staff, who was not responsible to parliament, but rather, directly, to the emperor. In the same way the emperor's private military office (*Militärkabinett*) acquired great powers of appointing and dismissing officers. It happened before 1914 that Jews would be refused commissions as reserve officers. The *Reichstag* would complain; but the war minister would be unable to give any details, since he was not, in that respect, responsible or even informed: or so, at least, he could plausibly pretend.

In important respects, Germany was thus 'a managed autocracy' as her enemies claimed. The *Reichstag* was elected by universal male suffrage, and yet it was constitutionally powerless in matters that counted as internal affairs of the states, while even in imperial matters its powers were very few.

True, it grew in importance, far beyond the role originally cast for it. As the economy developed, demands for central legislation also grew – weights and measures, company law, social measures, transport. In the later 1870s, a real tariff was imposed, at the behest of a majority in the *Reichstag*. This gave the Reich a serious income of its own, not just hand-outs from the states (although this effect was veiled). The budget rose. The demands of defence also grew very greatly – from a bare 100,000,000 marks in the early 1870s to 1,595,000,000 in 1909 and 2,405,000,000 in 1913/14. The *Reichstag* could make real trouble and the government had to take it seriously. If a chancellor lost control of it, as Bülow did in 1909 and Bethmann Hollweg in 1917, he would become a liability, and the emperor would have to let him go. But even then, Germany was a long way from being a centrally run country with a functioning parliament. The constitution was not seriously altered until the very last days of the First World War.

The reality behind Bismarck's constitution was Prussia. She was by far the largest state, having swallowed up several others in 1866, and she had a blocking position in the federal council, the *Bundesrat*, in which representatives of the states sat to discuss common matters. Her government was in practice often identical with the imperial one – to such a degree that, on one occasion, Bismarck, as Prussian prime minister, wrote in complaint to himself, as chancellor. Prussia had her own constitution. But it did not provide for universal male suffrage and bourgeois-democratic power: quite the reverse. As the nineteenth century went on, Prussia (and Saxony) became more and more clearly class-states.

The Prussian Chamber of Deputies (*Abgeordnetenhaus*) was elected, not by equal male suffrage, but by a complicated system known as the 'three-class franchise'. Voters in one area would be classed in three groups according to the amount of tax they paid. Those men who were responsible for paying the top third of the total tax collected from the area would be put into one class for voting; further down the line, the same principle prevailed. Voters in each class elected two electors (*Wahlmänner*) and these in turn chose the deputy. The inequalities of property were such that the lowest third accounted for ninety-two per cent of the voters. The Prussian Chamber thus vastly overweighted the votes of the well-off. Generally, it divided in thirds between the conservative, National Liberal and Catholic parties with a small number of left-wing liberals, although by 1914 the anomalies of the system even allowed through a handful of social democrats. The three-class franchise operated according to consti-tuencies, and since by now there were solidly working-class areas like Berlin-Kaulsdorf, even the top third of tax-payers there might well vote social democrat. In Berlin-Vossstrasse, the top third of tax-payers consisted of Wertheimer, owner of a large department store; his fiscal preponderance was such that he pushed even some former *Reichskanzler* into the third class.

In the 1850s and 1860s, a parliament representing only the rich would still produce severe disagreements between liberals and conservatives. By the 1880s, the rise of mass politics meant that both parties were almost equally scared of the left and the Catholics. Social democrats, who were elected to the *Reichstag*, promised to put an end to the Prussian world of Junkers and armies: they seemed to be anti-clerical, centralizing and contemptuous of the past; they promised to bring in a very large income tax and huge inheritance taxes. The politics of the Prussian parliament became, accordingly, a simple matter of upper-class representatives assembling to say 'amen' to assorted right-wing truths, and passing laws to reward themselves.

Junker families enjoyed a considerable preponderance in the administration. In Prussia east of the Elbe – the provinces of East Prussia, West Prussia, Silesia, Prussian Saxony (annexed in 1815), Poznania, Pomerania and Brandenburg – they had a wonderful time. The local administration was in the hands of a government appointee, the *Landrat*, whose doings were only barely affected by the existence of a local council or *Kreistag*. *Landräte* were usually Junker sons with a law degree (which in Germany could take seven years to acquire) and they co-operated with their local cousins. There were famous cases of such officials' conniving in the tax dodges of their cousins. In 1909 a spokesman of these Junkers, Elard von Oldenburg-Januschau, made the mistake of suggesting in public that the Prussian noblemen, unlike Jews, were distinguished by honesty in their tax returns. He wrote to the ministry of agriculture for details, and was privately informed by the minister, Count Arnim-Muskau, that tax evasion rose in Prussia the further east you went. Generally, in Prussia, investigation of tax evasion resulted in the further payment of 240,000,000 marks, or 4.5 per cent of the total tax bill; however, in the Junker heartlands east of the Elbe, the percentage was much higher – 7.7 in

Poznania, 8.6 in Allenstein and 11 in Bromberg. Prince Dohna-Schlobitten, for instance, had declared an annual income of 60,000 marks for the years 1903–10: he omitted from it sums that he was owed in one year and that he 'forgot' to declare for the year they were paid. These tax affairs attracted the attention of the chancellor's deputy, Hans von Delbrück; soon, he found that several conservative members of the *Reichstag* and the Prussian Chamber were involved, including the conservatives' leader, Ernst von Heydebrand und der Lasa.

These families also enjoyed a near-monopoly of civil-service posts in the Prussian provinces; indeed, part of the problem concerning tax was that the tax officials were, quite often, closely related to the tax-payers. In the army, similarly, the Junker class had considerable predominance. In 1914, fifty-two per cent of the colonels were of noble origin – a number that was higher even than in the noble-dominated army of 1866. In the 1880s, the then liberal war ministry had been forced, by an aggressive General Staff, to tighten up the provisions for intake of officers, who became more, not less aristocratic, in majority, as the century wore on. By 1910, many of the army's leaders were so anxious to preserve the nobles' near-monopoly of army commissions that they even opposed the creation of a larger army, which, by requiring more officers, would let in 'democratic' elements.

In economic affairs, the nobles' estates were subsidized by the government – whether through tariffs, direct grants, exemption from taxation, a complicated system of rebates in grain transactions, the *Einfuhrscheine*, or provision for artificial prices in the nobles' distilleries. The mass of the people in Prussia were thus paying for the upkeep of these Junker estates, and subsidizing the Junkers' various monopolies. Yet the Prussian parliament, consisting of representatives only of the better-off, would not intervene; and the *Reichstag*'s writ could not run in Prussia to counteract this. When the mass parties complained, they could, quite often, encounter violence from the police. The Prussian police force – and the lesser bureaucracy in general – acquired a

formidable reputation for petty-mindedness and vindictiveness. Its collective mind emerges in the following figures,
which were solemnly recorded by policemen in a Berlin
cemetery, standing by the graves hour after hour and day in,
day out:

Visits to the graves of the liberal rebels shot on 18 March 1848

Year	No. of visits	Wreaths	Wreath-labels removed by police, on grounds of offensiveness
1903	10,035	153	28
1905	7250	131	14
1906	15,500	212	2
1909	14,500	198	11

For eighteen months, a liberal *Oberbürgermeister* of Berlin,
Kirschner, was refused confirmation of his appointment in
the later 1890s because he had inscribed a memorial to these
rebels on the Friedrichshain Gate. The ways of the Prussian
police were shown in the Tacitean succinctness of their
instructions: menaces of violent punishment which, in their
effect, are incapable of translation into English, or indeed
any other language. In this world of crack-pot authoritarian-
ism, it was not surprising that many social democrats, who
otherwise would have slid easily enough into the kind of
left-wing liberal pose that their counterparts in countries to
the west adopted, went on feeling revolutionary. It was
difficult not to cry *à la lanterne* in these circumstances.

Social democrats might well feel that this police state had
been set up to crush them as part of the class-war which every
European country experienced after 1880. But in other
countries, police repression was weakened after 1900, as
indeed it was in the other German states, in whose chief
towns the social democrats held their annual congresses
(Chemnitz, Jena, Stuttgart etc.), because police interference

was less. The Prussian police state went back further than the industrial class-war. It owed much to the Brandenburg electors' imitation of the Swedish Vasas' North European bureaucratic absolutism and *raison d'état* (it was not an accident that, after 1618, the Hohenzollern dynasty was Calvinist whereas the bulk of their subjects were Lutheran). It had thrived particularly from its own success in the eighteenth century, when Frederick the Great added a large part of Poland to his possessions. For two-fifths of Prussia's population consisted of Catholics; and many of these were Poles. The real trouble with Prussia was that a colonial and a metropolitan administration coincided in Berlin. Its response to any problem was the harshest and most narrow-mindedly egoistic. The law of associations, for instance, forbade any assembly of more than half a dozen people without police permission; and if more than six people were present, then a policeman would attend, and the language of the gathering would have to be German, for his benefit. The Catholics were sometimes relentlessly perse-cuted. Their priests had to be approved by the State, their religious gatherings similarly. Catholics got nowhere in the Prussian bureaucracy – only one Prussian ministry, agricul-ture, was filled by a Catholic, and even then he had married a Protestant and brought up his children as Lutherans. Many Catholic town councils were Protestant monopolies.

In Prussian Poland there was a regular land-war. After 1854 seasonal labourers from the east – *Sachsengänger* – were controlled by a 'service rule' (*Gesindeordnung*) which banned strikes on pain of a fifteen-mark fine (in a wage of thirty) and a three-year gaol sentence; even when employees did not know beforehand the employer with whom they had signed up, they were forbidden to leave his service. In 1900, at the behest of Wangenheim, head of the landlords' association (*Bund der Landwirte*), these arrangements were tightened up, though in 1902 some of the anti-Catholic measures (the 'Jesuit Clause') were weakened so as to secure Catholic votes for another grain tariff.

In some, though by no means all, respects, the Polish

question in Prussia resembled the Irish one in Great Britain. The problem was twofold: first, the effects of the agrarian depression were such that Germans went bankrupt in the Prussian east, and their lands would be bought up by Poles who were able, through family farms, to work for smaller costs. The Catholic Poles also had a higher birth-rate, partly out of religious principle, and partly because they needed children's labour, since they were dependent either on family farms or on day-labouring in the Junker estates. From 1903 to 1907, over half of the pieces of land east of the Elbe, excluding Silesia, were sold. By 1907, in Poznań, there were 900,000 Poles to 760,000 Germans; in the industrial region of upper Silesia (centring upon Katowice) a Polish majority was emerging. Many Germans complained that Polish workers were sending back money to enable them to buy land from spendthrift Junkers; there was no doubt that the land, and much else, was being 'Polonized'. The landlords' league claimed that there was 'a state of war between people and people'.

Prussia 'fought back'. In the early 1890s a German league was set up, the *Hakatisten* (so named after the initials of its main leaders, the three landowners Hansemann, Kennemann and Tiedemann), to 'defend the values of Germandom in the East'. German liberals quite often blamed German noblemen for their 'plight': after all, it was the nobles who brought in Polish seasonal labour, and also the nobles who, by farming inefficiently, sold up to Poles. Max Weber wrote his first serious work on agrarian conditions east of the Elbe with a view to explaining this 'calamity'; in fact he resigned from the Pan-German League because it was not nationalist enough about this issue (although his attitudes became more sensible later on, as he grew up). The city centre of Poznań was studded with grim buildings, gigantic imitations of the castles of the Teutonic Knights; Kaiser Wilhelm II took part in ludicrous pageants at the restored Knights' castle, Marienburg, and dressed himself up as Grand Master. The Polish town of Inowroclaw was renamed 'Hohensalza', after a famous Grand Master and crusher of Poles. In 1886 the

Prussian parliament set up a fund to buy up bankrupt German estates and sell them to German migrants; the fund was increased in the 1890s; and in 1908 the national liberal leader, Johannes von Miquel, pushed through a law that would allow compulsory purchase of bankrupt or Polish estates: this at the very moment when British practice in Ireland was to force estate-owners to sell to their Irish tenants. The educational system was relentlessly Germanized, and in 1906 there was a huge school strike in Poznań, in which children, carrying candles, demonstrated through the streets at night.

The Prussian programme did not work. In the first place, there were many more Poles than Germans; in the second place, it was Germans who sold up: even under the *Lex Miquel*, 32,000 hectares were acquired from Germans, as against 2620 from Poles. Finally, the Germans themselves would not move back to the land once they had left it. German statesmen were given to romanticizing agrarian life. But they found few takers for the bleak existence of an east -Elbian farmer, as was shown yet again in the early 1930s, when the pre-Hitler régime attempted to settle the urban unemployed on bankrupt land in East Prussia or Pomerania.

A similar bitterness attended Prussian activities in Alsace, which had been taken from the French in 1871. The population there spoke, in the main, German (though in a difficult dialect). But it was also Catholic, and in some respects rather backward. It received a full dose of Prussia. The annexed region did not become a separate German state; rather, it was called *Reichsland*, and was governed as a colony. Its Catholics felt the weight of the *Kulturkampf*, and the military garrison behaved badly. Even a generation after 1871, in a German-speaking province, the bulk of votes went to Francophile groups; and although a representative assembly was given limited powers in 1911, the authorities stopped at that, because they feared an autonomous Alsace. Soldiers often behaved badly there. Civilian governors (*Statthälter*) sometimes had glimmerings of a sense that all of this was grotesque; even quite stiff-necked figures, such as Prince

Wedel or Count Dallwitz, would complain on their subjects' behalf. They would be told: these people only understand force. It was applied in a famous incident in the little town of Saverne (Zabern) in 1913, when a lieutenant gave outrageous punishment to the population for 'dumb insolence', an insolence which he had himself provoked by using the insulting term '*Wackes*' for Alsatians, a term which the *Statthalter* himself had forbidden. In any case, he had vastly exceeded his powers. In the upshot, he received public congratulations from the Kaiser, and the *Reichstag*, though it grumbled, allowed the matter to drop.

Prussia was, then, a harshly run class-state, with an aggressive foreign policy and a government that, for much of the time, was irresponsible. It was a state whose ideology was simply its own power; vainglorious fantasies appeared to be its rulers' stock-in-trade.

Bismarck, German nationalism, the constitution, or the weakness of German liberals were variously blamed for this. The fact was, however, that Germany did have a universal-suffrage parliament. It could, simply by blocking all government legislation, have insisted on constitutional change. In practice, the *Reichstag* never did this. True, the constitution gave great difficulties. They caused much head-shaking before the war. They were circumvented in forty-eight hours at the end of it. If the *Reichstag* did not function in a Western sense, it had to do, not with articles 15 (B) and 21 of the constitution, but with the attitudes of the parties. Had the left and centre combined as they sometimes did in Great Britain and as they usually did in France, the constitutional problem would have been solved along Western lines.

According to nineteenth-century liberal orthodoxies, peace and prosperity ought to have gone hand in hand with reform. The first paradox in Germany's constitutional development was that economic modernization did not go parallel with political modernization. Rather, by 1912, the country's political system was becoming chaotic, and a nationalist general spoke for much of the right when he said that the country needed the blood-cure. Germany's very rapid economic development created, on the one hand, a tense class-war in the cities; on the other hand, it embittered a great part of the agricultural and artisan community.

The politics of the *Reichstag* appeared to be complex. There were a great many parties (catalogued in Dieter Fricke's two-volume *Die bürgerlichen Parteien in Deutschland*) because there were many regional interests to be voiced. The Poles, the Danes of Schleswig-Holstein and the Alsatians had groups of their own; in the 1890s there were three anti-Semitic parties; Hanover, Hesse and other regions sometimes sent autonomists to the *Reichstag*. In general, these small parties made up a fifth of the German parliament. Usually, they were to be classed with the liberal middle, from which they took their votes.

There were five chief parties: social democrats, Catholic *Zentrum*, left-wing liberals (in southern Germany, *Volkspartei*), right-wing liberals (*Nationalliberale Partei*) and conservatives, who also had a small pendant in the *Reichspartei*. The left in the *Reichstag* consisted of social democrats and left-wing liberals, who in 1910 took the name 'Progressives' but earlier had been known as 'anti-clericals' (*Freisinn*). The proportions shifted in the social democrats' favour after 1890, but the combined *Reichstag* left took at most forty per cent of the seats. The same was broadly true for the right – conservatives, National Liberals and their small-party allies. Here, too, the proportions shifted from one group to another: by 1914, conservatives and National Liberals had fallen to around fifteen per cent each of the seats. The balance of power in the *Reichstag* was thus held by the Catholics, who usually had somewhat over a fifth of the seats (though by 1912, sixteen per cent). If the Catholics shifted to alliance with the left, then there would be a left-centre bloc that might achieve constitutional change: after all, the *Reichstag* had serious powers to obstruct the government, and these, if used, could have forced the government to concede reforms of a kind that had long been standard in other countries. In 1918, such a left-centre bloc did emerge; it constructed the

German Republic, and as such became known as the *Weimarer Koalition*. The essential political question of the Kaiser's Germany is negative: why was there no Weimar coalition before 1914?

The constant combination in the *Reichstag* was an alliance of right and centre – i.e., conservatives and national liberals (the parties of the *Kartell* majority in the later 1880s) with the Catholics. This combination was known as the 'Blue-Black Block' – blue for conservatives and black for Catholics. Given this majority, the *Reichstag* would not successfully exert itself for constitutional change. It never once vetoed the budget; its majority supported aggressive policies abroad, and indeed regarded the chancellors as weak-willed. With few exceptions, Germany's intellectual class had authoritarian and nationalist sympathies.

Many reasons have been advanced for this state of affairs. The Germans lacked a 'political class', i.e. people who would play pure politics in the English manner. There were no German Whigs; and the Junker element was entrenched in narrow-minded defence of its privileges. Except perhaps partly in Matthias Erzberger, a Catholic politician prominent in the creation of the Republic later on, there was no Lloyd George who could knit left and centre together, through plausible appeals both to Liberal industrialists and to Labour. It was also true, indeed a truism, that nationalism weakened liberalism. German liberals stood for empire, and even, though with strong reservations, for armies; a large part of the younger male middle class took considerable pride in being commissioned as reserve officers; the anti-militarism of the left offended them. The prominent liberal historian, Otto Hintze, who married a Jewess, remarked in an essay on German parliamentary development (1908) that Germany could not acquire proper institutions because they would not support the army; but the army was needed to defend the country against her ring of enemies; therefore the only way of acquiring a real parliament would be to defeat the French first, and so not to have enemies to face.

These factors, which had long origins, were complicated

after 1880 by two different crises, which reflected the very
rapid alteration of the country: the industrial class-war, and
the troubles of the *Mittelstand*, i.e., of the farmer-artisan
world. By 1912, a great majority of the working class voted
for the social democrats, who advertised themselves as a
revolutionary party; apart from a very small band of
Progressive liberals, the other parties were in almost
permanent opposition to them.

The National Liberals and their small-party associates
took money from industrialists and voiced their interests;
they took votes from the urban middle class and some – not
many – rural areas. Their share of the vote fell from a rough
third in the later 1870s to a sixth in 1912, and the party was
open to a jibe that it had become 'middle-class auxiliary
forces for the conservatives'. Like most Liberal parties in
Europe, it had difficulty in organizing. In the past, it had
relied on local 'eminent citizens' – *Honoratioren* – and it did
not adapt very easily to the requirements of mass politics. Its
central office in Berlin contained only three officials in 1902;
a general secretary had to circulate local parties with the
advice that they should not choose their candidate at the last
moment. From time to time, there were alarms. In the later
1890s, the National Liberals voted against the Kaiser's
proposal to imprison pickets; around 1903, some Young
Liberals tried to force the party to make a more serious
appeal to the 'new *Mittelstand*', these armies of clerks,
schoolteachers and officials whom the 1890s had called into
existence. That would have meant espousing a reform of the
limited suffrage in Prussia (or Saxony), accepting a social
democratic and Progressive partnership in the *Reichstag*,
and, probably, an advocacy of free trade. These policies
worried the National Liberals' industrial paymasters, as well
as the bulk of the Prussian deputies. They were heavily voted
down; and when the National Liberal leader, Bassermann,
seemed to be steering the party towards the left, he was
almost deprived of his long-held office. The votes of the 'new
Mittelstand' went elsewhere, even, in some places, to the
social democrats. German liberalism was therefore much

weaker than its French or British counterparts. In France, there was not a class-war of anything approaching German intensity; in Great Britain, outside Ireland, there was not that vast bloc of small farmers which provided the constituency both for Junker conservatism and for political Catholicism.

The National Liberals' left-wing rivals, the Progressives, were an even sorrier sight. They originated in a wide variety of places. A good part of the Jewish community in Berlin voted for them; so, in the form of the *Volkspartei*, did southern German democrats and anti-militarists; in the merchant towns of the Baltic, free-trading sympathies caused much of the local patriciate to vote for the left-wing liberals. They suffered, however, from problems of finance, in that their industrial supporters were not as comfortably off as were the National Liberals'. They also failed to organize, not least because their constituencies were so disparate. The patricians of the north were in favour of a limited franchise, and disliked social democrats. The South Germans could, at times, speak an irritatingly particularist language. The Berlin element, though often highly intelligent and, in the case of Eugen Richter, a leader in the 1890s and 1900s, mordantly funny in the Berlin way, tended to overrate its own strength. The left-wing liberals were great splitters. They divided over matters of free trade and empire – some of them for a great navy, others not. They divided in their attitudes towards the National Liberals: should they aim to capture these, or should they, instead, appeal to the social democrats? In 1902, the social democrats proposed to oppose the Bülow tariff by obstructing all *Reichstag* business. The Progressives would not have this, and forfeited social democratic support. In the early 1880s, there were already serious divisions. In 1884, a single left-wing liberal party emerged – using the title 'anti-clerical' (*Freisinn*) since anti-clericalism was about all that the party had in common. But when Bismarck raised matters of colonies, and, still more, when Caprivi undertook reform of the tariff in the early 1890s, the party divided yet again. By 1893 there were three left-wing liberal parties – two anti-clerical, and one

'South German *Volkspartei*'. In 1907, this element even made an alliance with the national liberals and the conservatives with a view to opposing both Catholics and social democrats: the years of the *Bülow-Block*. In 1910, the left-wing liberals came together once more as *Fortschrittliche Volkspartei* ('Progressives') and once more looked to socialist alliances. But in the election of 1912 they did not win a single seat on the first round of balloting, and survived, with under a tenth of the seats in the *Reichstag*, only through socialist tolerance. Together, all brands of liberal had taken half of the *Reichstag* seats in 1871. By 1912, they took a quarter.

But if the class-war, and the rise of socialism, pushed German liberalism towards the right, it was also incapacitated by the rise of a new right – partly in the form of German conservatism, but more particularly with the rash of small, crypto-Nazi parties which emerged in the wake of agrarian crisis, and stole liberal votes. Related to this (though of course not politically allied with it) were the further phenomena of Polish nationalism and political Catholicism. Each of these, in their way, showed the extent of discontent at liberalism.

Germany, by 1890, had become the dominant industrial power of Europe. But that industrial achievement tended to obscure the reality that there were two Germanies: the backdrop to the burgeoning factories of the Ruhr or Saxony was a world of farming and of small towns which, even in 1914, still accounted for forty per cent of the German population (as distinct from the English eight per cent). The great German cities divided, politically, much as did other European cities: right-wing liberal, left-wing liberal, political-Catholic and socialist. But the whole pattern was complicated by an agrarian dimension, with an independent-artisan aspect. Around 1900, German political discussion was dominated by the question of the *Mittelstand*. The famous economist, Gustav Schmoller, wrote a famous piece called *Was heisst Mittelstand* ('What is the *Mittelstand*'). The sociologist Tönnies contributed an equally celebrated work on *Gemeinschaft und Gesellschaft*, in which he contrasted the atomized and mechanistic world of the big city with the 'organic', unselfconscious world of the old artisan-peasant community.

Mittelstand did not mean 'bourgeoisie'. It applied, rather, to the world of independent farmers and craftsmen who stood between the old landowner and his peasants. In many respects, *Mittelstand* was the glory of northern Germany, as it was of most Protestant civilizations: striving to retain independence, sober, hard-working and proud, though also smug and 'Main Street' in politics. In many ways, the *Mittelstand* and big industry complemented each other (as they did in the United States). Big industry needed the craftsman-skills of the *Mittelstand*, and, at the same time, would sub-contract to independent artisans who, in turn, would buy industrial goods. Something of a caste system developed in Germany, as elsewhere. A Catholic proletariat – Irish in Great Britain, often Polish in Germany – would turn the wheels of heavy industry, directed and complemented by largely Protestant craftsmen, and the industrial success stories of this era, whether with Mannesmann in Augsburg, or Krupp in Essen – or for that matter Carnegie in Pittsburgh – showed only the vitality of this mixture. The achievements of the Protestant *Mittelstand* in Germany in the 1880s and the 1890s inspired Max Weber to write penetratingly of the links between Protestantism and capitalism; and, though his remarks can be contested for the sixteenth century, they apply practically without qualification to the late nineteenth.

So long as things went well, German liberalism took the votes of the Protestant *Mittelstand*. But, even in the 1890s, that loyalty was becoming weak. *Mittelstand* Germany had much to resent; and, by the early 1930s, it supplied Hitler with what was, by far, his largest single constituency. The beginnings of that process, and the consequent destruction of German liberalism, can be read back to the 1880s.

The agrarian aspects of this were clear enough. The decline of food prices affected Germany despite tariffs; there was a great flight from the land, which also drove up wages.

In the early 1890s, the worst point of the 'Great Depression' was reached, and farmers – Protestant and Catholic – complained violently. Each one tried to offset the fall of prices by producing more, and this caused prices to fall still further. At the same time, ingenious chemists were producing substitutes for goods produced by farmers. 'Saccharine' and 'margarine' made an appearance. Machines were invented to 'vend' bottles of beer at railway stations, which threatened the local brewers and tavern-keepers. The closer accessibility of foreign meat or vegetable markets equally affected German sellers, even in quite remote places. Even after 1896, when prices went up again, the agrarians were never contented, since their costs were also rising.

The agrarians denounced 'Manchesterism' – the liberal doctrine that goods and men should sink or rise to their natural market level, regardless of the damage that might be caused. Farmers wanted protection, and a great many of them went further – they wanted the State to guarantee credit at a low rate and even a market. There was also a considerable resentment against Jews. The Jews were thought to be profiteering out of the woes of agriculture. Horse-dealers in Hanover were usually Jews, and, at a time of falling prices, they were not often generous in their offers. Finance, especially at the visible local level, was frequently in Jewish hands; so was much of commodity importing and exporting. But, in many people's eyes, German liberalism as a whole was 'Jewish'. Many of its leading figures in the 1880s – including Lasker, Bamberger and Eugen Richter – were either Jews, half-Jews, or married to Jews. The *Freisinn* radicals of Berlin received their strongest support from the Jewish community. Jews seemed to be profiting from modern circumstances beyond any other group in Germany. In Prussia, for every 100,000 Protestant males, 58 went through higher education; in the Catholic case, 33; in the Jewish case 519.

But it was not only farmers who complained. The older kind of artisan – wheelwrights, cobblers, tailors, small metal-workers, textile out-workers and the like – also faced competition whether from foreign or domestic factory-made goods. As large department stores started off in the towns – the Tietz chain, for instance, which began with a Jewish shopkeeper in Rostock and spread out into large stores throughout Germany – small shopkeepers complained that they were being undercut and forced to work long hours. Here, too, were grounds for anti-Semitism, 'the socialism of fools' as an Austrian called it. There was a plethora of *Mittelstand* associations with portentous names, such as the *Deutsche Handelsgehilfenverband*, for commercial clerks. In the later 1880s, a *christlich-sozial* element came up, under the pastor, Stöcker, to knit such groups together. Anti-Semitic parties started up, though, once they had delivered their electoral charge of venom, they were unclear as to how to proceed, and quarrelled bitterly among themselves. Their votes came from the old liberal constituency. In 1892, an effort was made to capture the German conservative party. It held its meeting in the Tivoli Gardens in Berlin; anyone might attend, and anyone present had a vote for organization or leadership. Briefly, an anti-Semitic radical programme was imposed on the party, although its leaders were embarrassed at the crypto-Nazi rowdies, and many of them, having married Jews, disliked the racial anti-Semitic element. Within a short space, the party had been recaptured, and the rowdies expelled.

Even so, the *mittelständisch* agitation did turn the conservative party in a more radical direction. In the early 1890s, there was a concatenation of urban and rural trouble. Bismarck was dismissed because he would not appease the socialists by relaxing the anti-socialist laws. His successor, Caprivi, wished to curb agitation by relaxing the tariff on food – a move which would also suit the needs of industrialists, who otherwise would have been pushed to pay higher wages. Caprivi also hoped, in a manoeuvre which was quite characteristic of the complicated politics of the *Reichstag*, to gain left-wing votes for the army in exchange for a reduction of food tariffs. The right, as a whole, protested violently. Conservatives denounced this *Kanzler ohne Ar und Halm* ('Chancellor without sake and soke' is an accurate enough rendering of this expression). A conservative leader, Count Kanitz-Podangen, demanded a State grain exchange, with guaranteed prices to defeat the 'Jewish' free exchange. In 1893, a 'farmers' league' – *Bund der Landwirte* – came into existence. It speedily acquired a mass-organization, with its own press. It demanded, for instance, that margarine should be given a hideous gentian colour – the colour of the *Reichstag* skirting-board – to put the consumer off; margarine was also to have a horrible name, *Oeltalg*, meaning, roughly, 'oilslick'. A ban on 'vending machines' in railway stations was proposed, and, in Württemberg, executed. All of this went together with a portentousness that was uniquely German. The *Bund* issued its electoral manifesto in 1893 with the words, 'A slow but steady rise in the price of grain has been the hallmark of all the great civilizations.' Department stores were dismissed as an *Unwesen* ('monstrosity'); emancipation of women, almost all Poles, and Jews, were similar targets for abuse.

This agrarian and *mittelständisch* group received some of its support from defectors from the liberals. But it came to dominate the *Reichstag* in many ways because it acquired the alliance of conservatives and Catholics.

The conservatives were, from the start, a Junker party. They recruited most of their voters and candidates from the lands east of the Elbe, in which two-fifths of the land were held by estates over 5000 acres (as against one-fifth in Germany as a whole). The party was highly nationalist and arch-Prussian; it disliked parliaments; increasingly, it sought to use State power to buttress Junkers' economic position. True, there were some conservatives who looked to the English model – or even the model of the Catholic *Zentrumspartei* – and tried to open up the party. They set up their own party, the *Reichspartei*, to champion a more liberal, urban and 'popular' conservatism. Some industrialists supported it, but it never really got off the ground. In view of the attitudes east of the Elbe, there was not much room for such a brand of conservatism – a truth that was again displayed towards the end of the Weimar Republic, when moderate conservative parties were shot down almost as soon as they appeared above the horizon. By 1890, the conservatives were becoming markedly hysterical. The Junkers regarded themselves as the backbone of the country, Frederick the Great's *rocher de bronze*. But the decline of the lesser gentry in the 'Great Depression' was unmistakable. Junkers had fewer children as they strove to keep up appearances – in 1878, 3.85 per family; in 1888, 3.17; in 1910, 2.85. Lutheran nunneries were filled with Junker daughters whom the family could not afford to maintain or endow. For such groups, Thomas Mann's *Buddenbrooks* (1901) could serve as a parable, for it charted the decline of a merchant-patrician family – beginning with a four-square patriarch, proceeding through a run-down of financial and moral standards, and ending with Hanno, in the fourth generation, who is weak-willed to the point of spending his time passively enthusing over *Parsifal*.

Some Junkers became foolishly indebted; generally, the smaller the Junker estate, the greater the proportion of its value that would be mortgaged; and by the early 1890s, there were widespread demands for State assistance, in the form of a guaranteed State grain price, payable on a grain exchange from which private (mainly Jewish) dealers would be excluded except on the sellers' terms. When the private dealers boycotted this exchange, and established an independent one abroad, some of them were arrested. After 1896, even great estates came under pressure because costs rose. They began to follow the smaller estates into decline, as also happened elsewhere in Europe. The burden of debt became so great after 1900 that Junker spokesmen were desperate to find a new entail law – a way by which an estate could be preserved for ever in a single family, but without losing its capacity to act as collateral for a loan. The complications of this scheme preoccupied the Prussian parliament even in the last months of the empire. Even in April 1917, when Germany's leaders were desperately trying to parade their country as a parliamentary democracy, the conservatives in the *Landtag* took up most of its time in debate on the entail question. To frustrate the opposition of liberal deputies, they managed to tie the entail bill with a law concerning the daily attendance allowances of *Landtag* members such that opposition to the one would also mean opposition to the other – which, clearly, the liberal members could not afford. That same tactic was used in 1902 when the *Reichstag* debated Bülow's tariff, and the left threatened to obstruct proceedings. Similarly, there was a great scandal around 1900 when conservatives in Prussia, some of them very highly placed officials, obstructed proceedings in order to stop the government from building a canal from the Rhine to the Oder. This – the *Mittelland-Kanal* – would have let cheap grain into east Elbian Prussia. The obstruction was such that the canal was not properly started until after the war (and it was not finished until 1937). In such contexts, the Junkers' claim to superior virtue in matters of tax-payment could only sound hollow. Indeed, one of their leaders, Hammerstein, was convicted of a cheque-fraud in 1897. There was an uncontrollable *révolte nobiliaire*.

The *Kartel* of National Liberals and conservatives acquired a majority in the *Reichstag* because it had the alliance of Catholics. The *Zentrumspartei* – the name of which represented, not a political position, but rather a 'focus' for the Catholics – began as a confessional party in 1871, to defend Catholicism against liberalism. Had the party supported the democratic cause, that cause would have won. But its (rough) fifth of the seats was used in a different sense.

The Catholics' position was often misunderstood. Liberals quite often saw in the *Zentrumspartei* only a negative body – protecting Catholic education, and supporting regional causes. Socialists often assumed, more or less from first principles, that political Catholicism would be on the right. Neither assumption was quite accurate. Particularism was, sometimes, a cause of Bavarian Catholics; but the bulk of the party's voters came from Prussia (Silesia or Westphalia), and they were indifferent to the wrongs of Bavaria. Catholicism as a political cause certainly mattered, but after 1881 the Prussian state's war on Catholics – the *Kulturkampf* – was stopped, and the Pope himself asked Windthorst, the Catholic leader, to compound his quarrel with Bismarck. The *Zentrumspartei* was bitterly anti-socialist, but that was not, as many socialists supposed, an obvious matter. Half of Germany's Catholics (like most British Catholics) voted socialist in 1912; socialists and Catholics collaborated in the municipalities quite often, since both represented the masses, not 'the classes'. In the 1920s, Prussia herself was ruled by a coalition of Red and Black.

The Catholic party gained strength from two main factors, both of which counted for much after 1890. It could play 'machine-politics' to perfection, just as its equivalents did in other countries, especially Belgium and Ireland. But it also became a strongly agrarian party, and could line up the Catholic peasantry and artisans.

Its character changed in the 1880s. Old Catholic notables were pushed aside as the party acquired mass support: the princes and cardinals who had dominated it in the 1870s were replaced by middle-class lawyers such as Trimborn and Spahn, or even lower-middle-class figures such as the schoolteacher Josef Wirth, or Matthias Erzberger. These men faced a difficult political situation, for they had to combine a variety of differing social elements in the one party. Catholicism in politics appealed to the peasantry, the middle classes, the artisans, and the proletariat. It had its own trade-union movement (roughly a tenth of the size of the socialist one), the leader of which, Adam Stegerwald, could talk class-war to the dread of his allies. In practice, the party found it difficult to retain its working-class supporters; in the Ruhr, it also lost the loyalty of migrant Polish workmen, who founded their own party in resentment at the high-handed practices even of German Catholics towards them. More and more, the strength of the Catholic party lay in the small towns – with fewer than 2000 inhabitants – and the countryside. Of the ninety-one seats which the party generally won in elections, seventy-three were straightforwardly agrarian. These constituencies were usually far smaller than urban ones, for the constituency boundaries were not changed after

1871 despite the great growth of the cities – thus, for instance, Schaumburg-Lippe contained 10,707 people in 1912, Berlin NNW 104,460 – and this in itself gave many Catholic deputies every reason not to upset existing arrangements. In Saxony, where there was an intense industrial war, the Catholics even agreed, in 1904, to substitute a five-class franchise for the existing liberal arrangements. The new franchise virtually excluded social democrats; but at the price of excluding, also, many Catholics.

The Catholic party might count as an 'outsider'. But it found common ground with the right in matters agrarian. It too supported tariffs. True, it hesitated. After all, its working-class voters would not wish to have food prices artificially raised; and many Catholics also feared that the proletariat as a whole would be provoked by any 'Junker tariff'. In the early 1890s, the party voted, by and large, in favour of Caprivi's reductions of the tariff. But there was an agrarian revolt, parallel with the emergence of the *Bund der Landwirte*, and the party went into opposition again (which brought about Caprivi's fall in 1894–5). By 1902, it supported Bülow's tariff of five marks per hundred kilograms of grain.

It was true, as liberal economists like Lujo von Brentano pointed out, that the Catholic peasantry would lose from a grain tariff. They raised pigs, and so their costs would be increased. But there was a counterpart. Railway fares were rigged in such a way that foreign meat and vegetables became artificially expensive. There was a complicated system of 'hygienic inspection' at the border; indeed, in 1894 all foreign cattle was banned, on the grounds that it suffered from foot-and-mouth disease – only Swedish cattle was exempted, in effect because the Swedes also had iron-ore which Germany needed. The National Liberals and the conservatives already supported an industrial tariff – the 'alliance of blast-furnace and manor-house'. With the adhesion of pig-farmers, that alliance easily dominated the *Reichstag*.

It was, therefore, quite easy for the government to keep

the Catholics in play, provided it paid a high enough price. At times, it refused to do so. After 1890, the Catholics' great strength lay in their political machines, which clashed, in many parts of the country, with the liberals. Some Prussian cities were largely, though not wholly, Catholic; they were governed on three-class-franchise lines; and since the Protestants were usually better off than the Catholics, town councils tended to be heavily Protestant and liberal. Trier, for instance, which returned Catholics to the *Reichstag*, had no Catholic representative on its council until 1911; in Augsburg, there were in 1911 thirty-five liberals to three socialists and eight Catholics. The Bavarian government was in the hands of stiff Liberals (Lutz until 1875, Crailsheim thereafter). In the 1890s, both there and in Württemberg, a Catholic populist challenge declared itself. There was agitation for universal suffrage, which came, in stages, between 1895 and 1905. The Protestants and their liberal-Catholic allies were terrified of this – partly because it would put up the socialist presence, but particularly because it gave Catholic machine-politicians a wonderful field. They could act as they did elsewhere in Europe – putting up the rates on non-Catholic businesses, and using the money to create municipal services which would be filled with Catholic clients. A town such as Nördlingen, a Protestant island in a Catholic rural sea, responded bitterly to this (and in the early 1920s had become heavily Nazi). In Bavaria, the *Einschwärzung* ('blackening' or Catholicizing) of public affairs caused all other parties, from socialists to conservatives, to join in a *Grossblock* ('Great Block') against the Catholics; but despite electoral pacts, the Catholic majority in Bavaria, as at the same time in Belgium, fell only marginally. By 1912, the socialists were coming to terms with the Catholic machine. Soon, municipal services of all kinds were to be divided on these lines of *Proporz*. Declining artisans, tavern-keepers and farmers thus acquired their own version of the 'Junker miracle' – they could use political power to support a tottering economy.

The inroads of Catholics were such that, in the years

1907–9 the Bülow government presided over an anti-Catholic alliance in the *Reichstag*: there was 'a marriage between carp and rabbit', i.e., electoral pacts between conservatives, anti-Semites, Progressive liberals and National Liberals, which had the odd consequence that, sometimes, an anti-Semite would have to stand down for a Jewish Liberal candidate. This electoral arrangement – the *Bülow-Block* – was ostensibly provoked by the Catholics' denunciation of colonial practices; but it reflected the increasing desperation of liberals at the Catholics' penetration of public life, not least in the Polish provinces of Prussia. The *Block* disintegrated quite quickly. The Reich's deficit – largely because of armaments – grew so large that Bülow had to propose a direct Reich tax on inherited property. This revolted the conservatives, and they joined with Catholics in voting it down. By 1909, Bülow's successor, Bethmann Hollweg, was again having to run the *Reichstag* through a 'Blue-Black Block', which could blackmail him. It took great sleight of hand for him to pass the armaments law of 1913, with a tax on property to pay for it.

German politics were thus blocked. The *Reichstag* left was painted into a corner, and was unable, to the very end of the empire, to put through elementary constitutional reforms which might have changed the country's public character. For it was a part of the *Reichstag*'s tragedy that the social democrats could not extend their control beyond one-third of the electorate – the *Drittelsperre*, or 'barrier of one-third', which they encountered in the election of 1912. They gained most of the working-class vote, but seemed unable to go beyond that. At the same time, the party leaders – Karl Kautsky, Hugo Haase, August Bebel – made it their business to rein in the 'revolutionaries'.

German social democrats could be proud of their achievement. They ran the largest socialist party in Europe. Demonstrations would be attended, on occasion, by as many as 250,000 people – a figure arrived at in 1910 for protests against the three-class franchise. The trade unions contained, by 1914, three million people. In France and Italy, the socialist movement was badly divided, and trade unions were much weaker; in Germany, socialist solidarity was a by-word. Discipline was upheld, in ways that frightened Latin or Slav socialists: at conferences before 1914, the practice even grew up of 'timed applause'. Within its own terms, the party was extremely successful.

The trade-union movement was also quite successful, and second, in Europe, to the British. Strikes were a notorious feature of German public life. Their high-point came in 1905, when 510,000 people struck, for a total of 7,400,000 days. The trade-union leaders seriously considered a 'political general strike' to achieve immediate changes in the constitution. In 1906, 320,000 people struck, for 6,300,000 days; in 1910, 370,000, for 9,000,000; in 1911, 330,000 for 6,900,000; in 1912, 480,000 for 4,800,000; in 1913, 250,000 for 5,700,000. Monster demonstrations were organized, both in 1905 and in 1910, against the three-class franchise in Prussia, and the social democrats' left wing became agitated at a possibility of immediate revolution. By 1893, the social democrats had become the second-largest party in the *Reichstag*, by 1903 they took more votes (though not more seats) than any other, and by 1912 they had become the largest party in seats (just under one-third) as well as in votes.

How were they to use this power? The dominant tone in their assemblies was 'revolutionary': red flags, International, anti-militarism, workers' republic, taxation of the rich, nationalization of agriculture, hygiene, free love, and the irritating little word, *Genosse* ('comrade'). Social democrats would not join in the *Reichstag*'s *Kaiserhoch*; they would not attend court functions. The national party condemned any approach towards 'Millerandism', i.e., any move by social democrats in any part of Germany to support, let alone join, bourgeois governments. The Baden party was condemned in 1908 for supporting the budget, even though it contained provisions for welfare which an enlightened minister of the interior, Bodmann, had proposed. Equally, the party's leaders, and especially the trade unions, spoke against a revolutionary-violent policy. No political use was made of the general-strike weapon, and when the party voted for this (in 1905) the trade-union leaders opposed it, though in ambiguous language (two contradictory resolutions were adopted). The party's leadership – the 'centrists' who stood between left and right – had too much to lose. They had doubts as to the solidarity of the unions; and at bottom they felt that the party was bound, in time, to become the majority, or 'inheritor' party in the *Reichstag*. 'Revolutionary attentism' was their slogan; the immediate priority being to keep the party disciplined and together.

In Prussia or Saxony, which were harshly run class-states, revolutionary language suited the dominant mood of the working class. The industrial bosses, though sometimes patriarchal (in the manner of Krupp, at Essen), greatly resented trade unions. They brought in migrant workers, usually Poles, in Silesia, Saxony and the Ruhr to break strikes; they promoted 'yellow' unions (after 1910, in the mines of the Ruhr, these were more successful than the socialist ones); and the machinery of State, from armies to police forces, was used, often very cruelly, against the social democrats. Food prices were higher than elsewhere because of the Junker conspiracy. On the other hand, in southern Germany, and parts of Thuringia, attitudes were more enlightened. Bavaria, for instance, had universal (male) suffrage after 1905; there was every case, in Munich, for social democrats to take power by alliances with local liberals in the Millerandist manner. Indeed, revolutionary language might, by scaring off the potential middle-class or peasant allies, have a quite counterproductive effect.

After 1896, it became clear at least to some social democrats that Marxism was not working out as planned. Marx had expected capitalism to collapse in its own 'contradictions': the working class would become poorer, and capitalism would undergo crisis after crisis until the moment of collapse occurred. But the fact was that the working classes were becoming better off. In the 'Great Depression', real wages had risen; and although after 1903, and especially after 1910, the share of wages relative to profits declined, there was not much doubt that capitalism was surviving well enough. Eduard Bernstein, who had spent many years in London, gave voice to these doubts in a series of articles in the intellectual periodical, *Berliner Monatshefte* (1896–7), which he later published as *Die Voraussetzungen des Sozialismus*.

He argued for a 'revisionist' approach – i.e., to revise the original Marxist programme of Erfurt (1890). Clearly, he felt, the party should appeal to a wider section of Germany than the industrial proletariat. It should become a *Volkspartei* on the left, assembling the votes of all democrats, whether middle-class or agricultural, and to do so should moderate its strategy and political tactics. For instance, it could make an appeal towards the peasantry, and recognize the small plot (as the French socialists were to do). It might even accommodate patriotic sentiments in the matter of navy and empire, as British socialists seemed to do: after all, an enlightened Germany, democratically ruled, might have something serious to offer to backward parts of the world.

Bernstein was hotly opposed, and at congresses his line was always defeated. The 'centrists' were desperate to keep the party together, and had to avoid a split. They also had to appease the left, which had its own view. Rosa Luxemburg and (less forthrightly) Karl Liebknecht spoke for a revolutionary general strike. True, this might fail; but in the outcome of police repression, the working class would hate the State, and so would become a properly revolutionary force. The trade unions rejected this role, as did the bulk of the party. But that did not make for 'revisionism'. On the contrary, Bernstein's arguments were consistently turned down. Karl Kautsky, the party's *Chefideologe*, wrote a turgid work to show how he was wrong. Rosa Luxemburg and the Austrian, Rudolf Hilferding, showed, more interestingly, that he had been right only in a limited sense. The capitalist crisis, they said, was staved off because of imperialism. The booty which it provided was prolonging the life of capitalism. But imperialism had its own 'contradictions' – not least, it would provoke a great war, in which bourgeois society would collapse.

The 'centrists' did at least keep the party together. But this had its price, in 'immobilism'. Since no one agreed on an agrarian programme, the party had very little to offer the peasantry. Social democratic spokesmen spoke for free trade in food, and the elder Liebknecht even announced, in 1893, that he advocated this because it would ruin the peasantry – who would troop, broken, into the towns to become good social democrats. Until the mid-1920s, the only programme that social democrats could offer the peasantry was extermination, on lines laid down in the *Communist Manifesto* long before; that this programme was advocated in lower-class accents did not make it more palatable. In the same way, the party was sometimes contemptuous towards the migrant Poles, who responded by forming their own unions and political groups. In Bochum, for instance, only one-third of the vote went to the social democrats in 1912, partly because of populist Catholicism, and partly because there were so many Poles there. In the stricken Vogtland, where there was a natural social democratic constituency, the social democrats made no showing. Their vision was a narrowly industrial-progressive one, with little to offer to nationalities, peasants or remote and backward handicraftsmen.

Kautsky made a virtue of this immobilism. He was asked, in 1903, whether the Belgian socialists were right to proceed with a general strike for extension of the franchise. He replied that such a strike would probably succeed; but that the only result would be to increase the presence of political Catholicism in Brussels; socialists, to achieve anything, would have to make an alliance with the liberals; and that would mean abandoning the party programme, the revolutionary cause. Indeed, the Belgian socialists would maybe even find themselves being responsible for continuing capitalism. So, on the whole, it was better for the working classes not to have an equal vote. He added, with a quite characteristic touch, that since Belgium was only a dwarf of a country, it did not matter anyway. Such attitudes repelled the party's right. But since the right threatened to divide the party, it was powerless. The price of unity was immobilism, an obsession with matters of administration. By 1914, there were clearly two sides in the party; at elections, separate slates were presented; at congresses, the right often met on its own, in hotels. The leadership's answer was to impose greater discipline. Undated letters of resignation were demanded from deputies. Party spokesmen had to outline what they would say in the *Reichstag* before being appointed to speak in a debate. Yet, despite the revolutionary phraseology, the party abandoned much of its earlier isolation. In the International, it opposed any idea of a general strike to stop war. In 1912–13, it helped Bethmann Hollweg to pay for a great increase in armaments; in 1914, it voted for war credits, with only a few dissenting voices in the parliamentary party's meeting on the issue. In the July crisis of 1914, Bethmann Hollweg regularly consulted the social democrat leaders, Philipp Scheidemann, David and Südekum. Did they have any illusions as to what he was doing?

By 1912, German politics had reached an impasse. There were occasional hints of collaboration between social democrats, liberals and Catholics. In November 1913, over the Zabern incident, the three groups came together to denounce the government, but the coalition broke up when a vote of effective censure was proposed. The government went on relying, essentially, on the Blue-Black Block, and paid the price in concessions to the conservatives. After Bismarck's innovations of the 1880s, German social legislation thus remained some way behind that of Lloyd George.

Both on the left and the right, anger and desperation prevailed. There was not much prospect of serious reform; equally, the right could do nothing to prevent the social democrats from acquiring greater prominence, and their third of the vote terrified many conservatives. There was a proliferation of leagues, often overtly anti-Semitic, to defend the *Mittelstand*; military leagues also emerged to demand great increases in the country's military strength. General

Keim, leader of the *Wehrverein*, talked a language close to Fascism. Nationalist (and usually *Nationalliberal*) academics and businessmen collected in the ultra-respectable 'Pan-German League' (*alldeutscher Verband*) to promote the cause of empire. It was clear that many people close to the Kaiser and to Bethmann Hollweg thought that the internal problems of Germany could be solved only through imperialism – overseas, perhaps, but also through a conquest of Europe. The tariff problem appeared to be uncontrollable. Germany could not get rid of her tariffs, since there was a *Reichstag* majority in their favour. But they would provoke other countries to put up tariffs – as France, Russia and a substantial part of British Conservative opinion intended to do. That would mean serious damage to Germany's exports. Men such as Walter Rathenau, the extremely intelligent head of AEG, and a man of influence with Bethmann Hollweg, promoted the idea of *Mitteleuropa*. It would be a free-trade zone, of course dominated by German big business. It would incorporate the notion of 'Berlin-Baghdad'; fringe countries, such as the Netherlands, would be drawn into it; the raw materials of the Ukraine would be an important base for it. This free-trade zone, with its captured markets and raw materials, would solve Germany's social and economic problems. In 1915, a book, *Mitteleuropa*, was published in advocacy of this scheme. It became a bestseller several times over, and supplied a blueprint for Germany's war aims.

German foreign policy became increasingly aggressive after 1897, when Tirpitz produced his first plans for a great battle-fleet. Germany went on producing such plans, despite all the evidence that the British would respond to the challenge, and would take up semi-alliances with Germany's continental rivals if need be. In 1911, in the second Morocco crisis, there was a clear threat of war between the two blocs; and the atmosphere in the following years became more and more tense, with considerable arms increases everywhere. The German government did not respond to this with much sense of reality. On the contrary, it proceeded with plans to build ships which, in the event, spent most of the war quietly in harbour. Although the navy took up a third of the defence budget, the government could not resist plans to increase the army as well. In 1912, and again in 1913, military expansion was undertaken – in 1913, almost 1,500,000,000 marks being spent on it, paid for by a tax on property (*Wehrbeitrag*). Not many historians nowadays dissent from the proposition that the German government, egged on by its generals, deliberately provoked the war of 1914.

Was there a connection between the internal circumstances of the country and its aggressive policies abroad? In the old days, German historians usually argued for 'the primacy of foreign affairs', meaning that foreign policy should dictate the course of internal events. In the early 1930s, a penetrating historian, Eckart Kehr, argued the other way about – that foreign policy was designed for internal consumption, so that *Primat der Innenpolitik* had to count for more. He showed, as have other historians since, that one factor counting in Tirpitz's creation of a navy was that it would divide the *Reichstag*, and keep it powerless. In the same way, historians have argued that German foreign policy before (and during) the First World War was designed to preserve the status quo in Germany. When Bethmann Hollweg's foreign secretary, Kiderlen-Wächter, launched the second Morocco crisis by sending a gunboat, the *Panther*, to Agadir, he was doing so for the sake of the forthcoming elections: with a war scare, the government parties would do well.

There is sufficient evidence for at least partial support of these arguments. In the two years before the July crisis, Germany's leaders appear to have been gripped by a mood of desperation. In December 1912, for instance, a Crown Council quite seriously suggested that there should be war within a year and a half, that the press should be prepared, that military increases should be undertaken, and that the *Reichsbank* should build up a larger War Chest. All of these things were undertaken. The *Reichstag* could not control the government; at the same time, the Kaiser, surrounded, often enough, by hysterical generals and noblemen, lost any sense of cool *raison d'état*, of a kind that had distinguished some of his ancestors. It was the Bismarckian tradition to jump at opportune accidents, doctor documents, and send troops in. War squared the circles of German politics. Bismarck had had to conquer Germany in order to rule Prussia. Would Bethmann Hollweg have to conquer Europe in order to rule Germany?

3. Russia

Many of Germany's problems, and the impasse of politics there, came from her need to adjust inflexible structures to rapid economic change. In Russia, the case was much worse. Until 1880 she had been very backward by western European standards – the vast bulk of her people living from primitive agriculture. In the 1880s Russia began to catch up – slowly enough, but quite quickly in the 1890s and especially after 1908. By 1914, the delineations of the future Russian 'super-power' were clear to all who knew her. Sir Arthur Nicolson, in the British foreign office, blessed the fact that the two countries were now allies. The German chancellor, Bethmann Hollweg, remarked on 7 July 1914 that 'the future lies with Russia, she grows and grows, and lies on us like a nightmare'. He told his son not to plant long-growing trees in the family estate in north-eastern Germany because when they came to maturity, only the Russians, in occupation, would profit. Tsarist ministers, who in 1905 had thought that the world was coming to an end, recovered confidence. P.A. Stolypin, the tsar's strong man, told a foreign journalist in 1909, 'Give the State twenty years of internal and external peace and you will not recognize Russia.'

By then, Russia had become the fourth industrial Power in the world, having overtaken France in indices of heavy industry – coal, iron, steel. Her population grew from just over sixty millions in the middle of the nineteenth century to a hundred millions in 1900 and almost 140,000,000 by

1914: and that was counting only the European part, i.e., west of the Urals. Towns, which contained only ten million people in 1880, contained thirty million by 1914.

The trouble was that this very rapid change was imposed on a country that was much less well-adapted to it than Germany, let alone the countries of the West. The Russian system of government was that of an early-eighteenth-century absolutist state and both its forms and much of its personnel had been taken from the Germans. Its military ranks were straightforward copies of German ones – *Yefreytor* (*Gefreiter*) for 'corporal', *Feldfebel* for 'sergeant', *Vashe Vysokoblagorodiye* (*Euer Hochwohlgeboren*) or 'Your Highly Well-Born-ness' as a means of addressing a lieutenant-colonel; the tsarist army (and the Soviet one) had a highly stylized drill, including the goose-step, which was imported from Holstein. True, in the manner of eighteenth-century states, French was frequently used in the State, and continued to be spoken as matter of course by upper classes in the nineteenth century. But it was the German influence that was stronger. Men from Baltic-German or Swedish families – whose descendants went on taking a preponderant role in the higher ranks of the army – were used to conquer and exploit huge lands to the south of Moscow, the Ukraine and the steppe country of the southern Volga and the Don. Eighteenth-century Russia was a rich country, and Catherine the Great's St Petersburg was easily the most imposing of the eighteenth-century cities, though maybe, as was said, 'a combination of Wedgwood and cardboard'.

The difficulty was that this country had been made great by the State machine. The tsars' lands, vast, were under-populated – in the early seventeenth century there had been fewer Russians than Frenchmen – and there were very few towns. Peasants were enserfed to stop them moving away; and the nobility counted partly as farmers, in that they lived from the serfs' labour, and partly as bureaucrats, in that they administered most aspects of the serfs' lives, while collecting taxes as well. In eighteenth-century Europe serfdom had broken down – the better-off serfs could buy their freedom, and there were growing towns for others to escape to. In Russia, neither process happened on any scale. Serfdom did break down, in the middle of the nineteenth century, because the nobles, in changed circumstances, could not make much profit out of it, worked the administrative side wastefully, and provoked serf revolts. The difficulty was that whereas in western and central Europe the emancipation of the serfs came as the end of a process, in Russia it came as the beginning of one.

The mystique of the State, as built up partly by the Byzantine tradition of Orthodoxy, and partly by the Germanic Enlightenment, haunted the mind of any tsar or his ministers in this period. There was distrust of individual effort almost from top to bottom of Russian society, expressed in such acts as the prohibition, on the Russian stock exchange, of companies' floating shares in units of under 5000 roubles – the quite considerable sum of £500 – because it was automatically assumed that smaller shares than that would merely attract profiteers and speculators. The system of government was frequently arthritic because transactions had to go through several bodies, in several copies, because otherwise there might be a danger of corruption. Tsars virtually without thinking merely assumed that representative bodies would be divisive and corrupting – opening the great Russian empire, which had been built up by absolutism, to join in the fate of eighteenth-century Poland. Suggestions of a parliament were waved aside with little ceremony by successive tsars, until in 1905 Nicholas II was driven to allow one, which he then treated without respect. In a vast land like Russia, where Russians themselves made up only forty-five per cent of the people, there were dozens of other peoples with different traditions and languages. They could not be represented in a central parliament without its becoming a Babel; it followed that there would have to be federalism, for each people to look after its own affairs. That, to the tsarist State, was quite unthinkable. Ukrainian, spoken by twenty-five million people, was dismissed as 'jargon'; the Poles were a danger to

Russia. The greatness of Russia depended on keeping these peoples together: a parliament, dismissed by the tsar's adviser, K.P. Pobedonostsev, in the 1880s as 'the great lie in our times', would merely cause the State to fall apart. Law continued to be handed down from above, by a clumsy bureaucratic machine, and, in the early 1880s, public order was reinforced by a dismantling of Alexander II's provisions as regards education and limited policing. Had these liberal arrangements not simply led to his own assassination, in 1881, by an anarchist?

In the 1880s and 1890s, in the reigns of Alexander III and the first few years of Nicholas II, a police-state system prevailed. Governors-general, handing down martial law (and hence also death-sentences – not many – though they had been abolished in civil law), and police chiefs, whose repression needed authorization from the minister of the interior, not the courts, put down political opponents. The security department (*okhrannoye otdeleniye*, shortened to *okhranka*) though quite small and poor, made a name for itself by its relative uniqueness in Europe, where states had not maintained such forces since the 1850s.

There were efforts to shore up a crumbling social order. The ministry of education believed that education, beyond people's social status, merely created agitators – 'mirages of temples of science for peasants', as a minister of finance put it. The generous State scholarships of Alexander II's day were cut back; the number of non-nobles in high schools was reduced from fifty-four to forty-six per cent in the 1880s, and a grindingly classical curriculum was introduced. To maintain the nobles, a special Land Bank was created for them in 1885, where they could obtain credit at preferential rates. Efforts were also made to prevent the Jews from developing: they were held to be harmful to the State, were sometimes expelled from the main cities, and were the object of an increasing number of pogroms (the Russian word for 'devastation') in this era – the worst of them in the Bessarabian capital, Kishinyov, in 1903, which occurred with police support. In education, they faced a *numerus clausus*, i.e., a restriction – severe – on the possible number of Jews admitted. Jews could take examinations for the military schools (which had high prestige) only outside the system; only one Jew at a time (and one Pole) was admitted to the artillery school. The public educational system was made Russian, even in Poland, where village lads would be taken away to be trained in a Russian-language, secluded college for some years before being sent to teach Poles in Russian (the system did not work at all). By 1905, a third of Polish youth was being educated in the 'flying schools' organized by a voluntary Polish group, the ZET (*Związek Młodzieży Polskiej*). In Alexander II's time the Finns had been promoted; the Tsaritsa was very popular, and would, on her yachting expeditions in the Baltic, be received at Finnish coastal villages with receptions of 'champagne and sour clotted cream'. By the 1890s a great row was brewing between the Russian régime and Finnish nationalism. Efforts were also made to 'freeze' the peasant world. In 1893, peasants were not allowed permanently to leave their communes at all, and a system almost tantamount to State serfdom prevailed. The bureaucracy, from customs officials to the most exalted members of the Council of State, which deliberated as to laws, behaved with an arrogance that revolted everyone who had dealings with it.

This system, though on paper tyrannical, was self-contradictory – indeed, its mortal faults had really been spelt out to anyone of intelligence (which did not include either Alexander III, who was distinguished only by his bulk, meanness and uxoriousness or Nicholas II, though he had a certain cunning) in the 1850s. The State was too poor to afford much. The 'Security Police' in Moscow consisted of six officials with a budget of £5000 for the whole province, and even in 1900 it had not expanded by very much: indeed, by then, there were almost no political prisoners. The huge province of Penza had three police officers and twenty-one policemen, though a few more were added in the 1880s.

There was no way of preventing lesser nationalities from developing their own languages, as happened spectacularly in Latvia. There was also no way of preventing Jews from bribing ill-paid officials into letting them escape from the Pale of Settlement and do dealings in the capitals. The censors, overwhelmed by the '93,565,261' works they had read, let through Marx's *Capital* without noticing what it was about, though they took time off to read Tolstoy's *Kreutzer Sonata* and ban that. In military matters, the régime might try to extend military discipline to the whole country, but the results were quite funny. If the army conscripted everyone liable, it would have had to pay out endless sums merely for supply, which accounted for three-quarters of the military budget as it was. They therefore exempted four-fifths of the available manpower on various grounds: physical condition, the luck of the draw, 'family status', i.e., whether a man was a family breadwinner or not. In 1914, two million peasants got married in August: to the bewilderment of the authorities. By the end of 1915, the Russian army was actually smaller than the French or German armies, though the population of these countries was far smaller. The Nobles' Land Bank had far too little capital to shore up noble agriculture, and noble lands – for reasons to be discussed below – shrank, from 1861 to 1905, from over half of the agricultural surface to less than one third of it.

The system appeared to work roughly for two decades only because these were relatively quiet decades as far as popular protest was concerned. The peasants' land-war in the later 1870s had occurred as a delayed response to the emancipation of the serfs. In 1861, serfs had been given, as a rough rule, two-thirds of the lands they had previously used, and rented the remainder from their former landlord. They were also expected to pay a sum of money to the State, 'redemption dues' (*vykupniye platezhi*), to pay it back for giving compensation to the former landlord for the loss of his serfs' rent.

This whole business was an absurdity. In the first place, the former landlords had usually mortgaged their serfs to the State – a total of 700,000,000 roubles as against the 1,000,000,000 of 'redemption dues' – so the landlords received less than a third of the 'redemption dues', which really went to the State. The sum itself was quite small, certainly not enough, over forty years, to make the irritation worth it. Other countries, when serfs had been freed, had been much harsher. In Prussia, big peasants, *spannfähige Bauern*, had had to give up two-thirds of the land; had exploited new land; had taken over the village commons, and thereby deprived lesser peasants of grazing land without which they could not survive; had taken over the lands falling vacant; had prospered; and had then bought out their former lords. In Russia, such big peasants were far less evident. Tsarist Russia, which did not have to deal with a peasantry already 'differentiated' in the Prussian (or English) way, dared not deal too harshly with the peasantry, and 'redemption dues', which, on statistical average over forty years did not work out at more than 2½p per head per annum, were a gesture.

It was a gesture which was avenged several times over. The peasants were not held individually responsible for paying their dues. A lump sum would be assessed for each peasant community – the *obshchina*, which acquired administrative recognition – and the better-off peasants would have to pay more than their fair share. Besides, the dues, earlier payable by labour, now had to be paid in cash, of which there was little. Peasants fought back, and there were endless battles in the later 1870s as they did so. In Novgorod, the dues were 80 per cent of cash income, and Smolensk was 222 per cent in arrears. There were also battles over the demarcation of landlord and peasant land, and it came to full-scale riots as these issues were adjudicated in the later 1870s. In the 1880s, and in the 1890s, the land questions had usually (but far from always) been sorted out, communes were acquiring more land, and the State connived at the non-payment of 'redemption dues' because it had, in tariffs, an alternative source of revenue and because it dared not tackle the peasantry. The problems which had beset the last years of Alexander II therefore died away, and there were two decades of a wholly misleading calm, during which the temper of the country changed to 'stormy', in ways which, given the absence of representative institutions, cannot be quantified.

It was characteristic that the chief running battle in the last two decades of the nineteenth century was between the government and the institutions created in the 1860s, the county councils (*zemstva*) which, in the properly Russian (as distinct from Polish or Baltic-German) provinces were elected on a restricted franchise to carry out administrative jobs – fire insurance, road-building, lunatic asylums etc. Alexander II had seen in these councils, which were, to start with, dominated by the local gentry and only in the 1890s by other elements, a force for progress. They were allowed to collect a *zemstvo* rate. In some areas, they worked well with the central government. In others there were problems in endless matters.

The *zemstva* sometimes wished to levy a rate on local business which the ministry of finance regarded as injurious to enterprise; in others the rate was applied even to government concerns like the railways. The Tver *zemstvo* took the lead in demanding decentralization and liberalization. It was rebuffed and at the end of the century the *zemstvo* was locked in an endless and boring quarrel with the governor over matters such as the levy charged for compulsory fire insurance. The Perm *zemstvo* was penalized for commissioning a portrait of the long-service director of its lunatic asylum, a Dr Litvinov, to hang in the offices of the asylum. The Suzdal *zemstvo* suffered because it had devoted fifty roubles of reserve fund to its library. The police, generally, regarded the educated and decent – though muddled – *zemstvo* people as an enemy, to be harassed. There were even cases where the local lunatic asylums were searched for political suspects.

The *zemstvo* spokesmen made out that they were innocent martyrs, of a stupid and venal police and a bureaucracy that resented *zemstvo* enlightenment because it showed them up. But there was more to it. *Zemstva* were quite expensive, and did abuse their power to charge a rate. In Perm the rate even amounted to a third of 'the profit of the land'; landowners in Tver complained to the governor, Prince Golitsyn, that their rates rose from sixteen roubles in 1883 to eighty-three in 1898. Golitsyn accordingly had a long battle with the *zemstvo* Board (*uprava*) indicating that the hospital diet was too lavish, that roads were badly maintained, that suggestion-books were disregarded. In the event, the *uprava* was suspended over these matters. The *zemstva* took their role as liberals very seriously, and made a great fuss. Inquirers with some understanding of English local government in the Middle Ages – such as the Russians Paul Vinogradoff and M.M. Postan who brought much to the study of that subject – felt that the powers of the *zemstva* were such that a modicum of political sense would have given Russia a proper parliament, as the only way to shut them up. These Russians, though distinguished as regards English medieval history, were wrong as regards Russia. The problem was that the supporters of the *zemstva* did not have very much money. Tver, leader in the *zemstvo* movement, was also an area where gentry landholding had collapsed dramatically from 2,092,000 *desyatiny* (roughly, hectares or $2\frac{1}{2}$ acres) in 1861 to 704,000 in 1896. Tver liberalism was the complaint of the declining gentry, in Russian form.

So long as the ancient Russian opera line, *Narod bezmolst-vuyet* – the people are quiet – held good, these matters were almost shadow-boxing. The affairs of the empire were vastly complex, far too much for the simple brain of a Nicholas II to grasp. He was comfortable, on the whole, only with advisers who reassured him; his wife, a hysterical German, was no help; and indeed anyone who understood Russia would almost by definition have been a man ruled out from action, such as the extraordinary agronomist A.V. Chayanov whose understanding of the peasant question was incomparable, and who warned all régimes that it was so complex that nothing could be done about it. It was easy for tsars to relapse into the comforts of Orthodox spirituality, to shrink from the creative effort either of real repression or real modernization, and to indulge their tastes for English recreations, ministry-shuffling, and historical ceremony – at which they sometimes betrayed their nervousness. Nicholas II, like Louis XVI and Charles I before him, was a Hegelian mediocrity.

Still, he needed money. That, in the long run, was to destroy him, for it created new economic forms, extremely rapidly, which few of the tsar's ministries really grasped. From 1860, as part of the liberal State, the empire had built railways, and had 21,228 kilometres by 1881. The reactionary government continued this, and had 31,219 kilometres by 1892. The 1890s, more than the 1900s, also saw expansion, and by 1914 the empire had 70,000 kilometres of railway, including the Trans-Siberian. These railways were sometimes operated in a lavish way, being the pride of the State, and they quite easily paid for themselves, since at the other end of the line there were mineral deposits in profusion, especially in the Ukraine and the Donbass.

Russian industrialization was the usual mixture of continuity and imitation; the chief difficulty with it was that it was crammed into the 1890s and 1900s. People were taken to towns and factories for which they were not prepared, and which were not prepared for them. Ports like Odessa and Riga quintupled in size in two decades. The great, filthy oil town of Baku on the Caspian shot up overnight from a fishing village to the centre of Russian oil in the later 1890s; the same happened, more or less, with the Ukrainian coal and metal towns, Mariupol or Yekaterinoslav. In St Petersburg, to be discussed in detail below, conditions were probably worst of all, for they were compounded by a city administration of legendary apathy and incompetence.

Russian industrialization did have a base to build upon. There had been metal-working on a considerable enough scale for several centuries. In Moscow, there was a whole network of artisans, and 'the Moscow merchants' had a long history. When they turned to making textiles by modern methods in the 1880s, the Polyakovs, Ryabushinskys, Morozovs, Shchukins, Stakheyevs knew what they were about, and had a solid work-force to back them up. There were also many Russian technologists, for certain areas, such as Yaroslavl – north-east of Moscow – or the Mari people (on the Volga and near Kazan) had stood out for several decades, even centuries, for their literacy and engineering abilities. They had been among Russia's 'non-conformists'.

The circumstances of the 'Great Depression' provided the impulse for industrialization in Russia, as everywhere else: that is, the growth of towns provided a market, centrally organized manufacturing undercut many of the old local producers. Nails, knives, sacks, cotton were affected – the *kustar* industries performed in villages, at home. In 1866 in the Moscow region there were 66,000 cotton-weavers, but only 20,000 in the 1890s. Then again, the fall of agricultural prices and the run-down of gentry estates especially in the early 1890s (when between five and ten per cent of them came under the foreclosers' hammer every year) prompted the ministry of finance to think of something else. *Étatiste* bureaucrats like Sergey Witte, with whose name the industrialization of the 1890s is associated, had no difficulty in demonstrating that the State must take a more active part in organizing economic growth, and must establish priorities. His Italian counterparts were saying things not markedly different, for much the same reasons – that a largely agrarian state, faced with agrarian depression, should encourage the development of industry more directly than it had done in the past.

Railway building, planned by the State, followed; it generated a demand for iron and steel, as the construction trades had already done; a higher tariff supplied revenue. It added twenty-eight per cent to the price of manufactures in 1902, and forty per cent on other goods. Witte stabilized the rouble on the gold standard (1897) and invited foreign investment. Considerable sums, amounting, by 1914, to 8,000,000,000 roubles, came from abroad – part of the savings made in France and Great Britain from the 'Great Depression'. The money, at first placed in government bonds, was, after 1908, placed generally in industry directly. Foreigners also bought shares in mining and raw materials (such as oil), and French capital went into the banks which Witte promoted. There was nothing uniquely Russian in any of this. Italy, to take only one other case, underwent much the same experience. Both countries had the benefits and disadvantages of involvement with the 'multinationals' which were emerging long before 1914. Skills arrived from abroad in the form of Germans, who, on the whole, did not like Russia, and Englishmen who, on the whole, did. But they were ultimately responsible to foreign shareholders. In 1900 the Anglo-Russian Oil Company, *ARMO*, simply closed down its wells at Nikopol so as to cut worldwide production and thereby bring prices up again. Ten thousand Russians were thrown out of employment, and the town was ruined. It added a dimension to the resulting hatreds that the owners were foreign, though Russian owners would not have behaved differently.

In the early part of the 1890s, Russian industry continued the progress started in the 1880s on the basis of railway building, mining and construction. Witte built 25,300 kilometres of railway from 1894 to 1903, taking up thirty-seven per cent of pig-iron output. In the later 1890s, Russia had a boom, as every other country did. Harvests were good, prices were rising (for once) and transport to markets was becoming easier. But there was a fundamental instability in Russian industry at this time, which affected her in much the same way and for much the same reasons as Germany in the middle-1870s or Italy in the later 1880s. Banks, new to the business, were imprudent; there was a chaos of competition from inadequately experienced firms in heavy industry; there was a depression in Germany. By the end of 1899, interest-rates were very high; shares fell; two large banking and industrial groups went bankrupt; banks cut their loans to build up their reserves; firms were threatened with bankruptcy; they lowered their stocks, and prices fell: pig-iron, which had been selling for 80 kopecks a pood (16 kg) in June 1900, fell to 45 in December, coal from 9 to 6, oil from 17 to 4, and production fell from 177,000,000 poods of pig-iron, the basic element, in 1899 to 149,000,000 in 1903. In 1899 325 firms had been founded, with a capital of 363,000,000 roubles; in 1902, only 68 were founded, with capital of 73,000,000. Two-thirds of the companies quoted on the stock exchange went bankrupt or merged with others, and Witte lost his position in the ministry of finance.

At the centre of this there were two chief problems. The first, and more obvious, was the get-rich-quick mentality of the new concerns, which had been established for speculative purposes, and frequently through grants of State contracts. Beyond that was the instability of the market. Russia was still a very largely agrarian country, with three-quarters of her people living permanently on the land and many others still vacillating between town and country. The heavy industrialists combined (as, it must be said, they also did at this time in Germany and the United States). They formed cartels to share out the market; then they established a central office for these cartels to arrange who should produce which quantities on a quota system; then they branched out, through their banking supporters, to acquire firms that supplied them. Russia acquired some large cartels in this era – forty-seven in all, and later on twice as many (Germany in 1914 had over 200): *Prodamet* was formed to sell metal in common and thus keep up prices; *Tsentrosakhar* for sugar, *Med* for copper, *Krovlya* for roof-iron (in the Urals), *Prodvagon* for sales of railway material, *Produgol* to sell coal (which contained the producers of ninety per cent of Donbass coal). These cartels were not very efficient. The dividends they paid were considerably less than those paid by the Moscow textile manufacturers. They were not greatly different from anything being produced in the West, especially in Germany. But since many of their directors were foreigners they appeared to be parasitical. Theakston, D'Arcy, von Dittmar, Butler (though he changed his name to 'Butlerov') were an offence to nationalists as well as to socialists.

It was indeed a feature of Russian business life that many entrepreneurs were foreigners, or of foreign extraction. Sociologists like Max Weber at the turn of the century pondered this phenomenon, as sociologists pondered the phenomenon, so widespread, of the Scottish engineer in

Great Britain. When the Russians gave out contracts for shell in the First World War, well over half of the factories concerned were owned by men with foreign names, often German – Knoop, who ran the largest textile factory in the world at the Krenholm Mill, in Narva; Wogau, who dominated copper; the Elworthy Tractor Company at Yekaterinoslav; *Russki Renault* in St Petersburg; the König sugar refinery; 'Ayvaz', a Finnish firm producing optical glass; *Glaces du Midi de la Russie*, a Belgian-dominated cartel giving a quarter of Russia's glass; in Moscow the Bromley Brothers, Shanks (tailors), Goujon, 'Dutfua' (which is a transliteration of the German pronunciation of an exile-Huguenot name, Du Toit), Hübner, Girault. A great many of the engineers were, in fact, Poles. In emigration, after 1917, the Russians were not businessmen, on the whole, as Germans would have been, but lawyers, landladies or bankers. Why do some civilizations produce entrepreneurs, and others not? In Russia it is quite easy to give an institutional answer. The State, following a long tradition, made life difficult for entrepreneurs, and continued to discriminate against individual enterprise for decades after 1861, whether in business or in the stock exchange. Finance, when no one trusted anyone else, was very difficult; transactions which elsewhere might have been settled by a telephone call in Russia had to go through endless legal processes, in several copies. Labour was sometimes recalcitrant; markets insecure. But in the end these are not adequate answers. Jews (though surprisingly fewer in Russian than elsewhere), foreigners and men from Yaroslavl – who were the single largest provincial migrant community in St Petersburg in 1861, and the second largest, after Tver, in 1900 – did well. Others did not. In explanation, so far, we can offer only banalities. Max Weber charted a very hostile coast.

Certainly, there was a great gap between the world of the sleek foreign entrepreneur and his Russian banking outriders, and that of the Russian artisan and small-scale manufacturer. Industrial concerns, whether from abroad or originating in Moscow, tended to concentrate their skilled labour, their capital, their ultra-modern machinery so as to make the best use of them. The result was a set of gigantic factories. In St Petersburg, placed within the city boundaries there were 956 factories, most of them in the Spasskaya district or the northern shores of the Vyborg side, and 48 outside. Some of these factories were very large. The Putilov, with 30,000 workers, was largest, but the Nevsky, Obukhovsky, Treugolnik works were also huge places. It was here that a great part of Russian metal-working and engineering was carried on. In other parts of Russia, the same 'gigantism' went on, though quite often it was the case that factory-owners set up their works some way beyond the towns, near a coalmine or a centre of rural enterprise. In Kostroma province in 1911, 83 per cent of the 61,000 workers in industry lived outside towns.

In his account of the Russian revolution, Trotsky later on made a great play of these huge factories. A later authority, Olga Crisp, has questioned the whole theory. Orthodox Marxists, Lenin included, suggested that there were in Russia about three million factory workers in 1914. But these figures were based on tsarist census material which ignored factories containing fewer than twenty or at the least sixteen workers. The Factory Inspectorate, who themselves, in the whole of the central industrial region, amounted to about two dozen, said in 1900 that there were 18,000 factories, employing on average 93.6 workmen. The Moscow inspectorate confessed that it had not even seen 76 per cent of the factories from 1884 to 1900, and in the whole of European Russia, in 1899, there were only 251 inspectors. At the same time the business directorate of *Vsya Rossiya* said there were 142,000 firms, with an average of twelve workers. In any case, it was absurd to confine the term 'working class' to people in factories of considerable size, and Rashin, a modern Soviet authority, puts the figure at 15,000,000, after inclusion of miners, building labourers, railwaymen, Volga boatmen (of whom there were 500,000) etc. It is not easy to draw conclusions from all of this, though tentatively it seems clear that there were in Russia many large and many very small concerns, with not much between them. Yet in western Europe it was the middle-sized concern that made for economic growth and political stability. But to say that there were a great many small concerns is only to say that there were a great many peasants, living in relative isolation.

The first wave of industrialization ended in a confusion that foreshadowed 1917. Depression at the turn of the century threw many people out of work, and drove people at all levels of Russia to extremes of discontent – *zemstva*, nascent trade unions, educated youth, the nationalities. In 1902–3 the discontent was shown in a great wave of strikes in southern Russia, starting from the oil-town of Baku where Azeris, Georgians, Ossetes and Chechens joined with the Russian workers for a two weeks' fight – the kind of transnational industrial militancy that lacked virtually all counterpart in western Europe. In summer 1903 the great textile factories at Ivanovo-Voznesensk erupted in a similar manner, and the women workers collaborated with the men in a way that, again, did not have many counterparts in the West, where the women worked for less than the men, who did not see why they should not do so. This strike threw up a committee that ran the town for a week until troops arrived. In the end, these strikes followed a pattern well known in other countries: a depression, which embittered, followed by a gradual lifting of troubles, which gave the militant workmen a card to play. The strikes were all followed by wage-rises. Agriculture at this time had suffered from the urban depression. In the summer of 1902, and into 1903, there were peasant riots as well, not unlike those of neighbouring Romania four years later, against usurious leaseholders and estate-owners who exported grain while their villagers went hungry. The provinces of Poltava and Tambov were, for the greater part, devastated; manor houses burned down, animals mutilated. In 1901 there were 155 interventions by troops (as against 34 in 1898) and in 1903, 322, involving 295 squadrons of cavalry and 300 battalions of infantry, some with artillery. 1902 was the highpoint of the whole thing. Troops were used to crush the peasantry on 365 occasions. In 1903, for internal order, a force far greater than the army of 1812 was mustered. The Karlovka estate of the Grand Duke of Mecklenburg-Strelitz (who had taken tsarist service) and the Rakityanskoye estate of the Princes Yusupov went up in flames. In sixty-eight of seventy-five districts of the central Black Earth there were 'troubles' – fifty-four estates wrecked. The worst area was Saratov.

There was nothing particularly new in these things. In western Europe there was an ingrained sense of property, written into law, the further west you went. In Russia, everything combined to give a much wider sense of what land was about: to each his needs. A landowner who stocked even a modest quantity of grain or who left fields unworked for 'capitalist' reasons was not understood. Was it so very different in Ireland, also a land outside Roman law? The real difficulty is why the landowners did not develop as chief figures in an agrarian 'front' in Russia, as their counterparts, the Czartoryskis and Sapiehas in Poland, or, especially, the Eszterházys or Majláths did in Hungary. There is no easy answer to that; possibly we should look to priest, not landowner, for the key.

At all events, the peasant troubles coincided with a great growth in 'revolutionary consciousness'. This again is not peculiarly Russian. All through Europe, the depression at the turn of the century threw up political groups, or simply tighter political organization of existing groups – a British Labour Party, *Sinn Féin*, the French *Confédération Générale du Travail*, central reorganization of the German *Nationalliberale Partei*, and so on. In Russia, and especially by the exiles in Switzerland and southern Germany, 'parties' were organized. *Osvobozhdeniye* ('Liberation') was established in 1902 at Stuttgart by the political economist (and ex-Marxist) P.B.Struve. The social democrats, whose first small conference in 1897 had been arrested, established themselves as the *Rossiyskaya sotsial-demokraticheskaya rabochaya partiya* and had a famous conference in 1903 when they divided between

Lenin's followers, the majority (hence 'Bolsheviks'), and his opponents, the minority (hence 'Mensheviks'). The nationalities of Russia became more organized; there was a famous quarrel at this time between the Finns and the Russian empire; the Ukraine, Georgia, Armenia produced movements, mainly based on students, which attacked the Empire.

There was a counterpart in Russia to this: an all-Russian movement of 'socialist revolutionaries'. They emerged from rather similar gatherings in various parts of the land. In Tambov, on the middle Volga, a journalist, Viktor Chernov, and a teacher in the local school of adult education, A.N.Sletova, assembled a dozen people like figures from Dostoyevsky's *Besy* ('The Possessed'). In 1898 they held a 'peasant congress' and had eight peasants, a hatter, 'a representative of the intelligentsia' and some of the heretical milk-drinking *molokane* sect who would not attend their village assembly (*skhod*) because it was so drunken. In the grim Don town of Voronezh, one Gots had organized a similar group; one Gershuni started a 'northern group'. The socialist revolutionaries sometimes believed in terrorism and sometimes did not.

Terrorists of one kind or another did kill Vyacheslav von Plehve, the minister of the interior, his colleague Bogolepov at education, Grand Duke Sergey, the governor-general of Moscow, and a number of provincial governors in this era; there was a procession of pale, thin and often Jewish students to the gallows and Siberia, after spectacular trials. They, like the peasant rebels of 1902, could argue that the tsarist government would never have produced its steps towards moderation, representational bodies, and abolition of redemption-dues had it not been for the terror. For it *was* true that 1903 saw less illiberal ministers, and discussion of a consultative assembly ('the Bulygin *Duma*'). On the other hand, the other revolutionaries, and many, perhaps most, of the SRs, disliked terror for various reasons: it might be counter-productive, in that it stimulated the police into greater effort (as had certainly happened with *Narodnaya*

Volya two decades earlier); on the other hand, by bringing minor improvements in the government, it might stave off revolution; in any case, it was revoltingly cruel, and no business for decent socialists of any stamp.

These divisions over terror ran through the entire socialist revolutionary party; but such divisions came up more or less at every turn in its affairs. When revolution came in 1917, the party was strikingly ineffective, even though it gained almost two-thirds of the vote (mostly from peasants, who had been mobilized by the rural intelligentsia) in January 1918. The party's left wing broke off and made an alliance with Lenin to which the Bolsheviks owed their victory; the party's right stood ineffectually in coalition with the Whites; and, later, the Bolsheviks simply abolished their own erstwhile allies. This revealed the socialist revolutionaries' fatal weakness: for all of their democratic habits and their generosity of temperament, they had no real efficiency and no concept as to what they would do with real power; in any case, in the end, they represented a vast but isolated and fragmented countryside.

It was not altogether surprising that non-Marxist socialism of this kind did not appeal to more than a small section of the intelligentsia or, in the end, the working class. And yet Russian socialism depended, in large measure, on the intelligentsia's adaptation of Marx to Russian circumstances. It was Lenin's achievement to take from the socialist revolutionaries (and from the anarchists) an element of 'legitimate' violence which was allied to a 'scientific' Marxist understanding of Russian circumstances.

The intellectuals were more predominant in Russian socialism than anywhere else because they did not have to face such a great obstacle from trade unions as they did elsewhere. The party's money came, not from trade-union subscriptions, but from rich sympathizers and sometimes the proceeds of bank-robberies and sales of literature.

The relative absence of trade unions is easy enough to understand. Up to 1906, they were illegal, and after then they faced discrimination. The government feared that, even if unions were allowed to organize for 'friendly' purposes, they would simply divert the money to revolutionary purposes instead. By 1912, social reforms had been put through the *Duma*, to allow sickness benefits paid partly by an employer's contribution. Trade unions, or factory committees, would have some role in operating the scheme. But the government insisted that the whole thing should be under close police control (not surprisingly, when the workers came to vote for delegates to manage the funds, five-eighths were Bolshevik).

But, more generally, wages were too low (the average in 1906, around 250 roubles, was half of the German figure, itself a third below the British one). Employment was also irregular, and men would shift quite often to different provinces or to the land. In 1905 a calculation was made that only 52.7 per cent of the inhabitants of European Russia lived in the district where they were born; 16.9 per cent did live in the same province, but 30.3 per cent in another one altogether. In St Petersburg, almost two-thirds of the inhabitants in 1900 were 'foreign' to the province, and in other cities the proportion was not much less (in Odessa, 44.2 per cent). The vast amount of to-ing and fro-ing as workmen from the land returned in the summer was shown in the railway traffic of St Petersburg. In January, about 110,000 travellers would be coming and going; in August, 320,000.

There was, in fact, a huge, inchoate working mass, dependent on irregular employment, on low wages, and quite often drifting from town to country. Soviet authorities, having sensibly included the building labourers and similar elements not involved in these mesmerizing great factories, give figures of between 15,000,000 and 18,000,000 for the 'working class'; and of course Lenin addressed himself to people far beyond the great factories, including elements that, in Germany, were dismissed as *Lumpen*.

St Petersburg itself created them. Its industries expanded to include a thousand factories, most of them inside the city boundaries. Its population went up to over 2,000,000 in 1910, an increase of one-third in five years, and complicated

by the summer itinerants. The competition for factory space
meant that rents were very high. In the industrial areas of
Spasskaya ward, land was worth two hundred roubles per
sazhen (one-eighth of a square mile) but on middle-class
Vasilievski island, fifty. Prince Vyazemski's tenements were
filled with 6000 people, many of them living in a corner
(*ugol*). The rise in land prices was such that speculators had
every reason to delay building houses when the land might
easily be taken for factories; in the meantime, scarcity would
push rents up – and in St Petersburg, with the lowest wages
in industrial Europe, they were higher than in any other
capital city. Only a third of the metal-workers kept their
families in this city; drunks were everywhere; there was an
almost uncountable illegitimacy rate. In flats, the average per
room was 1.7 people, in cellar rooms, 3.9, and in the 'night
houses' (*nochlezhny dom*) there were five men to a single
board-bed, their places separated by chalk marks. The
problem of building speculation was such that no more than
700 houses went up in a single year, and no one knew how
to deal with it.

The city council was run by established interests, generally
official. By 1900, only 8000 men had the right to vote for it,
and most of them abstained. The police kept a close watch
over finance, which was run jointly with the local *guberniya*.
The city's debt, at £9,000,000, did not compare with
Glasgow's £50,000,000. Health regulations were rudimentary, and the canals were a well-known trap. Two hundred
and fifty thousand roubles were spent annually on cleaning
the city, a quarter of Berlin's figure, and an eighth of Paris's;
the educational fund was a quarter of the figure in Vienna.
Because of a wrangle over competence, an electric tramway
did not start until 1907, which had the effect of keeping the
city's concentration, of official quarters, residences and
shanty towns and factories, far higher than elsewhere in
Europe. It was not to be wondered at that intellectuals
became obsessed with root-and-branch reform, the creation
of a new world of shining modern cities, modern industries,
a clean, healthy and sober proletariat. Nor was it surprising

that, in the working-class movement, intellectuals would predominate. Marx appeared to offer a sort of Newtonian physics in politics; and although Russia could hardly count as an advanced industrial country, there were unquestionably good grounds for adapting Marxist ideas to suit her case. This was the achievement of Lenin, who inherited Russia in circumstances of extreme confusion in 1917.

Lenin (né Vladimir Ilitch Ulyanov) was the son of an inspector of schools in Simbirsk. Like many intellectuals in the later nineteenth century, he became disaffected; still more so when his brother was executed for conspiring to kill the tsar, in 1893. He suffered a term of Siberian exile, and eventually fled to Switzerland, where he joined other socialist exiles, men such as Martov, Plekhanov ('the father of Russian Marxism') or Axelrod, who eked out a living from selling socialist newspapers and periodicals, and who would also occasionally benefit from rich Russians' subsidies or from German and Swiss socialist charity. Russian socialists were a very varied crew. The earliest organized socialists had been collected by the Jewish artisans' *Bund*, in Poland and western Russia, but little organizations emerged all over the country, and would send representatives from time to time to discuss things with the exiles. Among the leaders, the working class was not represented at all, and theoretical discussion, often of great bitterness and intensity, was frequent.

Lenin himself was a constant theorist, and it is tempting to argue that his success in 1917 was owed to his 'correct' theoretical understanding of Russia's stage on the Marxist graph. The evidence for this is not very solid: when he first came west, he was still very young, and much of what he had to say about Russian capitalism was simply an echo of the German socialists' own Left: i.e. a theoretical argument for immediate revolution. That aim was his constant; and in his later theoretical writings, his arguments for it were sometimes inconsistent, both with each other and with German Marxism (for instance, he was much more flexible towards minority nationalism than Rosa Luxemburg). Still, his theorizing did give him mental discipline, agility, and a capacity to escape from the cramping influence of Western socialists, most of whom shrank back from violence.

Soon, Lenin had a clear vision of the party he needed. The founding of the Russian Social Democratic Workers' Party had occurred in 1898, but its participants were then, in the main, arrested. In 1903, in Geneva, Belgium and London, a second congress was held, at which about forty exiles and representatives from Russia discussed what to do. Lenin shocked orthodox socialists in the West by splitting this small group from the start. He 'packed' the committees, and arranged for elections and resolutions to be made while opposition people had been lured away. In this way, he obtained control of the party's journal, *Iskra*, and the committee; his contrived majority gave his faction the name *Bolshinstvo* ('majority') while the defeated side became 'Mensheviks' (after *Menshinstvo*, or 'minority'). This victory was soon upset, and Lenin had to set up a different journal, *Vperyod* ('Forward'). Both sides claimed to be orthodox Marxists, but they quarrelled bitterly, on occasion, as to what that meant. From then on, although the two sides re-united from time to time, there was continual tension. Lenin was blamed for his arrogance: he seemed to want a party consisting of picked people, pledged to obey any order from the centre, and also contemptuous of trade unions (whose spokesmen, the 'economists' and 'liquidators', he loudly denounced: for him, trade-union consciousness was not nearly enough for social and political revolution, since it could be bought off with a wage-rise).

Mensheviks wanted to imitate German social democracy, and they had their base in St Petersburg, where such things were at least imaginable – after all, there, too, there were big metals factories, as in Berlin, and there, too, the printers took a lead in trade-union activity, as they did everywhere in Europe. It made sense to adopt a Menshevik platform there: i.e., open the party to all comers, and choose the proper moment to ally with bourgeois liberals, of whom the *zemstva* and Struve supplied the troops. First, the bourgeois democratic revolution, and then social democracy – exactly what Kautsky said. Early Marxist texts bore this out. Marx had always said that capitalism had to create the new economy, of workers, machines, parliaments. Then the workers would take over. Kautsky had no difficulty at all in putting down (with Germanic arrogance) the young Russians who challenged him.

Lenin argued that in Russia the peasantry, far from being the doomed petty-bourgeois class Mensheviks said they were, were a revolutionary force. True, he saw this in full only after the revolution of 1905, and even then did not see what he was doing. Still, Lenin adapted Marx to show that where Marx had talked of a working-class rising, in twentieth-century circumstances his vision could be expanded. In the middle of the nineteenth century, in Germany and France, the peasantry had looked forward to owning their own property and supporting conservative régimes. But in the next century, the experience of imperialism changed everything. Countries overseas were exploited, and so money was passed back to the central countries which enabled them to 'buy off' their native revolutions. Still, the fruits of imperialism came through in the form of cheap food prices; that ruined peasantries in the metropolis; and therefore made them, despite their property, exploited proletarians. They survived only because they had sons who could trek off to the towns for navvying. Lenin therefore said socialism should speak to the peasantry. To be fair, Marx himself had said the same thing towards his death; in 1883 he died with three cubic metres of statistics about the Russian economy at his bedside. He himself was adapting his system, where the Germans wished to ossify it. First the German socialists, and then the Russian Stalinists, made a mystery of Marx's last years, when he was coming to terms with the fact that his ideas were likely to come to fruition in the very place he had never imagined twenty years before.

Lenin wanted a centrally dictated party to replace 'social forces'. People like Plekhanov warned him: a Russia that becomes socialist now will be a gangster state. It will mean handing the immense tools of socialism to gangsters. Did Lenin mind? Did 1917 foresee 1984?

Events went in Lenin's way. It helped enormously, as Lenin had foreseen, that his opponents would be seriously deficient in brains. The tsar, in the splendour of the Winter Palace, surrounded by sycophants, reigning, from his fantastic capital of St Petersburg, over a sixth of the world, succumbed to the romance of Holy Russia. The only outcome of the troubles of 1900–3 was the dismissal of Witte, and the taking-up of a quarrel with Japan over the Far East, which led to disastrous war – waged, with hopelessly inadequate armament, over a long distance, and with great defeats. It was a mad enterprise, and anyone who knew the facts of the Russian army protested.

Intelligent Russians looked on their government at this time as something out of a fable. When there was trouble in the universities the tsar's response was to replace the existing minister of education with a former war minister, Vannovski, who was in his eighties (1901). This was the outcome of a calculation quite characteristic of the times. The government was unable to control universities and many high schools, which produced strikes and demonstrations in the manner of 1848. The only answer appeared to be to conscript the students who made trouble – as students, they had been exempted. But the army authorities did not want to take in troublesome students. In any case many of the generals dated from the Milyutin era, when the army had counted as liberal, favourable to education. The only way round this, for the tsar, was therefore to make Vannovski, his ancient crony, take responsibility for 'order' and thus involve the army. It is only fair to add that the old man astonished everyone concerned by taking the students' side. He was therefore dismissed within a few months. It was also characteristic that, in the troubles of 1902, the minister of the interior, Sipyagin, should address to the president of the Academy of Sciences a lengthy memorandum in protest at the gradual abandonment of the picturesque but superfluous *yat* and 'hard sign' of the Russian alphabet. He saw this as 'contempt for the State'.

The government could not fail to observe the discontent all around. But it responded only with tactlessness and folly. It could not control its own lieutenants, whether Prince Imeretinsky in Warsaw, Admiral Alexeyev, viceroy of the Far East, Count Vorontsov-Dashkov, viceroy of the Caucasus, or General Bobrikov, governor of Finland. The tsar did not try to control these men through powerful ministers, whom, on the whole, he feared and abhorred. There was no regular cabinet or regular policy. Ministers individually dealt with the tsar, and on occasion came up with contradictory policies. There was an almost fabulous series of dim-wits in the ministry of the interior, and the tsar crowned all when he appointed to it the manager of the imperial stud farm (a comment at the time was that at least it was an advance upon Caligula). Because seniority, in this arthritic system, counted for so much, the men in charge were often extremely old. The period abounds in commissions of inquiry chaired (as in 1915) by octogenarians; the tsar's favourite chief minister was the ancient and foolish A.I. Goremykin, who ignored problems in the expectation that this was a positive step. Some of the generals and admirals were buffoons. Kuropatkin, the war minister who led an army against Japan in 1904–5, could not understand why Cossacks had been ineffective. He did not see that horses had become far too vulnerable against ordinary modern rifles; instead, he thought that the Cossacks lacked 'martial dash', and, to make them charge more effectively with their sabres, he proposed to remove their light rifles. Indeed, the whole war with Japan – a mixture of pretentiousness, incompetence, bad luck and governmental incoherence – demonstrated how far the system was failing to respond.

The government dimly appreciated that it was not popular. Like most contemporary merchants of *Sammlungspolitik*, a Chamberlain or a Tirpitz, its answer was to rely on the thrills of nationalism and the booty of empire. At one level this meant what Plehve, minister of the interior, called 'a merry little war' with Japan. At altogether different levels, it meant the encouragement of pogroms against Jews, and persecution of lesser peoples. Count Vorontsov-Dashkov busied himself with confiscating the belongings of the Armenian Church. The semi-independent status of Finland dated to 1809, when she had been annexed by Alexander I (as grand duke). The Finnish currency was separate; there was a Finnish parliament (which a little later had universal and even women's suffrage) to outrage autocratic sensibilities; customs were a problem; so was justice, since Russian political offenders were free, once they reached Finland, which was only a bus-ride away from St Petersburg.

The Finns did not suffer conscription either. The tsar sent General Bobrikov to put an end to these anomalies. He was shot; his replacement caused a great row; the principle of conscription was asserted, with the greatest force that the government could apply; and four Finns were conscripted in 1902, because the army could not afford the upkeep of any more, and anyway feared that Finnish conscripts might feel rather resentful. In this same era, a deputation of Buryats from the frozen Siberian north arrived at the Winter Palace to complain that tax officials were confiscating an undue proportion of the yak dung which formed an important part of their economy. They were turned away by the porter.

The *pièce de résistance* in this assemblage of doings was the war with Japan in 1904–5. Witte had presided over the construction of the Trans-Siberian railway, though there was still a considerable gap in it at Lake Baikal. Russian banking and railway interests had become involved in Manchuria, north-eastern China. A concession had been acquired at Port Arthur, which was used as a naval base. Russians took an interest in Korea. All of this brought them into conflict with Japan, especially over Korea but also over mainland China. A gang of adventurers associated with one Bezobrazov who had the ear of the tsar behaved provocatively, in the hope of profiting from timber trade across the Yalu. The foreign ministry, for fear of offending the British, said it would withdraw troops from Manchuria and then, for fear of offending Admiral Alexeyev, viceroy of the Far East, failed to do so. The bulk of the government felt that the Japanese, being Asiatic, did not have to be taken seriously. The war minister, Kuropatkin, produced a plan which ended with the phrase 'capture of the Mikado'. The Japanese, who had a proprietorial attitude to Korea and an interest in Manchuria, had their British alliance and American support. Early in 1904 they attacked Port Arthur.

The Russian army at this time could not afford hot breakfasts. It was also a long way away. The Trans-Siberian railway was single-track, and was very short of sidings; much of the bed was quite sketchy, which meant that trains had to travel very slowly indeed; and there was a hole in the middle, so that troops had to 'detrain' at one end of Lake Baikal and march to the other end to 'entrain'. It took a year for the Russians in Manchuria to attain the same strength as the Japanese, who had only to sail across a narrow strait. Half of the Russian generals had not reached the fourth form; and the average age of generals was sixty-nine. The artillery had not been properly modernized. Bronze guns, which were heavy and ballistically inadequate, were still the rule, because they were cheaper than modern steel guns of the type the Putilov factory was beginning to produce. There was not enough smokeless powder, for only the Okhta factory could produce it, and although its managers, with a very tsarist-Russian mania for useless exactitude, could tell down to the last ounce or *zolotnik* how much they had produced, it was still not nearly enough. Guns therefore fired very slowly, inaccurately, and with smoke billowing around to blind the gunners as in days of yore. The Russian army was continually worsted, pushed back. As a last card, the tsar played the Baltic fleet, which embarked for the Pacific, sank a few trawlers in the North Sea which were thought to be Japanese torpedo boats, wintered in Madagascar, and was destroyed in the Straits of Tsushima the following May. Witte was called back to head the government and a peace was patched up at Portsmouth, New Hampshire, in August 1905, on terms that were better than might have been expected.

In European Russia, these defeats made a tremendous impression. They also coincided with an inflation. The government had spent 2,000,000,000 roubles on the war, and that, coinciding with a lifting of the trade cycle, brought inflation, as did the government's entry into the textile market for uniforms and the rest. Russia in 1905 therefore saw a wild version of the crisis that everyone else in Europe experienced at this time. The combination of a lost war, unemployment and inflation proved almost calamitous for the tsar, whose survival owed more to the divisions of his opponents than to any surviving mystique of Crown and Altar.

On Sunday, 9 January 1905 a huge crowd of workmen and their families converged, from Spasskaya and the Vyborg side of St Petersburg, on the vast square outside the Winter Palace. They were led by a priest, Father Gapon, and sang hymns. They demonstrated for a proper parliament, and expected the tsar to help them in the cold and hungry winter. The mystique of tsarism was still considerable; and tsars prided themselves on their role as fathers of their people. Even Nicholas I had received up to 30,000 of the ordinary inhabitants of St Petersburg at his Christmas receptions in the Winter Palace. Tsarist police-chiefs, such as Zubatov in Moscow, had even patronized the workers' trade unions, in the expectation that the tsarist State was above the class-war and could easily take the workers' part. But, early in 1905, the rising temper of the masses was plain. Nicholas II's commander ordered the demonstration to be dispersed in Senate Square, and there was a wholesale massacre.

Nineteen hundred and five in Russia was the greatest of the social and political upheavals that Europe experienced at this time. The changes in Russia were coming so concentratedly that, for the first time, social revolution was in everyone's mind. The great cities produced movements comparable with those produced further west – strikes and demonstrations. The Russian liberals, using their base in the professions and the town and county councils, organized a campaign of banquets – in imitation of the French liberals before 1848 – to denounce the government. The government responded by hinting at parliamentary institutions (though without power) and by harassing the *zemstva*. In 1905, the liberals gathered their forces, and set up a political party, the Constitutional Democrats (for short, KD or Kadets) to agitate for political reforms. Some of them also wished to see agrarian reforms.

Russia in 1905 produced a revolutionary movement that had gone beyond the theorizings of German socialism. There was, first of all, the peasant element, with which orthodox socialists were not equipped to deal. There already was revolutionary violence. In June 1905, the battleship *Potyom-*

kin mutinied, in the Black Sea, and its crew sailed the ship to Romania and liberty. In the Caucasus, a peculiar movement developed which no one really understood. One Zhordania, theoretically a Menshevik, discovered, in this disintegrating society, that he could rally the peasantry for socialism, though they made him swear an oath to the Virgin before he led them in that direction. Moslem and Christian joined forces; a great part of the middle class supported Zhordania out of hatred for Vorontsov-Dashkov. This was an inchoate movement, which soon took to guerrilla warfare, and received much peasant support. It was an anticipation of Mao.

In 1905, with repercussions into 1906, the empire exploded. Every grievance was aired; chief cities like Riga or Warsaw went on strike; there were waves of strikes in January, March and October; the peasantry, especially in the central belt from Poltava to Samara, sacked manor houses as in 1902–3; there was a railway strike in October. That strike, which prevented the tsar from shifting troops, caused him to improve the constitutional offers he had already made. On 19/31 October he promised to set up a parliament, the *Duma*. Witte was recalled, briefly, to preside over the assembling of 'Fundamental Laws'. With a sigh of relief, the middle-class protesters settled down to work with the tsar. The French offered a large loan. On the whole, the army remained 'sound', and troops put down a rising in Moscow which was organized by the social democrats in January 1906.

The liberal chieftain P.B. Struve gave voice to the middle-class liberals' opinion of what was happening when he remarked, 'Thank God for the tsar, who has saved us from the people.' The strikes of October, especially, had terrified these liberals. For the Russian lower classes were to a large extent 'out of hand'. Instead of tamely following the liberals, they had, in St Petersburg, established a representative institution that was without a counterpart in Europe: the soviet. It was direct democracy at its most relentless, the hundreds of delegates being chosen and rechosen at short intervals. It acted initially as a vast committee to co-ordinate strikes, and to link the activities of trade unions. It soon took on a political role. On the whole, the socialist revolutionaries who dominated it were in favour of collaboration with the liberals; and the same was true of the social democrats, although the young Lev Bronstein (Trotsky) – at this time formally a Menshevik – sympathized with Lenin's denunciations of class collaboration, and with his warnings that the liberals would betray the social democrats. Still, conditions in 1905–6 were not what they were to be in 1917. The wage-rises granted to strikers were not wiped out in value by inflation; the food crisis eased; police and army remained under discipline. Stolypin, along the Volga, Meinhardt in the Baltic provinces, and Generals Möller-Zakomelski and Rennenkampf from opposite ends of the Trans-Siberian railway restored order through drum-head courts-martial and simple out-of-hand shooting. The Petersburg soviet was arrested in December 1905.

The *Duma* elections were held in April 1906; the government recovered confidence far enough to defy the resulting liberal-dominated parliament, dissolved it, held new elections for a second *Duma*, which met for a few weeks in 1907, and again fell foul of the régime in its efforts to obtain proper parliamentary privileges. On 3 June 1907 the tsar's strong man, Stolypin, had a piece of paper pinned to the door of the *Duma* overnight, to the effect that it was dissolved. It was a *coup d'état*.

Nineteen hundred and five had failed for many reasons. The armed forces had by and large stayed loyal; disloyal elements were demobilized, and mutinies remained isolated. The working-class movement had shown itself in great strike waves, but there were obvious limits to the duration of these. The peasant upheavals had spent themselves in 1902–3, and the recurrences of peasant troubles were quite local, in the Ukraine east of the Dniepr, and to some extent also in Bessarabia. Socialists had still not worked out their attitude to the peasantry; and they did not agree as to violence, so that the *soviet* in St Petersburg took no real action, and the Moscow uprising early in 1906 was again isolated. The railwaymen did not strike, so that troops could be ferried to put down that revolt. The liberals, to whom everyone looked for a lead, were divided, and in any case did not have the wherewithal for revolt. The October manifesto took the wind out of their sails. Against a government that would not concede very much, they were almost powerless. Now, Stolypin's *coup d'état* enabled him to 'pack' a new *Duma* with upper-class representatives.

The Stolypin era, or 'Monarchy of 3 June', was described by contemporary socialists as 'Russian Bonapartism'. This expression referred to Marx's *Eighteenth Brumaire of Louis Napoleon*: Louis Napoleon was held to have restored a version of the *ancien régime*, but with bourgeois adventurers taking the place of some of the 'feudal' element. He was also held to be putting down the workers' movement with main force, and to do so, made an alliance with part of the peasantry, through the medium of the Church. In some ways, 'Russian Bonapartism' was a good description of Stolypin's activities. He did introduce land reform; he preached nationalist causes; there was ugly official anti-Semitism; and, like Louis Napoleon in France or Prince Schwarzenberg in Austria, he tried to revive religion as a political force, building 5500 churches and appointing 100,000 new priests.

Stolypin did try to work with the *Duma*. The first two *Dumy* had been elected by a system quite close to universal male suffrage; there had been majorities for left-wing causes. But these bodies did not work well. As tsarist apologists had long foretold, a Russian parliament was a Babel of different nationalities and parties. No one knew how to manage it. Stolypin's *coup d'état* substituted a straightforward class parliament for the earlier *Duma*. By using Article 87 of the Fundamental Laws (which the tsar had drawn up) the government could do almost anything: in this case, it dissolved the *Duma*, and changed the electoral system. Liberal protests, and appeals for a tax strike, were ignored; the police state, in part, returned; and the third *Duma* (1908–13), like the fourth (1913–17) contained natural right-wing majorities. Their power was much the same as the Prussian *Landtag*'s. Even so, government ministers took offence even at these limited powers. In 1909, for instance, they became incensed at *Duma* questioning, and there was 'a ministerial strike'.

Apart from a handful of social democrats and other left-wing deputies, the *Duma* divided into three chief groups, with shifts from one to the other. The left consisted essentially of the Kadets, liberals in association with Pavel Milyukov (a republican historian); there was a centre in the Octobrists, the right-wing liberals whose main support came from the big industry of Moscow, and whose spokesman was an industrialist, Alexandr Guchkov. On the right were anti-Semites, 'Black Hundreds' (as the extreme nationalists were known) and an inchoate group called 'the rights' (*pravy*) who had their own moderate wing, later known as 'Nationalists'. To avoid any extension of the *Duma*'s power, the government only needed to knit together the right and centre. On the whole, it succeeded: it could offer programmes of nationalism (against the Finns, for instance) and great armaments. After 1910, Russia too experienced an atmosphere of *réveil national*.

Stolypin himself was not an old-fashioned or lazy figure like his predecessors at the interior ministry. He was a 'technocrat' – a conservative, concerned with efficiency. He might even have collaborated with the *Duma* liberals had he, on his own side, not had to keep his link to the right, the court and the seedy intriguers around the tsar, and had they, on their side, not been continually preoccupied with their links to the left. The government was overhauled. It even, briefly, departed from the tsarist practice of appointing aged men. It now amounted to a regular cabinet, with a proper chairman, and not simply to a collection of departmental chiefs meeting whenever the tsar felt like it. Various ministries' policies, which in the past could sometimes be contradictory, were now harmonized to some degree, while the shock of defeat caused both the navy and the army to bring a much needed reorganization and proper General

Staffs. Intelligent bureaucrats like Kokovtsov and Litvinov-Falinski in the ministry of finance began to explore ways in which the economy, as a whole, could be steered through State action. Above all, Stolypin made a great effort to give some answer to the Peasant Question – the greatest problem of Russia.

Stolypin proceeded from a political angle. No one who had seen the skies redden with burning hayricks and houses in 1905 could fail to do so. But there was a vital economic side. Without efficient agriculture, industry and towns would not have much of a market, food-supplies, exports with which foreign machines or commodities could be acquired; and would the quality of labour which reached industry from backward agriculture be such as to sustain industrial growth? Before 1914, everyone was concerned with the Peasant Question.

Taking German and American figures for comparison (the English ones are much higher), in the USA the yield per hectare of rye was 68 poods (16 kg), in Germany 100, in Russia 54, and of wheat 9.7, 21 and 6.4 respectively (it was much less hardy than rye). From 1901 to 1913 the Russian increase in these yields was slight, smaller than anything in Europe. Artificial fertilizer was used only on three per cent of the land even in 1914; and yet natural fertilizer was also much less in evidence, for the peasants were unable to keep cows on their land in any numbers because they needed the grain for themselves. There were 293 cows per thousand inhabitants in Russia in 1914, but 622 in the USA and 688 in Denmark; and Russian cows were also scrawny. In 1917 fifty-two per cent of households did not have a plough at all, and of the rest, a good many had a primitive plough only. In the Beryansk, Melitopol and Dnieprovsk districts of Taurida province, which was comparatively prosperous, only two-fifths of the peasant households had animals and a plough for them to use; a third had no plough at all, and the rest either a primitive one or no animals. This problem worsened because the population rose dramatically, and the land was supporting twice as many people in 1900 as in 1860. Russian industrialization depended on the imports of machinery and commodities, while the need for foreign money also dictated that the country should export her grain. It made up almost half of the value of Russia's exports in 1913, and amounted to 12,000,000 tonnes in a harvest of 70,000,000 (an unusually good, and therefore untypical figure). Russia's economic development depended on the continuation of this exporting, which was not popular among peasants who themselves had not enough to eat.

Already in 1902 a committee (of 184 men) had sat to discuss the agrarian question. In November 1906, and with subsequent legislation of 1910 and 1911, Stolypin tackled the heart of it, the peasant commune, which he and many others regarded as the single greatest cause of Russia's agricultural backwardness and her political restiveness. The commune, not individual farmers, formally owned the land. It was thought to prevent individual peasants from acquiring their own land and passing it on to their children; hence they had no incentive to invest in it. The land was also, generally, used in 'strips' of a size that could be ploughed in a single day, and most often these strips were not consolidated because the peasants shared them out according to the value of the land. Hence a peasant's effort would be dissipated over several strips, with much walking to and fro, and much waste of land on pathways. Some peasant families might have up to a hundred strips, and there was continual bickering in the village assembly, the *skhod*, as to who should get what, and when.

This system was not uniquely Russian. It had its counterpart in the 'rundale' of Ireland, the 'runrigg' of Scotland; even in 1945 a tenth of France was owned in common, not by individuals; there are still elements of archaic strip-farming in western Germany; and in the Balkans the *zadruga* of Croatia was very similar to the Russian commune, the *obshchina*. The point of the whole business was that it gave each peasant a chance of land. It did so at the expense of agriculture, since peasants in a commune did not invest in the land and make it produce more. In the eighteenth century, Protestant Europe – the British in the lead – attacked her own forms of commune, with laws as to consolidation and inheritance which, especially in England, were a success. Northern France and Belgium, and northern Italy, moved in the same direction, to produce individual farmers, though sometimes with vestiges of communal tenure. One of the central points of nineteenth-century liberalism was to reward individual initiative, and that had inevitable repercussions on agriculture. It helped, in all of these cases, that there were flourishing towns and industries to take any 'surplus' agrarian population, and the emancipation of the land was an indispensable preliminary to industrial growth.

An essential in this emancipation was that there should be, at peasant level, a class of farmers who would co-operate in dismantling communal arrangements, and buying out their poorer fellows – 'rural capitalists', though the expression hardly fits the case, who even within the formal commune had established hereditary title and consolidation. In Prussia of the later eighteenth century, the growth of markets, money and population had enabled some of the peasants to emerge in this way, and for them the formal freeing of the serfs was anticipated long before. A further essential was that on the land there should be estate-owners able to organize the whole process of consolidation and private property; to give a group of villages some kind of coherence in common matters (the harvest, which required back-breaking work, more or less continuously, by every man, woman or child in the area; or irrigation). In western Europe, the English legal system allowed a relationship between estate-owner and tenant that was flexible enough to take account of land prices, rates of interest, food prices in such a way that both parties proved, by the standards of the day, efficient. In Prussia, the landlords who took over from the 'pre-capitalist' Junkers in the first half of the nineteenth century imposed some rationalization on agriculture, and the 'surplus' peasantry went (in millions) to the towns.

It was an essential part of the Russian peasant problem that

the great estate-owners did not take a similar role. On the
contrary, after 1861 they were in a permanent decline. In
1914 there were still some spectacular great estates – 699 with
over 5000 acres. Most of these consisted of huge tracts of
mountain and forest, such as the 600,000 acres of the
Orlov-Davydov family or the hardly less fabulous holdings
of the Beloselski-Belozerskis, the Golitsyns or the Yusupovs
– although in each case these families were transferring their
real interest to the cities (the Beloselski-Belozerskis owned
Vasilievski Island, in the Neva at St Petersburg). In the old
Polish regions of the south-west, and in the Ukraine west of
the Dniepr generally, great Polish noble families maintained
a dominant presence. The sugar-beet lands of the Ronikiers
or the Czetwertyńskis were patriarchal empires of the kind
that were frequent enough over the Austro-Hungarian
border, with interests that spread out to include coalmines
and distilleries. But generally noble agriculture declined – as
it did everywhere in Europe. Nobles had had 120,000,000
desyatiny (hectares) in 1861, or just over half of the
219,000,000 in European Russia below the frozen north. By
1905, they owned 79,300,000. By 1914, they had 35,000,000,
and since a third of that was arable land, the nobles' share
of arable farming – the centre of the whole question – was
therefore less than a tenth in 1914. In Perm and Vyatka,
noble landowning amounted to 0.4 per cent of the arable
land.

The reasons for this were not difficult to see, and had been
at the root of the emancipation of the serfs in 1861, when
already two-thirds of the serf-owning nobility were virtually
bankrupt. It was exceedingly difficult to make money out of
Russian agriculture. In the non Black Earth regions, the soil
was very poor. Frosts prevented farmers from working their
fields in the Moscow region for all but two months of the
year. Drought and high winds affected the fertile areas of the
Black Earth region. Harvests were extremely irregular, and
every seven years there would be famine somewhere or other
– in 1891, fairly generally. Grain prices had fallen steadily in
the last quarter of the century. Transport, in much of the

country, was impossible, and even after the railways began, the shipment of grain could be expensive – so expensive that a shipment from Irkutsk to Riga swallowed up any possible profit. In Tver, which stood across the Moscow-Petersburg railway, an estate of 250 *desyatiny* would produce at best a profit of 1500 roubles – about the income of a middle-ranking civil servant, even then in a province which, like neighbouring Smolensk, had qualities that made it good for producing industrial crops such as flax. There was also the question of labour, which Tolstoy regarded as the centre of the whole business. Peasants with their own plots tended to work very irregularly for their landlords, and had to be dragooned. They also felt that they had been done out of land at the time of the emancipation, and there were some fabulous court cases. There was a fifty years' battle in the Bolshaya Yaroslava district of Ryazan over 2300 *desyatiny* between the heirs of Count Zubov and Prince Baryatinski on the one side, and several peasant villages, whose armed uprising ended in several imprisonments; in the Balashovski district of Samara, 253 private owners disputed an enormous tract with sixty-nine peasant communes; maps of the area in dispute took up several rooms, and took five days to peruse. This had been going on for several decades. In 1907 the Peasants' Land Bank took on 1891 estates as terrified owners sold up – more than in the previous eleven years.

Finally there was the matter of credit. Russia was too poor, and the banking system nowhere nearly developed enough; Alexander III's Nobles' Land Bank (and the subsequent sister foundation, the Peasants' Land Bank) did not have enough money. Even in 1894, the total sum advanced to nobles on mortgage – 4,000,000 roubles – was no more than a single year's turnover of landbuying by the bank.

Still, if the nobles were in retreat, they could be replaced by individual farmers of the kind who emerged in most other countries from the 'Great Depression'. It was not until Stolypin's time that the State encouraged individual peasant farming – indeed, in 1893 the communes were reinforced – but it was a cardinal point in Stolypin's thinking that there were 'sturdy and strong' peasants who could shove aside the 'drunken and weak' brothers. It was also a cardinal point for Lenin, though he was arguing towards a different outcome. In other countries the emancipation of the peasantry had been preceded by their differentiation into potential rural capitalists, smallholders and the rural poor: 'kulaks' with fifty acres or so, *serednyaki* or 'middle peasants' with about twenty-five, *bednyaki* or 'poor peasants' with ten, and *batraki* with no land at all. Lenin saw the 'proletarization' of the middle-to-poor peasantry and the emergence in Russia, before Stolypin but also greatly fostered by Stolypin, of a kulak class which had about three per cent of the peasantry already in 1900, both in communes and in private landowning. Subsequent Marxist historians stress that Stolypin was encouraging this capitalist class at the expense of the other peasants, whose revolt in 1917 then becomes comprehensible. Since we are dealing with three-quarters of Russia's population, the peasant-capitalist question really involves an inextricable mass of other questions – the nature of Russia's economic development, of her social system, of Lenin's ideology, of the role of the peasantry in the revolution and, by implication, of the subsequent development of Soviet agriculture, through collectivization to its present-day stagnation. The contours of the problem are clear enough: why did Russian agriculture remain backward, and why did the peasantry not respond to the revolution in the counter-revolutionary way in which European peasants generally responded to urban upheavals in so many countries since 1848?

There are many immediate reservations to be made. In the first place, it is dubious, in a huge country like Russia, if we can talk about 'the' peasant question at all. It varied from place to place, according to soil, climate, landholding, religious traditions, alternative employment in industry or handicrafts. The Baltic provinces had quite successful Junker estates – a quarter of the land – though the *Ostzeyskiye Barony* (as they were called in Russian) were not very popular. The heartland of communal agriculture was the central Black Earth region, sprawling over the Ukrainian east and the lands of the middle Volga and the Don. The Crimea was quite prosperous; so too was 'New Russia', the lands taken by Catherine the Great north of the Caucasus and the Black Sea coast. Around Moscow, market-gardening prospered; around St Petersburg, it did not: and the only reason advanced – though with characteristic implausibility – for the difference is that around St Petersburg peasant families were paid so much money for fostering the city's foundlings that they survived without bothering to grow vegetables.

Then again, the statistics on which any inquiry can be based are difficult, once we are below the level of noble estates. Until this period, it was only when the agricultural problem came up very seriously that even harvest figures were regularly collected, as in the 1850s and again after 1893. It was only in 1904 that any division of the provenance of the harvest was made as between rented, privately owned, communal, or co-operative peasant property, and according to the Soviet historian Kovalchenko, even the official figures were in the habit of exaggerating the amount of privately held land by about a third. Most Soviet historians assert that only the statistical inquiry of 1916 can count. Then again, communes varied greatly, some large, some small, some an administrative formality, some not recognized.

Stolypin wished to encourage rural capitalism by breaking up the commune. But it was not easy. Earlier, the government had used it as an administrative device. The village elders took some of the judicial functions of the old serf-owner. Since the entire commune was responsible for paying dues, it followed that no one must leave without the permission of the others; hence, communes could issue passports. Stolypin ran down the administrative side of the communes, increased the amount of money available to the Peasants' Land Bank, and sent a small army of assessors of land (*zemleustroiteli*) into the countryside to sort out questions of boundary (in ten years, they worked over 20,200,000 *desyatiny*, frequently a back-breaking job which had to be carried through in the teeth of rural resistance). He also cancelled redemption dues. These had sat, because of the collective responsibility, very heavily on the shoulders of the better-off peasants, and the sums owing, by 1900, were quite considerable. Some districts were several hundred per cent in arrears, i.e., they had paid so little even of the interest that at compound rates their debt was seven or eight times what it had been in the 1860s.

The government had been accused, by liberals, of maintaining the peasantry in communes because it needed to control them harshly, and to stop the 'sturdy and the strong' from flexing their liberal and individualistic muscles. There was some truth in that, but it was to ignore the character of much of the peasantry, which so greatly wished to maintain communal farming that, in 1917, when the peasants could choose, 95.5 per cent of them opted to go back to communes.

The reason for this, in most areas of communal tenure, but especially in the vast regions between the Dniepr (which bisects the Ukraine) and the Volga country, was quite a simple one. The sense of private property, so inseparable from the concept of property in the west of Europe for centuries past, did not exist with much strength on the Russian land. The abundant commodity in Russia was land – even in land-hungry Poltava, the average figure per household was 11 acres, and the lowest allotment (*nadel*) was 5, compared with the French average of 9.8 acres in 1815, or the half of Prussian peasants who had 4 and less. The scarce commodity was labour, and it was only after 1860 that the population expanded even remotely far enough to make the land populated sufficiently by some European standards.

The communes existed, for the greater part, to make sure that a man had enough land when he had the labour to farm it and the family mouths to be fed from it. In other words, the more children, the more land. Every twelve years, land (except for a man's original plot, round his house) would be examined by the village assembly, and those households whose children had grown up would lose some of their land.

It was in strips because, in that way, each household could have its share of good, bad, indifferent land. In such circumstances what Lenin and others said was true enough, that there was a section of the peasantry at the very top which would own much more land than the others. But the point was, and it was ignored by Lenin, that the 'big' peasants would generally lose it again. Some brilliant statisticians were at work before 1914 on these problems, A.V. Chayanov the greatest of them. Khryashcheva, in Yepifan district, found that from 1899 to 1911 two-thirds of the households with four horses were split up at the end of the twelve years. In the next bracket down, households with from nine to fifteen *desyatiny*, fifty-six per cent had been partitioned; in the next bracket, from six to nine *desyatiny*, half had been partitioned. Far from being necessarily a capitalist, and hated by his fellows, the 'big peasant' merely had many children, and became a 'medium' peasant once they were of an age to set up on their own. Teodor Shanin has assembled impressive statistics in this same sense, and believes that the phenomenon was not only quite general, but had much to do with the rise of population.

It almost followed automatically that the more children a man had, the richer he would be. A survey of Kaluga in 1897 showed that within the category of households of nine to twelve *desyatiny*, there would be an average of 9.8 people, with two *desyatiny* per capita; but in the category three to six *desyatiny*, there would be 6.6 people per household, with an average of 1.4 *desyatiny* each, and it was generally the case that, the more children, the more land. The statistician Knipovitch bore this out as regards animals: obviously, the more land the more animals, ranging from 0.5 horses on four-person households with two *desyatiny* to 1.5 horses for households above ten *desyatiny*. Another statistician, Shcherbina, looked at savings, and found, in Voronezh, that a household with five *desyatiny* and 5.17 members would have an income per head of sixty roubles per annum of which six would be saved; a household with from fifteen to twenty-five *desyatiny* would earn seventy-five roubles for each of its 8.53 members, of which they would save ten.

If Shanin's account is correct – and, in this difficult area it squares too many circles for it to be very far out – then we can see why the peasant commune proved so resilient. The 'big peasants' at the top of the whole system were not usually rural capitalists of a new type at all: for they forfeited much of their land when their children grew up, which means that the whole complicated business of sub-dividing land on inheritance, a western European phenomenon, did not happen in Russia in the same way. The 'big peasants' did, however, become capitalists of an old kind. Because their savings were greater, they had money to advance to other peasants in need, at high rates of interest. They became usurers, possibly with a horse and cart or tools to lend out. In that capacity, they were known as 'kulaks': an ugly word, meaning 'fist'; sometimes they were known as *miroyedi*, 'devourers of the commune' – but it had nothing directly to do with agricultural capitalism as such. As such, kulaks were quite happy to remain in the commune, because that was where they had their clients. In Voronezh, investigated by the Soviet historian Simonova, a third of the land 'freed' by Stolypin went, not to 'big peasants' but to landless ones: the kulaks preferred to remain as they were. The very word 'kulak' is therefore one of the great misnomers of this century. The Russian peasants' own word for 'big farmer' was *zazhitochny krestyanin* ('prosperous peasant').

Stolypin's 'technocrats' were, then, encountering problems with which 'development strategies' have since become, sometimes gruesomely, familiar. It was not at all easy to 'solve' the commune question, and the effort to do so caused a great deal of trouble. There are of course innumerable qualifications that can be made in this pattern. The above remarks do not hold good for several parts of Russia – the Crimea, for instance, where a combination of favourable circumstances led to communes' being an administrative formality; the lands of Stavropol, north of the Caucasus; most of the western provinces, including Poland; most of

Siberia. Quite possibly it is illusory to talk of agricultural modernization without reference to the factors that brought it about in the West – markets, seasonal migration, rural handicrafts, a centrally planning estate or (in Denmark) co-operatives.

Even so, in the great central belt from the Dniepr to the middle Volga, the area of the 'land war', Stolypin's reforms failed to work. The peasants saw in communes their chance of land; many workers in the cities, a great number of whom maintained their links with the communes, also saw their entitlement to land there as their security for disability or old age (that was what one minister of the interior, Prince Svyatopolk-Mirski, meant in 1904 when he made the otherwise absurd-sounding pronouncement that 'In Russia there is no social question').

Disregarding huge tracts of forest, tundra or mountain which belonged to the Crown, the Church, the State or to great families, the sown land in Russia amounted to 80,000,000 *desyatiny*. In the Stolypin time, about half of the privately owned land was transferred to peasants, largely through the Peasants' Land Bank; roughly a tenth (in one source, 11.3 per cent) of this land remained in estates in 1916; and of course a great part of that was let out to peasants, often to whole communes. Peasant land amounted, overall, to four-fifths in 1905, and nine-tenths in 1916, though there were variations – in the Baltic and Lithuania, around three-quarters, in the eastern Ukraine, 85 per cent, in the south-east almost all, on the middle Volga, 93.6 per cent.

Within the category 'peasant land' there are divisions to be made for which the statistical material is not adequate. It is generally asserted that eighty per cent of 'peasant' land was run by communes, though maybe some of these were formalities. The other peasant land was privately held, by smallholders (*khutoryane*) who lived in isolated farmsteads. Some of these smallholders, though no more than three per cent of all the peasantry, counted as substantial ones, independent farmers of the American type, i.e., hiring labour. There was a further category of peasant which

Stolypin sanctioned, the man who separated from the commune, taking with him a consolidated plot of land, but still lived in the village – in Russian, *otrubnik*. The question for Stolypin was, therefore, how many *otrubniki* would emerge from the reforms.

Plainly, it was impossible to take land from the whole commune unless a majority of the peasants agreed; if they did, then even the 'commons', for grazing or fuel, could be divided. Some of the communes were mere formalities, where no repartition of land on the twelve-year cycle had occurred for some time, and where the strips had already been consolidated. Such communes were formally dissolved in 1910–11. In others, there had already been a division of the peasantry, and the poor ones would sell their rights to the better-off. As soon as the relevant laws were passed, people took advantage; then the real problems began.

Numbers leaving their commune with land

1908	1909	1910	1911	1912	1913	1914	1915
508,300	579,400	342,200	145,600	122,300	134,600	97,900	29,800

It was significant that fifty-seven per cent of the peasants applying to separate came from the fourteen provinces of the north-west, the south, and the south-east, while forty-three per cent came from the thirty-two other provinces.

The reform's results showed this. In some areas, large numbers of peasants would manage to establish an individual title to their holding, and take it out of the commune. In Stavropol, for instance, a quarter of the peasants got out, taking a third of the peasant land; in the west-bank Ukraine half of the communal peasants left, with half of the peasant land; in St Petersburg, slightly under a third of the peasants left with much the same proportion of land, and that pattern was common enough in Smolensk, Tver, Pskov. In the Black Earth region generally, twenty-eight per cent of the peasants left, with eighteen per cent of the land; in the non Black Earth, fourteen and nine per cent respectively. In the north, almost no one bothered formally to leave the commune. In Ryazan, Kursk, Kaluga and Tambov, the heartland of the peasant question, roughly five per cent of the peasantry left, with five per cent of the land. In all, 2,478,000 peasants acquired rights to their land (only two-thirds of those who applied: in many cases the communes objected). 1,101,800 households (of the total 13,000,000 in European Russia at this time) sold up their small plots – 4,000,000 *desyatiny*, which were then bought by the better-off *otrubniki*; 17,000,000 *desyatiny* were thus acquired or retained by these million *otrubnik* households; and to them, as private peasants, should be added the pre-Stolypin smallholders, the 2,818,000 *podvorniye krestyane* or *khutoryane*. Land surveyors were sent out to work the boundaries.

Formally, then, rather above a quarter of the peasantry was not involved in communal agriculture by 1916. It would be wrong to deny that something had been achieved. These were years of good prices: rye, 55 kopecks per pood in 1901, reached 62 in 1912 and 70 in 1913; wheat at Odessa had been 86 kopecks in 1901 and reached 124 in 1912. The State advanced money to *otrubniki* at five per cent, lower than advances to other clients, and *khutoryane* could obtain hundred per cent mortgages. Siberia was opened up, and dairy-farming there was quite successful – supplying London, for instance, with much of its butter. The co-operative movement began to move forward in Russia as it had done in Denmark (a Danish expert called Köföd was employed to advise the ministry) and in the Raiffeisen system of Germany and Austria. Harvests were excellent – around 60,000,000 tonnes for most of the time, with 70,000,000 in 1913, of which 12,000,000 could be exported.

A fifth of the grain came from surviving private estates, though they had only a tenth of the sown area. These estates also were responsible for forty-seven per cent of the grain that was marketed (though often they acted as middlemen for peasants' grain), since the peasants took up most of what they produced. The question then was, could the newly independent peasantry produce surpluses?

Although there were hopeful signs here, they are subject to qualification. Siberia, for instance, took 3,145,753 people from the interior in the years 1906 to 1916, but 546,607 returned because they could not face the hardships, and because the bureaucracy muddled things so badly that 700,000 people were dumped in the wastes of Tomsk in 1909 with no preparation at all. The co-operative movement succeeded in areas where farming had already been 'modernized' or was starting from nothing, as in the Baltic or Siberia. In the Baltic lands, co-operatives had one hundred roubles' capital per head, but in the central agricultural region, five, and in the south, fifteen. The State contributed five roubles per head, but at interest of twelve per cent; and this hardly helped to buy a plough, of thirty to forty roubles, or a horse, of fifty to sixty. The credit co-operative of Ufa was worth eleven roubles per member, but the Raiffeisen ones in Germany were worth 7900.

Then again, to break with the communal traditions of the past was quite difficult. Despite the mortgages, many independent farmers could not survive: in these years there were 570,000 foreclosures, and arrears owing to the Peasants' Land Bank rose from 9,000,000 to 45,000,000 roubles for the 1,600,000 independent peasants who had their lands through the Bank. Quite often, there were cunning frauds – cases of men who acquired land, took out a mortgage, and then went on living in the commune, neglecting the land, but living as usurers in the village. Of the 20,200,000 *desyatiny* worked over by surveyors, almost a third was still in some form of communal tenure. If the independent farmers went on having children as before, their plots could become insufficient, and they would look back to the communes for a chance to obtain more. Sometimes, the independents were worse off than they would have been if they had stayed in the commune. In the Rzhev district of Tver, there were 1045 smallholding households, and half of the land belonging to them was with the three-quarters of them who owned less than five *desyatiny*; in the Toporetski district of Pskov, only a tenth of the smallholders had three or more horses, another tenth, none, and almost half, only one. Not surprisingly, there was a serious movement back into communes by 1914: there, a man was safe.

With all of these shifts, the temper in the countryside became worse. Troops were used on 13,507 occasions in January 1909, and on 114,108 occasions that year. By 1913, there were 100,000 arrests for 'attacks on State power'; the technocrats' actions provoked riots, and there were also attacks on bigger peasants' leaving the commune. The government did its best to show the advantages of the new system. Excursions were organized for peasants to see for themselves the well-watered Latvian smallholdings, the artesian wells of the Mennonites around Samara, the stone houses and stout roofs of the German settlements in Kherson. To a five-*desyatin* smallholder, these things only served to increase resentment. The 'sturdy and sober' Stolypin smallholder is one of history's saddest might-have-beens.

Another might-have-been of this era was Russian capitalism. From 1908 to 1914, Russia experienced a great 'boom', with a growth-rate of 8.8 per cent. The State's revenues doubled, to almost 4,000,000,000 in 1913/14. The number of banks doubled, to 2393; resources rose by 2,500,000,000 roubles, to reach 7,000,000,000; and the value of 'active operations' went up by 7,200,000,000 as banks invested, especially the thirteen large banks of St Petersburg, which dominated the process, such as the *Peterburgski mezhdunarodni* and the *Azovsko-Donskoy*. The rising prosperity was shown in a 250 per cent rise of ordinary bank deposits. Construction stimulated metal, which stimulated coal. Pig-iron output, the basic index, rose by sixty-four per cent in Russia as against thirty-two elsewhere in the world, and fifty in Germany; engineering and metal-working rose by seventy-five per cent as against forty-two in Germany. A chemical industry started in Moscow; electrical industries followed, and became cartellized in 1912 as *elektroprovod* (for cables). From 1910 to 1913, 757 new companies appeared, adding 1,112,000,000 roubles' share capital to the existing companies' 1,000,000,000. Merely in the statistics of the factory inspectorate, which seriously understated everything, a process of industrial concentration and the employment of more workers per factory is plain: 25,300 factories in 1900, employing 2,040,000 workers with 3,200,000,000 capital; 22,600 in 1908 with 2,500,000 workers for 4,300,000,000; 24,900 in 1913 for 2,900,000 workers and 6,600,000,000 capital. Coal output rose from 1,019,000,000 poods in 1901 to 2,200,000,000 in 1913, steel output from 133,000,000,000 to 295,000,000,000. In the south, energy input rose by 3.3 times, and productivity (per worker) therefore rose.

The amount of money lent from abroad in this period rose. But, as a proportion of Russia's investment, it declined from one half in 1900 to a fifth in 1914; and it shifted direction, away from government stocks which were safe but boring, into industry which appeared to be equally safe but was far less boring. In the old days, foreigners exploited Russia's minerals. Now, there was quite a healthy development of Russian manufacturing, even of machine tools, and the country had passed the 'take-off' point – if that has any meaning – in that it could generate its own investment.

Why? Russia's experience here was not unique, only on a much larger scale. Both Italy and Hungary experienced tremendous growth in this period, from a similarly 'agrarian' background. There, too, industry, sometimes heavy industry, emerged 'locally' – Milan, Csepel island in Budapest, Brescia, Resiczabánya – and had high growth-rates, with a gradual adaptation in some places to the new industries of the era, whether Italy, with her respectable place in the automobile industry, or Hungary, which in 1914 had the largest electric-lamp factory in Europe. Even the agrarian south of Germany began to 'industrialize' in this rather patchy way, with Württemberg and Catholic Bavaria acquiring both large concerns like the Mannesmann and smaller sub-contracting firms like the Mauser armaments works.

In all cases, the 'Great Depression' had worked calamitously. It had destroyed much of the traditional artisan class;

the fall of agricultural prices had wrecked traditional agriculture; there was not much of an industrial base to build upon; the State had been forced into a policy of encouraging foreign investment and extending the railway network; banks had been forced to become more modern; the easier, necessary, and imitable industries like textiles would come in, partly because the foreign imports had become too expensive.The recovery of commodity prices after 1896 produced, in all three countries, much the same phenomena. Their great industries, cartellized, became more prosperous. The demand from agriculture went up, and in all three cases agriculture accounted for three-quarters of the population even in 1914. Workers were sucked into the towns; and the combination of inflation, entrepreneurs' attitudes and the inadequacy of the State machine resulted in urban rioting that, in the end, produced, after 1917, a very serious 'revolutionary situation' in all three countries. The Russian 'boom' was therefore a phase of a Kondratiev long wave. The country still depended, essentially, on commodity prices. When these went down again – as they did, disastrously, in the later 1920s – crisis resulted, as it also did in Russia, despite her socialist system. For the background to the Stalinist collectivization of agriculture was a determination to export sufficient grain to pay for industrial machinery, at a time when grain prices fell, by 1932, to a quarter of their level in 1925, itself two-thirds of the level of 1913.

In the end, though the Russian 'boom' was impressive, it had weaknesses. Forty per cent of the work-force was still in textiles, working long and ill-paid hours in Ivanovo-Voznesensk or Łódź. The great profits went to textile firms, taking the place of imports. The turnover profit of the Moscow region in 1913 was, at 434,000,000 roubles, 2.3 times that of all Baku oil, 4.7 times that of the southern metallurgy concerns, and 14 times that of Donbass coal. There was a great weakness in Russia at the level of medium factories, and especially at the very base of society. A Russian provincial town, for instance, was not the lively and prosperous affair of the West: it would be a collection of pompous, neo-Byzantine ochre-coloured buildings, surrounded by mean back-streets, with squalid little bars and 'general stores' selling exactly the same bazaar of goods facing each other across the street; the inhabitants, where not in the nobility or the official class, wandering round in smocks and baste shoes. The Russian novelists' classic provincial places, 'Our town of Z', supported 1,200,000 traders, for a population approaching 150,000,000 in European Russia in 1914. In France, the *patente* tax on shopkeepers was paid by 2,300,000 people, with a population barely a quarter of European Russia's. The big men of Russia were certainly prospering as never before, but it only caused greater, not less, disintegration of the economy.

As regards Russia, it was common to hear that 'but for the First World War' she would have continued to develop along Western lines, i.e. towards capitalism and democracy. A similar view was taken in every country affected by the First World War: no Mussolini, no strange death of English liberalism, no Hitler. In the end such arguments, though maybe plausible enough, are unreal. The business of European states in this era was to prepare for war with Germany or to wage it. Their ways of waging the war revealed a great deal as to their character. It is not a test that tsarist Russia survives, for it becomes evident that she was not a society that could respond to the rapid changes of twentieth-century civilization.

That became plain in politics. Stolypin's technocracy disintegrated, overtaken by a hysterical nationalism that also affected a good part of the *Duma*. The (nearly) universal-suffrage *Dumy* had not proved workable. A new electoral law of 1907 substituted a class parliament, which met in November, with a lower-class fringe. On the whole, this was a body of landowners, officials, some (not many) spokesmen for industry, and professional men. The government treated it with some contempt: there was, for instance, a great crisis from May 1908 to April 1909 because the *Duma* had dared to arrogate to itself an invasion of the Prerogative in officer commissions. The fact was that the generals and admirals did not like members' scrutinizing their accounts which were none too Tirpitz-like. Indeed, the naval authorities were making the worst of a difficult hand: they were busy planning two great fleets, Baltic and Black Sea, vacillated hopelessly between one and the other, and ended up with two half-navies which did practically nothing in the First World War. The upper house was wheeled on to obstruct the *Duma*'s undesirable approval, and this absurd battle went on and on. Stolypin, defending the elementary rights of the *Duma*, made himself unpopular with the tsar, and some of his colleagues simply refused later to appear in the place at all.

The Kadets were quite eclipsed in all of this. The class parliament gave them 84 seats (of 442), and they could reign over a bloc, on occasion, consisting of the two dozen lower-class deputies (including a dozen social democrats), with left-wing Octobrists and the twenty-eight 'Progressists' allied with businessmen like Ryabushinsky, Tretyakov and Konovalov. The Kadets' own supporters were partly middle-class and high-minded aristocrat; but they also gathered many votes from the lower middle classes, despite the franchise that told so heavily against them. By November 1912, their supporters were pulling apart: the better-off ones were tending to vote for 'Progressists', the lower-class ones even for social democrats, such that in the second *curia* of St Petersburg the Kadets fell by two-thirds. In the election to the fourth *Duma* which met in 1913, the Kadets fell to fifty-nine, and conservatives of various brands were easily predominant. Even by 1909 the Kadets were in quite serious decline, hardly dared to have a representative congress, and when they held one, opened it to all comers. It goes almost without saying that the liberals split. Nekrasov, Gredeskul and Prince D.I. Shakhovskoy wished above all to preserve their link with the left. Milyukov, striving to keep the party together, proposed to restart it as 'the party of world renewal'. On the right, Prince Trubetskoy and Struve hoped instead to make up to the less repulsive parts of the nationalist right, and Struve explained that he was not so much anti-Semitic as 'a-Semitic'. In practice, the *Duma* came to be dominated by a large nationalist bloc, constituting a sort of *chambre introuvable*. The liberals' divisions, in reaction to their minority status in the parliament, are a subject of exaggerated importance and considerably exaggerated interest.

The landowners who made up a good part of the assembly were, by 1909, in a state of some alarm. After all, Stolypin had fulfilled one precondition for the title 'great conservative statesman' in that he stabbed his followers in the back. The nobles were losing more and more of their land; feudalism was ending, even if capitalism was not starting. Townsmen were making a great deal of money. They included many Jews, who had lost some of their formal disabilities in 1906. The bureaucracy, threatened by *Duma* criticism, and by Stolypin's recognition that a government effort was needed, stopped quarrelling with the *zemstva*. In the army, the new General Staff made life uncomfortable for the old gang. The nationalities were profiting from the boom years, and even the despised Ukrainians had produced a national movement that worried the landowners there, who were mainly Russian.

The response of propertied Russia, the element that voted for the *Duma*, was overtly nationalist, and nationalism carried along with it many of the centre group of Octobrists, some Progressists, and the whole of the right. In April 1909 the landowner Balashov founded a 'moderate right' group; in January 1910 it joined with right-wing Octobrists as *Vserossiyski natsionalni soyuz*, or 'all-Russian national association'. The seventh congress of the United Nobility (*Dvoryanstvo*) declared in 1910 that 'it is necessary to clear the Russian land of Jews, to clear it harshly and resolutely', step by step and 'by a plan worked out in advance'. In 1911–12, the case of Mendel Beylis, a Jew falsely accused of ritual murder, demonstrated that this attitude reached into the ministry of justice. Beylis was eventually acquitted, but only after a great international protest. A collection of outright gangsters called *Soyuz russkogo naroda*, centred in Kiev, and operated by one Dr Dubrovin, took the lead in anti-Semitic propaganda and pogroms. A Prince A.A. Shirinski-Shikhmatov founded a weekly, *Okrayni Rossii* ('The Fringes of Russia') to foster the campaign against restive minority peoples; the ministry of education, under A.I. von Schwarz, declared in 1908 that there were to be no further universities in areas where there was even a significant presence of the minority people (*inorodcheski* meaning 'people not like us'). The *Duma*'s time in 1911 and 1912 was taken up largely with discussions of three issues: how to curtail the rights of the Finns; how to make the Greek-Catholic people of Chełm province in Poland join the Orthodox Church; and how to get the Polish towns to pay for their administration without being represented seriously in local government (the 'Western *Zemstvo*' question).

In each of these cases, the government was some way behind the class *Duma*. Stolypin became very unpopular with the right, and the tsar came to treat him with little respect. Even in 1909, as a result of the *Duma*'s assertion of its rights in budgetary matters, Stolypin had lost the tsar's confidence, and he was retained mainly because only he appeared to know how to manage that body. But by 1911 a new confidence had seized the tsar, and he was prepared to dispense with Stolypin. In circumstances which have never been cleared up, the prime minister was killed in a Kiev theatre in September 1911. The assassin, Mordai Bogrov, had a police pass to the (heavily guarded) place; the tsar, before the occasion, had given Stolypin a public snub. Within two years, the tsar was back to his old game of appointing catspaws: the chief minister was, once more, the aged Goremykin, who could wheeze out platitudes to the tsar's satisfaction, and who did not listen even to colleagues who supported him, let alone opposed him.

Still, by now even liberals like Milyukov were talking the language of 'healthy egoism' in national matters, using the German expression *Staatsvolk* (*Gosudarstvennaya natsiya*) to describe the Russians, an expression which the right rendered in their own way as *narod khozyayin* which translated back into *Herrenvolk*. Struve, though believing that Finns and Poles should have some kind of autonomy, also thought that that made sense only in terms of a really great Russian empire. Other liberals had made the step of conversion to Orthodoxy and to nationalism. The *Vekhi* group, consisting of Struve, the writer Bulgakov, the Kadet Izgoyev and other prominent liberals was, in Lenin's phrase, 'an encyclopedia of renegade liberalism'. By 1913–14 the *Duma* was producing huge majorities for great armaments, naval and military, and had, seemingly, acquiesced in the running-down of parliamentary government. It had split into quarrelling sub-groups, was treated with outright contempt by the tsar's ministers, and dared not do anything to assert itself.

But beneath the trumpetings of revived military autocracy, the romance of expanding factories and booming shares, there was a rise in the social conflict which worried anyone who gave it serious thought. The boom had produced inflation, of roughly forty per cent since 1908 – again a factor not at all confined to Russia, but worst there. The average industrial wage rose only from 244.7 roubles in 1908 to 263.6 in 1914, with a slight fall in between, in 1911. It of course concealed great variations: in St Petersburg a skilled metal-worker would earn rather over 500 roubles, in Moscow or the Urals a third less than that, the southern factories most of all. Here again was a factor not confined to Russia – the tendency of factory bosses to retain profits at the expense of wages – and there were industrial troubles in Russia, as everywhere else:

Year	No. of strikes	No. of strikers
1905	13,995	2,863,173
1906	6114	1,108,406
1907	3573	740,074
1908	892	176,101
1909	340	64,166
1910	222	46,623
1911	466	105,100
1912	2032	725,491
1913	2404	887,096
1914	3574	1,337,458

The factory inspectorate which took the figures consisted, for the whole of European Russia, of 150 men and women; and if Leopold Haimson is right, the incidence of strikes is underestimated by about a fifth. A modern Soviet authority states that, in 1913, there were 3000 strikes, involving 1,463,000 people.

The revival of autocracy led to continual troubles of the kind that had preceded 1905. There were strikes and riots in the universities, provoked by police handling of prisoners; the funeral of old Tolstoy, on 9 November 1910, was the signal for huge demonstrations; in February 1912 came the Lena massacre. *Lenzoto*, a company partly English, exploited a difficult goldmine on the Lena, far from the railheads, in the *tayga*. Its workers revolted; there were arrests, further protests, and finally troops were called in who, on 4 April, killed 270 people and wounded another 250. This affair led to a whole series of strikes and May Day protests, which the government dared not ban. After that, there were many overtly political strikes, as for instance in June 1913 against the proposed execution of fifty-three sailors of the Baltic fleet, in July against press restrictions, and again in the following May, when 225,000 struck at the arrest of six workers of the Obukhov factory who were to be tried for striking. Just before war broke out, St Petersburg experienced a general strike, which started on 1/14 July: 12,000 workers gathered at the Putilov factory, and the police intervened. On 3/16 July, several workers were killed, and on 4/17, 90,000 went on strike. Three days later, virtually the whole capital followed, including shops and trams, and it went on until 12/25 July, with Moscow and Riga following. The tension came to an end only when it was diverted into the great wave of patriotism in the outbreak of war.

A debate began, later, as to the significance of all this: had Bolshevism already captured the working-class movement in 1914? There are insuperable obstacles to a straightforward answer. Elections were not particularly revealing, and several factors counted against the development of trade unions in Russia, as elsewhere on the continent (Italy or

Spain being obviously comparable cases). Wages in Russia were lower than anywhere else in Europe, employment was irregular, the police were often hostile (although the technocrat Kokovtsov could see that in Germany the unions were a factor preventing workers from 'hasty and ill-considered decisions'). In St Petersburg there were only 30,000 people in unions, 7000 of them in the largest union, the *metallisty*. Often enough, the difference between one type of socialist and another at ground level was impossible to detect.

Still, a fierce quarrel divided the socialist leaders at this time. It had its counterpart in most other socialist parties. To a Lenin, in Switzerland, the whole point of socialism was to create a new world altogether: there was no point in bothering about simple, piecemeal reforms – indeed, they might be counterproductive, since existing conditions would be improved by them. There was no sense in using the social democrats' handful of *Duma* deputies to make alliances with sympathetic liberals; that body should only be used to make propaganda. There was no point in appealing to liberals – a broken reed. There was every point in raising 'revolutionary consciousness', by provoking trouble in town and country, by terror if need be, and so encouraging a police reaction that would so infuriate the working class that its revolutionary sentiments would be heightened. Money should go, not to trade-union organization, but rather to propaganda (*Pravda* was established on 22 April 1912 in the wake of the Lena affair). The more trade-union minded socialists were appalled, and tried to organize trade unions with a view to establishing the kind of power they had in Germany. Lenin accused these people of trying foolishly to 'liquidate' the class struggle by piecemeal reform, and denounced them. He split the party over this. In the wake of 1905, it had united; but by 1910 there were again strains; and in January 1912, at a conference in Prague, the strains became public. Where Mensheviks (on the whole) would use, say, the workers' sickness-benefit contributions to promote sickness benefits, Bolsheviks (on the whole) preferred to use them for revolutionary purposes. Mensheviks' confidence in Lenin was not improved when they discovered one of his leading supporters, Malinovsky, was a police informer, as was the socialist-revolutionary, Azev. Just before the First World War, Russian socialism had again been divided, with the parliamentary group splitting between seven Mensheviks, led by Chkeidze and Tsereteli, and six Bolsheviks.

To the tsar, the great ceremonies accompanying the tercentenary of the Romanov dynasty in 1913 would only confirm his conviction that his empire could be great only through autocracy. The *Duma* had collapsed into quarrelling sub-groups, capable of uniting only for great armaments. Its use, by a handful of revolutionaries, for the purposes of propaganda was dangerous; it was responsible for the wave of troubles. He planned to reduce it to a consultative capacity. He built up the army, in the 'Great Programme' of 1914, to almost 3,000,000 in peacetime, and planned a vast naval force as well. Intelligent conservatives, such as Witte and Durnovo, warned against this. So did the tsar's confidant, the 'mad monk', Rasputin. But the generals were confident enough, and so was the foreign ministry, armed with its French and British connections. In 1908, Russia had been clearly unable to contemplate war. In 1914, though with much hesitation, she would respond to a German challenge.

4. Italy

If there was a continental statesman whom the great Gladstone admired, it was Camillo Cavour, the maker of Italy. The kingdom which was created in 1861 seemed to preserve sound classical-liberal principles: free trade, education, a powerful Chamber of Deputies, a constitutional monarchy. The administration followed a French pattern, of prefects supervising locals quite closely, preventing the abuses of decentralization (theoretically) which liberals abhorred. The liberals who operated this state were sometimes good Catholics, but they disliked many aspects of the Church, not least its inflated worldly claims. They were bringers of enlightenment, and Gladstone approved of them. The Italians responded, admired England.

In actual practice, their political class grew more and more either to admire Prussia or to sympathize with Bolshevism in Russia. For Italy demonstrated the fragility of liberalism in an extreme degree. There was a considerable economic advance from 1881 onwards, as there was in Russia, but it came together with a population boom, pretentious and inglorious imperialism, a disintegration of the agrarian structure, an alienation of many intellectuals, and a rise in the temperature of the class-war, which led to violence. By 1912, Italian parliamentary life was breaking down. Fascist voices were loud, speaking for 'integral nationalism' and 'proletarian imperialism'. In Italian socialism, extremists (like Benito Mussolini, at the time) won in the congresses; a socialist leader, Leonida Bissolati, was thrown out of the party for 'attending Court' to discuss the possibility of socialists' joining the government. In May 1915, when Italy went to war at the side of the Entente, parliament was not consulted, and was shoved aside by a conspiracy of king, generals and government. At the end of the war, Italy collapsed into the *biennio rosso*, and in 1922 Fascists established a violent and dictatorial version of the counter-revolution, which supplied Hitler with examples.

As happened in Russia, the industrial growth of Italy was impressive enough after 1880. In the 1880s, the State had promoted railways and given support – through a tariff, and sometimes through direct subsidies – for iron and steel and for shipping. The early 1890s were a bad time, at least for agriculture and banks, but after 1896 Italy 'boomed' as Russia did – more impressively than any other country in Europe outside Russia, in terms of growth-rates, and yet without Russia's mineral resources. Where in 1861 there had been 9000 industrial concerns, in 1900 there were 117,000, and in 1914, 188,000. Italy's foreign trade in the first half of the 1890s was at its lowest point since 1870; but from 1896 to 1914, foreign trade went up from 2,600,000,000 lire to 5,900,000,000, a rise that was faster than Germany's. In the old days, Italy had exported agricultural produce and some luxury goods. By 1914, manufacturing had a very substantial share. Italian motor cars (*FIAT*, Lancia etc.) did well; the new technology of the 1890s also made a good showing, especially in the electrical industry, in which Italy was a leader. Camillo Olivetti's typewriters started in 1911, Agnelli in 1899, Lanza in 1898. In 1898 100,000,000 kilowatt-hours were used; in 1914, 2,575,000,000. Italy needed this because, like France, she had to import her coal, and electricity allowed the development of all kinds of new industries. Heavy industry in Italy was less impressive, but the Terni works of the 1880s were extended to take in Tuscan Piombino, Elban Portoferraio to push steel production from 100,000 tonnes in 1890 to 1,000,000 in 1914. In general, industrial output rose by eighty-seven per cent from 1901 to 1911, a third above the average European figure.

There were, as in Russia, gaps in this general picture of advance. In the early 1890s Italy had a severe banking crisis, and suffered from the worldwide decline of commodity prices. At the turn of the century, there were depressed years, and in 1908–9 the new industries employing electrical power discovered that they had been over-competing and suffered a severe, though brief, recession. The years after 1909 were 'boom' years as they were everywhere else, with the standard accompanying phenomena of inflation and stagnating wage rates. These recessions, which occurred in parallel in other places, were accompanied by political crises – Crispi's imperialist fantasies in the early 1890s, the royal semi-dictatorship of General Pelloux in 1899, the collapse of Giolitti's left-inclined 'technocracy' in 1909, and the chaotic era of imperialism and class-war which ended in 1915, with the declaration of war.

There were not many mysteries as to Italian economic growth. The 'Great Depression' had slowly wrecked traditional agriculture and handicrafts: cheap grain from abroad, and cheap textiles, put an end to local economies. The government responded by promoting industry – iron and steel, railways etc. The banks were forced to take a different view of their activities, because the 'old' no longer made a profit. Some of them indulged in wild speculation in the Roman building boom of the 1880s, printed their own money (illegally) to finance it, and crashed resoundingly in 1891–2. The German example of 'mixed banks', which borrowed short and lent long, to industry, was then taken up with dramatic effects. At the same time, there was a flight from the land (including emigrants who amounted to 300,000 per annum before the war) which in some places forced agriculture to change. New estates in the lower Po valley, around Mantua and Rovigo, were built up with migrant labour, and the output of agriculture rose by one-third from 1896 to 1914, though the fraction of the working people employed in it fell from three-fifths to two-fifths. It greatly helped, of course, that commodity prices were on a long up-turn after 1896.

Given that northern Italy – Lombardy, Venetia and Piedmont – had a long tradition of skilled artisan-working, it was not surprising that once the artisans were pushed out of old ways, they could adapt skills to sophisticated industries. Prato, near Florence in Tuscany, had an unbroken tradition of economic 'seriousness' that went back to the early Middle Ages. After the recessions, Italian industry also 'cartellized', as most other European industries did. The *Istituto cotoniere* regulated cotton output; the *Unione Zuccheri* sugar-beet, like *Tsentrosakhar* in Russia; ILVA, emerging at the turn of the century, though not fully-fledged until 1911, covered much of iron and steel, and dealt with the Germans with a view to quotas. As in Russia, there was a dramatic rise in bank deposits – partly from new 'creative' lending, and partly from the withdrawal of savings hitherto kept in a sock. These deposits rose five times from 1899 to 1914. Savings, which had been nine per cent of the GNP in 1897, were sixteen per cent of it in 1914.

As in Russia, this rapid economic advance was imposed on a society that had been generally backward in 1870, with a sixth of the per capita income of France. Industrial towns such as Turin or Milan expanded very fast. For reasons not dissimilar to Russian circumstances, trade unions could not recruit widely. They were virtually banned until the early 1880s (in Depretis's left-leaning phase) and did not flourish as in Germany because of irregular employment, low wages, mistrust of union managers. True, the northern industries had a long tradition, and expanded fast enough to have a union tradition for some trades (inevitably, the printers) in the 1870s. These were tight little bodies, almost guild-like in their attitudes; and they disliked the patronizing intellectuals so much that they would not take the word 'socialist' in the early 1880s when they began to form a political group, the *Partito operaio italiano*. It was only in the crisis of the 1890s, with bank failures and political scandals abounding, that this crisis was resolved. At Genoa in 1892 an Italian socialist party was formed, though the name *Partito socialista italiano* was not used until 1895.

The intellectuals, such as Filippo Turati, son of a Catholic prefect, had great trouble in defeating the anarchists, many of whom would not join this bourgeois-dominated party. In fact, anarchists had an organization of their own. Osvaldo Gnocchi-Viani had learned about the *Bourses du travail* in France when he saw the *Exposition* of 1889 and joined with other socialists in promoting a new (Second) International. He proposed these institutions for Italy. Some municipalities helped, on the grounds that these institutions (in Italy, *Camere del lavoro*) could act as employment exchanges, though they also had 'recreation-facilities'. The anarchists took over these 'facilities', established a federation of *Camere del lavoro*, and used them, not as places to inspire particular craft unions, but rather as centres of agitation for the working class as a whole.

A degree or two further on, and these would have been soviets. By 1901, there were some ninety in northern Italy, breeding-grounds for 'anarcho-syndicalism'. Maybe their importance was exaggerated, but they did serve as meeting places for migrant and irregularly employed workers who could, there, rediscover people from their own home villages. Anarcho-syndicalists used them, and worried the trade unions. By 1900, the trade unions, fearing that they would lose potential recruits, joined their own organization, the *Confederazione generale del lavoro*, with that of the *Camere del lavoro*. But there was still a considerable division between them.

The trade unions were quite weak. Even in 1907, they contained 670,000 people only, a quarter of them in agrarian unions, and by 1914 they had still not reached the million mark. They were heavily concentrated in the north, the industrial 'triangle' of Turin-Genoa-Milan. Their power was very local, although, since they could lame important industries, it had to be respected. They had a certain capacity, even in the later 1890s and early 1900s, for attracting a large following – partly through the *Camere del lavoro* – and for proclaiming a strike which, since the police intervened very harshly, did 'raise proletarian consciousness' – as was unquestionably the case with the general strike of September 1904, called to protest against a local prefect's handling of a *Camera del lavoro* in Genoa. 'Five minutes of direct action have done more than ten years of parliamentary chattering,' said Errico Ferri, a revolutionary stalwart, to the applause of a Lenin or a Rosa Luxemburg. But the basis of such activities was that trade unions had not grown far enough to take on the kind of bureaucratic and administrative activities that distinguished trade unions in more 'mature' economies.

For Italian socialism, matters were complicated by the existence of a large peasant class which offered potential support. Of course, for socialists to court the peasantry was not Marxism as the Prussians understood it: Kautsky detested peasants in much the same way as Marx, most of the time, had done. But in Latin Europe, a link between the countryside and socialism was far from unimaginable. In the Romagna, especially, 'primitive rebels' had a long history;

there, in the 1870s and 1880s, anarchists had been at work. In the new estates of the Po valley, immigrant agricultural workers, *braccianti*, found themselves huddled together in villages that lacked schools, churches or proper housing. In Tuscany, towards the end of the nineteenth century, the old system of share-cropping, *mezzadria*, was breaking down. The head of the extended family, the *capoccio*, was losing his authority; the landowner tended to screw up his demands, and to shorten his leases; his agents behaved more tyrannically; and the presence of industrial centres such as Piombino or Livorno meant that socialist doctrines could penetrate the countryside. By 1919–20, Tuscany had become 'red' – as, in large measure, it still is. The extent of socialist penetration of the countryside was such that Emilia even became 'red' before its chief city, Bologna, did.

Still, Italian socialism had practically nothing to say about what was in many ways its greatest challenge, the south; in this, the socialists, as so often, were only repeating the experience of the liberals, who had similarly been bewildered. Southern Italy and Sicily were lands of great estates – in the 1870s, there were seventy of them in Sicily alone, containing over five thousand acres. The land was usually unrewarding, and irrigation, outside a few favoured areas, was extremely limited; and although the great estates did not usually function at all well, at least they guaranteed some kind of central organization. *Latifondo* and *minifondo* buttressed each other. In the latter part of the nineteenth century, the old landowning system ran down, much as it did in other countries. The cities filled up with rejects from the countryside, who lived crammed together in the *fondaci* of Naples. There was an epidemic of banditry. In the countryside, the poverty horrified northern inquirers, who would find people dressed in goatskins.

The 'Great Depression' in most other countries at least caused new life to emerge from the wreckage of the old. But in the Italian south, that new life emerged only very thinly; much of the area fell into fantasy. The educational system did not work at all well, not least because the southerners' language was a long way removed from Tuscan. Truancy amounted to two-thirds in Calabria, and in Sicily to over half. Illiteracy in some areas was nearly total. Taxes were not paid: in Calabria, seizures of property in lieu of tax amounted to one case in 114, whereas in Lombardy the figure was one in 27,416. The ills of Sicily could not even be laid at the door of the Church, since it, too, was next to powerless in most of the land. In the years 1892–4 Sicily erupted in a series of riots, the *Fasci Siciliani*, in which the petty bourgeoisie of the cities joined hands with workmen from the sulphur mines (who had lost their French market because of synthetics) and with peasants. The country passed, for a time, into chaos: sackings of tax-offices, assassinations of officials, plundering of stores. An *exalté*, De Felice Giuffrida, led crowds of peasants who, to the utter bewilderment of northern observers, carried portraits of the king and queen, of Garibaldi, and Karl Marx.

Socialists did not know what to make of this. Even Labriola, who was himself a Neapolitan, described the *Fasci* as 'Romagnolo banditry, only worse – a mixture of socialism, anarchism, careerism and the *mafia*'. In reality, the *Fasci* came from an old enough tradition of 'primitive rebellion', which had last surfaced in the widespread outbreak of brigandage in the south in the 1860s: then, bandit chiefs had advertised their loyalty to the dethroned Bourbon dynasty. Now, there were new socialist elements in the brigandage. But, on the whole, the Italian socialists did not wish for such alliances. Their 'Church' in Milan – as southerners dismissed the party leadership – took much the same line as the Mensheviks in Russia as regards peasant uprisings.

The socialist party itself divided between 'reformists' and 'revolutionaries' as all other European socialist parties divided. The revolutionaries' case was plain enough: no good to be expected from bourgeois society, therefore pull it down. The reformists' language was also quite deducible from first principles. A Bissolati could easily demonstrate that in Italian circumstances, a socialist vote in the chamber would bring about such-and-such a sympathetic government, with reforms in consequence. These two sides quarrelled at party conferences, and produced the expressions *massimalisti* and *minimalisti* which meant much the same thing as 'Bolshevik' and 'Menshevik' though not directly so. The party, like the German one, produced its strong 'centre' of intellectual northerners – Filippo Turati above all, who dominated it. They were determined to keep the party together. That meant preventing a Bissolati from going too far in the direction of alliance with bourgeois liberals; it also meant reining in the maniacs of the left, Errico Ferri, Antonio Labriola, ('a German, born by mistake in Naples', as he informed Engels) and in the end Mussolini. Up to the First World War, the party's tendency was unquestionably revolutionary, although from 1905 to 1912 the congresses passed 'reformist' votes, disapproving of strikes for political purposes. By the later 1890s, there was a wave of protest in Milan; it was incompetently crushed by a military régime, that of General Pelloux, in the *fatti di maggio* of 1898, when there were 500 casualties and 828 trials. After 1908, the rising revolutionary temper was clear enough:

Year	No. of strikes	No. of strikers
1899	400	
1900	1700	
1901	1671	420,000
1902	1042	197,000
1904	839 (231 agrarian)	210,000
1906	1649 (350 agrarian)	382,000 (118,000)
1907	1891	327,000
1908	1474	316,000
after a fall, post-recession, in 1909 and 1910		
1911	1255	327,000

Italian liberalism of the classical type – which still surfaced with the aged Saracco as prime minister in 1900 – was almost powerless against this phenomenon. The radicals in the

1880s had tried to deal with it partly by extending the franchise a little, and mainly by organizing a tariff, so that jobs would be protected and the government would have some money to spend. The strange figure of Francesco Crispi, a one-time republican who, in the later 1880s, became Depretis's successor, practised Italian imperialism in the hope that the problem of poverty and overpopulation would literally go away. In A.J.P. Taylor's words, he made Italy run in the hope that she would learn to walk. But his policies came to grief in 1896, when an Italian invasion of Abyssinia failed at Adua – not enough money for the army, hence a disaster, just as happened in other similar ventures elsewhere. After that, an effort was made to come to terms with Sicily, in that a Sicilian aristocrat, di Rudinì, emerged with a programme of decentralization. This led to nothing in particular; and the rising social temper prompted the king to name a general, Pelloux, in 1898. His tactics ('boom') were wholly counterproductive: the Chamber of Deputies would not follow him when he tried to rule by decree, and the massacres in Milan in 1898 merely made the masses more radical. In 1901, the monarchy called on radical liberals to find common ground with the masses, and first Zanardelli and then, late in 1902, Giovanni Giolitti were called in. The period up to the First World War was dominated by Giolitti, though his dominance was clearly weakening after 1909.

The greatness of liberal Italy had always been Cavourian, i.e., honest and hard-working makers of the State, who were prepared to override local interests for the sake of Progress. Giolitti came from this tradition, for he had been born in 1842 at Mondovi in Piedmont. He was a hard-working and ascetic, almost puritanical, legal bureaucrat. His political views were quite radical. In the early 1880s, when part of Depretis's *trasformista* government, he had resigned (as his colleague Zanardelli did) over the government's failure to bring in an income tax – which would have offended the rich – and a divorce law, which would have offended the Church. He resigned again from Crispi's government in 1889, as minister of the treasury, over frivolous financial management. He acquired, thereby, the support of liberal economists, men such as Pantaleone and Luzzatti, in the *Giornale degl' economisti*, who spoke for free trade, left-leaning liberalism. Giolitti also acquired respect on the left in general. In 1897–8 he had a public row with the 'Prussian' upholder of the right, Sidney Sonnino, who was arguing for a solution of the upheavals by force, and remarked, 'I deplore the class-war as much as others. But let us be fair: who started it?'

Giolitti's great strength was that he could talk to the left; in an almost revolutionary upheaval, such as the last two years of the century, when King Umberto himself was shot by an anarchist at Monza, Giolitti appeared to be the only way forward. Until 1912, he did in practice gain official, though tacit, socialist support.

But he had another essential ability: he could manage the kind of parliament that Italy by now was producing, parliaments where actual policies came to mean very little, and where parties as such barely existed. Until 1882 (Depretis) the vote had been very restricted, to five per cent of the population, and after Depretis to ten per cent. Even then, there was much abstention. In northern Italy, which had great cities (and rather more than a third of the 500 deputies), elections were usually open battles. Northern Italy's deputies divided, as might be expected from a limited-suffrage parliament in the early years of this century, along lines not unlike the Prussian *Landtag*: about sixty classical liberals grouped around Sonnino and nominated in rich constituencies; about the same number of Catholic deputies; and the same again for the left-liberals of the *Estrema*, with two dozen socialists to make up their number. These left liberals, 'republicans' or 'radicals', descended from the democrats of the 1850s, but, as happened everywhere else, they became 'respectable' in the 1900s, and, as usual, divided. The politics of central Italy were wild. Its hundred seats went only very partially to the same groups seen in the north (Rome produced a Jewish liberal mayor, Nathan, in 1900) for socialism was picked up as a cause for

areas that had ostensibly no business to be voting socialist –
regional autonomists in Ancona, protesting against taxation
and conscription; the countryside in Emilia, protesting at the
domination of Bologna. The other seats went to straightforward nominees of the local political machine, and they called
themselves *ministeriali*. Virtually all of the 200 deputies of the
south, and half of the central ones, came in this category.

In the later 1870s, the classical liberals of Cavour's *Destra*
had divided over railway nationalization, tariffs, finance. A
section of them had taken up alliance with the radical liberals
of the *Sinistra* – the alliance that produced, first, Cairoli and
then Depretis. These men, many of them from the south,
had started life as violent anti-clericals and even republicans.
They were 'transformed' by office into upholders of order
and empire. Their landowning bosses, beset by the economic
crisis, made an alliance with the tariff-minded northern
industrialists. This was the basis of Depretis's long domination of politics. Crisis in 1885–6 overthrew him; but he was
replaced by a figure not wholly different, Crispi, whose
government, briefly interrupted in 1892–3 by Giolitti's first
ministry, lasted until 1896.

Crispi had started off as an extreme radical in the 1850s.
He had been violently anti-clerical (to the point of commit-
ting bigamy), and he had the austere style of many
mid-nineteenth-century radicals (he died very poor). But,
like so many other radicals at this time, he had been
converted to the cause of imperialism, and took up links with
Germany so as to have Bismarck's (and later Great Britain's)
support for Mediterranean adventures. In home affairs, he
tried to square circles. He offered anti-clericalism to buy
northern support in matters of education, a high tariff to buy
agrarian support. He also continued where Depretis had left
off, and significantly reduced the powers of the prefects: he
allowed communes to elect their own mayor. In the north,
this perhaps did not matter very much. In the centre and
south, it meant that the older *notabili* were displaced, and
'new men', the *galantuomini*, took their place. It was a step

which turned power in the Italian Chamber over to the grubbiest elements in the south.

In southern Italy, it was said, 'the only industry is power'. In the 1880s and 1890s, the old landowning system of the south ran down. The *Fasci Siciliani* were evidence of that. Basilicata or Calabria were horrifyingly poor; in Sicily, leprous churches, an eroded countryside, crumbling great estates and communal agriculture produced nothing but children and, more and more, crime. A thin layer of parasites stood in for a bourgeoisie except in the largest cities, where there were more solid figures who demonstrated that it was after all possible to make a certain sum of money out of the very poor. The industries supported by the old kingdom of Naples and Sicily had collapsed once tariff-barriers against the north came down. Not much took their place. Messina exported citrus juice, and produced it by the most rudimentary methods even in the 1900s: men, women and boys huddled in a torrid yard, slicing the lemons, pummelling them, and squeezing them by hand into a jug, which would then have the pips picked out by sieving. If a business made any profit, it would be at the mercy of the local protection-racket. In 1902 there were two trials – one on the murder, by a Sicilian deputy, Palizzolo, of an incorruptible banker; one on the cover-up by a Neapolitan official, Casale. The Naples administration was dismissed fourteen times from 1861 to 1906.

The election of mayors by their own communes, in such circumstances, was simply an invitation to the local 'new men' to take some of the government's powers for themselves, and to augment their systems of clientage. It meant, in effect, that southern deputies would often be chosen for their capacity to 'lean' on the government and start horse-trading. One sign of this came in the elections of 1891. Crispi's government had a majority of 400. It then failed to roll logs properly. It lost a vote of confidence, within a week of the first session, by 400 votes. After Crispi's fall, his conservative successor, the marchese di Rudinì, endeavoured to shore up the landowners' power in the south, by decentralization – so that the growing link of *galantuomo* and government could be broken. He, too, lost 'confidence'. The king, in desperation, turned to his generals and then, in still greater desperation, his son turned to the radical-liberal 'technocrats'.

Giolitti inherited the strange result of Italian unification, that the south conquered the north. He, like Crispi, had to square circles. He had to content the *ministeriali*; he had to stop the socialists from suspending great parts of the country's economic life; he had to show the radicals of the north that he would promote education and modernization. He had also to deal with a new element in politics, clericalism – the origins of *Democrazia Cristiana*.

The Italian liberals had been violently anti-clerical, and had had a long running battle with the Pope, secluded in his Vatican 'prison', where he even rebuked cardinals for responding to Italian military salutes. But the mobilization of the Italian lower classes in politics gave the Church, in the 1890s, a very strong hand, and the Germans' political-Catholic machine showed the way. The Pope had, as a matter of principle, decreed that Catholics should not recognize the liberal State, but in practice he could not stop them from taking part in its affairs – at one level, to prevent a law on divorce, at another, to take advantage of the extension of local government. Industrialists like the bicycle-manufacturer, Prinetti, or the textile-owners of Brescia and the Veneto – who closely resembled the austere Catholic industrialists of Roubaix or Tourcoing in France – were only too anxious to have a political group. By 1905, the Pope needed Italian support in his quarrel with France; he encouraged the new clericals to join the Chamber ('not as Catholic deputies, but as deputed Catholics'). Leo XIII had already produced a famous encyclical, *Rerum Novarum*, in 1893, in which he spoke for 'social Catholicism'.

Italy thus acquired her own equivalent of the German *Zentrumspartei*, and somewhat later it was formally organized as the *Partito popolare italiano*. Some of its chiefs, especially Dom Sturzo, talked the language of social reform. This was a party with a strongly agrarian base in northern areas such as Bergamo. Since 1886, priests had been organizing savings associations and promoting the *cattedre ambulanti* which showed peasants how to use fertilizer. The party was frequently at odds with local notables, and promoted, in such cases, its own lower-middle-class candidates. It had a vociferous left wing; indeed, one of its priests, Murri, sat for a time on the socialist benches. It talked of land reform. One of its spokesmen, the Pisan professor Toniolo, worked out a complicated way round the class-war which involved the re-creation of guilds – *corporazioni*. To this, Mussolini owed his expression 'the corporate State' (which in practice meant a useless bureaucracy with the useless law degrees that have bedevilled Italy ever since).

With the complication of the grasping southern placemen, Italian politics therefore came to involve a group of varying sorts of liberals, a Catholic group, and, on the left, some fifty socialists (1909). If Giolitti united the northerners, he could outvote his own southern 'supporters'. He could block the Catholics by taking up an alliance in the south and, partly, with the left. He could silence the liberals simply by throwing responsibility at them. From time to time, the Chamber would become restive at Giolitti's long domination. Giolitti would then adopt a measure which he knew had no chance of success – a progressive income tax being his favourite – in order to improve his credibility on the left. He would be outvoted. Some liberal successor would come in – Sonnino in 1905–6, Fortis in 1909–10, Luzzatti in 1912, Salandra in 1914. They would last for a few months at most, since they lacked Giolitti's extraordinary capacity for remembering a man's price.

Giolitti benefited from the 'boom' of this era. Public revenues doubled. Giolitti put up the spending of the ministry of public works from 69,000,000 lire in 1901 to 123,000,000 in 1908 and 465,000,000 in 1912. This involved road-building and land-reclamation. He consulted the trade unions over this, and, in Emilia, handed them the responsibility. Sums sent to Messina after its horrifying earthquake were directed to local placemen, with predictable results. The ministry of posts and telegraphs, and the ministry of transport, were quite clearly targets for the political machines. They involved the appointment of countless small jobs in the State service, and hence were vital to the placemen and, increasingly, also to the clericals. Bonomi's 'Party of Social Credit' really existed only to obtain the post office by astute parliamentary manoeuvring, regardless of any actual issue. It was not even as if the parties had much coherence. Within them all, there were serious disagreements as to which alliances should be taken up. In one area, Catholics and liberals would co-operate; in another, liberals and left; in much of the south, liberals and placemen, or Catholics and placemen. Thus, groups within parties would break away from party policy if it risked offending their local allies. When issues involving matters such as shipping subsidies, or railway nationalization, or the nationalization of all forms of insurance – three great questions of Giolitti's time – came up, there were weird parliamentary combinations, to be ex- plained only in terms of extremely venal local practices. The fact was that much of the bureaucracy, i.e. the local prefects, now depended for their jobs on a ministry of the interior which could be occupied, or leaned on, by parties with a wholly local, often corrupt, interest. The bureaucracy became venal as well, though less so in the north than in the south. It connived at open electoral malpractice, such as the Molfetta bye-election of 1911, when the placemen's thugs kept opponents away by clubbing them.

This system began to disintegrate in 1910. The process of inflation was marked, in Italy, as in Russia; there were troubles accordingly in countryside and towns alike. The socialists swung back to a revolutionary line, dismissing Bissolati for trying to shore up the better aspects of the Giolittian system. Ancona, and other towns, experienced 'Red Week' in June 1914. Giolitti's initial answer to the disintegration of politics – which went beyond even his capacity for remembering prices – was simply to sit back. He did nothing during great strikes (just as in 1921 he went on holiday abroad in his last period as prime minister, when a general strike occurred). His only answer was to make politics still more complicated, and he promoted a bill for universal suffrage which, it was thought, would gain him Catholic and socialist support. The election of 1912 did in fact return seventy socialists and a mass Catholic party in the north, though in the south 'abstention' was considerable, and the placemen survived in force as 'liberals'.

It was a situation that could drive anyone of honesty to despair. The socialist revolutionary wing, which promised root-and-branch destruction of the system, attracted many intellectuals. Honest liberals often retired into hopeless pessimism. Others relapsed into hedonism, a rather sad aesthetics also characteristic of Vienna. Still others followed D'Annunzio and supposed that, since thought produced nothing beyond despair, the answer must be mindless activity, imperialist nationalism. From 1908, a group in Florence with a newspaper, *La Voce*, spoke a language of hysterical nationalism and tyranny: the precursors of Fascism.

When Crispi's system had disintegrated in the 1890s, he had indulged in imperialism. The creation of a foreign crisis would, he hoped, show how the government must not be upset: even the placemen might heed a patriotic appeal, especially if there were victories. Giolitti did the same, in 1911. After the second Morocco crisis, the Western Powers were at odds with Germany; each side bid for Italy's favour. The Russians, after a meeting in 1909 at Racconigi between Sazonov and Tittoni, Giolitti's foreign minister, sought Italian support for their own plans regarding the Straits. In the autumn of 1911 the Italians invaded Tripolitania, Libya, which, after trouble, they retained (treaty of Lausanne). This escapade whetted appetites. The army saw itself as bastion of order in the State; nationalists became worked up over the fate of *Italia irredenta*, the Italian-inhabited areas of Austria, and the Dalmatian inheritance of Venice. It looked as if Italian intervention would finish the Habsburg Monarchy in a few weeks. True, the Chamber of Deputies, in majority, objected. But few Italians had much time for these deputies. A combination of backstairs manoeuvring of king, army government and an orchestration of violent mobs demanding war swept the deputies aside. On 23 May 1915, Italy and Austria-Hungary went to war. It was not at all as easy as the generals thought. The war on the Isonzo was as horrifying and difficult as the war in the west; it proved to be the final step in the disintegration of liberal Italy.

5. *France*

The Third Republic stood out in Europe of the later nineteenth century as the only country where aristocracy was not predominant in politics. After the strange era of the *République des ducs* in the 1870s, the State was very consciously bourgeois. This was shown in an institution which, everywhere else, was extremely aristocratic, the diplomatic service. Even French ambassadors were sometimes middle-class. Their Russian colleagues, despite the Franco-Russian alliance, usually preferred their German opposite numbers. In London in 1914 the Austro-Hungarian ambassador, Count Mensdorff-Pouilly-Dietrichstein, the German ambassador, Prince Lichnowsky, and the Russian ambassador, Count Benckendorff, were cousins; they stood apart from their French colleague, Paul Cambon, who, like his brother Jules in Berlin or Maurice Paléologue – the archetypal 'funny little man' – in St Petersburg, was the unmistakable product of 'meritocracy'.

The Republic, hastily proclaimed in the confusions of 1870, acquired shape only with the constitution of 1875, and was free of clerical and *notable* domination only at the end of the 1870s. Almost by definition, it was 'bourgeois', since republics were free of the formal monarchies and aristocracies which, elsewhere, justified themselves on the grounds of good government. The French Republic, looking to its distinguished Dutch, Swiss and American predecessors as much as to the original Roman Republic that had inspired them all, was supposed to be a state in which one individual was as good as the next. It catered for the responsible self-government of the self-reliant individual, and its institutions were designed so that tyrannous régimes could not recur. It gave the United States the Statue of Liberty.

It was this principle which, in part, made the Republic's politics so confused. From 1870 to 1940 there were 108 governments (as against fifteen in Great Britain). Deputies could, on a 'snap' vote, overturn any government. The deputies themselves were so disorganized that no one could tell which way a particular group of them might go. In 1910 the *Chambre* tried to set up groups, and ten emerged, of which 'independents' were a prominent one. The others were hopelessly prone to splitting, and parties other than the socialist one had a very sketchy existence. The prime minister was unknown in law until 1934, and the president of the Republic had very little power. This system, bizarre as it seemed, worked quite well until 1914. Many people from other European countries would much rather have been born in France.

The French system of government, anomalous as it appeared, in an age of monarchies, was the expression of an old dream of radical liberals: the State looked after public utilities, education and defence, and then left people to get on with their own affairs. Parliament was an assembly of representatives of free men with some property; its powers were such that aristocratic, military and clerical tyrannies were ruled out. Of course there was a right, a left and a centre in France, and their roles in politics – their divisions, alliances, realignments over the main questions of the age – were not really very different from their counterparts in other parliamentary countries. Thus, in the first half of the 1890s, there were several confusing attempts, as in Germany under Caprivi, to come to terms with the social question: Tirard offering a reduced tariff, Freycinet a larger military effort, Dupuy the closure of the Paris *Bourse du travail*, Léon

Bourgeois co-operatives (*Mutualité*), Casimir-Périer the anti-'anarchist' *lois scélérates* etc. with other 'caretaker' ministries merely keeping going, while Jacques Méline endeavoured to build up an industrial-agrarian bloc based on a high tariff (1892) and *anti-Dreyfusard* imperialism (1896–8). In Germany, Italy or Great Britain, not to mention smaller countries, these issues came up within the framework of a single government. In France, the peculiarities of the system meant that the issues came up separately, under a series of short-lived governments which often contained the same personnel.

Governmental instability in France was not wholly dissimilar to Italian experience, and had similar causes. A deputy, with his extremely local interests in mind, would try to lean on the minister of the interior for some favour or other – the building of a road, a school-loan, decorations for his clients etc. If the minister did not give him what he wanted, he would join the ranks of the 'Outs'; without serious reference to any of the great issues of the day (imperialism, income tax, social reform etc.) he would try to overthrow the government on some 'snap' vote or other. As in Italy, political chieftains who understood the game and had considerable personal charisma would organize these men. Personal allegiance to a Clemenceau, 'the Tiger', cut across party boundaries.

But this process had far stricter limitations than in Italy or Spain. There, parliamentary politics became a game some way removed from important national concerns, and, in the post-war confusions, both countries fell under Fascism. In France, there was real universal male suffrage, and hence far less *caciquismo*, i.e., domination of local politics by a 'boss'. There was not much political violence. There was a puritanical republican intelligentsia. The Senate acted as a serious obstacle to governmental tyranny. The bureaucracy was not, on the whole, venal and, though there were some spectacular miscarriages of justice (in 1907 a man who tried to assassinate Dreyfus was sentenced to three months' imprisonment) the law could not be bought and sold. French deputies might often overthrow governments on trivial pretexts, but there was a left, centre and right which split, allied, realigned according to the important national issues (taxation, social reform, education, imperialism etc.) in ways that make French politics – if we judge in 'sets' of governments – not dissimilar, in pattern, from the politics of other European states that were rich and had a wide franchise.

Still, there were important differences. France broke many of the European 'rules'. Virtually everywhere else, liberals ceased to make up a majority in the parliaments in the 1880s: they were outnumbered by right (conservatives and clericals) and left (socialists) in combination. In France, this did not happen. The right and left took, between them, about two-fifths of the *Chambre des Députés*. It was possible for governments of the centre to go on and on – almost as one-party government, without the disciplines that serious opposition might have imposed. The governments changed frequently, but the ministers did not. Up to 1879, when men of the right had been in charge, there were sixty-three ministers, of whom only five served again. But from 1871 to 1914, there were in all 561 ministers, of whom 217 served in one government only, 103 in two, 71 in three, 48 in four, and 122 in five or more. Governments were central ones, though sometimes, to escape from excessive dependence on their own grasping supporters, they could move in a particular minister to make an appeal to right or left, and so dispense with the votes of some of their own followers. On the whole, the Third Republic was a régime of centre and left, with the right in opposition – not the usual European story at this time. It was only towards the end of the century, especially with Jacques Méline, that 'class-war' began to push centre and right together; and the process became clear only after 1910, when it caused great convulsions and the most rapid change-over of governments in the Republic's history (ten in four years).

By 1910, the sense of national emergency and the emerging menace from the left were such that serious politicians of the centre wished to have 'serious' government. The *Chambre* itself was forced to set up parties (ten groups resulted, the 'independents' being quite large). To end the dependence of governments on locally interested deputies from the *petites mares stagnantes* of remote constituencies, Aristide Briand made a great effort to impose proportional representation. In 1913, Raymond Poincaré was elected president, with a brief to increase the powers of his office. These steps were bitterly opposed, by a variety of clever devices, and, when war came, the political system of the Republic was in some disrepair.

It was, then, the emergence and survival of a centre so strong that it could dispense with formal disciplines that marked the Third Republic. Right and left were much weaker than elsewhere. This clearly reflected the social and economic conditions of France in this era. She was not a country of big business and trade unions. She broke many European rules. The population went up only marginally, from 36,000,000 to 39,000,000, at a time when other countries' populations doubled. At that, France supplied few emigrants, and took over a million immigrants. Yet she remained much more heavily 'peasant' than other Great Powers. In 1910, fifty-six per cent of the French were still living in places with fewer than two thousand inhabitants; she fell from second to fourth place among the industrial countries (overtaken by Germany and Russia, by an increasingly long head). Elsewhere, such a preponderance of peasants would have made countries poor. But France was rich: her wage levels behind England's, but above Germany's. She exported £2,000,000,000 in capital (to the British £4,000,000,000) or almost twice as much as Germany. In other countries, the high proportion of peasants would almost automatically have meant that politics varied from reaction to revolution. In France, the centre ruled, and its divisions dictated the political pattern.

France owed much of her character to her synthesis of two civilizations, Mediterranean and Atlantic, and that fundamental division underlay the Third Republic as well – as with the expression, '*c'est le Nord qui travaille et le Midi qui gouverne'*. Still, even here there were peculiarities. The base of French Protestantism was in the south, Languedoc; and many of the great industrial dynasties of the *Nord*, such as the Mottes of Roubaix, were austerely Catholic, to the point where, in Belgium and northern France, Max Weber's thesis falls on deaf ears. Regional oddities, inherited from the *ancien régime* and not blurred by 'modernization' as happened elsewhere, make generalization in French history a hazardous business. In the Doubs, a single village stood out politically because it elected candidates of the left, from Ledru-Rollin in 1848 to the communists after 1945; its neighbours voted for the right. No one could see any reason for this except that the village had had a republican priest in the revolution.

The tradition of the sturdy independent in industry and agriculture survived so strongly in France that socialism had to grow into it, adapt, and lose some of its industrial character. Large-scale industrial development was much less than in Germany. In the middle of the nineteenth century, France had acquired metal and textile industries using what was then known as 'the machine-system': there were obvious markets for both, and obvious sources for them to draw on. France needed to import a third of her coal, and did not, for some time, produce nearly enough of her own, which may have held back industrial development. Industry was confined to the *Nord*, parts of the east, the Rhône valley, and pockets elsewhere, such as the semi-rural mines of the Loire. On the whole, it stagnated in the 1880s, and large parts of it were quite stagnant thereafter as well. The economy grew at a slow rate – barely above one per cent during the Third Republic to 1914.

The reason for this was not, in the first instance, hard to find. France was peculiar among the industrial countries in that she was so heavily peasant. The proportion of her population which lived in towns rose from thirty-three to forty-four per cent in this whole period, and much of the growth was confined to Marseilles, Lyons and Paris – in contrast to Great Britain or Germany, where there were several very large cities by 1914. Although these were great modern cities, they concealed the reality that in France most people lived directly or indirectly from agriculture. Only one person in twenty lived outside the *département* of their birth, as against one in seven even in Russia. There had of course been a flight from the land – perhaps 800,000 people in the later 1870s and rather less than that in the later 1890s, but it was nonsense for a Jacques Méline, making propaganda for his tariff, to talk of *le désert français*. The villages did change – they lost many of their artisans during the 'Great Depression', since they were undercut from nearby towns, overcompeted, and could find jobs elsewhere. But the villages remained powerful. In 1906, over two out of five Frenchmen lived from farming, and another one in five lived from supplying them. The small country town (Céline's 'Eurcques sur Ourcques') survived well in France.

The real peculiarity of the Third Republic was the vast number of small market towns of from 5000 to 25,000 inhabitants – a feature inherited from the eighteenth century. They included several *chefs-lieux de département*, such as Tulle, Guéret, Gap, Rodez, Saint-Lô, Carcassonne. This feature counted especially in the Midi, hence the great numbers of politicians from there. France after 1890 was a southern republic.

France became a classic peasant country, where farmers worked small plots with their families: the republicans' dream. There had been 10,290,000 pieces of land in 1826; by 1881 there were 14,300,000. The amount of land held by properties above forty hectares ran down from 22,000,000 hectares in 1882 to 16,300,000 in 1908 as small properties took it up. In Great Britain, 2184 owners, with over 5000 acres each, had half of the country; in France, 50,000 owners with over 250 acres each had quarter. The extent of peasant ownership had still not reached Henry George's ideal in France, and the nobles survived quite well in some places – Maine, Anjou and Poitou in particular – while in three *départements* – Hautes-Alpes, Cher, Bouches-du-Rhône – the estates had over half of the surface, and in eleven others, including Var, not far short of half. But, generally, the large estates in a good third of the country, and to some extent beyond that, discovered a truth that their Russian equivalents knew far better: that if the potential labourers had small plots of their own, then these plots would come first. The battle had really been lost in the 1840s, if not before, and the 'Great Depression' completed it. By 1900, roughly a third of the country was held by substantial farms, such as the 8000 in Seine-et-Marne which supplied Paris, and the other two-thirds were divided between middling-sized and small farms. Smallholdings were naturally predominant in the poor soils – Creuse, Corrèze, Ardèche etc. There was, in France, nothing to resemble the huge landowning of Great Britain or Prussia, even though up to 1914 landed property still counted for more in politics than banking.

The strength of the 'sturdy peasant' with his own plot had many consequences. The first was that, in the small country towns, small family firms survived to supply agriculture and its dependants: whether with 'tertiary-sector' services or with goods that the peasants needed. Large industrial firms existed only in the industrial regions of the *Nord*; elsewhere, small firms predominated. The *patente* tax, paid by 1,750,000 'independent' shopkeepers in 1870, was paid by 2,300,000 in 1906 – almost twice the figure for the whole of Russia, although the French population had not risen by very much since 1870. Even in 'industry' so many workers were in fact independent artisans that a quarter of 'workers' declared themselves 'self-employed'. The situation would not change substantially until transport allowed cheap mass-produced goods to penetrate the countryside – which did not occur until the later 1930s.

The basis of the whole structure was simple enough. If the independents had had many children, their properties would have been subdivided, and would have become unworkable; besides, there would have been too many mouths to feed, a situation painfully taken out on French daughters. In Lot-et-Garonne, families were offered condolences at the birth of a second child. The unique French property structure depended on a limitation in numbers of children, which eventually produced a population decline between the wars. By 1891, there were alarms. A Dr Bertillon wondered what the government could do. There was a periodical on contraception called *La Génération consciente*, French equivalent of 'family planning'. The Church worried, and reproved the men, whose anti-clericalism will not have been lessened by the reproof. According to Eugen Weber, in the more primitive regions abortions were fed to the pigs. One counterpart to all of this was the ferocious saving of the French: 2,000,000,000 francs per annum. The rural masses often kept their savings in the legendary sock or mattress. Urban savers used the many savings institutions – not 'banks', which was a dirty word since the days of John Law's bold experimentation in paper money, but *caisses*, which were required to behave prudently with the money, and did so, to the apparent detriment of French industry.

In the 1880s France, not unlike Italy or Russia, with their great agrarian masses, stagnated. But the 'Great Depression' did its work in France as well, aided by State investments under the *Plan Freycinet*. Artisans moved from village to town; agriculture was to some extent rationalized. Wine-growers were affected by phylloxera, which brought French wine-production down by three-quarters from the middle 1870s to the middle 1880s; there was emphasis on dairy-farming and on the export of country-made luxury products, such as leather. The banks were forced to modernize, though not as dramatically as in Italy since firms met many of their own costs through *autofinancement*. *Paribas*, the *Banque de l'Union Parisienne* (Schneider in 1904) and the *Banque française pour l'industrie et le commerce* (Rouvier in 1901) took a long view of industrial investment, and, in the boom years before 1914, they flourished: *Paribas*'s profit being 35 per cent in 1914, as against 16.4 per cent in the more staid *Crédit Lyonnais*. Virtually all French banks, with their government's blessing, directed their clients towards Russian funds. Of 45,000,000,000 francs invested abroad in the fifteen years before 1914, a quarter went to Russia.

The 'Great Depression' did not affect French agriculture as heavily as it affected agriculture elsewhere because the French peasant, with far fewer children and with a stable market, was protected from its consequences. It did hit the artisan, since more cheaply made goods became available, and it hit the conservative bank, through declining interest-rates. The movement of the 1890s, when all of these things came together, was, to start off with, depressing, but, once capital and labour had been forced to mobilize, France produced new industries, using the best available new technology and her own old skills, which had a long history. The Lyons silk-workers, faced with Japanese and Italian competition, found a way of using silk-threads that earlier would have been thrown away (the *filés de schappe*). The problem of cheap energy was solved by electricity. The Rhône valley, and Lyons, the heartland of the French artisan, profited from hydro-electricity just as Milan did. The automobile industry, and aircraft, both of which suited the French capacity for tinkering productively in backyards, did extremely well. Renault started off in a shed at Billancourt, and by 1914 had two factories in Russia; Citroën began similarly, and by 1917 was able to plan, build and use a tank factory within six weeks. Panhard, Levassor, Peugeot joined in; and the multiplication of auxiliary services for motor cars, e.g. Michelin's tyres or *Zénith* (Lyons) with its V8 multi-cylinder engine, ensured that this whole region would do well. Lyons, under Edouard Herriot, was a very proud city, and its radical newspaper, the *Progrès*, like Toulouse's *Dépêche* was France's equivalent of the *Manchester Guardian* or *Glasgow Herald*.

A chemical industry developed as well, with the 24,000 workers, at St Gobain, where German techniques were used. To dispense with Sicilian sulphur, superphosphates were made from coal-gas and ammonium sulphate. The electrical industry also did well, and Bréguet used quick-fingered female labour to produce electric bulbs (as was the case with Philips in the eastern Netherlands). An electro-chemical industry developed as well: electrolysis produced the Hérault process for aluminium, and since France had bauxite, the basic material, she became the largest aluminium producer in the world. In the First World War, France, despite her weaker heavy-industrial base, made many more shells than Germany (11,000,000 per month in 1918 to the Germans' 7,000,000). The ultimate reason (beyond the labour mobility of 1914–18) lay in the success of her adaptation of the chemical and electrical industries. She led the world in aircraft throughout the First World War (though the first regular air service for civilians was, curiously, an Austrian one between Vienna and Kiev, started in 1918).

French exports, which had stagnated in the 1880s, recovered their levels of 1875 in 1897, and then doubled up to 1914. The new industries, the thriving banks, and exports produced a considerable boom before 1914, just as they did in Italy, only with a much stronger base in France. The growth-rate doubled between 1896 and 1914, to 2.4 per cent, and in the 'dynamic areas' identified by François Crouzet it rose from 2.97 per cent before 1896 to 5.2 per cent thereafter. Maybe the basis of all this was fragile. The collapse of international financial stability and the fall of commodity prices in the 1930s caused havoc in the French agrarian-based economy as it did in the Italian (or for that matter the Russian). Still, before 1914, it was associated with a *belle époque*.

The transfer of money from country to town and then the augmentation of the money in both after 1896 led to a building boom. Paris, having been restricted, in most of the 1880s, as regards height, added the 'mansard roofing' of Renaissance style that is nowadays so characteristic (the Hôtel Talleyrand, overlooking the Place de la Concorde, was bought by the Rothschilds, who added such a roof to its classical aspect). Hénard planned the extension of Paris, as Herriot and Augagneur did in Lyons; after the *Exposition* of 1900 the Champ de Mars, where the exhibition-pavilions had stood, was partly taken over by smart, tall blocks of flats just off the Avenue de la Bourdonnaye, and the left-bank *septième* became, like the *seizième*, the desirable place to live, as the bourgeoisie migrated from the 'city' areas of the *huitième*. The French capacity for exploiting themselves (and others) was shown in a growth of small shops, unhindered by any of the absurdly restrictive legislation that was imposed on opening hours in other countries. Boucicaut of the Bon Marché had already shown the way; Samaritaine and Galeries Lafayette followed, in the domain of department stores, but small shops also proliferated. From 1900 to 1914 the number of retail businesses rose from 198,000 to 226,000; the number of restaurants quadrupled; the value of retail businesses in Paris doubled. Far beyond this level, France began to develop in heavy industry. The Gilchrist-Thomas process allowed her to use the iron-ore of Lorraine (Briey and Longwy) despite its high phosphorus content. German coal turned it into iron and steel, whether in France or in Germany, and there was some international cartellization prefiguring the Iron and Steel Community. French iron-ore output multiplied by ten times from 1895 to 1914. Steel rose from 800,000 tonnes in 1890 to 1,500,000 in 1900 and 4,500,000,000 in 1914, and coal went up as difficult seams were exploited through electrical power – from 28,000,000 tonnes in 1895 to 40,000,000 in 1914.

By 1914, France could confidently face the industrial Germany which, earlier, she shrank from attempting. Still, the process of industrialization and modernization had given France a social problem which, earlier, she had barely known: a socialist challenge. By 1914 there were 103 socialists in the *Chambre*, one-fifth of the deputies. The trade-union strength had grown from 100,000 to almost one million in the past fourteen years; it was capable of laying low the economy, and there had been great strikes already.

French socialism had a longer tradition than socialism elsewhere, in that it stemmed from the great revolution itself. But, after 1884, it lacked the stimulus to violence that might come (as it did in Italy and Prussia) from living in a state that gave it no electoral chance at all, and harassed it through the law and the police. At the same time, it did not develop on the same industrial base as German socialism. In 1896, only

1.3 per cent of French firms employed over fifty workers, 13.5 per cent from five to fifty, and the rest four and less. Even in 1914, the party had only 90,000 members, and only one worker in seven had joined a union.

Industrial France – by and large – followed the pattern of other industrial countries of the continent. In the later 1870s, workers in the few existing trade unions combined to create a workers' party. It included intellectuals – in this case, a grim, middle-class figure, Jules Guesde – but the unions did not want to see their scanty funds used for political attitudinizing, and relations were tense. In fact, the early party (*Parti ouvrier français*) split into quarrelling groups, one of them orthodox-Marxist under Guesde, one semi-anarchist (the *Allemanistes*) and the other virtually indistinguishable from left-wing liberalism. Half of the fifty deputies elected in 1893 remained independent of any of these groups. For at best half of the socialists came from the industrial *Nord* or Paris; the rest were from non-industrial regions. One of France's peculiarities, in German eyes, was that in some areas the peasantry elected socialists: the Var, Creuse, Corrèze, Aveyron etc. In reality, it was not peculiar for peasants to vote socialist: they even did so, despite socialist discouragement, in Germany. People did not have to be in the working classes to understand that some new form of society was needed.

By the early 1890s, France experienced some great strikes, in the Carmaux mines in 1892, the Commetry mine on the upper Loire, at Fourmies in 1891, when shooting killed nine people during a May Day demonstration. These strikes, in mines, occurred for much the same reasons as elsewhere: employers trying to reduce wages as prices fell. At Carmaux in 1893 there was a huge mining disaster, and a strike followed, to which the government was grotesquely unsympathetic. The place elected the socialist, Jean Jaurès, as deputy after a hard campaign. It all prompted a degree of unionization. A *Confédération Générale du Travail* was formed. But it contained only four unions. Invitations were sent out to every other union, and each, however small, was promised an equal vote – thus the 'fifty *comtiste* cooks of Caen', who would count for virtually the same as the unions of railwaymen or miners. The TUC in Great Britain adopted exactly the opposite policy. Since it already contained most unions, it was concerned to have the larger ones control the smaller ones, and therefore took up the 'block vote', enabling the secretaries of large unions to swamp any meeting. This was done, in the British case, to ensure responsibility; in the French case, to ensure membership.

The revolutionary side of these unions was reinforced, as in Italy, by the *Bourses du travail* which, like the *Camere del lavoro*, were subsidized by sympathetic municipalities to act as employment exchanges (*bureaux de placement*) and as general meeting-places for the working class. They were taken over by anarchists, such as the journalist Fernand Pelloutier, and they had their own federation. It talked the language of revolution, though the anarchist newspaper, in an age of vast circulations, took only 7000 subscribers. Towards the end of the century, the *Bourses* and the CGT joined hands, and their revolutionary language – 'revolutionary syndicalism' – sufficiently alarmed the Establishment. In 1906, with the *Charte d'Amiens*, the CGT pronounced in favour of an 'economic struggle' independent of political parties – just the programme of the revolutionary syndicalists, for whom the deputy was a traitor ('*homme élu, homme foutu*'). There were, indeed, many strikes: in 1902, five million days lost, more than in the previous ten years; in 1903 a lull; in 1904 a thousand strikes involving 270,000 people and a loss of four million days; another lull; in 1906, 1309 strikes, with 440,000 people, each striking, on average, for nineteen days. In May 1906 there was a strike wave, which affected building-workers, printers (for the eight-hour day) and the *métro*. The police, with the *Manège Mouquin*, demonstratively kept control, as something of a *grande peur* developed among the Paris bourgeoisie. Then, although railwaymen struck briefly in 1906 and 1910, there was a lull until the First World War.

The names of Griffuelhes, secretary of the CGT, Pataud,

leader of the electricians, Pouget, a journalist-anarchist, Merrheim, a puritanical *chaudronnier* (boiler-maker) from Roubaix, and Pierre Monatte, editor of the *Revue syndicaliste*, scared the bourgeoisie. But how effective were they? The CGT contained only a third of the unions (with in all 350,000 members), and the main unions – Keufer's printers especially, but also Basly's miners – were constantly against a general strike for revolutionary purposes. It was really advocated by the smaller unions, of artisans-under-pressure – men not unlike the German tailors with whom Marx had started off. The six smallest unions, with a combined membership of twenty-seven members, had the same voting weight as the six largest, with 90,000. In the executive committee, a third of the votes were proxy, because the unions concerned could not afford to send a delegate. Even ostensibly large unions turned out to be unrepresentative: the builders, for instance, had 9000 members in 1905, and 30,000 in 1908 – a small fraction of builders' strength.

'Revolutionary syndicalism' was, perhaps, merely hot air – the kind of language talked in isolation by sectarians – but it did, unquestionably, reveal a degree of discontent which the existing republican system could not contain. Employers in France who were often, themselves, from the working class, did not wish to recognize unions. The government itself would not let its servants join them. The railways, which were partly nationalized, were exploited. The government held down fares, and wages dropped in relative terms. By 1900 engine-drivers had a wage equivalent to that of a navvy. They worked harder; and, on the *Nord* lines, there was an accident every day. The drivers were generally retired at fifty years of age; and the largest element in the railwaymen's union (*Cheminots*) was precisely the drivers aged over forty, who forfeited their pension if they struck. The post-office employees (*employés des PTT*) were badly paid, though their work rose in volume by one-third between 1900 and 1906; primary schoolteachers were notoriously badly paid. It was a sign of the times that the radical Clemenceau, a voice of the People in the 1870s, given to attaching the suffix *-socialiste* to his radicalism, should have suppressed the rail strikes by conscripting the railwaymen, thus placing them under military discipline, and by arresting and dismissing the *instituteur*, Nègre, and the post-office clerk, Quilici, when they threatened to strike. French industry was too poor and disorganized to set up a really large-scale movement of trade unions. But discontent was certainly enough to create a large socialist party. After the socialists' unification in 1904–5 as *Section Française de l'Internationale Ouvrière*, they won 76 seats in 1910 and 103 in 1914, their strength concentrated in the central *Nord*, Paris and the south-east.

Strength in these three regions summed up French socialism. Part of it was industrial; part metropolitan; and part peasant. The unification of these three elements had been difficult; and once achieved, it made for a party that tended to divide (to the point where, in 1914, half of the socialists were 'independent'). In rural areas like the Var, socialism spoke for something much wider than an industrial cause: it might mean freedom from the domination of local radical 'machines', and it grew out of the habit, in wine-country, of collecting endlessly during the summer to grouse in cafés. By 1914, fifty of the constituencies represented by socialists were really agrarian ones. This mystified the Germans, though it need not have done. The socialist congress of Limoges in 1906 had stressed the need to consider 'the just demands of the peasantry' – a far cry from the collectivization of agriculture which German socialists appeared to be contemplating. Equally, the French party contained a great number of intellectuals. This again was understandable in French circumstances. The professions, and education at every level, discriminated against the young and not-well-off. There was no retiring age in universities, and Chairs were sometimes filled with extraordinarily aged, futile figures. The teacher-training *École Normale Supérieure*, in the rue d'Ulm, was a training-ground for intellectual socialists. Its librarian, Lucien Herr, carried over the positivist approach towards rational government, i.e. socialism, which would mean planning and welfare in this chaotic world. His most prominent disciple was the socialist leader, Jean Jaurès.

There were three strands in French socialism, as there were everywhere else – a revolutionary one (itself divided between the revolutionary syndicalists and the politicians), a central one, striving to keep the party together, and a 'reformist' one. The reformists had taken a lead in Europe when one of them, Alexandre Millerand, spoke in 1896 for an alliance with left-wing liberalism (the Saint-Mandé speech, picked up in Germany by Bernstein). In 1899 Millerand had joined a government of the allied left, and he was a prominent figure in politics thereafter. At the time, some socialists sympathized with him. After all, in his job as head of the labour office he could decree many things of value to workers (such as the imposition of a *numerus clausus* on the number of immigrants the government would employ in its direct work). But the bulk of socialists were scandalized: here was a man using the power of a revolutionary cause to get himself a job in a reactionary government. Aristide Briand, and Viviani, followed Millerand's path, to the same effect. Up to 1904–5 Jean Jaurès co-operated with the left-wing liberals of the *Bloc* era, and after that several of the united socialists persisted in voting for measures of which they approved. By 1914, the division of the socialists was such that, as in Germany, great armaments were voted for, provided they came together with a progressive income tax, as indeed occurred. By then, the French party was held together mainly by Jaurès, who had great personal appeal. He was clever enough to allow a programme (*chronologique*) which stated the aim of revolution but postponed it *sine die* and meanwhile allowed socialists to participate in electoral alliances and the parliamentary power-game, in exchange for reforms. This offended the revolutionary purists, who looked to a complete overthrow of capitalism. But it offered allies to left-liberal republicans who could use them (as was not the case in Italy) to free themselves from dependence on venal supporters. Joseph Caillaux, in particular, looked to

Jaurès as an ally in the march towards 'technocracy', especially in matters of tax reform. Socialists did not mind voting for a large army if it also meant social reform, in the matter of taxation of income. They were really too isolated to achieve anything more on their own.

In these circumstances, no great centre-right bloc was created, on *Sammlungspolitik* lines, to challenge the left. On the contrary, much of the centre looked to Jaurès as an ally against the right. In the Third Republic, a continually impressive feature is the weakness, isolation and ineptitude of that sector. The historian, remembering the cleverness of a Miquel or a Salisbury, can only award the French right the Charles X prize for public relations, and pass on. It generally did badly in elections: in 1898, in a reasonably favourable time, the three parties associated with the right gained respectively forty-four, thirty-five and fifteen seats – in all, some hundred – a quarter of the *Chambre*. Their proportion marginally rose up to 1914. The original right was confined to isolated country, where the *notable* would be voted in (the more so as voting was not behind a screen until 1913), in the *bocage* country of Loire-Inférieure, the Massif Central, the Pyrenees, the Ardèche above 1000 metres, and Brittany.

Conservatism elsewhere survived because it struck a bargain with the business classes. French conservatism failed to do so. It stuck to an old-fashioned Catholicism and monarchism for the early part of the Third Republic, and then drifted dangerously into the hysterical *anti-Dreyfusard* demagogy of the *Action Française*. Catholicism in France failed to develop a popular political side, as it had done elsewhere with conspicuous success. There were of course working-class Catholics in the textile north, but Catholicism remained a cause on the whole identified with the upper classes, and in this it differed mightily from Catholicism in virtually any other country, where lads of the village could become bishops, and lead electoral flocks towards a single Catholic party. In France – perhaps because of her stability – the Church remained conservative in a very narrow sense. It had already supplied the Bonapartist régime with NCOs to organize the plebiscites. It had a very favourable Concordat, by which tithes were paid for the upkeep of lands, and the State paid salaries, while the Church ran much of education. There appeared to be a clerical mafia at work. In 1876, candidates for the examinations of the *Grandes Écoles* who came from the Jesuit school of the rue des Postes did well, because they had apparently had foreknowledge of the questions. Prefects, even under the Republic, were appointed for their faith; so too were many *généraux de jésuitière*, for the army became more, not less, aristocratic as the 1870s and 1880s went by. The Church defended its position in the 1870s, and it proposed a national crusade, in the spirit of the newly discovered Lourdes, to regenerate France. The Pretender, Chambord, sympathized. It was an attitude that revolted even many liberal Catholics, and their defection to the republican cause did everything, in 1875 and later, to make a reality of the Third Republic.

Towards the end of the 1880s, the Church began to fear that it would be overtaken by socialism; and besides, the Pope wished to have a French ally in his fight with Italian anti-clericalism. He published the encyclical *Rerum Novarum*, a foretaste of 'social Catholicism', in 1893, and in 1892 addressed the French faithful with *Au milieu des sollicitudes*. The Cardinal-Archbishop of Algiers, Cardinal Lavigerie, appealed for Catholics to support the Republic, not a monarchy, and to form a party. Upper-class Catholics responded. The liberal Catholic, Jacques Piou, organized a group of like-minded upper-class figures – the comte d'Haussonville, the banker Hély d'Oissel, the Prince d'Arenberg (who, from his estates at Louvain in Belgium and in Westphalia could well appreciate political Catholicism) – to promote a 'joining' (*Ralliement*) of the Republic by Catholics. But pope, nuncio, cardinal, banker, prince: none could push through the hatred of the French bishops for the Republic. They denounced it, the persecuted speaking the language of the persecutor. They wanted control of education; they were scandalized by divorce; they saw no way forward in *Ralliement*. An *Union de la France chrétienne*, under the veteran monarchist Chesnelong (whose earlier headquarters had been, aptly, in the *impasse des Chevaux-légers*), denounced the *Ralliés*, with the bishops' support. The group won twenty-five seats only in 1893, and hardly more than that up to 1914, when it called itself *Action libérale*. The constituencies dominated by the right continued to vote for *notables*; the *Ralliés* could gain places only where they were themselves *notables*, and in the face of the extraordinary strength of French liberalism, such places were not many. France failed to develop a conservative party, based on the alliance of religion and business. Few businessmen in their senses could espouse the French right. In France, the democrats were not Christian, and the Christians were not democrats.

French politics were thus dominated by the centre – a centre which, because of the stability of occupations and the gentle rise in middle-middle and lower-middle-class prosperity, did not lose to right and left as it did in other countries. On the whole, Big Business remained liberal, looking to the left. This centre was made up of innumerable political groups. In the 1870s, it consisted of men who were essentially classical liberals, who would have accepted a constitutional monarchy provided it had not been burdened with socially-divisive clericalism. Many of the greatest figures were Protestant: Say, Jauréguiberry, Freycinet etc. In the 1880s, these classical liberals – *Opportunistes* or *Modérés* – had themselves frequently been opposed by radical liberals, such as Clemenceau. The radicals were businessmen who wanted government to take a more active part in sustaining the economy, and who looked to greater democracy, rather than balanced budgets. These radicals also had a train of deputies who were, within certain limits, interested purely in local issues, and who would overthrow any government, of whatever composition, if it did not satisfy these. There were also some radicals who, to reinforce their commitment to democracy, added *-socialiste* to their title. It meant nothing beyond low-class sympathies. Hence, in the mid-1880s, politics was reduced to a game; and the confusions that resulted were sufficient to encourage a general, Boulanger, to dream of a new Bonapartism, an alliance of lower-middle-class radicalism and the army, with the right tagging along. He made some headlines, but the system closed against him, and his candidates won only three dozen seats, while he himself could not persuade fellow-generals to rise against the Republic which paid their pensions. By 1889, he had been ousted. The elections of 1893 represented a standard pattern: 122 radicals, 50 *Républicains*, i.e. conservative-minded *Opportunistes*, 32 *Ralliés*, 56 conservatives and 250 *Républicains gouvernementaux*, meaning, usually, deputies with a local interest in view, with 50 socialists.

Even though, after 1895, the French economy changed, parties were not significantly different in 1910, when the *Chambre* rules forced deputies to form groups. There were 20 'independents', 19 *Groupe des Droites*, 34 *Action libérale (Ralliés)*, 75 *Progressistes* (right-wing liberals, in effect conservatives), 72 *Gauche démocratique* (right-wing liberals, in effect liberals), 113 *Gauche radicale* (radical liberals), 150 radicals (left-wing liberals), 75 official socialists and 31 independent socialists. There was still a huge preponderance of the centre, although, increasingly, a new combination of right and centre was settling in. But, until the modern issues of social reform and progressive taxation of income were properly launched, such a combination proved impossible.

In the 1880s and 1890s, as the class tension mounted, men of the right hoped that they could come to terms with the more right-wing elements of the centre. The obvious way of doing so was to use scandals. A system like the French one was peculiarly prone to these. After all, a large number of deputies were there to advance local interests and their own cause. Many radicals were ex-peasants, ex-journalists, ex-anything, with only prospects and a rich wife to their names. Like Lloyd George in Marconi, they had business contacts, and the intention of making money. Their political friends would help them. The son-in-law of President Grévy was found to be selling decorations. In 1891–2 a great scandal broke when it was shown that the bankrupt Panama

Company had been paying deputies – the *chéquards* – for 'publicity'. In practice, the deputies involved, who included the radicals Clemenceau and Rouvier, were innocent: they had only bought shares preferentially. But there was a rumpus. It did not deter the electorate from voting left in 1893, though some shady Jewish financiers committed suicide along the way.

Anti-Semitism proved to be the occasion of the next scandal, the greatest of the Third Republic, and one exploited shamelessly by the French right: Dreyfus. Late in 1894, a Jewish General Staff officer, Alfred Dreyfus, was falsely accused of espionage for Germany. The charge was fragile, the motive quite unclear, given that Dreyfus was rich. Still, out of hatred for the newcomer, the Jew, the 'not born', a coalition of aristocratic officers conspired to suppress the truth, to convict Dreyfus falsely and deny him a fair trial for several years. A great scandal resulted, since Dreyfus's family, with the help of honourable officers, discovered that he had been convicted on the basis of a forgery. By 1898, the forger, Colonel Henri, had killed himself. In the meanwhile, intellectuals of the left, including the novelist Zola (*J'accuse*), had vigorously denounced the government of Méline and the upper-class officer-milieu, for keeping Dreyfus on Devil's Island in the knowledge that he could not be guilty. The right responded with a display of Catholic France; the Assumptionist order, with its journal, *La Croix*, made common cause with vulgar anti-Semitism, encouraged by the immigration of Jews from Russia in the 1890s. In the event, the folly of the right in this matter was such that Méline's efforts to make a bridge between right and centre failed. He was repudiated in the elections, and Dreyfus was brought back and 'pardoned', in 1899. Some years later, he was formally exonerated and taken back into the army.

It is not too much to say that the outcome of the Dreyfus affair provoked all the discontents of France. The republican system had ossified. In the 1870s, it had meant freedom from Bonapartism and clerico-monarchism. Yet, in many ways, the old right had built up its power in other ways. A third of the prefectoral corps was *anti-dreyfusard*, outspokenly so. The army recruited its officers to a large extent from the aristocratic Saumur, St Maixent and St Cyr – the *cyrards* – including the Clermont-Tonnerres, du Paty de Clams and Rohan-Chabots who had taken such an important role in denouncing Dreyfus, the outsider. Some Protestant and 'technical' officers took Dreyfus's part, and there were some royalists who refused to participate in this vulgar campaign, but they were not many; and the anti-*Rallié* element of the Church had an extremely bad record.

But if the system had allowed the right a greater preponderance in the State than might have seemed possible in the outcome of the *seize mai* crisis of 1877, it was part of a greater ossification. Many social reforms, of a kind taken up as a matter of course elsewhere, were simply ignored in a France so heavily dominated by the small individual. The educational structure had gone on with its heavily classical *baccalauréat*, and ignored modern subjects, such as languages and science. There was no retirement age in universities, and professors lived to a very great age. The professions were stacked against the young and not-well-off. In the judicial civil service, for instance, young entrants had to serve unpaid for several years until they were lucky enough to secure a permanent employment – itself then ill-paid. The average annual civil-service salary, at 1500 francs (£60), was about that of a navvy, and the highest salary, that of a prefect, at 35,000 francs, was less than was paid to the floor manager of the Bon Marché in Paris. The provision of public health was pitiful. Léon Bourgeois's much-trumpeted *Mutualité*, though made into law by Méline in 1898, boiled down to a contributory pension, for old age or infirmity, of £3 per annum and the possibility (not often used) of bathing once a week. Standard provisions for limitation of working hours which were made in other countries had no appeal in France. The proliferation of small concerns, and the survival of agriculture, meant that most people were used to exploiting themselves, working, in the shops, from 7.30 a.m. to 10 p.m., with a three-hour break in the middle. Proposals for an eight-hour day, such as prompted the printers to strike in 1906, met incomprehension on the part of the vast majority of liberal voters; the idea of a paid holiday, or a non-contributory old-age pension, or a compulsory retirement age, met similar resistance. It was not until the Popular Front of 1936 that France achieved some (not all) of the social reforms which other countries had had even, in Germany's case, fifty years before. The fact that so many Frenchmen were independent meant also that there was no hope of paying for social reform through the taxation system. Progressive income tax, such as Prussia had had since 1891 and Great Britain since 1893, was nearly unthinkable. As Clemenceau remarked, a Frenchman would give his life for his country, but his money – never.

To many people, the Third Republic had become a system by which small-time interests became preoccupied with their political game and ignored the ossification of the system, while a clerical conspiracy reserved important places to upper-class Catholics. These Catholics were, now, quite closely connected with the old *Opportunistes* who, in the previous decade, had been their enemies. An Edmond Blanc, for instance, though a radical in politics, was a rich man whose daughter married a Radziwill and whose sister married the Catholic Hély d'Oissel. There always had been a social-climbing element in French radical liberalism; its radicalism had stemmed partly from the constant snubbing which 'trade' had met in the Faubourg St Germain. But even the French aristocracy was not wholly without a sense of survival, and in this era there was a great deal of intermarriage: Heines, Foulds, Mirès, Rothschilds, and their non-Jewish counterparts, were desirable acquisitions for aristocratic sons and daughters. The 'Two Hundred Families' or the *Grandes dynasties bourgeoises* had achieved a position of seeming indestructibility: the *mur d'argent*, as it was later known. Around 1900, there was an anticipation of the *Front Populaire*. In the election of 1902, right and left fought on clear lines, and there were only nine three-man ballots.

Jacques Méline had tried to 'collect', German-fashion, the parties of property against the left in 1896–8. He provoked powerful opposition, not least within the parties of property. The upper-middle-class republicans, *Modérés*, had been badly defeated in the election of 1893, and saw their support slipping to the radicals, who wished to reform the system and 'democratize' it. Not all of these *Modérés* (whom Méline re-formed as *Progressistes*) had any stomach for a costly and futile class-war. Men like the rich lawyer, Raymond Poincaré, who represented the Schneider-Creusot armaments interest, or Waldeck-Rousseau, another rich lawyer, or the imperialist Eugène Etienne or Rouvier or Georges Leygues or Louis Barthou – all of them prudent financiers – disliked the *clérico-nationalistes*, and came round to Dreyfus's cause. It was easy for them to find common ground with the radicals. The radicals were, after all, a party of businessmen, some of them very rich, like Edmond Blanc, Klotz, Deschanel, Doumer or Clemenceau himself. True, there was a fringe of ugly placemen in the radical element, and there were radicals who tacked on the suffix *-socialiste*. But were they not to be controlled through entangling alliances, rather than opposition? Finally, there was clear evidence that, within the socialists, there were many people who would adopt a programme of reforms which would improve capitalist society rather than destroy it with collectivism. In 1899, Waldeck-Rousseau managed to knit together his own *Grand cercle républicain*, later *Alliance démocratique*, of *Républicains de Gauche*, with radicals and radical-socialists (who joined hands in 1901–2 in a huge, ill-organized group called *Parti républicain radical et radical-socialiste*) and some socialists – including Alexandre Millerand, the 'revisionist'. He sat in cabinet together with General the Marquis de Galliffet, who had taken part in the suppression of the Commune in 1871.

Waldeck-Rousseau himself dropped out in 1902, and was replaced by the radicals' leader, Emile Combes, whose majorities were arranged by the *Délégations des Gauches*, chaired by the pompous radical, Sarrien, with whom Jean

Jaurès co-operated. This bloc ran France, in various ways, until December 1909, when Clemenceau was forced out after a premiership of three years.

This bloc was extremely fragile. Its right and left wings were scared at the presence of each other in the cabinet: some socialists could not take the Marquis de Galliffet; some liberals could not take Millerand, who endeavoured to make employers recognize trade unions. On matters of economic policy, the group was disunited; it would certainly not adopt the progressive income tax which alone could have paid for serious social reform, and proposals for such a tax failed. Reform of education was agreed upon, and a modern *baccalauréat* set up. The number of students was increased from 30,000 to 40,000 in a few years. Something was done for women's education. A few, timid, gestures at welfare-legislation were made: a voluntary old-age pension, provision of communal assistance for the aged and infirm, though it amounted to only 34.9 francs per head to the British 180, which, besides, was paid to two times as many people as in France. An effort was made to improve conditions in the civil service, but most radicals saw it as a parasitical body. Civil servants were allowed to see their personal files: which meant that the files became empty of anything other than chronology.

Still, there was a revenge on the upper-class *anti-dreyfusards*. Towards the end of the nineteenth century, the Church and, to a lesser extent, the army officers counted as bulwarks of Reaction. The *Dreyfusard Ligue pour la défense des Droits de l'Homme*, with its 240,000 members, was the spearhead of a large and vociferous anti-clerical movement. In many villages, there were masonic and secular organizations which united people against the Church. At the unveiling of Dalou's statue, the *Triomphe de la République*, there was a great parade of these organizations, headed by the Masons, with aprons and hammers. On the anniversary of Louis XVI's execution, people sat down solemnly to eat *tête de veau*. The *Bloc* had an easy target. The army came under the control of a republican general, André, who steered military appointments to create his own clique of masonic generals (such as Sarrail and Joffre) against the *capucins bottés* (such as Foch or Castelnau). Efforts were made to democratize the officer-corps. For instance, the provisions that kept it upper-class were dismantled. Officers' wives no longer needed a dowry of 1200 francs; they could work; they were no longer forced to travel first-class. In the event, a scandal involving André's use of masonic spies to report the views, in the mess, of officers – *l'affaire des fiches* – provided a pretext for the right to break off from the *Bloc*. In Emile Combes's time, it was cemented by jobbing. Combes built up his own office, with eighteen *adjoints* and fifteen *chefs de bureau*. His son showered medals. Georges Leygues, in the south-west, deployed 'kilometres of purple ribbon', or *les palmes académiques*. Radical (and some socialist) bosses had a wonderful time issuing tobacco licences.

The greatest of such efforts, and one which occupied parliamentary time, was the separation of Church and State, accomplished with much turmoil in the years 1905–7. The Church had made itself very unpopular; it had also stood for social divisiveness in education. The annual fees of a Jesuit college in Paris were 1400 francs – almost as much as a civil servant's salary – and the products of this Catholic education were clearly better placed to do well in professions than the children of State *lycées*, not because the education was better (quite the contrary – the standard in State *lycées* was often much higher) but because of 'contacts' and superior manners. The *réguliers* who taught now numbered 162,000, two-thirds more than in 1789; there had been a similar expansion of *séculiers*, or ordinary priests. French literature does not recall the members of the regular orders with fondness: almost uniformly, they appear as crazy bigots. The Church was also alleged to have done well with property, to have a *milliard* – 1,000,000,000 francs. Clearly, it had used the State's 40,000,000 francs of annual salaries to produce a private empire which was then used against the republican State.

Discussion of this issue squared various circles for the

radicals. It took up parliamentary time, so that the socialists' embarrassing schemes did not have to be considered; and even Jaurès went along with anti-clericalism since, like the British socialists on the Irish issue, the whole business had to be removed from the agenda if serious matters of social reform were to be taken up. The Church's property could also satisfy the itchy fingers of the radicals' shadier clients. If God had not existed, His Church, at least, would have had to be invented for the sake of radical purposes. In 1904 the French equivalent of English public schools were closed down: in Lyons, the orders' schools were stopped, and forty per cent of the Lyonnais secondary-school pupils were shifted to State *lycées*. In December 1905, separation of Church and State was decreed, the details being worked out by 1907. The State was no longer responsible for clerical salaries or buildings; both depended on the faithful, though in practice the municipalities sometimes helped out. The Church, for its part, no longer needed State approval of its appointments. Church property was nationalized, and sometimes sold off. The Grande Chartreuse monastery was sold off to Cusenier, the liqueur-maker, at a very low price, perhaps because the State's valuers had been bribed. Harmless orders of nuns were swept out, setting up in England or Belgium, as did Jesuits. There were ugly scenes in Brittany as villagers gathered to defend their Church. By 1907, the State had relented to some extent, and a working compromise occurred over issues of property; and thereafter anti-clericalism, like non-conformity in England, was a dead issue.

After 1907, the radicals were left confronting the problem which anti-clericalism had so successfully enabled them to sidestep: the question of income tax, and of social reform generally. The radicals did well in the elections of 1906: 247 seats (forty-two per cent) to the SFIO's 59, the old liberals' hundred (*Alliance démocratique*) and the right's divided 80. Clemenceau became prime minister until December 1909. He promised seventeen reforms, and carried out only one. He repressed strikes with vigour, so much so that his own party expelled him (though, since he had never applied for membership, he did not notice). He was especially heartless after the Courrières mining disaster, which killed 1100. He went on until the radicals let him go, out of fear for the liability of having him lead them into the next election of 1910. He governed with much noise and vigour; he tried hard to find in foreign policy an issue that would stand in for the anti-clericalism of which the radicals' own success had deprived them. Clemenceau was an old radical: a doctor, contemptuous of the right's morality (he was divorced from his American wife, and harried her unmercifully to the point where she was driven to taking parties of tourists round Paris, and was once imprisoned by her extremely unfaithful husband, when he was minister of the interior, for adultery). But Clemenceau was rich. So were many other radicals. Once the older issues had been swept aside, the socialists' and left-wing urban liberals' questioning as to the French taxation system could not be avoided.

After Clemenceau's fall at the end of 1909, matters of taxation and rearmament and social reform came up in France as they did everywhere else, in an atmosphere of increasing social tension and international war scares. On the whole, the nationalists were anxious not to have an income tax, and the advocates of social reform were anxious not to have militarist nationalism, although the socialists were mainly patriotic in that they would accept a defensive war against Germany.

The elections of 1910, and still more those of May 1914, indicated how far the old radical heart of the Republic was declining. Underneath the kaleidoscope of misleading party labels, and the crowding of deputies on left-hand benches, there was a notable shift to the right. In 1910, there were 76 socialists, 85 of the right (including the *Action libérale*), 60 *Progressistes*, or right-wing liberals; in the centre were 93 *Républicains de Gauche* and 225 radicals; in 1914 the radicals' decline was marked, for they fell down to 172, while the socialists (including independents) amounted to 126. The radicals could now govern only with serious support either from right or left.

The radicals, like other liberals, were seemingly incapable of serious organization. In 1914, there were 238 radical deputies, but only 172 accepted the authority of the rue de Valois. Their party dated to the turn of the century, but its central body was vast, and its conferences were open to all comers (who had a right to vote). The conferences, which were ignored by deputies, voted for standard left-liberal themes – even women's suffrage. But a third of the constituencies refused to pay their 200-franc subscription or, in 1910, to acknowledge the 'programme'. The deputies ignored conference strictures, and continued to vote for Clemenceau after his expulsion, or for Barthou in 1913 after his proscription. The radicals were partly a party of well-meaning schoolteachers and officials – they supplied the militants, in the name of *laïcité*. But they were also a party of local machines. The rise of socialism in the towns confined the party more and more to small towns and southern rural constituencies, where the decline of agriculture made the rural 'machine' important in economic matters. There were also rich radicals; and they, vigorous denouncers of past evils, now adopted imperialism with a vengeance. Albert Sarraut, deputy for the Aude, became governor-general of Indo-China in 1911; he had been preceded by Paul Doumer, who had also taken an interest in the Yunnan railway. Léon Mougeot, who had attacked the *Compagnie Occidentale* in Madagascar, became Combes's minister of agriculture and bought land in Tunisia; after which he saved the *Compagnie Occidentale*, which was under a younger version of himself. Justin Derchot ran *Le Radical* after 1909, and enriched himself in buying land which the State had confiscated in Morocco.

A Clemenceau, vigorously repressing strikes with a view to building up his credibility on the right, might be disliked by the mass of his party. Still, what else was there? In measures of social reform, curious delays were made. Old-age pensions, for instance, dragged on until 1910, when a very timid scheme was at last made law. Characteristically of France, only a third of those eligible actually contributed. Socialists and radicals, with some help from the centre, could certainly pass more, and more generous, such laws. But where was the money to come from? This question, and the related arms bills, coincided with a manful effort on Briand's part to clear up the 'stagnant little pools' of small-town and rural constituencies by introducing proportional representation. The result was a kaleidoscope of governments after 1910, when the parties themselves split: after Clemenceau, Briand; again Briand; a stockbroker, Maris; the left-liberal technocrat, Caillaux; Berteaux; Poincaré; Deschanel; Briand again; Barthou; Doumergue; Ribot for three days; Viviani, who presided over the outbreak of war. The main feature of this age was that some radicals could be squared for whatever programme provided that they obtained one of the great 'clientage' posts, PTT, the interior, transport etc. In the meantime, parliamentary business could be swamped by unexceptionable but, in detail, complicated little laws – e.g. 'the inalienable family home' (1909) which stopped discussion of income tax. Aristide Briand was a master in the art of getting the Senate to vote down things which the *Chambre* did not have the courage to vote down itself: although in practice the Senate was a fossil, which could have been (and on occasion, was) overborne by use of the *décret-loi*.

Still, with the second Moroccan dispute of summer 1911, it became clear that France would have to make a great arms effort if she were to remain a Great Power. Her population did not allow her to keep pace with German conscription; if she wanted an army as large as Germany's, she would have to have three-year military service, not two-year (as had been the case since Combes in 1905). That would mean a great increase in the military budget. How was it to be paid for? Already, finance made problems. Even without the burden of the new pension, expenditure had risen by a fifth between 1900 and 1909.

The tax system had been inherited from far back. In the

early days of the Republic, it had appeared suitable enough
to a largely agrarian world. The system was indirect, on land
or building, and tariffs made up an important part of
revenue. Some areas paid more than others, and the whole
system, by hitting goods of ordinary consumption, affected
the poor more than the rich.

Many people groaned. The alternative was a tax on
income, going up by steps. But this, in France, encountered
great difficulties. The preponderance of the 'independent'
sector, of farmers and shopkeepers, meant that most people
kept their own books, if any, so that their incomes could be
judged only by painful inquisition, of a kind the Republic
was supposed to be constructed against. Why take more
money from the successful, and thus penalize them?
Sixty-five projects for such a tax failed before 1909, including
one from Rouvier, a veteran. The Senate rejected two others,
in 1907 and 1910. It was not until 1913, thanks to the needs
of national defence, that the tax went through. It exempted
farmers altogether. The tax itself was quite small, taking
between three and four per cent of incomes above 5000
francs, with a slight surcharge above 25,000.

Of the three great reform measures, income tax and the
three-year-service law went through in 1913, but proportional representation, the centre's weapon against shady local
notables, failed, in part because of its proponents' disagreements as to how it could be realized. But, now, the centre-left
coalition on which the Republic had been based was ending:
its dissolution was marked in the kaleidoscope of governments since Clemenceau, as they wrestled with combinations
of the three main issues, or with specious postponements of
them. The French right now claimed, successfully, the
nationalist cause for their own. After 1911 came the *réveil
national*, an era of parades and trumpetings. There were
gigantic demonstrations for a military law to bring France up
to Germany's level. *Action Française* spoke for the authoritarian, nationalist right, with overcurrents of anti-Semitism.
The appointment of the outspoken *revanchard* Poincaré as
president in 1913 meant that France now had an active

president, not a figurehead. He encouraged France's Russian ally into a forward policy in the Balkans, and promised that France would go to war whatever the pretext (August 1913). In 1913, the three-year law went through. It was challenged at the elections by the left, who promised to reverse it. But in May 1914, when it came to a vote, of the 602 deputies, 325 were still in favour – and they included socialists as well as 100 radicals. The liberalism of the Third Republic was ending in a Strange Death; and, after the First World War, France became once more a fatally divided country.

6. *Austria-Hungary*

The Habsburg Monarchy was a minor version of Europe as a whole. It sprawled across central Europe from the Swiss border to the remote Bukovina, on the Russo-Romanian frontier, from prosperous, sedate places like Salzburg in the Austrian west across the industry of Bohemia to the poverty-stricken Jewish villages of Polish Galicia and into the Carpathian districts of Hungary, where a desperately poor mountain population had to be exempted from conscription because, at the age of twenty, men's voices had not broken since their diet was so poor. It was a land of enormous estates, inherited from the days when a Hungarian Count Eszterházy owned more land than the king of Württemberg; but there were also great modern cities – Vienna, with two million inhabitants spread out over the largest city-area in Europe; Budapest and Prague, each with a rapidly expanding population in the later nineteenth century – Budapest virtually a newly built city, with some baroque elements on the Buda side of the Danube; Prague a baroque and Gothic masterpiece – today still almost intact – matched only by Cracow, the centre – though not the capital – of the Austrian part of Poland. In the Habsburg Monarchy, mobilization posters went up in fifteen languages; but there was a sameness to it all, shown in the town architecture. A Znojmo or a Brno in Moravia, a Zagreb in Croatia, a Kolozsvár (Cluj) in Transylvania: onion-domed churches, ochre semi-classical buildings, a large market square where, on Sundays, the military band would play to strollers on the nearby *corso*; sometimes, in the heart-towns of the Counter-Reformation, like Eger (Erlau) in upper Hungary, a vast baroque cathedral reigning over a huddle of little houses; or, in the old Calvinist centres, a much more modest Protestant *Templom*, such as the central church of Debrecen in eastern Hungary where, under the protection of the Calvinist Bethlens of Transylvania, Scottish exiles had promoted the cause of their grim international.

The Habsburg emperor, Franz Joseph (born in 1830), had inherited the mantle of the Holy Roman empire, reaching back a thousand years to his ancestor, Charlemagne. He had the Mandate of Heaven; and his domains were studded with huge cathedrals and monasteries, such as that of Kremsmünster or Melk, overlooking the Danube above Vienna, to remind him of the role of his dynasty in the Counter-Reformation, when the Habsburgs had reconquered central Europe for Catholicism. The stiff, Burgundian rituals of the emperor's *Hofburg* in Vienna – though, *ancien-régime* fashion, tables of precedence varied in the Budapest *Vár* or the *Hradčany* of Prague – reminded the present generation as to how far back this empire went, beyond the days when its Spanish ancestors were awarded, by Papal decree, half of the world. Servants of the dynasty behaved as if they had their portion of the Mandate of Heaven: cabinet meetings' minutes were couched in an extraordinarily dignified language, with all the sequence-of-tense subjunctives and vast sentences of German reported speech, the twine that bound the documents being coloured differently according to historic land – black and yellow for matters imperial, such as the army; red-white-green for the apostolic kingdom of Hungary; red-white-red, the colours of the Babenberg Crusaders, for matters of inner Austria; brown and yellow for the newly annexed Bosnian lands. Franz Joseph spoke nineteen languages – though the Viennese satirist Karl Kraus opened a book to record the imperial and royal platitudes he uttered in them on public occasions – and did his best to reign in an even-handed way over his peoples, described by one foreign minister as *eine besonders farbenprächtige Kollektion*, in the untranslatably ironic language that was second nature to anyone who lived in the Monarchy. Fifteen languages: but an uncanny sameness everywhere.

It was the ideology of the Counter-Reformation that politics were a version of Original Sin: a judgement abundantly confirmed by Franz Joseph's experience since his accession in the winter of 1848. As a boy of eighteen, he had been crowned, in a castle in Austrian Silesia, by the dynasty's saviour, Prince Schwarzenberg. The young emperor was expected to sort out the chaos of the liberals' revolt – a chaos to which his predecessor and uncle, Emperor Ferdinand, had been unable to oppose anything other than continual irony, some of which was almost Hungarian in its defeated intelligence. ('It was not necessary to have me abdicate in order to lose so many battles and provinces,' he later remarked.) Still, Franz Joseph had had to adapt to liberalism. He gave up the effort to rule the Monarchy as a single Greater-Austrian state (*Gross-Oesterreich*), and in 1867 it was divided into two parts. The historic kingdom of Hungary, twice as large as present-day Hungary, was ruled from a parliament in Budapest, and the rest of the Monarchy, a huge semi-circle of a state that took in Italians, Germans, the Czech lands, Galicia and the Bukovina as well as Slovenes of the Adriatic littoral, had its own central parliament in Vienna, the *Reichsrat*. The historic 'kingdoms and lands' of this Vienna-ruled state had their own parliaments, *Landtage* (usually called 'Diets'). The non-Hungarian part of the Monarchy had an extremely cumbersome official name, and was not called 'Austria' until 1915, though unofficially that had been its name since the start. There was a complex constitution, 'Dualism'. The two states were formally separate, but they had some things in common: a tariff, foreign policy, the Common Army. From time to time the ministers for these would meet the Austrian and Hungarian prime ministers in a Common Ministerial Council. Decisions in common matters were referred to 'delegations' of the two parliaments, which assembled alternately in Budapest and Vienna. It was characteristic of the nonsensical disputes between Austria and Hungary that in 1889 there was a great row over a conjunction. The Common Army was known as *kaiserlich-königlich*, its central organization as *Reichskriegs-ministerium*. *Königlich* showed that the emperor was also king – of Hungary, Bohemia, Croatia – and therefore put the other kingdoms on a level with semi-separate Hungary. The Hungarians disliked that intensely, and they also disliked the expression *Reichs-* because it implied that there was one vast Habsburg *Reich*, not two states. After a fuss, the conjunction *und* was inserted between the two 'k's' – making *k.u.k.* – and in 1911 *Reichs-* was dropped, to be replaced by *k.u.k.* which, by implication, put all the Austrian lands into one imperial 'k' and the Hungarian territories into another, royal but equal one. Henceforth, *k.k.* meant 'Austrian'.

Austrian politics reflected the fact that Austria was a modern country (on the whole) and followed the European pattern: that is, a confused criss-crossing of liberals and clericals in the 1880s, an attempt to silence the discontents of the lower classes in the early 1890s, a reversion to the right in the later 1890s and early 1900s, a landslide to the left in 1905–7 when universal male suffrage came in, a few years of left-leaning 'technocracy' and then, after 1909, the same political disintegration as went on in other countries. Austria went to war in 1914 with the Vienna parliament already closed down.

Hungary was a different matter. In Austria, economic weight was distributed relatively evenly between Germans, Czechs, Poles, Slovenes and Italians, so that even in a parliament with a retricted franchise, the German two-fifths of Austria, though by some way the richest element, were not a majority in the *Reichsrat*. Oppression of other nationalities was therefore not practicable. In any case, the Habsburgs themselves were not in favour of it. Franz Joseph wished to be a father to his peoples, and the Church reinforced his belief. His ancestor, Emperor Leopold II, had funded a Chair in Czech at Vienna University; Emperor Franz's censors had forbidden parts of Franz Grillparzer's play, *König Ottokars Glück und Ende*, because they presented Czechs in a bad light. In the 1860s, the Habsburg Monarchy promoted the Polish cause in Galicia whereas the Prussians and Russians, in their parts of Poland, became more and more oppressive, to the point of forbidding education in the Polish language. Count Taaffe, the long-term clerical minister-president of the 1880s, happily promoted the use of Czech and Slovene, both of which flourished in this era, and Franz Joseph himself, in common with most of the Church or the nobility, would happily have seen his Austrian state turned into a set of cantons of the Swiss model.

The difficulty was that, in the historic 'kingdoms and lands', nationalities were intermingled. One third of Bohemia was German – 'the Sudeten Germans', as they were called (in 1902), though in fact the Sudeten Germans were only the most prominent of the Bohemian and Moravian and Silesian Germans. These Germans lived mainly on the fringes of the Czech lands, but there were also substantial language islands at, for instance, Iglau (Jihlava). The Prague Germans had shrunk to a few thousand by 1910, but Brno, the capital of Moravia, was still a largely German city in a Czech countryside, and the towns of Silesia were often a mixture of German and Czech, or, in the case of the coalmining town of Tešín (Teschen), German, Czech, Polish and – to judge from the census returns of 1910 – 'inter-Slav'. In Slovenia there was a lesser version of the same pattern. In Galicia, the Ruthenes, or Ukrainians, or Little Russians made up a third of the population, concentrated in the east but with a fringe in the mountains of southern Poland. In Trieste, Slovenes and Italians co-existed; in the southern Tyrol, around Trent, Germans and Italians. The areas of the 'hereditary lands' of the House of Habsburg – roughly the territory of modern Austria – were a Germanic block, but even then there were peculiarities: Vienna had received so many Slav immigrants that she was almost made the capital of independent Czechoslovakia at the end of the First World War. In time, some of these Slavs became German nationalists: the Nazi head of Vienna was called, absurdly, 'Odilo Lotario Globočnik'.

It was, indeed, the Vienna *Reichsrat* that convinced the young Hitler, who lived in Vienna for several years before the war, that parliaments were useless; and Russian conservatives had no difficulty in pointing to that body as an instance of what would happen if their own *Duma* became a reality. In states with several nationalities, a centralized parliament would simply become unworkable. The language disputes dominated everything else. If a particular national group wished to push the government into accepting a measure, it could simply obstruct the *Reichsrat*'s business. Thus, in 1895–6, over the question of a Slovene grammar school in the mainly German town of Celje (Cilli), and again during the Badeni crisis of 1897–8, when the government gave Czech and German equal status within the Bohemian bureaucracy, the Slav side and the German side obstructed: immense speeches, sometimes in Russian (from a Ruthene deputy); cavalry bugles; an exasperated hurling of heavy law-books and ink-wells. Against such obstruction it was impossible to pass house-rules that would have prevented filibustering – a problem that the British (with the Irish), the Italians and the Hungarians also experienced.

In the 1880s, there had been a limited franchise, slightly augmented in 1882 to include the 'five *Gulden* men'. This meant a middle-class parliament, in which Count Taaffe could get by with shifting majorities – sometimes liberal, sometimes clerical. In the 1890s, as more people came on to the electoral roll, a much stronger lower-middle-class element reached the *Reichsrat*, and its representatives were more radical. A Karl Lueger, speaking violently anti-Semitic language, or a Karel Kramář , leader of the 'Young Czechs', were demagogues. The 'Young Czechs', who swept the poll in the Czech districts in 1890, were ruthless and confident of their future: quite uninclined to compromise with the

German minority. The *Reichsrat* gained universal suffrage in 1907, since the emperor hoped to introduce social democrats who would talk money rather than nationalism. But that, too, did not work. Over the nationality issue, the social democrats themselves divided, and by 1910 there was an independent Czech party. By then, the Austrian Catholics, too, had ceased to have joint meetings: they held separate ones for the 'kingdoms and lands'. The only way to run the *Reichsrat* was by constant use of the Constitutional Article 14, which provided for rule by decree in an emergency. Article 14 was used for the budget and most legislation.

It was a preposterous way to run the country. The only possible answer would have been to construct a federation of nationalities. But that solution was illusory, since so many of the federal units had their own nationality problem. Indeed, since 1880, the units had gained in weight relative to the centre. The Bohemian *Landtag* and the *k.k.Statthalterei* in Prague presided over considerable sums of money, a large bureaucracy, and surprising autonomy even in supposedly central matters, such as the railways. But the *Landtag* was even more difficult to manage than the *Reichsrat* itself; and the same came to be true elsewhere, in Istria or the Tyrol, with its large Italian element.

Bohemia was the worst instance of fighting. In the old days, German had been the language of commerce and the towns; Czechs had learned it as a matter of course (and Giskra, a prominent German liberal of the 1860s, though an opponent of Czech-language education, was himself a Czech). But the expansion of the population brought many more Czechs to the towns than before. The expansion of education was such that Czechs became a majority in schools and universities. In the 1860s, over half of all students in the Monarchy had been German; a generation later, two-fifths. The heavily classical education of the early nineteenth century had encouraged men from the non-German nationalities to absorb the Germanic culture; some of them spoke and wrote with distinction in German (as did the Czechs' leader, Tomáš Masaryk). But it was quite unrealistic to suppose that masses of doctors, engineers, lawyers would ever acquire sufficient mastery of German to be able to perform well in their technicality. Besides, the Czechs, being almost by definition a middle-, lower-middle- and working-class people with a large peasant base, had a higher birth-rate than the Germans, whose strength lay in their grip of middle-class professions and the upper classes. Like every other 'respectable' section of Europe at this time, they had a lower birth-rate: 7.8 per thousand in the 1870s to the Czechs' 10.5, then 6.8 to 8.8 in the 1880s, and similarly from then on. Prague became confidently Czech, and bred a tremendous national revival; towns like Plzéň (Pilsen) or Mlada Boleslav (Jungbunzlau) acquired dominant Czech populations.

Bohemia and, to a lesser extent, Moravia, were the most prosperous parts of the Monarchy. Bohemia contained over a third of the Monarchy's industry; and the glass of Jablonice (Gablonz) or the shoes of the great new Bata firm, managed by the Protestant Slovak Tuša family, had European reputations. Industrialization here, as elsewhere, was mainly a reflection of continuity. Bohemia, with her outlet to the sea along the Elbe to Hamburg, had always been a centre of skills. The coal of nearby Silesia, and an entrepreneurial element, allowed an expansion of heavy industry, and subsequently of textiles, shoes, chemical and electrical plants. It cannot be wholly coincidental that Bohemia, like Belgium – also an industrial but Catholic country – was on the fringes of the Counter-Reformation world. Both countries had a strong anti-clerical underground which made for radicalism in politics and success in business once the liberal revolution in politics and economic life had been launched.

If it had not been for the problem of nationality, then Bohemian politics would clearly have followed European 'first principles': a three-cornered battle between left, clericals and classical liberals. In practice, the electorate did usually respond by putting the non-national issues first. There was a large Agrarian party; there was a radical-liberal element, the 'Young Czechs'. Up to 1891, there had also been a powerful Czech-conservative group, the 'Old Czechs' – men of unshakable rectitude, like Palacký or his son-in-law, Rieger, who were usually bilingual in German, respectful towards the aristocracy, and, on the whole, classical-liberal in economic outlook. In the 1880s, Czech politics had been modified by the irruption of a lower-class element, and the Agrarians, though not formally clerical (in Bohemia, the Church was not 'national' as it was in Poland, and its own party had little success), were in practice respectful towards the Church and became a Czech equivalent of the *Zentrumspartei* – the largest and, after 1918, usually the governing party. The same radicalism which had created the Agrarians also created the 'Young Czechs'. They were businessmen, usually from nowhere, journalists, lawyers; much like the radicals in France. They sought a 'national' link with the new working class; they resented aristocracy and Church, as did their French counterparts; they were intent on securing places in the bureaucracy for people who could speak only limited German; they were also determined to prevent the German-language schooling which could so easily turn little Czechs into adult Germans. That a number of 'Young Czechs' were schoolteachers contributed much to this.

The 'Old Czechs' were unthinkingly loyal to the Monarchy, virtually always to the Church, and always to their patrons, the Bohemian aristocracy. They were men of great respectability, who, in their frock-coats, looked askance at the shirt-sleeves and constant smoking of the 'Young Czechs'. In 1890, an effort was made to sort out the language question: a very decent *Statthalter*, Count Franz Jaroslav Thun-Hohenstein, almost gained a compromise. It was upset when the 'Young Czechs' won a landslide victory in the election of 1891; and after that, even the parties whose main interest was not national were sucked into a battle between German and Czech blocs.

The battle concerned schools, bureaucrats, money. Germans knew that their towns had a good chance of remaining German if the schooling was in their language; Czechs,

besides wishing children to be educated in their own
language, sometimes considered that their birth-rate would
lead to Czech domination of all Bohemia within a generation
or two. The issue was complicated because some Czech
middle-class families (and not only they) wanted their
children to be taught in German, to make them 'respectable';
and Czech nationalists (like nationalists everywhere else) had
to contend with considerable apathy, and even with a hostile
element in their own camp, especially in Moravia. Two
'school associations', collecting money, fought it out. The
heart of the whole problem was that for a Czech to learn
German was a step up in the world; for a German to learn
Czech was, in many regions, to take up the language of the
servant class. German students could be especially arrogant
about this; mocking the accents of their Czech peers, putting
up notices on their clubs – 'the Czech language is not spoken
here', and the like. In 1880, when some German students
from Prague went on an outing to Kuchelbad, they were
attacked by Czechs, armed with stones, and as their boats
passed back to Prague under the bridges, they were pelted
with rubbish. In 1898 the student quarrel became so serious
that Czechs even invaded the German hospitals to riot against
the public use, there, of German. In three-quarters of the
Czech schools, by 1913, German was not taught; and Czech
was taught only in 124 schools out of thousands of German
primary ones. The school question was never sorted out in
Bohemia, but in Moravia, in 1905, a compromise came
about. There, the German minority, paying more than its
due share of the taxes (because it was generally richer) had
fought for German schooling; and many Czechs, in this
quieter part of the Czech lands, also wanted their children
taught in German schools: a similar later anomaly, in nationalist eyes, was the little place of Hlučin (Hultschin) in north-
western Bohemia, where the inhabitants, though a Czech
language-island, were as enthusiastic German nationalists as
the Germans of the nearby *Egerland*. In Moravia, the
Germans, for the sake of peace, agreed to a compromise:
Czech children were forced to attend a Czech school in any

community where there were forty Czech families, even if
that meant a lengthy journey by bus or on foot. By 1910,
German schools could be sued for admitting Czech children.

But in Bohemia, the national attitudes, hardened by the
migration which heavy industry encouraged, were more
clear-cut. The German Establishments in the towns fought
in the 1880s. In the town council of Budějovice (Budweis),
there were nine Czechs and twenty-two Germans. Speeches
in Czech were allowed only if the chairman, a German, knew
that the speaker had inadequate German. Czechs whose
German was good enough did in fact use Czech; were
overruled; carried the case to the administrative court of the
kingdom; were supported; Germans then carried it to the
administrative court of the State; and, by a narrow majority,
were defeated. Riots followed. They did so also over a case
in 1890, when a Czech businessman, presented with a
customs receipt in the Prague customs-house in German,
complained. The greatest of such riots occurred over the
Badeni language decrees of 1897, which specified that
German and Czech could be used on equal terms throughout
the Bohemian bureaucracy: i.e. no civil servant could refuse
to accept a document in Czech from a colleague. This was a
sensible enough provision. Indeed, it was superfluous since
Czechs, who accepted the low bureaucratic salaries more
readily than the Germans, made up (by 1914) 92.5 per cent
of the Bohemian civil service, three-quarters of the higher
ranks of the *k.k.* financial service, and much more than that
of the lower ranks. But the Badeni decrees prompted rioting
on a scale the Monarchy had not yet seen. Germans in
Slovenia joined in, since they faced a similar problem; Slavs
elsewhere responded, until the *Reichsrat* and various Diets
became quite unworkable. Governments succeeded each
other, and Article 14 was used to run the country.

These nationality conflicts were multiplied: Poles versus
Ruthenes, Italians versus Slovenes, Germans (in Carinthia
and Carniola) versus Slovenes, Italians (in the Tyrol) versus
Germans. In each case the problems were the same:

modernization of the economy, migration, a class-difference between the 'ideal types' of the two peoples, a great gap in birth-rates, a quarrel over schooling, the language of public affairs, and an insane concentration on minor issues (such as the renaming of streets in one or other language). Dux (Duchcov) forbade Czech tomb-inscriptions; Trieste did the same for Slovene. When the Tauern railway line was ceremonially opened just before the war, the official party was bemused to find that the station at which it arrived, with ceremonies laid on, had no name. The Italians would have rioted if it had had the Slovene name, 'Gorica'; the Slovenes would have rioted if it had not had that name; and the Germans would have been perturbed had 'Görz' been missed off. So 'Gorizia' remained without a name. So, in the 1880s, did Eger in Bohemia (Cheb). The claims of rival nationalities were couched in a pseudo-historical language, and 'Bohemian constitutional law' (*böhmisches Staatsrecht*) became an almost unrivalled bore of the later nineteenth century. By 1914, the Bohemian Diet was suspended (after the *Anna-Patent*) and the Vienna parliament, to which the disputes were transferred, was closed down *sine die*.

Franz Joseph was not particularly surprised at the politicians' inability to find an answer: he had adopted parliamentary liberalism under duress, and with scepticism. The Habsburg Monarchy was consciously 'above' the nationality quarrel; and Franz Joseph felt he could voice the 'true' opinion of the moderate majority which was undoubtedly at some distance from the hysteria of the nationalist extremists. Most Czechs, for instance, might sympathize with the school troubles, and might also find the local Germans unbearably arrogant. But they were also flattered to be part of a great state, looked forward to its pension, and, generally, had a great many other things to think about in politics than the perennial nationality issue. The radical 'Young Czechs', though taking the bulk of the lower-middle-class vote in 1891, were hammered at the universal-suffrage election of 1907 and never recovered. By 1914 the nationalist Kramář counted strongly as a man of the right, his political opinions much the same as those of Alexandr Guchkov, or, for that matter, Clemenceau. The Agrarians and the Czech socialists might find it formally difficult to associate with their German counterparts, but in serious matter they had a great deal of agreement. Besides, Bohemia was the centre of Europe: a land fought over. Were the Czechs not better off in a Great Power, which could protect them from Germany or Russia? Most Czechs thought so until 1917–18.

The Monarchy itself had a genuine claim to 'supra-nationality'. In the army, for instance, a very commendable effort was made to prevent any nationality from feeling out of place. It was true that the officers were, two-thirds of them, of German origin, which corresponded to the weight of Germans in the educated and better-off elements. But they had every encouragement to learn their men's language, or languages. Recruits learned the dozen or so words of the *Kommandosprache*, and, if they could, the few dozen words of the *Dienstsprache* – e.g. words for parts of a rifle, which obviously had to be part of a common vocabulary. For all other purposes, the *Regimentssprache* was used. Where, in mixed districts, regiments contained two or three different nationalities, officers and NCOs used all of these languages. In the peacetime army, this worked very well indeed. In the wartime army, odd ways out were found. One regiment, which contained Hungarians, Germans and Slovaks, was commanded in English because the officers knew it from school, and the men came from a district with such a high number of emigrants that English had become the standard language for men of the area to learn. The British army in India was run on not dissimilar principles, and managed, similarly, astonishingly well. The officers, if they made a fuss over their 'German-ness', were expelled; and a third of the officers were of Hungarian or Slavonic origin. The Croats supplied more than their due share of the officer-corps, as they had done since the Counter-Reformation; Czechs (who had included the great Marshal Radetzky) provided roughly the same proportion as they had of the population as a whole;

only the poor and backward Ruthenes were barely represented at all, because virtually any Ruthene with military
ambitions would pass himself off as a Pole, or even as a
German: Taaffe's language ordinances were violently attacked by the 'German-liberal' Professor 'Konstantin
Tomaszczuk' from Czernowitz.

An effort of marvellous complexity was made to overcome
the problem of nationalities: innumerable committees and
reports, couched in inextricable legal jargon, in the hope that
the Bohemian problem could be sorted out. The principle of
Landesüblichkeit ('customary to the province') was developed
to defend use of one language or the other, and both Czech
and German bureaucrats devised endless schemes to shut up
the nationalists. There was, in Austria, a tradition which
went back to the Counter-Reformation but which owed most
to Emperor Joseph II, that bureaucratic action would solve
everything. By the later nineteenth century there was even
a feeling that the mere engagement of bureaucracy amounted
to a solution: after all, if everyone were employed by the
State, then nationality problems would disappear because no
one would want the State to be upset. Where the industrial,
Protestant countries tried not to nationalize, and ran town
halls largely with a single man with a good memory and a
telephone, the Austrians operated with endless bureaucracy
and endless taxes. Taxes took three volumes, each of six
hundred closely printed pages, to explain. There were, in
1914, well over 3,000,000 civil servants, running things as
diverse as schools, hospitals, welfare, taxation, railways,
posts etc. A single tax-payment required the attention of
twenty-three different bureaucrats. The 'Young Czech'
businessmen complained at this, as did the German nationalists, for both of them were heavily taxed to put up with this
baroque nonsense. But so much of the Bohemian population
was directly interested in the bureaucracy that to attack it was
as hopeless as to attack Giolitti's machines. The problem of
multiplying bureaucrats was that there had also to be
duplication for different languages. More than a quarter of
German students, just under a quarter of Czech ones, and

over a third of Polish ones studied law, the preparation for
this career; underemployed law students and graduates were
the heart of the nationality movements, as they often were
of the anti-Semitic movement. So much money was swallowed by administrative complications that there was not
much left for the army itself; by 1913, it received less money
than the infinitely smaller British army (£25,000,000 to
£28,000,000).

That problem was made worse by the autonomous position
of Hungary. That country did not develop in the Austrian
manner. She too had many nationalities, making up a rough
half of the population – Germans, scattered around in
communities of settlers which, in the case of the Transyl-
vanian Saxons, dated back to the twelfth century; Slovaks
mainly in the north; Ruthenes in the north-east; Romanians
in the east; Serbs in the south; Croats, with their own
kingdom in the south-west, and ruled by a governor who
took his orders from Budapest. Each of these peoples
developed in the manner of the later nineteenth century,
though there were great variations in pace: the Ruthenes, in
the Carpathians, and many of the Catholic (as distinct from
Lutheran) Slovaks remained illiterate.

Greater Hungary was a unitary state. The parliament had
a franchise that embraced about five per cent of the
population, and it had the wildest anomalies in Europe. The
arch-nationalist class was the gentry, most of which depended on political power for their incomes. Fully a quarter
of the voters were men whose surnames figured in the
electoral roll for the old Diet of the 'feudal' era before 1848:
that constituted their right to vote. In most cases this
bocskoros nobility owned little, and sold it up after 1867. Fifty
thousand of them obtained jobs in the new semi-independent
state, and as many again found a place as 'lawyers'. Their
representatives converged on politics, and supplied the
backbone of the Hungarian liberal party, which was led by
a Protestant count, Kálmán Tisza. His machine – the
'mamelukes' – operated like all of the others. It fixed
elections, and the deputies could obtain places in the

railways, the banks or the new industries. In 160 of the constituencies, those far from the centre, the government's placemen, with the help of the local police and bureaucracy, could arrange an election with no difficulty, on occasion establishing a police cordon round the polling stations to keep honest voters away. In about sixty other constituencies, the representative of the local magnate family was automatically nominated, and the parliament had its quota of Apponyis, Károlyis, Majláths, Zíchys, Andrássys, Pálffys, Szapárys who saw themselves quite often as Whigs. In 200 other constituencies, there would be a genuine enough contest, and the government would have to win fifty of them to obtain a working majority in the parliament. Many of the voters, here – and in Budapest, half – were Jews, who flourished in Hungary, to the point where they made up a quarter of the population of Budapest and practically monopolized its banking and commerce, as well as much else.

In practice the government could 'make' elections easily enough, though like its Italian counterpart it had difficulty in supporting its own supporters. Politics was an industry, with a great deal of money attached. In regions inhabited by other nationalities, an effort was made to promote the use of the Hungarian language: no nonsense there about giving towns and villages anything other than their Hungarian names, even in Croatia, which was supposed to be respected. Old Hungary did know the rule of law, and there were limits to the amount of persecution that minorities experienced (in the 'treason trials' before 1914, defendants got away with light, though unjust, sentences). Even so, in the league of central European nationalities crazily persecuting each other, Hungary was first off the mark. The Habsburg dynasty was powerless: the Hungarian parliament, unlike the Austrian one, hardly contained representatives of the other peoples, and so Hungary appeared to be less chaotic than Austria.

The Monarchy expected Hungary to share 'common' expenses – the army, above all. But Hungarian governments were reluctant to increase their contributions, and from 1889 the army badly lacked money, to the point where it was dissolving regimental bands in order to have more infantrymen. The system of conscription failed, because there was not enough money to support universal military recruiting. Not more than a third of the available manpower was taken to serve and many of these men were 'sent on permanent leave'. Hence, when the young Hitler evaded his call-up, the military authorities let him go without much fuss, after the usual 'physical' had been used to eliminate him. (It was also used in the case of Erich von Stroheim, who was born Erich Stroh in the vicinity of the war ministry in the Stiftgasse, grew up with a fascination for things military, but discovered that it did not survive more than a few weeks' concrete experience.)

The Hungarians' objection to the army was, at least in part, that it was dynastic, not Hungarian. It tolerated languages which the Hungarian State discouraged; an imperial general of Romanian origin was even imprisoned when he protested at the disabilities in public life that Romanians had to endure. In the atmosphere of radical nationalism around 1900, Hungarian politicians, many of them of quite recent Magyarization, made a fuss: they wanted the Hungarian part of the army to use the language and insignia of Hungary. In 1903, they put up a nine-point programme to this effect. They were supported by a band of industrialists who wished to have a tariff against cheap Austrian and German goods, and to build their own cartels in the wake of the turn-of-the-century depression. Political life became chaotic: after 1897, arrangement of the Hungarian 'Quota' of joint expenses was held up; obstruction ruled in the parliament. The government, under Tisza's son, István, lost control of the Whigs and its own placemen, and threw responsibility at them in the election of 1904, which was deliberately lost.

To restore order, Franz Joseph appointed a general, Fejérváry; he closed the parliament, and ruled by decree. In this era, the emperor and the Austrian prime minister, Baron

Gautsch, elected to promote the cause of universal suffrage in Hungary, to 'Get out of the House of Deputies these elements – arrogant oligarchs, advocates, clergymen, small noblemen – who for some 150 years have been making up the Hungarian parliament and ruling it and which for the same period have been throwing up always the same sterile constitutional questions' (in Fejérváry's angry words). Kristóffy, the minister of the interior, cultivated the small Hungarian socialist party; there were social troubles; there was an air of nationalist intoxication in Budapest, as people boycotted Austrian goods and wore a tulip in their lapel to advertise this fact (the tulips were made in Austria). With universal suffrage, Greater Hungary would have reproduced the problems of Austria in worse form. The nationalists drew back, accepted office, and until 1909 there was political stability. The 'Quota' was met, even increased.

Still, the Hungarian problem was not solved. The system there disintegrated as it did everywhere else before 1914. The radical nationalists of the independence party were strong in Budapest; some of the great noblemen sympathized; and the ruling liberals (re-formed by Tisza as *Nemzeti Munkapárt*, a Hungarian rendering of the Germanic *Arbeitspartei*, meaning 'party of work') were quite divided. In 1912, when it came to another military bill, the government passed it only by carrying the opposition out of the building. Hungary, though ostensibly solidly unitarian under the Tisza régime, was in practice much more unstable than Austria. When the Monarchy disintegrated, the independence of the Austrian nationalities was a matter largely of a few telephone calls. In Hungary there was civil war and communism.

Still, if the effect of Hungarian autonomy was to reduce very greatly the military effectiveness of the Monarchy, the example of Hungary also raised the expectations of lesser nationalities to a degree incompatible with the survival of the Dual system. It was in the South Slav lands that the Habsburg Monarchy came to grief; and it was through the South Slav question that the problems of Austria-Hungary came to provoke the First World War.

The Croats had been, in the old days, the most loyal of all the Habsburgs' subjects. They were aggressively Catholic, and aggressively military; they had supplied the Habsburgs' equivalent of the Cossacks, and, like the Cossacks, had acquired land for that. They had some rights, guaranteed in 1868, vis-à-vis their Hungarian rulers. These rights were not respected; and the Croat voters responded by dividing. Some wished to appeal for the old Habsburg absolutism; others hoped for Hungarian enlightenment (a hope squashed in 1908 when the Hungarians, by asserting the primacy of their language in the railways of Croatia, effectively barred Croats from jobs in them). As the country developed in the last third of the century, a radical element came up: a peasant party, led by Stepan Radić, and secular youth. There were Croats in Austrian-ruled Dalmatia, who were sometimes oppressed by the Italian minority of the old Venetian towns of the Adriatic. They spoke a still more radical language than did their counterparts in Croatia.

There were also, quite heavily intermingled with the Croats, 2,000,000 Serbs. They and the Croats differed in religion (except for the Catholicized Serbs in southern Hungary), and in Croatia proper, where a quarter of the population was Serb, there was tension for much the same reasons as there was tension between nationalities everywhere else. In Dalmatia, Croats and Serbs were more remote from their capital cities, and in 1905 they resolved, at Rijeka (Fiume) that Serbs and Croats should ally against their oppressors. The Croats of Croatia proper, who had set up the Resolution, did not carry very much weight in their native land; but their Dalmatian brothers did.

The Serbs of Dalmatia spoke for their own nationality. It had its own independent spokesman, in the shape of the kingdom of Serbia, which had wrested its independence from the Turks three generations before, and, after 1900, aimed to unite all Serbs (half of whom lived in Austria-Hungary). The Serbian State was not particularly bothered with the Catholic Croats: the Serbian prime minister was much more interested in acquiring Macedonia with a population that could not be properly described: Bulgarian or Serbian?

Still, the Austro-Serbian problem came up decisively over the lands of Bosnia and Herzegovina, where social and national questions were intermingled. They were Turkish provinces between Serbia and Dalmatia, and had been occupied by the Austro-Hungarians in 1878, as part of the same Berlin arrangements that had given Cyprus to the British. Before Ottoman days, Bosnia had belonged to Serbia, and, now that the Serbian renaissance was vigorously under way, Serbians and Serbs who lived under Habsburg rule generally hoped for unification in 'Greater Serbia'. As Turkey disintegrated in the Balkan wars of 1912–13, Serbia doubled in size, and her nationalists promoted the cause of the Bosnian Serbs. In their *Okkupationsgebiet*, the Austrians had presided over a muddled process of 'modernization' – 4000 kilometres of railway, 5000 schools, some roads and public buildings in the chief town, Sarajevo.

There were severe limits to the effectiveness of this. The Hungarians, who did not want Bosnian agrarian produce to compete with their own, insisted on the Bosnian railways' having a narrower gauge than the Hungarian lines, so that everything had to be shifted from one train to another at the frontier-station of Brod. The school programme had made only half of the population literate, but it did create a need for primary teachers, who often sprang from the peasantry. The agricultural system created trouble at the peasant level. The Austrians had taken over a Turkish share-cropping structure, in which a mainly Serb peasantry (*kmets*) worked for mainly Moslem landlords (*Agas*), dividing the crop between them in exchange for tools supplied by the landlord. That system broke down under Austrian rule, for much the same reasons as share-cropping broke down elsewhere: the chance of emigration broke up share-croppers' families and their patriarchal father's authority; some landlords wished for a better return on the land, and made greater exactions; the population grew, but had to be supported on land half of which, traditionally, was left fallow. As happened with the

Stolypin reforms in Russia, government efforts to help the peasants to acquire land were not very successful. By 1915, only nine per cent of the *kmets* had been 'redeemed', and they were already some way in arrears to the State which had supplied the loan to 'redeem' them.

In Bosnia and Herzegovina, the situation was further complicated by the existence of a considerable Croat, Catholic minority, and of a much smaller, Moslem one. Serbs, Croats and Moslems wrangled, and the Serb element looked more and more to Serbia. The Austrian régime – which was itself divided between a civilian in the *k.u.k. Finanzministerium* and a military *Landeschef* in Sarajevo – was perplexed. To challenge Serb nationalism, the Austrians launched a tariff war in 1906, and in 1908 they decided to end Serbian (and Turkish) hopes for a recovery of Bosnia by annexing the country. They gave it a constitution, which then turned out to be largely unworkable; by 1912, as the Serbian army won its great victories against the Turks, the Serb nationalists in Bosnia were in a state of ungovernable ferment. Students, who had their counterparts in the Russian socialist revolutionaries or the Ukrainian nation-alists, crossed over to Belgrade and received training from sympathetic Serbian officers, some of them very highly placed.

This coincided with a growing problem in Croatia. By 1910, a new radicalism had affected the Croat peasantry and students. A South Slav movement emerged, in which Serbs and Croats collaborated, in the hope of overthrowing the Hungarian régime. The Croat Diet, the *Sobor*, had to be closed down, and it was not until 1913 that a new governor, Skerlecz, reopened it; he had to close it almost at once. Students shot at Austro-Hungarian dignitaries, and General Varešanin was killed in Bosnia (his successor, Oskar Potiorek, remained confined to his quarters in the *konak*, the old Turkish government building, and communicated even with his chief of staff on little pieces of paper).

It was certainly true that most Croats regarded themselves as being a cut above the Serbs: their capital, Zagreb, had

taken its ways from Vienna and Budapest, whereas the
Serbians had languished for centuries under the Turks. But
events were pushing the two peoples together. The Habs-
burgs and most Austrians would much rather have set up
some kind of southern Slav unit in the empire, on much the
same lines as Hungary – the 'trialist solution', rather than the
Dual one. It would have meant uniting Croatia with other
South Slav lands. The heir to the throne, Archduke Franz
Ferdinand, favoured this, for he approved of the Catholic
Croats, and detested the Hungarians to the extent that he
forbade one chief of the General Staff to learn their language.
He gathered around him men who spoke the language of
reform: indeed, as his aged uncle grew older, Franz
Ferdinand's own military office (*Militärkanzlei*) became
almost a second government, in which great Bohemian
aristocrats planned for the future. Was he going to restore
Gross-Oesterreich, and cut down the powers of Hungary by
appealing to the non-Hungarian half of that land? Certainly
there was much talk of Franz Ferdinand's appointing his
military secretary, Brosch von Aarenau, as chancellor, with
full powers to effect a reform. The Hungarians were
extremely apprehensive, though of course they had survived
this kind of threat before, and did not intend to abdicate their
control of Croatia.

In June 1914, military manoeuvres were to take place in
Bosnia, where 15 and 16 army corps were being prepared for
the eventual invasion of Serbia. Archduke Franz Ferdinand,
as army inspector, went to supervise these manoeuvres; it
was natural enough for him to pay a courtesy visit to
Sarajevo, although he had forebodings. He and his mor-
ganatic wife travelled there on Sunday, 28 June, which
happened to be the Serbian national day, marking Kossovo.
The security arrangements had been badly handled by
Potiorek, a gloomy homosexual, who had a grievance against
the archduke because Franz Ferdinand had promoted his
rival, Conrad von Hötzendorf, to be chief of the General
Staff. No doubt, in view of the strained finances of the
military government, he did not want to face criticism from

Vienna at overlavish security. There was a very thin military cordon as the archduke drove to the *konak*; and a bomb was thrown from the crowd. It bounced off the back of the car, and the archduke drove on, in a rage, to the governor's residence. Shortly after midday, he drove off again to see an officer who had been wounded in the bomb explosion. His driver took a wrong turning, into a narrow street where he could not manoeuvre the car. Waiting there was another assassin, Gavrilo Prinčip, a Bosnian Serb who had obtained training and weaponry from Serbian nationalists over the border. He had given up hope of reaching his target, because of the failure of the earlier attempt. Now his target drove up to him, very slowly, and stopped. Princip fired several times before he was overpowered; the archduke and his wife were dead.

IV

WAR AND REVOLUTION, 1914–18

1. 'Gift from Mars'

The murder of the archduke came as the culmination of a
quarrel between Austria-Hungary and Serbia. Count Berchtold, the Austro-Hungarian foreign minister, had no doubt
that the murder had been organized on Serbian soil, and with
the connivance of influential Serbians; there was even a
suspicion (unfounded) that the archduke had been disposed
of because he threatened to solve the South Slav question
within the Monarchy. The assassins had been given encouragement from extreme Serbian nationalists; they had also
been given discouragement from those members of the
government who had heard of the plot. But it was not
difficult for the Austrians to guess that the assassins had
trained and obtained weapons from Serbia. Potiorek in
Sarajevo had been arguing for some time that the Bosnian
crisis was insoluble in its own terms; there would have to be
a 'disciplining' of Serbia. But the Serbian affair symbolized,
in Vienna's eyes, much of what was otherwise going wrong.
The time had come to reassert the Monarchy's prestige, to
unite the dissident peoples by a dramatic stroke. The
Habsburg generals, Conrad above all, saw themselves –
rightly – as the core of the empire, and had been wanting such
a dramatic stroke for some time. They had been restrained
– paradoxically – by Archduke Franz Ferdinand, and by
their German ally. In the second Balkan war, of summer
1913, Berchtold had become alarmed at the extension of
Serbian power. He had had to protect the newly created
Albanian state from Serbian and Montenegrin incursions;

but throughout the crisis Bethmann Hollweg had refused to support any scheme for war. In November, the Kaiser himself told Berchtold that there should be no war for six years; some other solution must be found for the Serbian question. In January 1914 there was a row between Vienna and Berlin over future policy: Berchtold spoke for alliance with the defeated Bulgarians, which the Germans did not like. But now, with the archduke, the Kaiser's friend, dead, would Berlin not accept the Austrians' case? It was, the Austrians' Serbian experts, Giesl and Forgách, agreed, 'a gift from Mars'.

Germany held the key to all of this. Austria-Hungary was too weak to act on her own. The Habsburg army, with $48\frac{1}{2}$ infantry divisions, had to face the Serbians' eleven, and conditions on the ground made that difficult enough. But Serbia had her protector, the tsar. Already, in the winter of 1912–13, there had been an Austro-Russian crisis when Vienna had threatened Serbia. The Russians had patronized the Balkan League that had fought Turkey successfully, and they themselves were ambitious for the Straits. They were building a great Black Sea fleet, and their foreign minister, S.D. Sazonov, argued in a memorandum of December 1913 that Russian interests required a seizure of Constantinople soon – he suggested 1918. In January 1914 the tsar's ministers had agreed that war would be inappropriate at that time, though Zhilinsky, the chief of the General Staff, believed that it could be sustained (unlike in previous years) if need be. It was quite likely that Russia would support independent Serbia; and with $114\frac{1}{2}$ infantry divisions and a French ally, Sazonov spoke with force.

Accordingly, the Germans had the decision: they alone could guarantee Austria-Hungary – which, in a sense, they had already done in March 1909 when, with an ultimatum to Russia, they silenced her complaints at the annexation of Bosnia. During the Balkan wars, the German voice had been one of restraint. Now, in July 1914, it became one of encouragement. Just after news of the archduke's death arrived, the German ambassador in Vienna, Heinrich von

Tschirschky, spoke on his own authority to restrain Berchtold – which he assumed, from past experience, would be the right thing to do. He was at once told by Berlin not to take such initiatives again. Austria should 'act'. An Austro-Hungarian diplomat, Count Hoyos, went to Berlin and saw the Kaiser on 5 July; Bethmann Hollweg was consulted. Hoyos was told unmistakably that the Austrians should go to war with Serbia.

Perhaps the First World War would not have broken out if the archduke's driver had not taken that fatal wrong turning. But the fact was that, since January 1914, a great many Germans had been arguing for a war. The constants which had secured peace in Europe were changing.

It could almost be said of European liberalism that, in the words of Count Czernin about the Habsburg Monarchy, 'We were bound to die. We were at liberty to choose the manner of our death, and we chose the most terrible.' In the old days, the liberal 'consensus' had counted very strongly against armies. Great Britain, the arch-liberal country, had only six divisions in Europe. The German liberals had made continual trouble for Bismarck and Caprivi over the amount and the timing of army finance, and until 1911 army budgets did not substantially increase. It was true that the French republicans were keener to spend money on their armed forces. Republicanism inherited the Jacobin tradition of 'the nation in arms', and justified itself implicitly by the need to reverse the judgement of 1871, and to win back the lost provinces, Alsace and Lorraine. It mattered a great deal that the French officer-corps was recruited from 'democratic' elements which scarcely figured in the German or British armies at all.

Liberals could be brought to vote for navies. They were not nearly so threatening to internal peace as armies, and they were supposed to bring tangible economic benefits. Every historical work without exception made the point that the British were prosperous and peaceful because of their navy; the United States, the last Gladstonean country, constructed a huge battle-fleet in emulation. Germany, too, had built a battle-fleet, starting with the naval bill of 1897. It was clearly designed for a possible war with Great Britain, to act as a constant blackmailing weapon; that became plain in the second naval bill, of 1900. The motivation was obvious, that Great Britain should be compelled to help Germany acquire an overseas empire. During the First World War, there was a veritable explosion of colonialist dreaming inside the German government – 'German central Africa', colonies here, there and everywhere. That was not coincidental.

This threat was the single greatest factor in creating another constant of Edwardian Europe: Anglo-German rivalry. The British had been looking for colonial agreements with France and Russia (and the United States) because their resources were strained enough as it was. They could not, for instance, guarantee their own status both in the Far East and in the Mediterranean as they had done in the nineteenth century. The Entente with France in 1904, and that with Russia in 1907, reflected the fact that France and Russia had something concrete to offer, while Germany did not. But there was always more to it; the British feared the expansion of Germany for economic and military reasons, and strove to preserve a balance in Europe. They were terrified that Germany and Russia might make common cause, for instance in the Middle East ('such a nightmare', said Sir Arthur Nicolson). It made sense to indicate to Germany that there were answers to the naval blackmail.

A naval race then developed. In 1905–6, the first all-big-gun ship, *Dreadnought*, was launched. It made all earlier battleships obsolete, and was itself greatly improved up to 1914. Tirpitz made further demands on the *Reichstag*, which were accepted, and in 1908–9 he even went behind the *Reichstag*'s back to build by stealth. The fact became known to the British, who experienced a naval scare. They pursued their earlier policy of building two ships for Germany's one, and in 1909 Lloyd George's budget catered for eight, not four, capital ships (though in part this was to smuggle direct taxation past right-wing liberals). The British attempted to sort the issue out by compromise. In 1910, again in February

1912 (the Haldane mission), and again, sporadically, in the years before 1914, noises to this effect were made. But Tirpitz was adamant. To scale down his naval demands would mean accepting that the whole scheme for a navy was a failure. On the whole, the Kaiser supported him. The Germans would answer only that they would stop naval building if the British made a pact of neutrality. Virtually everyone in London understood that, in that event, the Germans would attack France, and then settle accounts with the British. Agreements were made about extraneous matters – even the Berlin-Baghdad railway – to indicate goodwill, but no pact followed. On the contrary, the British supported France in both Moroccan crises.

In these circumstances, a balance of power worked. The German army might threaten France. In 1905, when Russia was weak, the threat was very real. But the Germans were deterred by the thought that Great Britain would intervene; the German navy was not at all prepared to defeat naval intervention, and, besides, the suspension of German trade by a British blockade could well throw Germany's cities into confusion. After all, in 1905 the social atmosphere in Germany was very tense indeed. Sazonov remarked in January 1914 that 'Germany clearly appreciates the danger that if there is British intervention she would be exposed within six weeks to complete internal social catastrophe': there would be bread-riots, from which socialist revolutionaries would profit. That same fear haunted British thinking about war. The suspension of trade would cause terrible social troubles; and the government's strategy was based, extraordinarily, on the slogan 'Business as usual'. As soon as war broke out, the board of trade engaged a hundred more people and rented premises in Cheapside to advise traders how they should set about conquering the vast, previously German-dominated, markets. In Germany, the Kaiser's reaction to the first Moroccan crisis was that no forward policy could be undertaken without 'first shooting the social democrats dead'. In Russia, the conservat strongly advised against war in 1914. That factor still counted with a British cabinet minister, John Morley, who resigned upon the declaration of war in 1914: 'The atmosphere of war cannot be friendly to order, in a democratic system that is verging on the humour of [18]48.'

Left-wing socialists sometimes argued that war broke out because the Establishments wished to stave off a social crisis. No doubt it was true that an important argument for imperialism was that it would achieve this: places to ship the surplus proletariat, captured markets and cheap raw materials to make the metropolis prosperous. Such thinking was clearly present in the war itself, when war aims were being elaborated, and in Germany there was a great deal of such talk among bankers and industrialists before 1914. It is impossible to pin down such considerations in the July crisis itself. The documents of the main countries, and even the private papers of anyone who took part in the chief decisions, indicate only a concern for questions of prestige, strategy, 'high politics'. Far from being launched to stave off a social crisis, the war owed a large part of its immediate origin to the feeling that, if the facts of the country's 'case' were properly presented, then the socialists themselves would accept it. Bethmann Hollweg informed the social democrats throughout the latter half of the July crisis as to what was happening; they accepted it, as did their counterparts elsewhere, with few exceptions, and the patriotic atmosphere of August 1914 brought euphoria to monarchs and statesmen who had feared quite the opposite.

Governments in the West had the measure at least of the social democratic parties and the trade unions. In France, a third of the socialists elected in March 1914 had voted for the three-year military service Act even though their party's official stance had been against it; in Germany, in summer 1913, the socialists had voted for the taxes which allowed a very great increase in the strength of the German army. Still, the official attitudes of parts of parties were one thing; the reactions of the masses were quite another thing, and it would be naïve to suppose that statesmen who spent most of their time discussing finance would not regard their country's prosperity as a vital consideration. Inside Germany, there were growing fears after 1910 that the economy could break down. Exports accounted for a third of the gross national product, and if they stopped there would be vast unemployment. They would stop if other countries put up tariffs. But the Germans themselves had a tariff; they could hardly complain if Russians and French imposed one as well, as both seemed likely to do; while the constant talk in British right-wing circles of abandoning free trade caused a shiver of alarm throughout German business. Increasingly, there was discussion inside Germany of building up a middle-European block, the idea of *Mitteleuropa*, where Germany would have a vast tariff-free zone, one more solid than her existing territory. Conferences to establish that were arranged in Budapest and Vienna in April 1914. This would knit together the Habsburg Monarchy, Balkan countries, perhaps Italy and Belgium, in a huge *Zollverein* such as had made for Prussia's economic greatness seventy years earlier. This programme was difficult to realize, since German agrarians feared the competition of cheap Hungarian grain. But it was to figure very largely in Germany's war aims. It was an essential feature of the July crisis that Bethmann Hollweg received not even routine objections from businessmen, whether of the free-trade *Hansabund* or the tariff-supporting *Zentralverband*. On the contrary, the cleverest businessman of them all, Walter Rathenau, was an outright supporter of *Mitteleuropa*, and its chief architect.

A further 'constant' which changed before 1914 was the liberals' attitude to armies. In the 1890s, liberals had been converted to navies and empire. But they remained hostile to armies which were often seen as tyrannical and wasteful. In Germany, an alliance of left-liberals, social democrats and Catholics prevented any increase in the army budget for many years after 1893, and almost one-half of Germany's young men escaped conscription by one means or another. That factor still counted for much in 1905. But after then, military leagues made inroads on liberal consciousness, as can perhaps be seen from the great flood of war literature that emerged at this time. The enthusiasm of August 1914 speaks for itself. The State had a romance and a mystery of its own; military service allowed even the national minorities, the lower middle class, the Jews to join in. The State became a great machine, in military matters as in others; a machine to which the liberal 'technocrats' had already contributed much. It was not a romance that remained confined to the middle classes. For much of the working class, the army proved to be very attractive, and that, perhaps, accounts for the surprising amount of military theorizing that went on among socialists. Jean Jaurès in France wrote a book about militia armies; Reinhard Höhn in Germany catalogued the often extremely knowledgeable interest displayed by the SPD. When the British called for volunteers, they had their best response in aggressively working-class districts, e.g. the Rhondda.

Before 1911, the army chiefs themselves were often anxious to avoid taking working-class recruits. Proletarians were said to be physically unsuitable; probably more to the point, they did not put up any too easily with the kind of rigid military behaviour that the peasantry was supposed to tolerate. Russians, Germans, Austrians had used this argument as a reason for confining conscription largely to the peasantry. After 1911, that changed. The Prussian war ministry was pushed to accept the thesis of Colonel Ludendorff, that Germany needed to have a mass army, even if that meant accepting officers who would not have found a place in the old, aristocratic, days. In December 1912, the chief of the German General Staff argued for a great extension of the army. Now, the danger of war from some Balkan quarrel was unmistakable, and Moltke wished to be properly ready. Germans' sense that they would now have to protect their central European interests was combined with an accurate enough notion that the army no longer needed to be confined to peasants and Junkers. Besides, Bethmann Hollweg himself egged the soldiers into demanding more money so that he could deny it to Tirpitz, whose plans were ruining Germany's chance of a neutral Great Britain. The way was then open, not just to a naval race, but to an arms race in general which would go beyond anything that had hitherto been experienced. In 1913 Germany expanded her peacetime conscript army to 665,000 (from 530,000) and planned to expand it still more in 1914. This cost 1,465,000 marks and required a special direct tax, the *Wehrbeitrag*, paid by property. In the context of this the French, in order not to lose pace, reintroduced three years' service, so that they trained as many conscripts in peacetime as the Germans. The Austro-Hungarian army took 160,000 men per annum, not 100,000, after 1912.

Most of this occurred in the context of another changing 'constant': Russia was becoming very strong indeed. In March 1914, the German press, including the semi-official *Norddeutscher Anzeiger*, made a great fuss about this. A constant theme in internal discussions of the Germans at this time was the need to defeat Russia before she, France and Great Britain became an insuperably strong coalition.

There were two elements in this calculation, both of them logical enough in their own terms. The first was the strength of the tsar's army. In backward days, Russia had not been able to afford to conscript more than a fraction of her manpower, and the Russo-Japanese war had shown how weak was the equipment. But as the budget expanded, expenditure on the army could rise from 473,000,000 roubles in 1909/10 to 528,000,000 in 1912/13 and 581,000,000 in 1913/14, while naval expenditure doubled. That expenditure did not include 'extraordinary' sums, given as capital grants for this and that: the 'little programme' of 1908 and the 'reorganization' of 1910 gave the army 700,000,000 roubles altogether. In 1913, a further 'Great Programme' was discussed (it became law in June 1914) to supply a further 140,000,000 roubles per annum and a capital grant of 432,000,000 to enable the army to expand its capital base, and to allow it to increase its number of recruits from 450,000 per annum to almost 600,000 – giving a peacetime army three times as large as Germany's, and armed with 6700 mobile guns to the Germans' 6004. True, the Russian war ministry and artillery department made spectacular errors in the use of this money, and much of it was frittered away. But the days when Germany could automatically count on a weak Russia were over. By 1917, said the military experts, Russia alone could challenge Germany on equal terms.

The German panic involved not only the strength of Russia, but also the speed of Russian mobilization. The General Staff's response to the alliance of France and Russia had been logical enough in the 1890s, under Count Schlieffen. Russia did not have too many railways, and because of that she could not mobilize her army at all fast, in contrast to the Germans, who could use lines that might accommodate as many as 700 military trains a day (it took thirty-six trains to carry an infantry division). The Russians responded to this by building what they thought were safe fortresses, which swallowed a large proportion of their budget, and were stuffed with immobile guns useless in the field. That meant that Germany would have, in wartime, several weeks, and perhaps even months, to attack France while Russia was not ready. Schlieffen responded to this with a plan to overthrow France while leaving the defence against Russia to a very weak force and to the Austrians. Because the French had developed very strong defences along the border, the Germans would have to bypass them through neutral Belgium – a plan worked out, not coincidentally, in 1897, just as Tirpitz planned his battle-fleet against the British. After 1914, Schlieffen was criticized, since the plan went wrong.

Any advance in the speed of Russian mobilization would undercut this plan. Such advances duly happened. The Russians built railways in any event, since Poland was an important part of their economy. But some of these were purely strategic in purpose, and the expansion both of building and capital equipment was such that the Russian army could mobilize quickly enough. In 1912/13, the French offered Russia a loan of 500,000,000 francs to allow the Russians to construct strategic railways. That loan speeded things up, but it was not vital, since the Russians would be able to find the money themselves. Danilov, the effective head of Russian planning, kept having to revise his mobilization-schedules upward. In 1900, Russia could not even manage 200 trains daily to the west. By 1910, 250. By 1914, 360. By 1917, 560. This allowed the Russian army to mobilize, not under the arthritic arrangements of plan no. 18, dating from 1905, but under plan 20, due to take effect in September 1914, when the mustering of seventy-five infantry divisions on the western borders would be over by the eighteenth day of mobilization – only three days later than Germany. In the summer of 1914, the old plan ('19, altered') was still in effect, and mobilization took thirty days. That gave a German army of ninety-five divisions just the time to defeat France before Germany herself was invaded by a Russian army group, held off by only twelve divisions. If Germany had not gone to war in 1914, she would have had to rethink her entire military operation; and yet Moltke, and virtually everyone else, could see no alternative to it.

But in any event, the Germans knew that they could not rely for much longer on their Habsburg ally. Already at the time of the Badeni crisis, there had been a widespread fear that Austria-Hungary would break up. The French and Russians, at that time, had tightened up their alliance, and made it, in effect, an aggressive one in the event that Germany took over the collapsing Monarchy. Every twist of the Austro-Hungarian internal crisis since then had evoked similar fears. Now, the murder of the archduke brought them to life again. Beyond this, there were German fears over the future of Turkey. Russia's protégés in the Balkans had carved up her European possessions (except for Albania and a slice of Thrace) among themselves. German efforts to find a place in Turkey had led to the despatch of a military mission, under General Liman von Sanders, in the winter of 1913–14. The Russians had protested at the presence of a German general commanding the Straits, through which half of their trade found its way. Liman himself was eventually given a rather different post, but the point was still clear enough (January 1914), and the row between the two countries was noticeably worse than in the past. But it was above all the imponderable: what would happen to eastern Europe? which caused tension between the two. It even caused Sazonov, in June 1914, to argue to the tsar that he must make some effort to accommodate the Poles who, otherwise, might gravitate towards the Central Powers.

When the Austrians asked Germany what they should do about Serbia, the answer was quite clear: deal with Serbia; and if there is trouble with Russia, then better now than later. In that sense, the answer to 'the origins of the First World War' is obvious – Germany. At the time, Bethmann Hollweg and others had to conceal what they were about. The British, it was hoped, would be neutral. The social democrats had to be squared, and they would not buy 'Prussian militarism', or more exercises in Ems telegrams. It all had to look as if an injured Austria sought proper redress from a semi-barbaric nation. Bethmann Hollweg himself even pretended to be on holiday in the early days of the crisis. But he was incautious enough to indent, later on, for his expenses: and they reveal that he took a journey to Potsdam on every one of these days, except 1 and 3 July, to advise the Kaiser. Similarly, he had an expensive telegraph installed on his estate, and indented for the cost of every last syllable. The Bavarian and Saxon military attachés faithfully reported back to their capitals what was going on: preventive war, included. Just after the war a communist government in Bavaria published these and similar documents. Upon the counter-revolution, their editor was sentenced to a long gaol sentence (far longer than Hitler's) for 'treason' – i.e., telling the truth.

On 5 and 6 July, the Austrians were left in no doubt as to German views, and the delays came on their side, not Germany's. They had to overcome Hungarian opposition: Tisza feared a Romanian revolt if it came to war, and was probably overborne only when his friend, István Burián, the Hungarian minister in Vienna, told him all of the details concerning German support. By mid-July, Vienna had worked out its plan: send demands on Serbia, ostensibly reasonable but in practice unacceptable; reject the answer; declare war, with injured innocence. These things were done – ultimatum delivered on 23 July, answer rejected on 25 July, and war declared on Serbia on 28 July. The Germans were informed at every stage, and they were sometimes demanding earlier action by their hesitant allies (whose nervous inability to bring themselves to the point of mobilization caused them much trouble later on).

By 28 July, European war was plainly on the horizon. Sazonov showed willingness to concede; he urged concessions on the Serbians; he would accept British mediation. But he would not see a vital Russian interest treated without ceremony. Since 1913, he had been under strong pressure from the French, in the full flood of their *réveil national*, not to draw back under threats – indeed, in August 1913 the French president, Poincaré, had been keener on Balkan actions than Sazonov himself – and although we do not know what was said in the State visit paid by Poincaré to St Petersburg just before the war broke out, it seems safe to guess that it followed earlier lines. The Russian military were confident enough, though not as confident as they expected to be after the realization of the 'Great Programme' in 1917. Sazonov decided to give a warning; partial mobilization against Austria-Hungary. It was to be announced on 29 July, and the Germans were warned in advance.

This, and an increasing suspicion that the British would not be neutral, caused some wobbling in Berlin. The Kaiser came back from his holiday and (as Bethmann Hollweg had foreseen) drew back from the crisis: he told the chancellor to tell Vienna that there were no grounds for causing a European war. Bethmann Hollweg weakened the instruction, but did inform Vienna late on the twenty-ninth and early on the thirtieth that Germany 'could not let herself be involved in a world conflagration by Vienna without regard for our advice'. This ran counter to everything he had said before, but it perhaps showed that the prospect of British intervention had become clear. Whatever the case, these manoeuvres – whether failures of nerve or tactical calculations – failed. The Russian generals appreciated that, if there were only partial mobilization, they could be in terrible danger. They would send half of their army, according to plan 19 variant 'A', against Austria-Hungary; that would expose the other half to a German thrust, at a time of terrible complications on the railways. The only answer was: total mobilization, which the tsar accepted on 30 July at 3 p.m. for proclamation the next day. But in any case the German generals were making not dissimilar calculations: if they were slow off the mark with their mobilization, then Russia would have a head-start and the Schlieffen plan would be unworkable. Bethmann Hollweg had terrible difficulty in keeping them still on 29 and 30 July. In fact, under pressure from Moltke and the war minister, Erich von Falkenhayn, he agreed to proclaim German mobilization at noon on 31 July. It was only a chance that Russian general mobilization was proclaimed first. On 31 July, the general mobilization of Austria-Hungary, Russia and Germany was a fact. Germany sent an ultimatum to Russia, and declared war on 1 August. The French, in pursuit of their alliance, mobilized on 1 August (with effect from 2 August). An excuse was found for declaring war on them, on 3 August. The Schlieffen plan then went into effect. German armies occupied Luxemburg, and pushed into Belgium.

It was the signal for Great Britain. Her military and naval chiefs only wanted an excuse. The Germans' invasion of Belgium involved Great Britain as guarantor of Belgian neutrality. The attack on a neutral (which experts had seen coming) gave a perfect moral argument with which the cabinet dissenters could be silenced, and on 4 August, an ultimatum went off from London. War followed.

2.   The War, 1914–18

'War is the midwife of history': an appropriately Hegelian sentiment for a German war. 1914–18 was an obvious moment of Hegelian 'suspension', when one era changed into another. But it took four and a half years of war, ten million war-deaths, and tens of millions of deaths indirectly brought about by the war, to finish that world.

The war ended in ways that anticipated 1940: tanks and aircraft, used in an almost *Blitzkrieg* fashion by the French in their offensive at Villers-Cotterêts in July 1918. But the war began in ways that reflected 1870, with cavalry-charges, individual heroism and grand manoeuvring. No war ever began with such extraordinary misapprehension as to what it would be like. The crowds in Europe cheered off their young men to war. The British overwhelmed their own military authorities at the extent of volunteering. On the continent, reservists rushed to the colours with a small shortfall that had the authorities quite unprepared, for they had expected to have to send military police around to collect the recalcitrants. So many Austro-Hungarians turned up at the depots even before formal mobilization that they had to be sent away again, because nothing had been prepared to take them in.

One reason for the war's lasting so long was the paradoxical, and significant, one that everyone expected it to be short – in the manner of nineteenth-century wars. The Austrian social-welfare offices even refused to pay bounties to the families of reservists on the grounds that the soldiers would soon be returning to their jobs. The preamble of the Russians 'Great Programme' in June 1914 had read that 'The circumstances of Russia's neighbours rule out the possibility of a long war'. By this was meant a familiar European theme.Exports, international trade were thought to be the guarantors of prosperity and internal order. Interruption of trade for any length of time would mean riots, revolution. The industrial Powers would have to make peace after six months, or at most a year. Financial calculations acted in the same sense. The treasuries assumed that their credit would be exhausted after a few months, although the British, with their huge overseas investments, were rather more sanguine. The Hungarian finance minister remarked in the Hungarian cabinet that he could see his way to financing the war only for three weeks – i.e., not even to the end of the mobilization of the Austro-Hungarian army. After that, credit would be exhausted. No one seriously supposed that the war could be waged with paper money. Sir Frederick Shuster, called upon to advise the British government on this point on the bankers' behalf, said that if an effort was made to fight the war with *assignats*, French-revolution style, 'You will not get very far.' Without a solid currency, there would be terrible inflation and unrest. The banker was right. But he was wrong in supposing that, in most countries, inflation would ruin the war effort.

The generals themselves planned, without exception, for a short war, and so did terrible damage to their chances of fighting a long one. They threw away extraordinary numbers of men who could more sensibly have been used to train other men, not for fighting the wrong battles. Of course, this corresponded to the needs of the Alliance system as well as to the mood of 1914. Germany had to knock out France before the Russian army was really in the field: in other words she had to plunge into Belgium, outflank the French and surround them, in the Paris region, within thirty days – after which the Russians would be well and truly launched into East Prussia, and perhaps beyond the Vistula, only a hundred miles from Berlin. The Austrians, similarly, set themselves to knock out Serbia. The Russians did their best to muster a North-Western Army Group for invasion of Germany on 'M 15' – the fifteenth day of mobilization. The French General Staff had been quite prudent in its planning up to 1911, but Joffre had substituted 'Plan XVII' in 1911–12 for an offensive into Alsace. He did so in order to support the simultaneous Russian attack into East Prussia, which could now be realized.

All of these initial offensives came to a bad end. They relied on four factors: cavalry, enormous masses of infantry, bombardments by shrapnel (which exploded in the air), and tactics of massed bayonet attack. Cavalry proved to be the first casualty of the war. Horses charging could, in the old days, have moved faster than guns could fire – in the Charge of the Light Brigade, for instance, the cavalry had at least reached the Russian guns, though only after large losses. The quick-firing revolution in artillery in the 1890s put paid to that; indeed, a well-aimed rifle could knock out a horse one mile away. Besides, cavalry divisions even without opposition were very difficult to supply, because horses ate a great amount of grain – so great, in fact, that fodder for horses accounted for fully half of Russia's military transports, and more British shipping than was sunk by submarines. Nine Russian cavalry divisions cantered grandly across the Prussian frontier on 15 August, ran out of contact with each other, made a muddle of their supplies, and caused a nervous breakdown in their commander, the aged Khan of Nakhichevan. Thereafter they clogged the supply lines to such an extent that the Russian First Army could barely move, except towards a textbook siege of the fortress of Königsberg. On the Austrian side, ten cavalry divisions rode out into Russian Poland, again on 15 August. Within a week, they were back – the men leading the poor animals, whose skin had been rubbed off their backs by a saddle that gave a fine seat, but suited only cavalry horses, not the requisitioned ones.

The mass infantry attacks were not usually any more effective. The standard tactic was a simple and stupid one: to bunch the infantry together and move them forward as fast as possible. This was justified by reference to *élan vital* or some such incantation, and none of the armies (except the Serbian, which had some experience) thought up anything else. Generals were promoted on the basis of their capacity for eating fire, and Russian infantry was commanded, at army level, usually by cavalry generals like Rennenkampf. The idea was to create a Napoleonic 'lozenge' – the great square-shaped formations that Napoleon had employed (to self-destructive effect) at the battle of Wagram in 1809. This was a crazy thing to do. In the first place, rifle-fire was far faster than it had been in Napoleonic days: the highly trained British soldier, a professional, could manage eighteen rounds in a minute – i.e. firing, slipping in the next bullet, working the bolt and firing again in three seconds. Machine-guns (though they often broke down) complemented this; and the revolution in artillery was also such that an infantry attack could be broken up two or three miles off by well-aimed guns, and in less than two miles even by badly aimed guns. The French offensive into Alsace broke down with 500,000 casualties in a few days after 15 August. So did the Austrian attack on Serbia, on 16 August. So did the Austrian attack on Russia, which began in bizarrely late circumstances on 21 August, and continued until retreat from eastern Galicia, on 11 September (the 'battle of Lemberg'), with the loss, again, of 750,000 men on both fronts.

The other two offensives came to grief, though in rather different circumstances. Six German armies moved west (while one defended the Alsatian border). Since the French had concentrated to the south, the German army occupied empty territory. It encountered, first, a Belgian army that made mistakes. The Belgians had built up a fortress, Liège, just on the border, and proposed to rely on a subsequent one, Antwerp, if need be. But fortresses (in which the Russians also invested great sums) proved to be a trap for the defence. They offered an obvious target for the very heavy guns that all armies now possessed (though the Germans, for Liège, had to borrow some from the Austrians). The defence, by contrast, was pinned: it could not show any flexibility in defending the fortress. Events showed that the only way to defend fortresses was to give them up, and to defend them (as the French did at Verdun in 1916) from a line of trenches outside, which the enemy artillery could not 'spot' so easily, and which could be supplied with reserves from concealed communications-trenches. In August 1914, that counted as alchemy, and in Russia before the war General Sukhomlinov had been accused of treachery for suggesting that the whole expensive fortress-network should simply be blown up.

Liège – like Antwerp in the west, Przemyśl, Ivangorod and Nowogeorgiewsk in the east (and a ring of others in 1915) – collapsed after some heavy shelling, and put the Belgian defences into chaos. The Germans moved remorselessly through Belgium, occupying Brussels on 22 August and 'masking' Antwerp. The French responded with another futile offensive, in the north-east, where they attacked head-on and again lost a quarter of a million men. In the way of the German advance stood the British Expeditionary Force, and it gave a good account of itself at Mons before retreating, again and again, in view of the French crisis. By 1 September, German armies were poised to take Paris; the French government went to Bordeaux, and the Germans entered Amiens, Noyon and, almost, Rheims. They bombarded Soissons and damaged the cathedral, as they had destroyed the historic library of Louvain in Belgium.

They crossed the rivers Somme and Marne. If it had been 1940, that would perhaps have been that. But the Germans could not obtain supplies at all easily. There were, in all of the army, forty-seven lorries, and all of them broke down incurably in Belgium. The railways were not working. There was no telegraph to tell Moltke in Koblenz what was going on. The troops were very tired from their endless marching across Belgium and northern France. The French, though very hard hit by their enormous initial losses, retired towards railheads which spread out from Paris, the centre of the whole system. The taxis of Paris volunteered to ferry men to the front. But the taxis, though a Dunkirk-gesture of magnificence, were essentially a propaganda-feat.

In the confusion, one German army, Kluck's First, tried to go west of Paris while its neighbour, Bülow's Second, went towards the east – partly in response to appeals for help from its own neighbour, Hausen's Third, as it stumbled into stiff resistance in the rolling country of the Marne. The French commanders, Joffre overall, and Galliéni in Paris, took advantage of this. Kluck was isolated and very bewildered.

His western flank was attacked, and he turned to face the attack. A gap then opened between him and Bülow: the British Expeditionary Force found itself there, and received (with surprise) an instruction to move forward. The flank of the German Second Army was under attack, and it too moved back. Out of prudence, Moltke, who received alarmist reports from his personal representative, Hentsch, told everyone to withdraw. On 11 September, that withdrawal was undertaken. The 'battle of the Marne' ended with a German retreat to the line of the river Aisne, which could be defended easily enough.

The Russian invasion of Prussia was a similar story, but because of the Germans' strange belief that they must be Teutonic Knights, legendry was woven around the 'battle of Tannenberg' with which it ended. Two Russian armies, each about as strong (on paper) as the single German Eighth Army in the region, invaded the province, one from south, one from east, on 15 August. They were preceded by a cavalry screen, which was of course nearly useless. They moved at the rate of two miles a day, and telegrams from the High Command (*Stavka*) arrived in brown-paper parcels, by motor car, all the way from Warsaw. The eastern force collided with the Germans at Gumbinnen on 20 August; German attacks were bloodily fended off. The southern army, Samsonov's Second, meanwhile came up very slowly towards the Germans' rear. The German commander proposed retreat. He was dismissed for the insight, and was replaced by the team of Paul von Hindenburg as commander and Erich Ludendorff as chief of staff, who took over the very efficient East Prussian team – Hoffmann, the *General-Quartier-Meister*, with Grünert, Grallert, Marquardt, the artillery expert, Bruchmüller and a set of commanders and chiefs of staff who served Ludendorff right through until the end.

Hoffmann organized a retreat – half of the army to go by rail to the western flank of the Russian Second Army, the other half to march south-west as fast as possible, to get away. That half could only go on foot because the railway was occupied otherwise. In marching south-west, that half collided with the eastern flank of Samsonov's bewildered force. The other half of the Eighth Army attacked Samsonov's other flank; and the bulk of the Russian Second Army was engaged in heavy fighting (at which it did well) in the centre. The flanks closed; and 100,000 Russians became prisoner by 30 August – the battle of Tannenberg, though the place itself, scene of a great medieval battle between Poles and Teutonic Knights, was some way off. The other Russian army, beset by supply problems, could not move to help Samsonov, and in any case did not know what was going on. It, under German pressure, evacuated East Prussia.

By mid-September 1914 the pattern of the war was set, and for the next three years it did not much change, although great efforts were made by both sides. The great manoeuvres of 1914 had been based on a misapprehension on the generals' part: that the war had to be won in a short time. There was almost a tacit agreement to ignore reality. Infantry tactics had been based on precepts that were absurd and destructive, the mass attack. The only justification for such attacks was that soldiers were too stupid to do anything other than form a crowd and move forward at speed. This corresponded to pre-war ideas of the profession. Generals supposed that it took years and years to make a soldier, and that the two years' training was wholly inadequate for this. Primitive infantry tactics continued, though they were rather less primitive, after the battle of the Marne, than before.

In particular, the Germans discovered the war-winning weapon of 1914–18: the shovel. Artillery had become so powerful that the only defence against it was digging. Troops who dug themselves a trench and threw up a parapet would be protected against bombardments, because it was very difficult for guns to pinpoint such a target, and even if they did pinpoint it, shell was often inadequate. Most armies had laid in shrapnel, which exploded in the air above a mass attack, and did terrible damage. But shrapnel was powerless against a trench, if the men kept their heads down and hid in the dug-outs. High explosive was needed. But even then it had to be fired from very heavy guns, for it needed an inordinate amount of high explosive to get through a dug-out ceiling. The trenches became more sophisticated, the ceilings thicker, as the war went on.

In the old days, it would have been very dangerous to place defenders permanently in a trench system, because, once there, they were immobile. If an attacker got round the flank, he would enfilade the trench, i.e. his guns would fire sideways into it, with devastating effect. But, in 1914, on the western front, there were no flanks. So many men were conscripted that the line ran continuously from the Channel to the Swiss frontier. Of course it took time for this to become evident. After the Marne, the Germans retreated to the Aisne, and were attacked, dug-in. Then the French tried to find the western flank; were opposed by a counterstroke near Arras on their own western flank; which they themselves countered by another flanking strike. By the end of the year, the fighting had reached the sea, and the British Expeditionary Force found itself holding what was left of Belgium, a position around the shattered town of Ypres, where the British line formed a 'salient'. Salients were an important feature from then on. They were sectors which jutted out into the enemy lines. Theoretically they could be used to funnel troops for an immediately effective attack; but they had the considerable drawback that the enemy guns could fire from three sides into a tightly packed mass of troops. The Ypres salient saw very heavy fighting in the spring of 1915, again in the Paaschendaele offensive of summer 1917 and again in the German offensive of April 1918. These attacks cost hundreds of thousands of casualties.

A final feature made this war, in principle, quite different. There was very little mobility. In the old days, horses could carry battles at a good speed. Now, they were far too vulnerable, and though armies maintained considerable forces of cavalry, they were next to useless in the field unless the enemy had been demoralized to the point of paralysis – as did happen with the Austrians in June 1916, during the Brusilov offensive, and to a lesser extent with the Germans in the last moments of the war in 1918. Yet, the horse could not be replaced. The internal combustion engine had not developed far enough to take a very great weight of armour plating. The tank, which all armies considered and which the British took a lead in producing (for the Somme offensive in 1916), was very slow – at the outside, it travelled at nine miles per hour, though in 1918 the French produced light tanks which could move somewhat faster. The tanks were always breaking down, and even the stoutest of them could not withstand a direct hit from a well-aimed gun. Thus, armies moved at an extremely slow pace; troops had to be loaded with supplies to carry them some way; and the sixty pounds of equipment and supplies made men move more slowly still. In August 1914 the Russian Second Army had advanced at the rate of two miles each day, and its commander expected congratulations.

Here was a situation without parallel, except perhaps in the lengthy sieges of the Dutch Revolt or the War of Spanish Succession. Armies had no difficulty in recruiting huge numbers of men, and in feeding them; after a few months, there was not much difficulty in equipping them with everything they needed, although corners had sometimes to be cut (the French used cast-iron shell-casings, and the Germans took their explosives quite literally from the air). But once these fabulously strong forces reached the front, they could not move.

What was to be done? The generals, in all countries, have had a – usually, wholly deserved – bad press. It was said that Douglas Haig, the British commander, was the best Scottish soldier because he killed the most Englishmen. The tsar's chief of staff, Alexeyev, told Brusilov in 1916 that his own son had written to him from the front to explain that there was not a single commander who had any trust at all from the men. In the early part of the war, especially, the generals were often callous buffoons, and in the tsarist army their grip on the promotions machinery was such that they merely replaced each other. In August 1916, when the tsar's army played what turned out to be its last card, a 'Special Army' was formed, composed largely of the two Guard infantry corps and the Guard cavalry corps, and assigned to the tsar's favourite, V.M. Bezobrazov. He trained it in the methods of 1877, and threw it into a succession of attacks known as 'the massacre of the Kowel marshes', which achieved nothing. So many Russian corpses lay on the German barbed wire that the Russians asked for a truce to bury the dead. The German commander, von der Marwitz, refused, on the grounds that these heaps of corpses would deter the Russians from attacking again. Yet Bezobrazov's diaries, like Haig's, show a fabulous indifference to losses. They – like Haig's – are astonishingly taken up with social trivialities: who will get which medal, whether the tsar liked a particular sycophantic gesture, who will get which job etc.

Still, at this remove, we can afford some sympathy for the generals. They faced an exceptionally difficult task. We can now see that an important part of the problem lay in the training of infantry. Tactics had to be revolutionized for this war to be won; artillery and infantry (and, later, tanks and aircraft) had to be made to work together. But that took time; it also meant using the existing trained troops to train others, rather than to fight a costly battle. The generals supposed – and in this they were supported, indeed overwhelmed, by the politicians – that their task was to win the war as fast as possible. Training programmes were therefore short and primitive, sometimes of only a few weeks' duration, and it was not until 1917 that the men were properly trained in modern infantry tactics. These, rather than numerical superiority or tanks, allowed the war to become mobile again in 1918. But it took an unconscionable amount of time to get there.

Faced with the western front of winter 1914–15, generals responded with a declaration of bankruptcy. Frontal bayonet charges at the barbed wire failed. The answer was thought to be: rain shell down on the enemy, obliterate the trench system, and send in the infantry to pick up the wreckage. This was, in essence, the method applied by the British and French in the spring of 1915 (Artois and Neuve Chapelle), the autumn of 1915 (Loos, Champagne – Chemin-des-

Dames), the long Somme campaign of summer and autumn 1916, and the 'third battle of Ypres' – or 'Paaschendaele' – in the summer and autumn of 1917. It was also the method used by the Italians in the eleven battles of the Isonzo (1915–17). These offensives were all failures, in the traditional sense of military victory. They would gain a few hundred yards at astonishing cost to both sides, though the attackers nearly always lost a third more than the defenders.

It took a tremendous effort of organization to build up and supply these hundreds of thousands of men at the front, and to feed the guns with the enormous quantities of shell that the method was thought to require (in the ten days' bombardment that preceded the Somme, British guns fired three million shells – three times more than had been fired in the whole of the Russo-Japanese war of 1904–5). The generals felt that they deserved congratulation, not abuse. Still the bombardments were not a success, except in the absurd sense that they killed so many men so indiscriminately that the Germans, who did not have as many men as the Allies, were bound to suffer, proportionately, more heavily.

The bombardments would churn up the ground, so that 'no man's land' became almost impassable. It was likely, especially in the early days, that the enemy trenches would be wiped out, and they would be occupied by the infantry. What then? The defenders would have a second line, and a third line, to which they could retire. The bombardment would then have to be staged all over again, this time on targets that had not been properly 'reconnoitred'. The infantry, meanwhile, would be in a salient and would, besides, be tired out; always, the second set of attacks would thus be a failure. On the first day of Neuve Chapelle, in spring 1915, the British did occupy a mile of line; but when they tried to get further, they found a strong line ahead, and were massacred. On 25 September 1915 the French offensive in Champagne did result in a breakthrough, the capture of ninety guns and 25,000 men. But that was that:

the breakthrough could not be exploited. Enemy defenders arrived by train to seal the gap, while the French pushed into it slowly and on foot, with all manner of supply problems. On the Somme, the British lost 59,000 men on the first day, 1 July, because the enemy guns had not been knocked out even by ten days' bombardment. Thereafter, generals simply relapsed into a policy of endless bombardment; keeping the German line under attack constantly. These methods, which were applied with rather more sophistication the following summer, were hideously costly, the more so when the Germans adopted a new system of 'defence in depth' – taking most of their men away from the front line, and relying on strong-points (often with concrete) which could harry the attackers, and leave them vulnerable to counterattack once they had made a few hundred yards' progress.

The heart of this whole problem was that the generals were mesmerized by shell, and could imagine nothing other than vast quantities of it. They did not trust their men who, after all, had been civilians up to a short time before; they relied on infantry tactics that were primitive, because they did not have the NCOs to allow the troops to move in small groups. 'Waves' were sent over the parapet, their officers showing the way, their sergeant-majors studded along behind, ready to shoot a man who fell out of line. It was only in 1916 that the Germans, who could afford loss less easily than the numeri-cally stronger Allies, began to devise other tactics; and only in 1917 that the British Captain Liddell Hart printed his manual on 'fire and movement', in which small parties with an NCO in charge would hop from shell-hole to shell-hole, giving other parties covering fire from time to time. These tactics kept losses down, and 1918 was less costly to the Allies than 1914. But in the early years, generals simply wanted enough shell to wipe out everything in sight. It was the only way to protect the highly vulnerable 'waves'.

The shelling was in many ways counterproductive. It gave the enemy warning; he could shift troops out of the front line (as the Germans did in the latter stages of the battle of the Somme, and especially in the third battle of Ypres) and in particular he could bring up reserves. It was this factor which prevented any 'breakthrough'. The attacking troops might indeed establish themselves in the enemy line, but they would be too tired, and fresh troops would themselves become tired as they stumbled up, under fire, to reinforce the original ones. The defenders' reserves would arrive by rail, to a line they knew, and the gap would be sealed off. It was not until March 1918 that a way round this was found in the west, though an enterprising Russian general, A.A. Brusilov, found it in the east in summer 1916. On the western front, all was stalemate.

There were indeed efforts to escape from the tyranny of the vast offensives. In April 1915, at Langemarck ('second battle of Ypres') the Germans used poison-gas for the first time, and its initial effect, on unprepared troops, was of course devastating: but it stopped the Germans themselves, and so the victory was limited. On 21 February 1916, and until July of that year, the German commander, Falkenhayn, found what he thought was a way to destroy the French. He attacked the fortress system of Verdun, knowing that the French would not give it up; his aim was to rain heavy shell on them there, without involving his own troops in 'no man's land'. This offensive succeeded, for a while, in its brutal form of cost-benefit analysis. The French did lose twice as many men as the Germans. But the German commander, the crown prince, lost his head, and supposed that the point was to take Verdun. He sent troops in, in an effort to capture it, and the French heroically held on, although their supplies had to move up through a narrow and exposed road over the Meuse, the *Voie Sacrée*. The Germans began to lose more than the French, the whole battle costing a million casualties. This battle, and the Somme for the rest of 1916, destroyed the old French and German armies.

In 1917, generals made an effort to think out the problems, at least in part because they now had to go more carefully with their men. In the spring of 1917 there was a widespread mutiny in the French army. The French commander, Joffre, was replaced by the younger Nivelle. But, Nivelle's attack of April 1917 was a failure. In its latter stages, there were cases of men going 'over the top' baying like sheep, and in some divisions men started marching to Paris to demonstrate that peace must come. An able general, Pétain, calmed them down, and the Germans did not even notice the mutiny at the time. But it was a sign – and there were others, such as the British mutiny at Étaples – that the soldiers were not simply automaton figures. From then on, there were serious efforts to think the problems through: in spring 1917 a British surprise-attack at Arras, in July a brilliant mining operation by the British at Messines, in November, at Cambrai, the first use of tanks (which were highly successful at first, though they broke down too easily, or outran their own infantry). Once this kind of cleverness was applied consistently, and in strategic matters, the war became mobile again (in March 1918, at the 'Ludendorff offensive').

The generals in the west were endlessly criticized for their concentration in France: was there not a way out? Especially, there were great hopes in the 'Russian steamroller': these alleged millions of willing troops. It was said that, if the Western Powers sent out war goods, then the Russians would win the war. Certainly, the war in the east was more mobile than in the west. There were not so many railways there to ferry reserves that could seal gaps; the front was over twice as long as the French line; and there were also far fewer troops. Of course it was paradoxical that the greatest population in Europe should supply comparatively few troops, but the Russian army, before 1914, had exempted two-thirds of its possible conscripts because it could not afford to feed them. It was not until November 1915 that a new law was passed to admit 985,000 conscripts to be taken in annually. The Russian army, for most of the time, had fewer divisions than the 'Central Powers' opposite them. Thinly held, inadequately supported fronts distinguished the eastern war. It was possible to 'find flanks', and to break through, in ways which could not occur in the west. After confused warring in Poland until May 1915, the Germans reinforced their Austro-Hungarian allies, broke through at

Gorlice in western Galicia, and, for the next few months, drove the Russian army out of central Poland. Then the German effort was switched back to the west (after a campaign to overthrow Serbia). In June 1916, the Russian commander on the Austrian front, Brusilov, made his name with a cunningly staged offensive which disrupted the reserves of the Central Powers and brought two Austrian armies to collapse; the Romanians entered the war on Russia's side in August. But although it was a situation of great tension, the Germans again raised reserves, supported the Austrians against the Russian battering-ram of the Kowel marshes, and occupied most of Romania by the end of 1916. After this, the eastern front saw only sporadic and small-scale action, since in March the revolution began, and was associated with the most serious mutiny of them all.

It was quite illusory to suppose that the east offered an easy way out. In any case, the Russians' war economy, though slow to start (because of excessive reliance on already busy foreign suppliers) did in the event produce reasonable quantities of shell – a million rounds per month by September 1915 and four million a year later (which compares with the Germans' seven million and the Austrians' one million). The army was never lavishly supplied, but by 1916 Russia was manufacturing her own war goods in reasonable quantity; Russian aircraft had a high reputation. In August 1916 the German commander at Kowel said that fighting in the east 'now resembles western circumstances' – the same stalemate.

Other war theatres offered little prospect of victory. In May 1915 Italy declared war on Austria-Hungary; again, despite a considerable superiority in numbers, the Italian effort was soon stuck, and although the Central Powers did successfully launch attacks in May 1916 (Asiago) and in November 1917 (Caporetto, which caused a lengthy retreat to the Piave) this front, too, reproduced many of the problems of the eastern front. A British effort to seize the Straits in 1915 failed for similar reasons (Gallipoli), the more so as armies that were supplied by sea could not rival those that were supplied even by the limited Turkish railways. As far as the land-war was concerned, there was no easy way.

At sea, it was a similar story. The Allies blockaded Germany, more to stop exports than imports, so that British goods could take German markets. Only in 1916 was serious pressure put on indirect imports (through neutrals) and even then the British blockade only achieved what Prussian conservatives, through tariffs, had long demanded. The blockade really succeeded only in 1918, and was powerfully seconded, in its effects, by the doings of the Prussian ministry of agriculture. The German navy, which was heavily outnumbered, dared not sail out except rarely: in May 1916 a great naval battle was fought off the Danish coast (Jutland), and it ended indecisively – more British ships sunk than German, but so much damage done to the German fleet that it did not emerge again until the very end of the war. It was a curious reflection on pre-war ways of thinking, not least in matters of gunnery, that these great ships could do nothing much; and yet for the price of one big ship, Germany could have had forty submarines. Before 1914, these had been neglected. But in 1914–15 the British blockaded Germany, and in retaliation German submarines sank British shipping and neutral ships in the 'war zone'. Neutrals protested; the Americans were incensed at the barbarities of submarine warfare, and there was a great row over the fate of the British liner, *Lusitania*, in May 1915. The row might have been less had it been more widely appreciated that she was carrying munitions. The United States were loud with threats, and for a time the German submarines were instructed not to sink neutral ships. The campaign was resumed in February 1917. In the summer months, so many ships were sunk that the British admiralty almost lost its wits. For some weeks, it rejected the historically well-founded policy of convoy. But the organizing of convoys, in which trading vessels could be shepherded by destroyers, defeated the U-boats, of which the Germans had, in any case, too few. In April, the German campaign provided the United States with a reason for intervention at the Allies' side.

The Americans supplied the Allies with great quantities of material; eventually, they were also required to finance much of this ordering themselves (America turned from debtor to creditor as a result of this). When, in March 1917, the Russian revolution began, the whole future of the Entente became doubtful: if Germany could concentrate on the western front, would the French survive? Many influential people in the United States wanted to throw their weight behind the Entente. They were given a present by Zimmermann, the German foreign minister: he summoned Mexico to ally with Germany, and attack the United States. His telegram-code was broken by British intelligence and was eventually shown to the Americans – the final factor in prompting the intervention of the United States.

The United States' intervention was not immediately effective, for an army had to be trained and sent over; it was not until the autumn of 1918 that the Americans were present in great numbers, and their losses – 100,000 – did not compare with the French figure, 4,000,000. Ludendorff, who since summer 1916 had become the effective German commander, planned to destroy France before the Americans could arrive. He staged a series of great offensives, in March, April, May and July 1918.

He was greatly helped by the collapse of Russia. In March 1917 the tsar had been overthrown, and Russia's internal condition became much worse as the summer went on and there was no end to the war. In November, the Bolsheviks seized power, and asked for an armistice. A delegation arrived at the German headquarters in Brest-Litovsk, and on 3 March 1918 a peace treaty was signed there. It was a dictated affair. The Soviet delegation was forced, by a threat of German occupation, to recognize the loss of a large part of European Russia. The Ukraine was to become independent; and similarly Poland, Lithuania, Finland, perhaps also the Caucasus states and the Baltic peoples. These creations acquired German protectors and exploiters: the Ukraine, especially, had to be garrisoned by a large force under Eichhorn, who was assassinated; and Germany acquired a large eastern empire, although it was through satellite states, not direct annexation that she (mainly) ruled. German-Soviet collaboration went on until in November 1918 the victorious Western Powers required Germany to abrogate the treaty of Brest-Litovsk.

One of the great might-have-beens of history is in fact the Allied recognition of Brest-Litovsk. By the winter of 1917–18, after the Bolshevik revolution in Russia, there was quite serious talk of a peace settlement between Great Britain and Germany, on the basis of a division of the world between the Sea and the East. Conservatives in many countries were terrified that, as the strain of war went on, there would be revolution. The moderate left, similarly, feared that communists would take over everywhere. In 1917 there was considerable pressure from many quarters for a 'neutral peace', or 'a peace without annexations or contributions'. There were also, in that year and in 1918, a great many strikes in Germany and Great Britain, which clearly had a powerfully anti-militarist element.

There had indeed been discussion, earlier, of peace. In 1915 and 1916, Bethmann Hollweg had tried to bribe one or other member of the enemy coalition to abandon its allies. In December 1916 the four Central Powers had appealed for peace. This was a manoeuvre. If the Allies refused, they would be discrediting themselves in American eyes; if the Germans then used the submarine weapon, would the Americans not understand? In practice the Allies simply said that they wished to know Germany's terms. Their own, they told President Wilson, were simple: self-determination. The Turkish empire, the non-German parts of Germany, the Habsburg Monarchy (by implication) would disintegrate. This was of course hypocritical language from Powers that controlled large tracts of other peoples' territory. The British and French planned to divide much of Turkey between themselves (a provisional arrangement of March 1916 was negotiated by Sykes and Picot, and, late in 1917, the Balfour Declaration established a Zionist 'home', which was intended to be a British client-state). It was far from clear that

British and French plans for central Europe were any more 'moral' than German plans for eastern Europe at Brest-Litovsk. The 'Czecho-Slovak' or 'Yugoslav' states which, by 1917, the Allies were promoting, each contained large dissident minorities, and even the majority peoples were very far from being solidly in favour of independence. Such states were as artificial as, and perhaps even more than, the Germans' 'Flandria' or the Ukraine of Brest-Litovsk.

Still, the Allies' war aims did make a greater appeal in the United States than did the Germans' aims. The Allies at least had to make compromises with each other and the Americans; the Germans had to bother only with their own allies, who carried little weight, given that, militarily, Germany was easily preponderant. In September 1914 Bethmann Hollweg had sketched out a programme ('the September memorandum') for *Mitteleuropa*, the permanent weakening of France; later, the main lines of Brest-Litovsk were also sketched out as regards Poland and the destruction of tsarist Russia. A key to the western position was German control of Belgium, and almost to the end of the war, no public renunciation of Belgium was made; indeed, very few private discussions within the government and the army showed that there was the remotest willingness to abandon that country. Against France, the German intention was to annex at least the iron-ore fields of Longwy and Briey, in Lorraine; there was certainly no intention to surrender Alsace-Lorraine, except maybe a tiny part, around Mulhouse.

War aims, especially in Germany, became an object of internal politics. The chancellor's hands were tied in Berlin; and the kind of statement that might win tepid approval from the parties of the right and centre there could easily be reproduced almost verbatim as Allied propaganda. It was true that, in June-July 1917, Bethmann Hollweg was ousted; the *Reichstag* did pass a resolution for peace (19 July) in reaction to the Russian revolution, the failure of the submarine campaign, and the possible defection of Austria-Hungary. But the resolution was ambiguously worded, and when the military situation improved (as it did in the autumn) the *Reichstag* ceased to complain for several months more. Indeed, Ludendorff himself was consulted, not only about the wording of the resolution, but also as to Bethmann Hollweg's successor – and his influence led to the nomination of a preposterously unsuitable candidate, the aged Michaelis.

In such circumstance, the 'peace moves' of 1917 were unproductive. The Habsburg emperor, Karl, who had succeeded Franz Joseph in November 1916, had ambitions to sort out wartime hatreds, both inside and outside the Monarchy. He sent his brother-in-law, Prince Sixtus of Bourbon-Parma, to talk to the French president and, later, to Lloyd George (April-May 1917). He indiscreetly talked and wrote about possibly 'just claims' by France to Alsace-Lorraine. In reality, this move encountered great difficulties. Karl would not cede anything to the Italians, and the Western Powers could not get Italian agreement to a 'neutral peace' – even though Lloyd George assigned Italy a good part of the Turkish empire to gain her willingness. Then again, the impossibility was manifest of gaining German agreement to the cession of Alsace-Lorraine short of crushing military defeat.

These discussions about peace were all effectively concerned with the possibility of a bargain: Germany to abandon her western claims, the West to abandon its protection of the East. The Anglophile German secretary of state for foreign affairs, Baron von Kühlmann, made almost explicit proposals to that effect in September 1917; in August, the Pope, launching his own peace appeal, had encouraged the discussion of such questions. But the Kühlmann peace move also ran out of energy. No German statesman would publicly renounce Belgium, and perhaps even Kühlmann did not wish to do so. At the same time, not many Western statesmen regarded the prospect of a Germany with a free hand to exploit the resources of Russia as anything short of a nightmare. The peace moves also encountered the difficulty that at each stage the Western Powers would feel bound to reveal their discussions to their own allies; the Kühlmann move was ended when Balfour revealed the German sounding to the Allied ambassadors in October. By then, the two sides were driven further apart than before; and Lloyd George, in response to Kühlmann's remarks on Alsace-Lorraine, adopted that French claim as a British war aim. In 1918, at least after January, the peace movement died away; there were far fewer strikes than in the latter part of 1917, and peoples everywhere again looked to the battlefield for salvation.

Ludendorff could, now, rely on a temporary superiority in the west, since he had taken German troops from Russia. He knew very well that time was running out. The blockade had disrupted his war economy, and although he could exploit conquered Romania and the satellite Ukraine, there were difficulties even there. It would of course have been far more sensible to continue the defensive in the west and to hope that the Allies would fall apart at the prospect of yet another series of hideous battles. But this was not a war about sense: and, the more it went on, the more it fuelled itself: even in Russia, when Lenin spoke for peace, he was denounced by a demonstration of war cripples.

Ludendorff, or rather, his assistant Colonel Wetzell, had worked out a method which, in the west, was quite new, though Brusilov had applied it on the eastern front in 1916. The military problem had become clear enough: how to stop enemy reserves from sealing gaps. That meant: surprise, which in turn meant only a brief, though intense, bombardment, and threats to several parts of the line at the same time. If infantry tactics were properly worked out, then a breakthrough in these circumstances was possible, and enemy reserves would be disrupted, since they would not know where to go until too late. Ludendorff's men gave special training to groups of infantrymen (*Stosstrupps*) under battle-hardened NCOs. Several offensives were prepared: from the region south of Ypres to Verdun. The first and largest of these was aimed at the junction of the French and British lines on the Somme, north-east of Amiens.

It began on 21 March. Ludendorff calculated correctly.

The British Fifth Army was broken through by a combination of guns and *Stosstrupps*. There were problems in shifting reserves, and these were not really sorted out until Haig at last agreed to the creation of a Supreme Command, under the Frenchman, Ferdinand Foch. In this battle, the British lost 300,000 men, one-third of them prisoners. Two German armies almost reached Amiens, the heart of British communications, and for a time the British and French were in danger of falling apart. Ludendorff persisted; and in that he made his greatest blunder. The Brusilov offensive had shown in 1916 that even if an enemy army had been quite overthrown, the victors could still not advance at all easily over a wrecked battlefield, without supply lines, and against fresh enemy troops. Early in April 1918, the Germans ran out of steam on the Somme.

On 9 April, Ludendorff tried again. There was a minor version of the earlier offensive, this time south of Ypres. There was an immediate success; Kemmel Hill was taken; and the British were very alarmed. But French reserves again arrived, and sealed the gap. In the meantime, the Germans were caught in two large salients, without fortifications or supply lines. To draw off the accumulation of enemy reserves in Flanders, Ludendorff tried a further attack, this time on the French front at the Chemin-des-Dames, north of the Marne, on 27 May. Here he encountered tired troops who were badly led; they collapsed, and in the next two weeks, to everyone's amazement, the German armies again crossed the Marne and threatened Paris. But there was a repetition of the earlier pattern, and by mid-June the Germans here also stood in an enormous salient. They had lost a million men, and Ludendorff needed all his remarkable powers of self-delusion to suppose that he could win. On 15 July, he tried one last time to break through; and this time his forces were too weak (Rheims-Soissons). Indeed, Foch had seen that stroke coming; and he organized a counteroffensive on 18 July, at Villers-Cotterêts. It was the start of an Allied advance that went on virtually without pause until November.

Foch profited from Ludendorff's mistake. Even if an attack succeeded, then, in the odd circumstances of 1914–18, it should be broken off, and resumed elsewhere. In that way, enemy reserves could not be as effective as they had been hitherto: they would have to move from the sector of initial defeat to face the new threat. The methods of breakthrough were to be the same as on the German side, although Foch could use tanks and aircraft in combination, in a way denied to Ludendorff. The Allies also had lorries (and London buses) to shift reserves, while the Germans' transport system was based on the great railway artery leading through industrial France to Metz, in Lorraine.

Once the strategic problem had been solved, and once a proper combination of artillery and infantry had been arranged, then the Allied offensives could succeed – and would have done so in 1916 if the right calculations had been made. Foch counterattacked on the Marne salient, at Villers-Cotterêts, on 18 July. His attack hit an open German flank, and the Germans had to evacuate the whole salient to avoid being cut off. Foch then stopped the attack. On 8 August 1918, the British attacked at Amiens, again into a flank, recaptured much of the ground lost in March, and again stopped. Two weeks later, the French general Gouraud attacked the St Mihiel salient, which threatened Verdun. This was the first large-scale use of US troops. Two weeks after that, the British broke through 'the Hindenburg Line' in French Flanders. By late September, there was a further French offensive in the Argonne, which caused a German collapse. In October the British broke through north of Cambrai and in Flanders; a French offensive was aimed at Metz. The secret behind these successes was that at no stage did the Germans have time to draw breath and send in their reserves. In fact, fully one-third of the German army, at this moment, spent its time travelling by train from one sector to another.

Ludendorff's nerve cracked just after Amiens in August. He soldiered on, automatically, for a time. But with the western defeats, his allies clearly lost heart. In mid-September, the Austro-Hungarians appealed for peace; on

28 September, the Bulgarians asked for an armistice. Ludendorff himself responded hysterically, and said that the game was up. Hastily, the Kaiser appointed a liberal chancellor, Prince Max of Baden, and he appealed to the Americans for 'mediation'.

The war in the west went on for a further six weeks while the Americans, the Allies and the Germans wrangled about terms. In four notes, President Wilson demanded not only German recognition of the 'Fourteen Points' of his peace programme (which dated back to 1917–18) but also a radical change in the German government; a change tantamount to the Kaiser's abdication. The Kaiser resisted, and there was some shocked ultra-loyal talk for a time. Ludendorff himself was dismissed; *Reichstag* powers were dramatically increased; there was even discussion of extending the franchise in Prussia; and a 'parliamentary' government, in which moderate socialists participated, was introduced.

The German Establishment resolved on a final, desperate stroke: they ordered the navy to sail out. The sailors had been doing little during the war, and in some ships greatly resented their officers. There were mutinies, and sailors arrived in Berlin to demonstrate (4 November). That led to great strikes. The local commander, Linsingen, behaved with folly; and the temper of Berlin was 'revolutionary' in the accepted sense. Left-wing socialists proclaimed a republic. To forestall their success with the masses, right-wing socialists and moderate politicians also agreed to proclaim a republic. It cut the ground from under the Kaiser. Protesting to the last, he abdicated, and took a train to asylum in Holland (9 November). In the meantime, a German delegation arrived in the West to seek an armistice. On 11 November 1918, it came into force.

The Habsburg Monarchy also disintegrated. Here, in October, Karl tried desperately to keep his inheritance together. But the victors in the West had no intention of helping. Karl had failed to free himself from the Germans; some of his Slav troops, taken prisoner in Russia, had agreed to fight for the Allies; and they, in turn, recognized the national councils in exile as future governments. In France, and, latterly, in Italy, Slav troops fought against the Central Powers. From 20 October, as chaos mounted, the Habsburg peoples declared their independence – Czechoslovakia, Yugoslavia came into existence; Romania acquired her co-nationals (and much more) in eastern Hungary; even the Austrian Germans demanded attachment to the German Republic, although in the event they were turned into an independent Austria. In Hungary, Count Tisza was assassinated, and a republican government, under Count Mihály Károlyi, was instituted. Here, too, came a demand for armistice. It was signed at the Villa Giusti in Padua, and, after it, the chaos in northern Italy was such that the Italians captured hundreds of thousands of Austro-Hungarian soldiers, in an affair known as 'the battle of Vittorio Veneto'. Karl would not abdicate; he only agreed to 'withdraw from participation in government', and he stayed on outside Vienna until 1919.

The capitals of the West were afflicted by a crowd-mania when news of the armistice came in. But the First World War ended in chaos: starvation in central Europe, a worldwide influenza epidemic which killed more people than the war itself, civil war in Russia, almost uncontrollable inflation in many countries, and a whole rash of social disorders. The American President Wilson was seen, in the West, as saviour.

A 'New Europe' came into existence with the peace treaties. On 28 June 1919, at Versailles, the new German Republic accepted its own version of Brest-Litovsk. Alsace-Lorraine went back to France, together with the Saar coalfields. The new Polish state acquired a large part of eastern Germany, and subsequently part of Prussian Silesia as well. Denmark regained the (mainly) Danish part of Holstein – an area which still contains German war memorials. The main provision of the treaty was somewhat unclear: the demand for 'reparation' of the damage done by the German military effort in Belgium and France. It was altogether inherent in the atmosphere of Versailles that an act of outright vindictiveness should be concealed in semi-moral language. The German people as a whole were saddled with responsibility for the behaviour of their government in July 1914, with the 'war-guilt clause'. The German representatives did offer to pay for the damage caused by the invasion of Belgium, and the great battles in France. But the French and Belgians, in particular, wished for much more than that; they wanted a steady tribute from Germany for generations to come, which would – it was supposed – prevent the German economy from ever flourishing again. The figure itself was not worked out until much later (April 1921), and the story of 'reparations' was to contain many surprises, but, in 1919 itself, a helpless republican Germany had to accept liability for an unstated amount. She also accepted Allied occupation of the Rhineland, which the French had hoped to annex. A 'League of Nations' was set up to provide rules for the conduct of international affairs. Hopes were curiously invested in it.

The division of the Habsburg Monarchy was completed in the treaties of St Germain-en-Laye (September 1919) with Austria and of Trianon (June 1920) with Hungary. An independent Austrian republic was established; it was accorded the largely German part of western Hungary, the *Burgenland*. It was not accorded the German-speaking parts of Bohemia and Moravia. It was not allowed to join Germany, as virtually all Austrians had expected and desired. It lost the southern Tyrol to Italy, and German-inhabited parts of Slovenia to Yugoslavia. The inhabitants of the Vorarlberg, who voted to join Switzerland, were not allowed to do so although, mysteriously, the inhabitants of Liechtenstein were allowed independence under one of the great Habsburg magnate families, which drew most of its money from Bohemia. Hungary, shorn of east, west, north and south, shrank to half of her former size. Later, the Balkan and Turkish questions were given a solution (in the case of Turkey, temporary) at Sèvres and Lausanne.

3. 'Red Dawn'?

The First World War was a dramatic end to an unparalleled era in European history, an era of civil and, on the whole, international peace. It is quite possible that the civil and military casualties of both political and international collisions in the century after 1815 did not exceed, in number, the figure for a single day's losses in any of the great battles of 1916. July 1914 inaugurated a generation of political and military slaughtering; ironically, it often occurred for the sake of 'Progress'; ironically, too, the most self-consciously Progressive movement of all, communism, owed its origin to a huge protest at the cruelties and absurdities of 1914–18.

The Bolshevik revolution of November 1917 set off, at some remove, a series of left-wing upheavals. In Germany at the end of the war there was a great battle between left and right: the Spartakist risings of December 1918 and January 1919; a communist régime in Bavaria, headed, until his murder in February, by the idealist Kurt Eisner and lasting until May 1919; and sporadic revolts, up to the late autumn of 1923. Hungary experienced a Bolshevik régime, under Béla Kun, for four months in the spring and summer of 1919. In Italy, the years 1919–21 were a period of strikes, near-anarchy and virtual civil war.

In Russia, the Bolsheviks survived military counter-revolution in their civil war of 1918–21, and they also survived large-scale intervention by the British, French and others. Elsewhere, the communist experiments, though greatly exciting to the Bolsheviks' Third International, did not survive. The Spartakists, and then the Bavarian *Räterepublik*, were defeated by the military 'Free Corps' (*Freikorps*); foreign intervention and the counter-revolution of Admiral Horthy defeated Béla Kun (who fled to Russia and was eventually killed in Stalin's purges). In Italy, Mussolini's Fascists – again, a body made up, overwhelmingly, of ex-officers and ex-soldiers – took power in 1922, and bloodily ended the left-wing threat to 'order'. At the same time, a general, Primo de Rivera, took over in Spain. In all of these cases, it was an effective end to the rule of law, although no one, until Hitler's accession in 1933, was as forthright in that as the Nazis were to be. Why should Russia have been unique in the success of Marxism, in its Leninist form?

The 'negative' answer to this – the bankruptcy of everything else – is easy enough to see. By March 1917, the war effort was breaking Russia. It was commonly put about at the time, and in the Stalinist era, that this had occurred for the simple reason that tsarist Russia was a 'backward' country with insufficient industry – an argument which appealed both to Stalinist 'modernizers' and to generals or statesmen who had done badly. This version was not altogether true. Russia, in 1914, had substantial industry. She took time to convert to a war economy, and hence was slower in producing war goods; but by the autumn of 1915 she was producing them in reasonable quantity: four times as much shell as the Austro-Hungarians, and more aircraft than the French. The railway network was expanded, by 4000 kilometres, during the war; coal-production rose by a third; there was a considerable expansion of chemical and engineering industries. Even the harvest, with due qualifications made, ought to have sufficed to feed the populace and the army, given that exports stopped. Russia was not backward in the same sense as, say, Romania.

Still, Russia was easily the largest country in Europe, and the simple statistics of the war effort cannot conceal the weakness of it all in terms of Russia's size and potential. There were huge pockets of backwardness, untouched by 'modernization'. The main coal-basin, in the Donbass, was far away from the industrial regions of Moscow or Petrograd; the railways were strained when they had to take coal from the eastern Ukraine rather than from Poland or from British exports, as before, and they were again strained when foreign imports arrived via the frozen north. The greatest such strain came when a third of the rolling stock had to be used for military purposes, especially when the army authorities misused trains and left them idle for a good part of the time.

Wartime dislocation grew with the evacuation of Poland in the autumn of 1915, during which many factories were shifted to the interior, along with floods of refugees. The movement of ordinary goods to and from the countryside became disrupted. This coincided with (and partly caused) a process of inflation: the main common feature of any country which, at this time, produced a 'revolutionary situation'. By March 1917 the rouble fell to a quarter of its gold value, and by November, to less than a tenth.

Wartime inflation reflected, in part, the scarcity of commodities in the world. There was a great demand in Europe for material to fuel the war efforts, and prices of, say, copper rose – a matter again complicated by transport. Inside the warring countries, manufacturers who wanted to attract labour also put wages up – so much so that a chief complaint, everywhere, was that the working classes were becoming so well off that they refused to turn up on Mondays, so that they could recover from their drinking bouts (hence the British licensing laws). The only way for these wage-costs to be met was, in the end, through bank credits. The government, on its side, had to spend more and more on the war effort. The Russian budget went up from 4,000,000,000 roubles in 1913–14 to almost 30,000,000,000 in 1916. It could be paid for only by printing money – theoretically by taking loans from the State Bank, which would accept a fiction that the government's IOU would count as 'security'. Printed money in Russia went up from 2,000,000,000 roubles in 1914 to almost 20,000,000,000 in October 1917. That in itself was only a small part of the money supply, since the banks were also issuing credits on a scale that, before the war, was quite unimaginable – they had to finance their clients, and the extent of their doing so is, as yet, uncalculated. This was a process which Germany, Austria and Hungary were also to experience in the early 1920s. In all three cases, printing money appeared to be the only way to guarantee production and employment, and in all cases this practice went on until

1923. In other countries, especially Great Britain, high taxes
and war loans kept inflation at least within reasonable bounds
(the pound lost two-thirds of its value by 1919, the franc
three-quarters). That was not so in Russia. In fact, the tsarist
government could not imagine creating the machinery for an
income tax in wartime; it did not want to deter 'business';
and even after such a tax was introduced, a prominent figure
of the post-revolutionary provisional government, the industrialist Konovalov, resigned in order to push his colleagues
to abolish the tax. In the inflationary circumstances, war
loans also failed – in the case of the last, 'Liberty', loan of
1917, so disastrously that the government had to print money
and lend it to the banks, at a premium, for them to buy the
war-loan stock. In no country was war finance a happy
business, but in Russia it was a complete disaster.

The consequence was an inflation which sapped at the
whole economy. Prices generally rose by four times to
January 1917, and after that in 'stratospheric' fashion (until
1922–3, when, with the new *chervonets* rouble, the Bolsheviks even reintroduced a form of gold standard). The
need for printed money became such, in summer 1917, that
the quality of the paper was considerably lowered; and there
was not even time to put numbers on it: clients had to be told
to ink in the numbers of the notes themselves.

Inflation turned the already strained Russian economy
into a nightmare, in which separate elements were no longer
to be distinguished. The peasantry already suffered from
lack of labour, tools and farm animals to supply natural
fertilizer. In inflationary times, they could hardly resort to
savings banks. It was true that the price of foodstuffs rose
very greatly; but since two-thirds of the peasants were
themselves in the market for these, there was no profit there.
In any case, the country's transport arrangements were
complicated, and the transport of grain involved a set of
middlemen – at village level, the 'kulak'; beyond him, maybe
an estate-owner, a grain-dealer in the nearest town; and
beyond these, a bank. It was to the middlemen that profits
went. To the inflation, the peasants in the end responded.

The harvest of 1916 was not, in reality, significantly less than that of 1914. But it did not reach the market to anything like the same extent as before the war. Peasants preferred to give it to animals, and to eat it themselves; it was their response to the impossibility of commerce. One sign of this was that the numbers of cattle went up, in three years, by half, while the number of pigs doubled. Another sign was that, for the great cities, deliveries of grain ran down. Moscow had had 2200 wagons of grain each month before the war. In January 1917 she had less than 900, in February less than 700. In Petrograd, it was still worse: the figure sank, in February, to just above 300. A Moscow 'food basket', costing 24.23 kopecks in 1913, cost 49.47 in 1916 and 87.51 in January 1917; even then, it contained only half of the pre-war quantities of meat and one-third of the potatoes. A pood (16 kg) of bread cost 2.50 roubles in January 1917, and 4.80 by July. In January 1918, it cost 80 roubles.

The collapse of the grain supply complicated everything. The railways were directed towards new sources of grain, but did not have the coal reserves that might enable these to be exploited; while the diversion of trains held up deliveries of coal, and used up the rolling stock to a point, often, of irreparable damage. In the cities, food-rioting fuelled the various stages in the revolution of 1917, and in the army, too, supplies ran down to a point where troops lived off bad fish and rotting meat. Such was the background to the Bolshevik revolution.

On 8 March 1917, a wave of strikes in Petrograd (which had their counterpart in Moscow) culminated in rioting. There had already been unrest which the secret police regarded as extremely serious. At the turn of the year, agitation among the politicians and the upper classes was tantamount to a Putschist atmosphere. Already in the summer of 1915 the *Duma* had protested at the running of the economy, and its protests were supported even by the commander-in-chief of the army, a grand duke. The tsar had sidestepped this problem, for he himself had taken command of the army in August 1915. But, in the winter of 1916–17, the agitation was resumed. There was a plot to murder the tsar's confidant, the monk Rasputin, who was (absurdly) blamed for the troubles. It became common talk among the working classes that the *Duma*, and perhaps also the army, would support a coup. There was a succession of strikes, as workers blamed, alternately, the government for the breakdown of supplies, and employers for their unwillingness to pay wages that might enable workers to compete on the black market.

These riots led to army mutinies. The soldiers of the garrison were bored, and very disgruntled with the endless war. Russia did not have the barracks and transport to keep them in the provinces, as other countries could have done, and there was a fear that Germans would attack the capital by sea. The soldiers, knowing that they might be sent at any moment to the front, and knowing, too, the unimpressive circumstances there, had listened to anti-militarist propaganda to the effect – not inaccurate – that this was a 'bosses' war'. Khabalov, the governor of Petrograd, called on the soldiers to act. He proclaimed martial law (and, in character, did not have glue with which to put up the posters). The soldiers, instead, fired on their officers. Even Cossacks fraternized with the rebels. Within a few days, it was over. The *Duma* set up a committee, from which there emerged a 'provisional government' in which the chief figure was a radical liberal, Alexander Kerensky. To damp down the agitation, his colleagues, and some of the generals, asked the tsar to abdicate. The tsar duly did so, on 15 March.

None of this was very greatly different, in essentials, from events in Germany and Hungary at the end of the war in the winter of 1918–19; indeed, in both cases, a Russian vocabulary was adopted, of 'councils' and 'people's commissars', in the name of a workers' revolution. But Russia developed her revolution in her own way. The main distinguishing feature was the creation of 'soviets', or councils for representation of the working classes in the cities. In March, as the provisional government emerged from the *Duma*, a soviet was set up to co-ordinate strikes.

Soviets spread to every other place of importance, and to some villages as well as to the army, where even the officers had them. They were elected in various ways, sometimes by acclamation, but generally by the representation of factories according to their size. The deputies would then elect an 'executive committee', itself cumbrous (in Moscow, seventy-five members) which would in turn elect a 'presidium' of seven. The soviets of the whole of Russia eventually set up an all-Russian soviet, to take in the deputies of workers, peasants and soldiers. The main theme of the Russian revolution is the turning towards Bolshevism of the soviets: by September, many of them had Bolshevik majorities in their executive committees, and in October, these soviets, with their 'Red Guard' volunteers, were in a position to order the arrest of class enemies, and the sequestration of their property.

These soviets produced imitators abroad – *Arbeiter- und Soldatenräte* in Germany, *tanácsok* in Hungary. But abroad these bodies lacked reality, except very briefly. In Germany the soldiers' councils were established in the wake of the armistice to help keep order in the evacuation of France; and similarly in Hungary. The soldiers and their officers at the front collaborated extremely well. German officers did their work, and the councils did good service, as was true, in the main, in Hungary. The German soldiers' councils in the south even elected Marshal Hindenburg as their president. As to the workers' councils in Germany, almost at once they ran into trade-union opposition; and the same was equally true for Italy and Bohemia.

The German trade-union movement contained 3,000,000 members in 1914, and though numbers had run down in the first years of the war, as men were conscripted, they rose again in 1917–18 and by 1919 had reached 7,000,000. The unions were well off; able to finance both strikes and benefits; armoured with a bureaucracy; capable of dictating to the socialist party (which in February 1919 won almost two-fifths of the vote). The unions had nothing to gain from a challenge to their authority from workers' councils which might duplicate what the unions were doing, only to destructive effect. In a time of chaos, the essential was to ensure that exiguous food supplies went round, which was also the task of the unions in Bohemia (the independence of which was virtually effected by unions). It was undoubtedly true that a great part of the German working class wished to change Germany very radically. But why do so through the revolutionaries whose example, in famine-stricken Russia, was hardly conducive to imitation?

The trade unions in Germany, more than in France or Great Britain, had acquired considerable powers during the war. To gain their collaboration in the war effort – the intensified effort of the *Hilfsdienstgesetz* or 'Hindenburg plan', which involved conscription of both sexes late in 1916 – the unions had been allowed control of hiring. Army generals, the *stellvertretenden Generalkommandos*, had a central place in arbitration of disputes; and on the whole their voice could fall quite often on the workers' side. General Groener, the key figure on the military side (who replaced Ludendorff as effective chief of the army late in October), had the confidence of the trade-union heads, Legien and Stegerwald, both of whom were very competent labour-bosses who knew how to handle their men. Both of them strove to keep order. Just as the workers' and soldiers' councils met in the *Zirkus Busch* in Berlin to elect a government, Legien and the chief German industrialist, Hugo Stinnes, signed a pact by which trade-union rights were guaranteed – together with the eight-hour day – while 'capitalism' was also guaranteed, i.e. private ownership of most of the economy. To control the left, the chief socialist, Friedrich Ebert, telephoned Groener in Spa and was assured that the army would support the new republic. This was a natural enough outcome for an era when officers and trade-union bosses discovered each other's virtues – a discovery repeated in Great Britain during the Second World War.

The German left was itself a fragmented affair. In 1916, a minority of the *Reichstag* socialists had jibbed at further recognition of the government's need for war credits. In the autumn, they had set up an independent group, which formally became an 'independent social democratic party' (USPD) the following April, just after the Russian revolution. They took the more idealistic older leaders; they appealed to the kind of trade union which was doing badly in the war inflation (e.g., older-fashioned textiles). The unions' collaboration with the State irked many of the workers in inflation-struck Berlin. At the end of the war, conditions there, in Leipzig, Nuremberg, the grim industrial towns of Thuringia and Saxony, and the ports of Bremen or Hamburg were desperate. From Berlin, people would go up-river along the Oder to steal the farmers' potatoes and apples and load them on to rafts. The crass behaviour of the Berlin garrison commander, Linsingen, almost invited protest. The factories had also seen wage rates, differentials altering with the introduction of semi-skilled labour and machinery – though that appears to be a feature of working-class revolutionary consciousness that has been much exaggerated – and increased use of machinery had led to a dramatic rise in the number of industrial accidents. The Berlin factories produced their own shop-stewards' movement (the *revolutionären Obleute*) – a chief figure was Richard Müller – and it was this that led the workers' demonstrations which led to the proclamation of the Republic on 9 November.

To keep control, the leaders of the main social democratic party (*M[ehrheits]SPD*) held their meeting in the *Zirkus Busch*, and, in imitation of the Bolsheviks, set up a government of 'people's commissars'. It consisted of three majority socialists and three independent ones (who resigned within weeks). The Berlin revolutionaries rapidly became isolated. In voting for central representation of the various councils, the extreme left hardly made any showing at all. Rosa Luxemburg, the chief figure of the left, was not voted for; she had to be co-opted. Meanwhile, the trade unions regained control; and the government collaborated with sensible civil servants of the old order to keep food supplies moving. A conference on 25 November agreed to restore the old federal states. The decision was taken to convene a parliament which would undertake to compose a constitution.

The background to this was a feeling that the revolutionaries were in hopeless isolation. Especially, they did not have control of the army; and there were next to no military mutinies, the army becoming demobilized by December (for the greater part). The countryside, outside isolated areas like the radical southern tip of Oberbayern, showed no interest in revolution, and before the war had voted almost wholly for Catholic or conservative (or crypto-Nazi) parties. Most farmers feared – rightly – that a socialist government would out-do the Kaiser's government in taxation of, and detailed interference with, the farmers' produce. The example of hungry Berlin mobs in Brandenburg was such that, quite soon, the peasantry supported upholders of 'order'. When in March 1920 a paramilitary group under General von Lüttwitz marched on Berlin to overthrow the republic and institute a Putschist régime under an East Prussian conservative, *Generallandschaftsdirektor* Kapp, it received food and good wishes from the peasants of the surrounding countryside. In Austria, as she emerged in her new guise of independent republic, the socialists, whose rhetoric was revolutionary, also encountered this problem. Otto Bauer, Karl Renner and the trade unions also adopted the cause of parliaments, not councils, because they feared that the peasantry would simply starve the cities out if a Red Revolution were proclaimed. In Hungary, their counterparts were driven to proclaim a Councils' Republic in March because they were driven to distraction at the thought of the country's disintegration at the Allies' dictation, and hoped for Russian help. In Bavaria, a similar collapse took place, and the trade unions (who were weaker in the south) allowed Kurt Eisner to run an extreme-democratic independent state for a time (he was assassinated in February 1919) though Eisner's own party took only a tiny fraction of the vote. Munich was then run, briefly, by a group of revolutionaries, who were brutally crushed in May by a combination of trade-union and military efforts. In all of these cases, one common feature was the revolutionaries' failure to find anything to appeal to the peasantry. Even Georg Heim's Bavarian Peasant League (BBB) which, before the war, had spoken radical, anti-clerical language ('We want no priests, no professors, no lawyers, no *Herr Doktors*', etc.) did not support the Councils' Republic. In Italy, despite agrarian upheavals in the valley of the lower Po, and in Poland during the Soviet invasion of 1920, the peasantry generally responded to their priests' promptings, and supported order.

In Germany, then, revolution was not a fruitful cause. The left, aware of this, became divided: whether to influence the majority socialists towards revolution, or to oppose them in their drift towards 'moderation', the parliamentary republic. A section of the left broke into revolt in Berlin on Christmas Day. That revolt was repeated for a few days in January 1919, the 'Spartakist rising'. It was, in miniature, the story of the Paris Commune all over again. The government, by now free of the independent socialists, handed power to a trade-union stalwart, Gustav Noske – another highly competent labour-boss. He used his links with the army to recruit volunteers to restore order in Berlin: the *Freikorps*, recruited from ex-soldiers with little else to do, marched into the capital and defeated the left. Rosa Luxemburg (who had disapproved of the rising) and her associate, Karl Liebknecht, were murdered, the bodies thrown into a canal. A month later, in February 1919, parliamentary elections were held, and the republican parties – socialists, Catholics and left-wing liberals – gained three-quarters of the vote. The new *Reichstag* assembled in the quiet little town of Weimar, centre of the German Enlightenment, because it would be less riotous than the capital. 'The Weimar constitution' – for a parliamentary republic – became law.

This was not the end of the German revolution. In Germany, no one dared to reform finances – to stop the government spending and the cheap credit that kept the working classes in employment, and the bosses in profit. The result was a tremendous inflation, which was cured only by drastic action, in November 1923, when, once more, army generals and trade-union officials collaborated to set up a new currency, the Rentenmark. In the confusions of this era, the left, embittered, re-formed as a communist party. In the early 1920s, on orders from Moscow, there were risings; in 1923, in Thuringia, 'the German October' occurred, with Béla Kun advising on tactics. But the republic was solidly enough based outside these little 'communes' of the left, and the socialists, whatever their quarrels with the other parties, would not give serious support to communist risings. Indeed, the single largest German state, Prussia, was run by a coalition of socialists and Catholics, and the socialist minister of the interior, Karl Severing, set up the beginnings of a 'secret state police office' – it soon turned into *Gestapa*, and ultimately *Gestapo* – which compiled the lists of communists from which, eventually, the Nazis made their arrests in February 1933.

In Russia, Petrograd – Baltic, puritanical – might talk a language resembling that of Germany, but Moscow, and, still more, the expanses to the south-east, were quite different. Trade unions, countryside, councils, inflation, soldiers, officers all took roles quite different from their counterparts in Germany. In Russia it was the counter-revolution that was isolated, not the revolution. An effort was made at counter-revolution early in September 1917 when the army's commander-in-chief, General Kornilov, misunderstood what Kerensky told him, and marched troops on Petrograd. These troops consisted mainly of the 'Savage Division' of Caucasus mountaineers and a cavalry corps. It might be compared, perhaps, with the forces with which General Franco started his successful counter-revolution in Spain in 1936, part of which consisted of Moorish cavalry; its German equivalent would be the *Freikorps*. It was characteristic of Russian circumstances that as Kornilov approached the capital, his troops deserted, and fraternized with the workers. Kornilov and his colleagues, high and dry, were arrested. A military counter-revolution did develop in Russia from the winter of 1918–19, and it gained support from the victorious Western Powers. Admiral Kolchak organized eastern Siberia with Japanese help; General Denikin set up in the north Caucasus with British patronage; General Yudenitch gathered a force in Estonia, again with help from the British (and also from the local Baltic-German *Landwehr*); the British landed at Archangel and Murmansk, initially to protect the stores from the Germans in the summer of 1918. Denikin, in particular, was given millions of pounds' worth of surplus stores.

Each of these forces, for a time, won successes. Kolchak approached the Urals in autumn 1918 (incidentally discovering the remains of the tsar and his family, who had been butchered at Yekaterinburg in July 1918). But Kolchak's one strong force was the 'Czech legion', some 50,000 men who had volunteered, from the prisoner-of-war camps, to fight for an independent Czechoslovakia. These forces left to fight in the west; and Kolchak's own troops disintegrated, leaving him to a futile internecine quarrel with his local Siberian allies, who arrested him. Yudenitch's force similarly disintegrated late in 1919, despite British help. Denikin did well for a time in the spring and summer of 1919, and reached Tula, only 250 miles south of Moscow. Then his troops, too, disintegrated. His strongest force, the Cossacks, had gathered so much booty that their military manoeuvring was impeded; other forces deserted. It was with battalions made up of officers that Denikin had to fight his last battles. By March 1920 his forces were evacuated from Novorossiysk, their main port.

That evacuation was a nightmare of confusion. As the Bolsheviks approached, there was a scramble for the gangplanks. The rearguard failed to cover the rear. Shells exploded into the mêlée, through which moved stretcher-bearers, clergymen evacuating the convents and the Church treasures, and Cossacks on horseback; while, very characteristically, a mad colonel flourished a sword in an effort to recruit 'a national army for the regeneration of Russia'. He recruited twenty-five men, whom the Bolsheviks arrested

next day. The final White effort came in the Crimea, under
French protection. Denikin's successor, Wrangel, was
rather more competent. He enjoyed success in the southern
Ukraine for some time, partly because the Red Army was
distracted by events in Poland, where it was defeated in
August (the 'miracle of the Vistula'). But Wrangel ran into
the problems that had defeated Denikin and the others. His
men were liable to desert; whole battalions had to be made
up of officers. He had no real welcome in the villages. The
Whites did, at last, respond to this. They produced a scheme
for land reform. It was extremely complicated, for it was
compiled by Krivoshein, who had been Stolypin's minister
of agriculture. The White *Azbukha* (intelligence) officers
then went into the villages, selling their scheme to the
peasants for fifty kopecks.

By the winter of 1920–1, the Red Army could move again
on the south, and Wrangel's troops were evacuated. Altogether, the White emigration amounted to 2,000,000 souls.
It was an extraordinary comment on events in Russia that the
counter-revolution had made such a poor showing – an event,
or rather non-event, that is unique in the history of Europe,
although, as events have shown, it was not to be unique in
the subsequent history of Asia. Were not Shanghai in 1949,
or Saigon in 1975, a vast replay of Novorossiysk?

To write the history of a disintegrating structure, especially on the enormous scale of Russia, is almost by definition
impossible. After the spring of 1917, the country passed into
increasing chaos. The first provisional government did not
last for long. Its foreign minister, the Kadet Milyukov,
offended the soldiers by pledging 'war to a victorious
conclusion', and demonstrations late in April (the 'April
Days') drove him out. A second coalition, and a third,
equally failed, since economic confusion, class-warfare, and
the military mutinies caused still greater loss of control. The
army leaders believed that the one sure way of restoring order
was to launch a new offensive; and the 'Kerensky offensive',
late in June, was fought on the Austro-Hungarian front. It
did not succeed; on the contrary, the army was driven out

of East Galicia, in August. Soldiers who refused to go to the front mutinied in Petrograd in mid-July (the 'July Days') and there were fears of an anarchist attack. The government imposed some, brief, control; Lenin fled to hiding. In August, Kerensky appealed to moderate opinion, holding a great conference in Moscow of 'the vital forces of the country'. The Moscow workers, in defiance of their own soviet, struck. Early in September, a German offensive took Riga, and, in response, Kornilov attempted to restore order with his march on the capital. It was a failure; but it had the effect of galvanizing the soviets to defend themselves against a military counter-revolution. In this, the Bolsheviks took charge. A 'military-revolutionary committee', dominated by the Bolsheviks, was the sole body that might give orders to the Petrograd soldiery. Late in October, the provisional government was wholly dependent on the soviet. Lenin and Trotsky, whose followers dominated it, decided, in the night of 7–8 November, to arrest the government. There was a brief foray at the Winter Palace, where the cabinet was barely defended. A subsequent film of the event caused more casualties than the capture of the Winter Palace had done.

The Bolsheviks established themselves in government, and put an end to the more immediate manifestations of counter-revolution. They arranged an armistice with the Germans in December, and made peace for a time the following March, at Brest-Litovsk, even though this meant the cession of a third of European Russia to Germany's satellites. In the spring of 1918, Trotsky began to organize a Red Army, which eventually won the civil war.

A chronicle of events confuses, rather than clarifies: for the background to everything in Russia was economic disintegration. To begin with, the situation of March 1917 had superficial resemblance to that of November 1918 in Germany. The soviet, when it emerged to co-ordinate strikes and to 'observe' the government, was, in majority, quite moderate. The socialist revolutionaries, a non-Marxist party which spoke for the peasantry and some of the lower middle class, occupied an overwhelming part of the soviet executive committee, in alliance with the Mensheviks. These parties did have their divisions. The 'left socialist revolutionaries' were close to anarchism, and ended in alliance – brief – with the Bolsheviks. The 'right socialist revolutionaries' were effectively a sort of small-peasant liberal party. The Mensheviks, too, split: between the 'defensists' who believed in fighting the war to a victorious conclusion (in which they were not unlike the German SPD), and the 'internationalists', whose chief was the pacifist Leonid Martov, 'the conscience of the revolution', who resembled Kurt Eisner. In the first few months of the revolution, Kerensky was able to rely on support from the more right-wing elements of both socialist revolutionaries and Mensheviks. The Mensheviks were quite soon discredited. The great Serpukhov factory gave them a subscription of 849 roubles in June but only 53 in August and 9 in October.

The trouble was that, once the tsarist system was removed, there was nothing solid to take its place; indeed, the Bolsheviks could claim, quite plausibly, that they were the only force likely to restore any kind of order. The Russian army, for instance, passed into a condition of chaos. Because of the generals' belief that they could do nothing against the German army, two-thirds of the Russian soldiers had done next to nothing since the battle of Lake Narocz in March 1916; and the others had been extensively bled in the Brusilov offensive and its tragi-comic sequel in the Kowel marshes and in Romania. A 'Nivelle mutiny' on a huge scale gripped the army in spring 1917. The Petrograd soviet was blamed for this, in that it had caused the abolition of the more archaic pieces of military observation. But beneath this was a disintegration of the officers' authority, even over the NCOs who, in the Russian case, unlike every other, became a strongly revolutionary element. Supply services became inadequate; and the soldiers' pay could not make up the gap, except for illicit drink, which flourished. In the army bases at Minsk there were vast, drunken brawls where officers might be killed if they strove to control the men. There was a considerable rise both in desertion and in the number of men reporting sick; there was much traffic – according to one account, of 800,000 men – towards 'delegations from the front'. True, the soldiers were still patriotic enough. It was incorrect to assert that the army had dissolved before the Bolshevik revolution. The soldiers might desert, but they came back to the front, and a Soviet historian has even discovered a *Stavka* document for November 1917 that reveals that the army's ration-strength, at the front, was greater in this month than at any other preceding time. The soldiers went home after the December armistice; and after then, the army did not exist.

A similar disintegration affected the Russian countryside. There were resentments at State exactions of grain (which the provisional government repeated); there were, in some (limited) areas, attacks on the stocks of the surviving estates; elsewhere, peasants fought with each other, and with men who returned from the towns, to obtain a share of communal land. That process became worse as the soldiers returned to demand their share of the land, and in 1918 the land battle went on again. This war among the peasantry was a constant which grew worse from spring 1917 until 1919; to divide it into phases on the lines of anti-landlord and anti-kulak, or to encourage the poor peasantry in committees (*kombedy*) as the Bolsheviks did, was an artificial exercise. The land's decisive contribution to the revolution was negative: the utter failure of counter-revolutionaries, including priests, to organize anything that might resemble the revolutionaries' nightmare of an 1849 or a French 1871. In these circumstances, the food production of 1917, and still more in later years, was so low that the towns starved, and became deserted. The Bolsheviks could get by only by impounding urban goods and bartering with the villages.

Again, the declaration of 'liberty' in Russia caused a disintegration of the country's structure of nationalities. Every separate people, from Ukrainians to Turkic nationalities and even the remote Siberian Yakuts and Buryats, revolted against the tsarist tyranny. There were demands for linguistic freedom, for an autonomous state. In the Ukraine, nationalists (usually with an anti-Semitic tinge) established their own council (the *Rada*, Ukrainian equivalent of 'soviet'). But Kiev's population was almost half Russian. The Ukrainian cause was that, essentially, of students, some small peasants and, in the end, of pseudo-Ukrainian counter-revolutionaries like the German-invented Hetman Skoropadsky, an adjutant of the tsar's, and a great land-owner, who had to learn the Ukrainian language while he was in his German-protected office. In the western Ukraine, in reaction to the Polish landowners and middle classes, Ukrainian nationalism certainly made sense. East of the Dniepr, it was different; that area was speedily overrun, without resistance, by the Bolsheviks in the early part of 1918.

The provisional government did not have much sympathy with Ukrainian nationalism; nor did any Russian party except the Bolsheviks, and they, too, were rather hypocriti-cal. The greatest might-have-been of Russian history – the emergence of a national challenge from the non-Russian peoples – turns out, in the end, to be a false question. The Russian Whites later blamed themselves for not recognizing the right of nationalities; indeed, *Yedinaya Rossiya* ('One Russian empire') was their great slogan. But, if E.H. Carr is right, the Ukraine was too weak in terms of its own people's consciousness. Nationalist intellectuals, such as Vin-nichenko, complained at the peasants' indifference. De-mands for linguistic autonomy could be met, by simple administrative changes. In the end, Russians were not hated in the Ukraine as widely as, say, Germans in Bohemia. The Germans' satellite state in the Ukraine was a failure, as Eichhorn himself saw, when he arrested his own satellite government and replaced it by a conservative Russian dictator.

It was undeniably true that Finland, Poland, the Baltic states and Lithuania – all of which differed in religion and in many essential customs from the Russians – made reality on the ground. True, some of them had a civil war between left and right, which in Finland was decided in 1918 by the intervention of a German army under General von der Goltz. But there was no doubt of their desire for separation. In the circumstances of Brest-Litovsk these nations re-emerged, with German garrisons, although they had to wait for the withdrawal of the Germans, in most cases, to obtain formal independence.

Still, in none of these cases could the provisional government look for support. Even in the winter of 1918–19, when Yudenitch came closer to capturing Petrograd than any other White general did, he had no help from the Estonians, who feared him more than they did the Bolsheviks. Lenin also came to terms quite quickly with the Finns, whose independence, in 1945, even Stalin was prepared to recognize.

In the summer of 1917, as Petrograd dissolved into chaos, the masses became much more radical. The Mensheviks and socialist revolutionaries who ran the soviet could only appeal for co-operation with the government. These appeals made no sense to the Petrograd working classes and the soldiers, who saw themselves as victims of a senseless war, and of cruel economics. The Kornilov coup brought into focus the animosity to which the disruption of food supply gave rise. The soviet acquired a Bolshevik majority. By mid-September, as the Germans advanced into Livonia, there were fears that the government would abandon the revolutionary capital to the enemy.

In other countries, perhaps trade unions might have been able to organize some common activity to restore some order. This, after all, was the story everywhere else in revolutionary Europe at the end of the First World War. But in Russia, the process of industrialization had gone so fast, the industrial population had been so mobile, and the government had been so discriminatory that the trade-union presence was very feeble. Trade unions in 1914 contained 100,000 men and women in all: a tiny fraction of the working class. It was the factory committee that made sense in Russia, and, to a lesser extent, the factory-based benefit committees. These bodies were very small. They were also, often, rivals. In the chaos of 1917, trade unions were difficult to organize, and, when they were organized, it was generally from a basis of factory committees. But, in these committees, and in the benefit committees, the Bolsheviks soon had a majority – they were the first bodies to become Bolshevik (April 1917). The subsequent 'district soviets' – and even 'tenement soviets' – also became Bolshevik, at a comparatively early stage in the revolution. By September, in the Moscow suburb of Bogorodsk, workers organized their own forces against crime, and these were led by Bolsheviks. Similarly, they took over the new unions. What made the Bolsheviks stand out was that, in all of the chaos, they had an idea, and offered a way forward. Lenin won because he offered the vision of a new world. It was this that gave his followers, as it had given the Jacobins and the Calvinists before them, a long-term sense of purpose and an ability to undertake, and to look beyond, the boring day-to-day work of miniature committees. Army, peasantry, nationalities, trade unions, factory committees, bureaucracy, women's movement: each contained its Bolshevik element. When the soviet came under Bolshevik control, the communist revolution was a fact.

The great strength of Lenin in the summer of 1917 was that he had all the answers. It was pointless to suggest that the Bolsheviks were in a minority (in January 1918, at the only free democratic elections Russia had seen since 1907, they won only a third of the seats, the socialist revolutionaries winning most of the rest). No serious revolutionary party had ever expected anything else. It was almost the definition of a 'revolutionary situation' that immense confusion would reign, both in the world and in people's heads. Indeed, political apathy, in the sense of helplessness, has been an outstanding hallmark of past revolutions, and in revolutionary Russia, most people did not know what to do. In Moscow, at the districts' council election in September 1917, the Bolsheviks won a large majority; but only a third of the electorate – 387,280 – bothered to vote. The socialist revolutionaries who were the Bolsheviks' main opponents had no programme, no tactic, no organization; they could not even prevent their left wing from adopting a Bolshevik alliance at a decisive stage.

Lenin had argued two theses before 1914. The peasantry, not the middle classes, must be the party's ally. Peasants were being 'proletarianized' by the development of the imperialist world economy, which turned small peasants from property-owners into a form of wage-slave. There was unquestionably enough truth in this to let Lenin make an appeal to the rural world, even if it had to be done under the slogan 'land to the peasants'. All of Lenin's opponents were quite unable to answer his propaganda to this effect. They knew that it was hypocritical. Mensheviks like Plekhanov followed the German SPD in despising the peasantry; they warned – not incorrectly – that the cession of 'land to the peasants' would make impossible difficulties for a socialist economy later on. But there was no Menshevik policy towards agriculture, and there were no Menshevik peasants. The socialist revolutionaries never did understand what they meant with their land programme; and their representative in the provisional government, Viktor Chernov, distinguished himself with appeals for 'order', and the decision of the constituent assembly as regards land reform. These appeals fell on hungry peasants and deaf ears. The Bolsheviks prided themselves on their freedom from bourgeois morality, and Lenin openly told Western sympathizers that he had adopted his land programme only in the expectation that the decisive factor was to win the revolution as fast as possible. The land programme meant, at the very least, that the peasants would be too busy fighting each other to fight the Bolsheviks. It was bloodily terminated by Stalin in 1929–33, with 'the socialist offensive' of collectivization of agriculture.

This same contempt for 'bourgeois morality' led Lenin to organize the Bolsheviks in a centrally dictated way. The Mensheviks had broken with him over this, in 1903. But Lenin's argument was simple enough. There was a revolution brewing in Russia; the party must be disciplined enough to take advantage; and if people were allowed to argue with central-committee decisions, then there would be chaos in the party's ranks. Indeed, that chaos did happen to the Mensheviks. Some of them followed a line not unlike that of the SPD, to support bankers and generals. Others took the USPD's stance, lamentingly torn between revolutionaries and SPD. Such were the Plekhanovs and Martovs whom Trotsky, dismissing their protests after the November revolution, consigned 'to the dustbin of history'. Sometimes, even Bolsheviks would protest at the party's dictation, its overriding of well-argued opposition even by utter loyalists, its endorsement of the cruelties of soldiers against officers, agrarian atrocities and the abandonment of the national cause against the Germans (as happened with the debate on Brest-Litovsk). To all objections, Lenin had a cruel answer: the revolution first. It allowed him to quarrel bitterly with his own friends, to purge them from the party, to establish a secret police, the *Chrezvychaynaya Kommissiya*, and to replace the Old Bolsheviks with gangsters and opportunists whom he could trust not to think – and whom it took a Stalin to control. By 1920, there were already labour camps in Russia, and they contained not only 'White Guardists' but also former socialist allies. Perhaps, when Lenin denounced Stalin from his deathbed in 1923–4, he had some idea of what he had done.

Bolshevism, like Italian liberalism, Jacobinism, or Dutch Calvinism long before, had been the creed of a classic 'creative minority', imposed on a confused and divided majority. It was the ideology of the machine – ultra-rational. It was contemptuous of the past, and highly respectful towards science and technology – a factor that came through in the art of the 1920s, and in 'social engineering'. It despised anarchic individualism, whether in economic matters or in matters of nationality. Once in power, the Bolsheviks could always quote Lenin if they wished to proceed towards Stalinism.

The influence of Lenin's success, in other countries, was equally calamitous. Revolutionaries in Germany, Italy, Spain were thrown back by events in their own countries.

The Communist International, founded by Lenin, won roughly a third of the socialist parties there and in other countries when it came to a test in 1920–1. Thereafter, the moderate social democrats in each case had to face a rival for the working-class vote. There was a three-way division in European socialism, and inside the trade unions. The left was Leninist: occupation of factories, revolutionary general strike, violent takeover. The right believed in collaboration with liberals or Catholics. The centre believed in holding the party together; it divided between left-leaning and right-leaning elements. In Italy, the wrangles of Nenni, Serrati and Turati prevented any common action against Mussolini. In Germany, the trade unions' and socialists' defence against Hitler was fatally weakened by the existence and the tactics of the communists in Prussia. As the Italian revolutionary, Malatesta, said: 'If we do not go on to the end, we shall have to pay with tears of blood for the fear we are now causing the bourgeoisie.' He went into a fascist prison.

New Structure: the Cultural Revolution of 1900

In 1902, a French minister of education, Georges Leygues, faced demands for a reform of the *baccalauréat*, the crowning examination of the French schools. He defended the traditional syllabus, with its heavy stress on the classics: 'The classical spirit belongs to all eras and all countries, because it is the cult of pure Reason, of the disinterested search for Beauty.'

In old Europe, these words would probably have been understood automatically. In the twentieth century, they were becoming a meaningless incantation. In the last quarter of the nineteenth century, as school systems everywhere expanded very rapidly, there was a steady fall in the proportions, and even in the absolute numbers, of students who wished to study the classics in universities. Dead languages, which had been a popular subject before, were kept going by the schools, as a matter of obligation. In Russia in the 1880s, schoolchildren had to take as many as forty periods per week in Latin and Greek, which were judged to be educationally superior (as the tsarist government saw it) to the 'modern' subjects, with their dangerous political connotations. By the 1890s, the classics were widely seen as a tyranny. In the context of the national efficiency campaigns in many countries, there were demands for a modern school-leaving examination in which science and modern languages should have their proper place. These demands bound the political left and centre together, in the name of 'technocracy'. After 1900, Latin and Greek began to lose the institutional hoops which had kept them in place. It was the end of a large part of the European cultural past. Within a few years, other 'non-practical' subjects were to experience a similar decline. George Orwell remarked of the later 1930s that the new generation did not know the Bible, but read *Picture Post* and knew the magneto.

To the new European townsmen of the later nineteenth century, the countless articled clerks and engineers, classics amounted to an affair of an ultra-élite: it was a language of the *Herrenvolk*, to be combated and resented in much the same way as German-language teaching in the Charles University in Prague, or French-language teaching in the University of Ghent. Utilitarianism, the essential creed of radical liberalism, provided arguments against the 'mumbo-jumbo' of the past. The practical arguments for classics were derisory. They were studied for their own sake, or for social acceptability, precisely because they had no immediate practical applicability. They had no immediate significance, but, like mathematics and 'scripture' – as the teaching of religion, defensively, became – they supplied a sense of structure beyond the self. With such a sense, students were expected to unify various branches of knowledge, to absorb several subjects, some of which were extremely demanding. Classics and mathematics supplied a background to many scientists, whether 'moral', 'social' or 'natural'. The results, in terms of the very wide general culture that prevailed in most universities before 1914, were very impressive. It is probably fair to assert that Europe, before 1914, produced virtually all of the ideas on which the twentieth century has traded; the rest being mainly technical extension of these ideas.

Even so, by the early years of this century, it was clear that the aesthetic background to European education was crumbling. The German philosopher Friedrich Nietzsche (1844–1900) in one of these intuitive leaps that led him towards the intellectual world of two or three generations beyond his time, remarked that when we have got rid of grammar, we shall have got rid of God. He was well placed to sense a connection. He had been born the son of an austere Pietist pastor in Saxony. His father died when he was very young, and his mother brought him up on severely Protestant lines (in all of which he resembled some of the figures of the Scottish Enlightenment). He became a professor of classics at a very early age, in the highly reputable University of Basel. But he lost his faith. Quite soon, he found classical scholarship devoid of significance; he took up, and then ran away from, Wagner. In the years 1873–88 he produced a series of brilliantly written, often aphoristic works of philosophy, of which *Beyond Good and Evil* (1886) is the most succinct statement, but his health declined, and his emotional life became so warped that he ended in madness. Nietzsche had to contend, in his own life, with the Death of God, the meaninglessness of scholarship, and a new understanding of the nature of the individual. He was precluded from taking the hedonistic way out, though not from black humour, and he tried to find a new morality that would replace the Christian one – the surviving forms of which he despised.

'It is only as an aesthetic phenomenon that existence and the world are permanently justified,' he wrote. He and his many disciples promoted a new irrationalism: the Self being so confused (*'Je est un autre'*, in place of the Romantics' *'Je suis autre'*) that only a *Brutalitätskur* could achieve unity in it. 'You say, a good cause justifies any war; I say, a good war justifies any cause.' Nietzsche's works did not sell well in his own day, but by 1900 he had acquired a European reputation, and his influence both in France and Germany shaped the development of existentialism. In the course of his writings, Nietzsche anticipated many of the twentieth century's concerns. He had interesting things to say on the philosophy of language; he wrote penetratingly, in *The Birth of Tragedy*, on the central place that music would have in the future, since it supplied a unifying element in culture that the linguistic or mathematical subjects could no longer constitute: in place of religion, classics and words, music, action and symbols. Nietzsche, to adapt his own expression, gazed into the abyss, and it duly gazed into him.

Perhaps it took a Nietzsche, living under the weight of

unbreakable rules, but unable ever to feel part of the structure that dictated them, to anticipate the nature of the century to come: the Kafka world of internal dissolution and outward absurdity to which the only possible response was that of a Céline or a Waugh, satire. In some ways, Nietzsche had been anticipated by the Scottish Enlightenment – particularly by its oddest product, Byron, whose influence on the continent has consistently been stronger than at home. The Scottish Enlightenment had been the first consistent European effort to come to terms with the waning of religion. Its leading figures were quite often sons of a (widowed) manse, who lost their faith early on, and strove to find new, secular absolutes – though, in this case, they turned out to be the utilitarianism which revolted both Dostoyevsky and Nietzsche in its two-dimensional smugness.

In the middle years of the nineteenth century, there had been a considerable revival of religion (as the extent of church-building in European cities testifies). Religious morality dictated private lives in the Victorian manner (although always with an underlying Sancho-Panza element) and Churches were well to the fore in politics. Towards 1870, the European mind was becoming secularized just the same, in that organized religion no longer commanded unthinking faith. Charles Darwin's challenge to scriptural authority was mortal; and the Protestant Churches, which were inclined to greater rigidity in matters of sexual morality than the Catholic Church, and which, in their ceremonial, had far less capacity for subconscious appeal, suffered decline. Once the institutional and legal framework of religious education was removed – the substitution, in most countries in the 1870s, of 'secular moral instruction' – these Churches were clearly on the defensive. By 1882, a decline in their attendance was noted. Spectacular neo-Gothic churches, constructed for congregations of hundreds or even thousands, were not half-full by 1900, and a few years later, they were quarter-full. The dissenting Churches in England used their rich supporters' money to construct a great rival, opposite the House of Commons, to Westminster Abbey. But even in

1900 they complained that, whereas they had provided for well over eight million places in pews (the figure was worked out with scrupulous exactness), not more than a quarter of these was constantly in use.

True, there were, around 1900, some spectacular intellectual conversions. The Catholic Church, which upheld orthodoxy at its most absolute, and which drummed out 'modernists' such as Abbé Loisy (in 1911) from the *Institut Catholique*, provided a fixed point in a shifting universe. Some products of the French secular system, who had experienced the Nietzschean abyss, became Catholic and nationalist: Charles Péguy in France being a notorious case. In Russia, after the failure of the revolution of 1905, the *Vekhi* group of intellectuals became, in Lenin's words, 'an encyclopedia of apostate liberalism' and rejoined the Orthodox Church: Struve, an ex-Marxist economist; Bulgakov, a magnificent novelist and playwright; the Rakhmaninov of *Vespers*. In Vienna, there were several prominent Jewish conversions to Catholicism: they included Gustav Mahler – whose 'Resurrection' Symphony (1894) belies suggestions that the conversion was carried out only for convenience – Arnold Schönberg, and the brilliant satirist, Karl Kraus. In the latter two cases, the conversions did not last; and in few of these cases did the conversion do much to lessen the converts' woe.

In the years 1900–5, it became plain that an almost completely secularized world had come into existence. It naturally took up the products of the Scottish Enlightenment – the engineering cast of mind on the one side, and a sometimes stupefying hedonism on the other. Not surprisingly, the chief figures in this cultural revolution were generally apostate Calvinists or apostate Jews; and it was the latter factor that made 'Vienna 1900' such a fertile place for the invention of the new century. That city's most notorious figure, Sigmund Freud, summed it up when he remarked: 'Honour, power, wealth, fame and the love of women – the aims of Life.'

Around 1900, a series of works, of all kinds, appeared, to

an effect that was intended to be, and has been, revolutionary. By the end of the nineteenth century, physics, architecture, painting, music, philosophy and – though less dramatically – economics and history each saw violent changes. Of course, like all revolutions, this one had roots that can be seen some way back into the past; in the 1880s, there had been clear anticipations; and, as with all revolutions, this one could even be ignored for some time after it by people of a traditional approach, working in some isolation from the 'modernist' world. Still, the years from 1897 to 1910 saw a violent reversal of much that had hitherto been accepted, and the creation of new orthodoxies.

The central doctrine of nineteenth-century liberalism had been the moral responsibility of the individual. In the past, there had been a religious sanction to this; in the latter part of the nineteenth century, secular sanctions had prevailed; and by 1900, these ceased to count for as much as before. The individual-as-entity was questioned: how could sexual morality survive Freud's identification of an inner, animal world in which repression would create neurosis? His *Interpretation of Dreams* (1899) and his *Three Essays on Sexuality* (1905) – which he regarded as his most important work – prompted a fully fledged theory of the subconscious (1912). The counterpart to this disintegration of the moral individual was a greater consciousness of the various ways in which society counted. 'Sociology' at this time came properly into existence. The German, Max Weber (1864–1920) wrote his work on capitalism and the ethic of Protestantism in 1903, in which he explored the relationship between ideas and social development, and after that he devoted his life to an exploration of the principles of sociology. His near-contemporary, the Frenchman Emile Durkheim, disposed more forthrightly of ideas, believed that sociology needed no philosophical justification, and in 1897 published a work on *Suicide* in which he called attention to the inverse relationship, in societies, of murder and suicide.

Society was becoming 'functional'; it was losing any but the most utilitarian moral content. At its most hysterical, this new attitude was expressed by the Italian futurist, Marinetti, who wished to consign all of his country's museums and monuments to the dustbin, and to build up a new world based on steel, concrete and the machine. Painters abandoned the late romanticism of the impressionists; instead, they developed a new desire to go beyond the immediate image, and to explore structural patterns which had an appeal almost impossible to explain. Cézanne's geometrical approach gave way, in 1907, to what may be described as the first abstract painting, Picasso's *Demoiselles d'Avignon*. By 1912, abstract themes made the running in both the German and especially the Russian expressionists. It was only the gauche and provincial – such as the young Adolf Hitler – who neglected the 'new art'. Charles Rennie Mackintosh, and the Vienna *Sezession*, attacked the older painters for pomposity, vulgarity and inconsistency. They reverted to styles that were primitive – in Mackintosh's case, the sinuous line, which owed something to the Celtic style, to memories of La Tène. But these styles somehow made sense only in terms of geometry. It is this which stands out in the *Sezession*: the anticipation of baldly geometric ways, and the absence, altogether, of ornamentation. The older artists, Klimt in particular (who, like Wagner, had started off quite respectably in the historical pageantry of the *Burgtheater*), might remain essentially with the language of late impressionism, but he, too, by 1900, was turning to abstraction, the imposition of mathematical patterns.

Elsewhere in Europe – to a very large extent, independently of the Austrian experience – painting had also moved some way from representational themes, 'views' which made sense in terms of the conscious brain and commonsense reason. In part, there was a tendency to 'express' something – hence expressionism, the pioneers of which were Van Gogh and the naturalists. If, to create a mood, the object had to be distorted, its dimensions wrenched apart, and its colours distorted, then that should be done with conviction. In this sense, the Norwegian painter Edvard Munch could express the miserable, guilt-ridden world of the Ibsen or Strindberg play in a painting. Other painters, throughout Europe, learned from Cézanne. He, first in Europe, imposed geometrical patterns and subtle arithmetically calculated shadings of colour to create a structure. The German schools (*'Blaue Reiter'* or *'Brücke'*) learned from these French *Fauves*. They aimed at pure aesthetics, almost unconnected with the object in view: hence Franz Marc, or the extraordinary Russian group, mainly in Moscow (Abramtsevo) at this time, or Malevitch – whose 'cylindrical' peasants, gathering a 'cylindrical' harvest, showed how the Russian peasant was being turned into a half-pig, half-machine – or Rodchenko, or Larionov or Tatlin, who soon abandoned representation of any kind and pioneered the 'constructivism' or 'futurism' which went beyond the 'cubism' of the early abstracts. These artists became fascinated by the machine, and Tatlin devised a workers' suit which could, with adjustments of geometric planes, do either as dungarees or as dress suitable for a Park of Rest and Culture. In this sense, the expressionism of a Kokoschka or a Schiele in Vienna was the last, despairing and grimly sensual phase of the representational tradition.

A sense that mathematics alone could count as certainty also affected architecture, music, philosophy and economics. Its most obvious demonstration came in 1903, with the publication of Albert Einstein's *Relativity*. By the later nineteenth century, theoretical physics had fallen into something of a slough, when it appeared that all questions had been neatly answered, and all that remained was technical elaboration, whether by chemists or engineers. Physicists with a strongly mathematical bent, such as Henri Poincaré in France, or Einstein himself, felt disquiet as they had to deal, theoretically, with speeds that approached the velocity of light. They built on the earlier work of Ernst Mach and James Clerk Maxwell. Einstein himself was a rather isolated figure – the (wholly unbelieving) son of a Jewish merchant in Ulm, who did not do well at school, disliked Germany, spent much of his early youth in Italy, and found employment as advisory clerk in the Patent Office in Berne. While there, he worked out the mathematics of

relativity: by use of the Lorentz transformation, he demonstrated how light could give evidence for the 'relativity' of
both space and time. Technical adaptations of Einstein's
final equation, $E = mc^2$, i.e., that mass and energy are
equivalent, produced at least theoretical appreciations of the
explosive potential of nuclear fission in the Cavendish
Laboratory at Cambridge before the war.

The new mathematical approach to philosophy resulted in
a new departure around 1900. Bertrand Russell's *The
Principles of Mathematics* of 1902, and his *Principia Mathe-
matica* of 1910 (in collaboration with Whitehead) symbolized, and shaped, a set of new developments, both in
mathematics and in philosophy. Philosophy abandoned its
old concerns with metaphysics and morality. Instead, it
became preoccupied with its own technology, logic – both in
mathematics and, rather later, in language. Since, as regards
metaphysics, the only remaining question of much interest
was why metaphysical problems occurred at all, the philosophers became concerned with the nature of language,
regarded by Wittgenstein (who collaborated with Russell at
Trinity College, Cambridge, even before 1914) as 'a map of
the mind'. The Swiss, Ferdinand de Saussure, applied this
in matters of literary criticism: to understand what works
really meant, it was necessary to examine the various
meanings of the words that were used, meanings that might
only be dimly understood by the authors themselves –
'structuralism', as it came to be known.

Architecture equally displayed a new 'mathematization'.
In the 1880s, late-nineteenth-century bombast had been the
(unfortunate) rule. Earlier architects' Gothic or classical gave
place to a great variety of pseudo-historical styles – pseudo-
Dutch, Danish Renaissance, neo-Romanesque, Vittorio
Emanuele monumental. The constructions of the Ringstrasse in Vienna (or Budapest) that appeared in the later
1870s and 1880s were distinguished by a combination of
coyness and dull monumentality; parts of Berlin were
wrecked by structures such as the vast Lutheran cathedral,
which showed Hohenzollern frogs trying to be bulls. Already

in 1906, so much of historical, classical Berlin had been knocked down to make way for these pompous buildings that the first work lamenting the destruction of a city in the name of modernism was published. The author particularly lamented what had happened to the Alexanderplatz, near the city's centre – a square that has suffered again and again with every twist of this century's purported modernism.

Even in the 1890s, many intelligent architects were becoming restive. They looked for a new simplicity, based on function, and gaining authority through use of mathematical proportions. Architects in Bohemia and Catalonia were given a great deal of money by local industrialists in these two areas, which lacked a pseudo-historic style of any conviction. There, in Prague and Barcelona, a new architecture was pioneered – art nouveau, as it became known, or *Jugendstil*. In the later 1890s, buildings that were much simpler than before were put up. They still had decoration, but it was considerably less than before. The brutal and functional shape of the buildings would be broken up by clever variations of window, balcony or corner; new materials, such as glass, iron or concrete, were used with intelligence. Charles Rennie Mackintosh achieved considerable fame on the continent in his adaptation of art nouveau to his own rather grim North European tradition. He (uncomfortably, but appealingly) married applied and fine arts, both in the houses and schools he designed and in his furniture. Cities such as Prague, Barcelona or Glasgow (and even, to some degree, Moscow) did not usually have the pompous requirements of capital cities; on the other hand, they were the centres of a powerful tradition, and they flourished greatly with the industrialization and commerce of the later nineteenth century. Enlightened businessmen in all of these cities promoted art nouveau architecture of distinction: the Ryabushinsky house in Moscow, the Villa Stoclet in Brussels (1904), the art nouveau cafés of Prague, the *Wiener Werkstätte* or Olbrich's *Sezession* building on the outer ring.

But art nouveau was too much of a hybrid to survive for

too long. By 1905, its exponents were anxious to pursue functionalism more forthrightly. The Viennese architect, Otto Wagner, was a leader in this respect. He showed, throughout his life, considerable adaptability – or perhaps a lack of serious roots. He began in the later 1870s with commissions for pseudo-historical buildings. He collaborated briefly with an interesting Viennese, Camillo Sitte, who wished to prevent the destruction of city centres by huge monuments (as had happened with the Ringstrasse) and who preferred the more intimate world of the late medieval city (he restored the Piaristenplatz in Vienna's VIII district). But Sitte, like his near-contemporary, William Morris, had no long-term appeal to city planners of the new type. Otto Wagner was anxious to make use of new materials – especially, concrete. After 1897, his buildings became increasingly functional. His churches, the famous tenement on the linke Wienzeile, and the equally famous Postal Savings Bank on the Cochplatz, were in the best art nouveau style. But after 1905, he fell for a much balder style, as did his contemporaries, Adolf Loos (who regarded ornament as criminal) or the unjustly neglected Josef Plečnik. In 1911, Wagner wrote a work on *Die Grossstadt* ('The City') in which he took together the trends of architecture and town planning, and laid the groundwork for 'The City of Towers' that has become so familiar ever since. He looked forward to cities built of glass and concrete, in which vast roads led to different 'zones', and in which the internal combustion engine would supply cheap and easy transport. Other planners at this time also considered 'lateral' cities, clustered horizontally along railway lines, in a lozenge-shape. Even before 1914, sparely functional architecture had come to dominate architects' thinking. Especially in Prague, interesting experiments were made to ally the new functionalism with cubism, in a planned contrasting of planes which anticipated the art déco style of the 1920s.

In music, too, a new mathematical approach emerged; again, mainly in Vienna (Arnold Schönberg's *Harmonielehre* of 1911 was followed in 1912 by a symphony celebrating the end of the bourgeois God; its second half is known as 'Totentanz of Principles'). Music had evolved in a way curiously parallel to the development of architecture, from late-nineteenth-century bombast to disquieting severity. Schönberg thought of himself as a new Monteverdi, simplifying the bombastic polyphony of his predecessors.

Music had consciously discovered the subconscious: a world in which morality, obvious forms, consistency had not much meaning, and to which subliminal appeals could be made. That discovery had been made in music by Richard Wagner forty years before. The Wagnerian revolution did of course have its precursors, notably Berlioz, but it was still a very nearly unique moment in the history of music. Music no longer existed in an apparently enclosed and self-explanatory way. It was consciously adapted by Wagner to moods, and he exploited all of the resources of theatre and orchestra to create a *Gesamtkunstwerk* with a resonance that was far from purely aesthetic. Robert Donington has argued that the *Ring* can only be understood with reference to the 'archetypes' of the psychologist Jung, i.e. the permanent spiritual realities of which human experience is often a distorted version. Richard Wagner himself was not far from saying much the same, only, of course, in different (and much-inflated) language. Donington and Deryck Cooke may indeed have a good case for suggesting that there is a 'language of music' which can be codified. Even on a stringed instrument, which is more accurate in registering harmonic intervals than keyboard instruments, a theme played in one key varies subtly from its sound in another key, since the tension of equivalent chords will vary slightly and, to the conscious ear (except in rare cases) inaudibly. Wagner himself exploited this, especially in *Tristan und Isolde*, where continual use of chromatic almost destroys a sense of key.

Wagner's influence on the later nineteenth century was immense. Huge, often fanatical audiences flocking to his temple at Bayreuth were unmistakable evidence that, in his blending of masculine and feminine, he had discovered a power to which nineteenth-century consciousness (and twentieth-century consciousness) could respond as to no other, although perhaps Schumann's early piano music had produced a similar exercise in harmonization of opposites, if on a much smaller scale. Wagner's (and Schumann's) enemies called it hysterical: Nietzsche was first a friend (in the 1870s) and then an enemy (in the 1880s) of this 'emotionalization of the intellect'.

The Wagnerian influence was particularly heavy on Claude Debussy. His *Pelléas et Mélisande*, of 1902, was a kind of 'anti-Tristan': the emotional drive made elegant and spare, but the dreamlike quality of the opera reinforced by chromaticism and tensely intricate changes of key. It was the Austrian Gustav Mahler who exploited the possibilities of Wagner to the full. He used music quite consciously and deliberately to express the shifting, indefinable and often contradictory inner world of dreams, memories, fantasies, ironic reflection and loneliness. For his Second Symphony, the 'Resurrection' (1894) he even wrote a 'programme', and did so for others of the symphonies, although he confessed that words were almost useless (and sometimes quite funny) when they attempted to describe what music was about. In the course of his expositions of his own inner world, he would often employ contradictory techniques. A Mahler score is a strange blend, in which ever larger orchestras will strive explosively towards a difficult shift of key – from C minor to E flat, say – with frequent little musical ironies, for instance, a reminiscence of some popular tune. Probably, the Sixth Symphony (1907) is the most successful of these inner tableaux. But Mahler's achievement was self-destructive, both of himself and of this kind of music: it could not be repeated. Oddly, in the course of his music, he had begun to develop anti-harmonies – a twisted and frequent use of the famous *diabolus in musica*, the diminished Fifth. Something of a revolution occurred when Schönberg, having started off as a respectable exponent of Mahlerian music, pushed on after *Gurrelieder*, in 1901, into an a-tonal music which disposed of the old harmonics altogether. Igor Stravinsky shocked Paris in 1913 with his *Rite of Spring*, in which he percussively allied sophisticated disharmonies with evocations of the pagan Slavonic gods.

The self-regarding self may have had its finest hour in Vienna around 1900, but it could be sterile, and even self-destructive. The future of music lay, not in central Europe, but in France, where classical aesthetics had a long history, or in Russia, and to a lesser extent Bohemia, where the power of native Slavonic musical tradition became allied, in Prokofiev, Stravinsky or Janáček, with the sophistication of the West.

Literature, by its nature, could not be 'mathematized' in the same way as most other matters. Instead, there were two different strands: self-contemplating, hedonistic narcissism on the one side, and 'socialist realism' – or its beginnings – on the other. In the later 1880s, most countries produced vast and grim works of social content, in which the background counted for much more than the chief characters. The French writer, Emile Zola, defender of the miners (*Germinal*) and of Dreyfus, had a huge following throughout Europe. Some cultures took naturally to grimness, as with the implacably realistic Scottish novels of this era, G.D. Brown's *House with the Green Shutters* (1900), or J. McDougall Hay's *Gillespie* (1911). Both of them owed their strength to a Calvinist Vengeance of the Lord theme, although both concerned the disruption of old communities by economic change. The social-realist approach distinguished the Russian, Maxim Gorky (a pseudonym that means 'bitter'); while Anton Chekhov, Henrik Ibsen and Anton Strindberg were concerned more with the collapsing integrity of the established classes.

The social-realist approach was in decline before 1914, and self-contemplating decadence, in one form or another, became the dominant theme.

In the heartlands of the West, the disintegration was sensed in a more internal, sophisticatedly and self-consciously aesthetic way. It was probably Arthur Rimbaud, the sadistically homosexual son of an army-captain father and a rigidly bigoted mother, who started Europe towards the dangerous path of words without meaning: a poetry in which the resonance, the almost subconscious impact, of words counted for everything, and their formal meaning for nothing; a startling anticipation, by a boy of seventeen a generation before, of the structuralist concerns of later philosophers. It led straight towards self-conscious decadence, a flight from the disintegrating intellectual world into hedonism, to a-morality, to the nightmare world of an Oscar Wilde's *Salomé*, an Aubrey Beardsley, a Gustave Moreau, a Huysmans, a world of castrating women, Medusa heads, Terrible Mothers, who had driven them to find the feminine in the masculine (Wilde found it, in the form of Lord Alfred Douglas, with a vengeance). Survivors of these nightmares were usually received into the Catholic Church, though both decadence and conversion were etiolated.

This 'decadence' was too dangerous. By the turn of the century, it was being 'aestheticized' into a world-weary, consciously *fin-de-siècle* 'good taste': Hugo von Hofmannsthal was at his best in the splendidly pastiche-eighteenth-century *Rosenkavalier* (1911) which so captured the Berlin public's imagination that special 'Rosenkavalier trains' were run to the opera's performances at Dresden. But there was a certain limpness to it all. Strauss and Hofmannsthal's later collaboration was not nearly so successful: their *Ariadne auf Naxos*, though beautifully ironic in its first act, even degenerated into overblown late romanticism in its second. Probably it was in Russia that elegance, theatricality and power went most successfully together: Diaghilev's *Ballets russes*, with Bakst's sets, were dazzlingly opulent, although, in the end, they were an exercise in narcissism that destroyed many of the participants.

Aesthetic narcissism is in fact the phrase that best sums up this moment in European culture. Writers cultivated the phrase, the 'effect', rather than the matter; and there were a great many people who sensed, beneath it all, the coming collapse. Thomas Mann's *Death in Venice*, written in 1911 (in Munich), was a little parable about the destructiveness of aesthetics, divorced from consequences; Hermann Broch's (later) essay on *Hofmannsthal und seine Zeit* was an evocation of the 'emptiness of values' (*Wertvakuum*) into which the cultural world had fallen. There was final, brief flowering in the 1920s. It is perhaps arguable that except in old-fashioned parts, such as eastern Europe, literature ceased to have the central role it had enjoyed before 1914.

In the early years of the twentieth century, then, there was an intellectual and cultural revolution. It did not particularly affect the world of popular culture, which had a vitality that defied this destructiveness. But the old world of nineteenth-century absolutes had been dealt a mortal blow, long before 1914. It is curious to note that, in the very years this occurred, there were political and social upheavals all over Europe – the progressive landslide in Great Britain, the rash of strikes in all countries, the first Russian revolution. In 1905, as the second generation of migrants to the towns became mature, there was a ferment in most areas of life, whether in the universities, the factories, the professions, or even the family. It was characteristic of the times that a women's movement made its appearance in all countries. The relative decline of the bourgeoisie after 1896 made life difficult for daughters. Some of them might passively accept that their families could no longer afford to keep them, and might make an unsatisfactory marriage; others might enter a nunnery; others would, in a genteel way, accept the ill-paid employment thrust upon them. Some responded in a different way, such as the 'suffragettes' in Great Britain, or the early feminists in Germany. In Vienna, in 1905, Rosa Mayreder wrote a classic of the feminist cause, *Zur Kritik der Weiblichkeit*, in which she reviewed some of the more outrageously anti-female literature (it included statements such as 'study makes women grow bald'). Sensibly, she remarked that the bicycle had done more to emancipate women than anything else. What H.G. Wells called 'the new woman' made her appearance. It was a phenomenon quite closely linked with the doctrines of Sigmund Freud.

Like so many others, Freud emerged from the strong nineteenth-century tradition of positivism: in medicine, of detailed experiment and observation, which owed its origins to the Scottish Enlightenment and had flourished especially in Paris, with Auguste Comte and Claude Bernard in the middle of the nineteenth century. Of course it was an error to suppose that empirical observation, without guiding principles, would lead anywhere (which was the foundation of Dostoyevsky's ultra-conservative hatred for the 'Mills and Bernards' who figure in such caricatures in his *Notes from the Underground*). Still, for a time, nineteenth-century positivism was a healthily destructive force. But there were ghosts in the machine. Freud, who went to Paris in the 1880s to study under the French neurologist Charcot, was closely involved in the study of madness. In true positivist fashion, he tried to cure his patients by standard physiological means – indeed, he made the terrible mistake of using cocaine, which almost killed a patient; on his return to Vienna, he tried hypnosis, which, again, was a failure.

It was only after his father's death, in 1896, that Freud began to understand something more. He owed a great deal to an absurd figure, his friend Wilhelm Fliess, who had in the middle of a theorizing that often out-did the wildest flights of gypsy tents, a sense that spiritualism and dreaming meant something. By 1897 Freud developed his 'project': a diagram of the workings of the brain which even he – though he was low on humour – did not publish because he feared his audience might find it funny. It was indeed funny: the brain consisted of energy which, if it did not find release in sexuality, would find release somewhere else, in the form of neurosis. 'Repression' (*Verdrängung*) – to which he gave a narrowly physical definition – was the 'cause' of his patients' troubles (it cannot be wholly accidental that, in 1897, in May, Freud, aged forty-one, last made love to his wife and never committed the sexual act again). Any of his followers, such as the patrician Swiss, Jung, who suggested that sexual repression might be one symptom of complications that 'spirit' and the conscious brain could deal with, provided that they were understood in less mechanistic ways, would be rudely ostracized by Freud, who was an extremely good hater. (At the end, in 1938, he said that now, at last, he could come to real blows with his enemies. His interlocutor supposed, obviously enough, that he meant the Nazis. Freud answered, gruffly, that he meant the Catholic Church.)

Still, whatever his absurdities along the way, Freud had expressed a discovery that did more to shape the personality of twentieth-century man than any other: the consciousness of a world within, of which the thoughts and doings that other people saw were merely a reflection. The subconscious was not a new concept. Even in 1818, Schopenhauer had pronounced upon it. In the 1880s, the Spiritualists, like the Theosophists Gurdjieff and Madame Blavatsky, were well aware of a new dimension. Freud looked into dreams, saw in them sexuality – sometimes preposterously so – and after 1900 had a fertile six years in which he examined the function, for instance, of jokes, or the meaning of certain expressions. He took up a theme that poets had known long before, that we are all, in a sense, the victims of our parents. He invented the 'Oedipus complex', the boy's so-great love for his mother that he can never adapt on 'normal' terms to another woman. The cases with which he dealt passed into folklore – 'Anna O', the 'Rat Man', the 'Wolf Man' etc. He spent hundreds of hours listening to his patients talking about Me, a favourite twentieth-century subject. In the end, he reverted to an absurdly mechanical view of the personality: super-ego, being the intelligent part, ego, the conscious personality, id, the subconscious drive (*Das Ich und das Es*). He saw the origins of character in sexuality, and the origins of sexuality in the baby's earliest upbringing: the area of its body with which it first made a sensual response ('the vagina is taken on lease from the rectum'). As with many such twentieth-century doctrines, there was sufficient truth in what Freud said to put him a long way ahead of his peers; but his doctrine was also, in the end, an extremely destructive one, in that it consigned moral responsibility, and a great part of the European past, to the rubbish heap.

Both in the new hedonism, and in the new mathematics, Vienna around 1900 was the chief centre. Of course it was not alone. It had counterparts in Prague, in Munich – the then cultural capital of Germany, where Thomas Mann lived before 1914 – and, though only to a limited extent, in Budapest. Paris, though not as crushingly predominant as before, was still a vital centre, even if, in literary matters, she suffered from a growing sense of inferiority to the Germans. London went its individual way; St Petersburg, in the years from 1900 to 1930, had a cultural moment that was all its own, but which, for some reason, had a greater resonance in England than in other European countries. But it was in Vienna that most of the twentieth-century intellectual world was invented. Practically in every field, from music to nuclear physics, Austro-Hungarian subjects were leaders.

Why? There have been distinguished works on individual themes within the overall context of 'Vienna 1900', but not yet a successful general treatment of it. The intellectual tradition of the city was not particularly strong: music, the most intimate of the arts, had flourished in the Habsburg world, but Austria had not led the field in anything else – on the contrary, she borrowed extensively from Italy or France. By most European standards, Vienna was rather a backward place – cosmopolitan, in that immigrants arrived from the rest of the Monarchy, but also highly conservative, in that the great aristocracy, the Monarchy, the Church and the army dominated the capital. The spirit of positivism, of unremitting experiment and endeavour, had arrived together with Austrian liberalism in the 1860s, and the University of Vienna – like other Austrian universities, notably that of Czernowitz in the remote Bukovina – flourished in this era, as did the universities of south-western Germany. Vienna was also (despite absurd romantic legendry) a rather harsh city, in which people of like mind gathered together for protection. Clubs, seminars, café-society flourished, and people met frequently to exchange ideas or to play instruments. Some of the writers in Vienna were also acutely aware that they, like their counterparts in St Petersburg, were living in a doomed world.

But the truly outstanding feature of Vienna before 1914

was the extraordinary preponderance, in cultural matters, of Jews. They were not religious Jews. In many cases, they were even converts. Karl Kraus, Gustav Mahler, Arnold Schönberg were converted to Catholicism (although, except in Mahler's case, it did not last, and in the Nazi era Schönberg reverted to Judaism). Ludwig Wittgenstein, though, as was said, Jewish *pur sang*, had a Protestant father. Freud himself, though by origin a Moravian Jew from a very strict household (he seems to have hated his partriarchally bullying father, just as Mahler did), gave up Judaism early on and hated religion with total consistency to the end of his many days. Arthur Schnitzler was a patrician, secularized Jew. Hugo von Hofmannsthal had a Jewish ancestor – Hofmann – who had made money, married 'out', acquired a title of nobility ('von Hofmannsthal'). None of them were Zionists (a movement that started in 1897, promoted by a rich Budapest Jew, Theodor Herzl). Most of them disliked Judaism. They were all, Schönberg apart, men who found relations with women very difficult indeed; they were all extremely unhappy, tortured people. Otto Weininger, the archetypal 'self-hating Jew', wrote a book about all of this in which he unintentionally related the upbringing to the secularized Judaism, the changing roles of father and mother, the consciousness of 'marginality' and the sexual disorder; Weininger himself was another Viennese suicide, shortly after writing his remarkable book in 1903.

Probably there is not much that can be meaningfully said on this theme until we know a very great deal more about it, and can discuss the missing links with more knowledge and confidence. But, in this period, everyone was well aware of the tremendous explosion of Judaism. Jews were the great success story of the later nineteenth century: whether religious, or, more generally, secularized, they brought seriousness, energy, an ability to appreciate contexts, and a desire to achieve to whatever they touched. This caused great resentment (the *Protocols of the Elders of Zion* was spatch-cocked together in 1903 by some Russian anti-Semites) although it also caused great admiration. Max Weber,

Werner Sombart and Ernst Troeltsch wrote extensively on the economic translations of religious psychology, and both appreciated the Jewish contribution to capitalism. Both of them also saw the analogy which could, partly, explain the phenomenon.

Max Weber's *The Protestant Ethic and the Spirit of Capitalism* was written at the start of his fertile later thirties and forties (1900–20). He started with the twisted background that appears to be more or less inseparable from serious achievement in this century. His father was a Jehovah-figure, his mother a decent, Calvinist soul. The father was a National Liberal deputy in the *Reichstag*, one of these self-righteous and two-dimensionally forceful followers of the later Bismarck, a Lutheran from Bielefeld in the Ruhr. South-western Germany, where Weber mainly taught, was the country's intellectual centre; not accidentally, though it was mixed in religion, it had been the area of the most rigid Protestantism in the seventeenth century. Weber started off as a German nationalist, in imitation of his father. He took up the 'national economics' preached in German universities – a complicated and uninteresting effort to ally Adam Smith to the mercantilists – and set off to study ways by which the Polish peasant population of east Elbian Prussia, and the hundreds of thousands of hated Polish seasonal labourers, could be defeated. It was all very National Liberal stuff, designed both to defeat the Polish 'hordes' and to upset the Junker lords who were responsible for bringing the immigrants in the first place. Weber's study of the rural problem of east Elbia, written in 1891, is still a very decent and reliable source, an important complement to the equally old work of G.F. Knapp on the Prussian *Bauernbefreiung*. On the strength of it, Weber was given the Chair of Economics by the Baden government, which gave him extremely enlightened support. He needed this, for, in the end, he was far too intelligent to succumb for ever to the German nationalist stuff preached at him by his father. He had a nervous breakdown, lasting for four years – the 'mid-life crisis' that Jung, later, identified. He did not read at all in that period.

When he recovered, in 1903, it all fell into place, and an astonishing one-man effort resulted.

The sociology of religion held him fascinated. No observer of the later nineteenth century could fail to see that, whatever the secularization in the meantime, the areas inhabited by people of different religions were dramatically different. To understand the Reformation, Weber only needed to look at contemporary south-western Germany, at, for instance, Bavarian *Mittelfranken*, or the *Wormser Ecke*, which produced far more than their fair share of dour, energetic artisans and businessmen. He never made the mistake of arguing – as the vulgarizations of him had it – that the Calvinist religion was a sort of dictation to make money and get ahead. He argued, much more subtly, that the attitude to things of this world, to worldly success, was different in Calvinist ideas on 'justification', different not only from Catholicism, but also from Baptism, or Methodism. He would have regarded with contempt any effort to discover, in seventeenth-century sermons, an injunction to their flocks by divines to make money. Indeed, he quoted with great approval from John Wesley, who had seen the whole problem long before: that extreme Protestantism, once it was released into a metropolis, would be better at making money because of its earlier isolation and its theological outlook; the money would then cause its makers, and their children, to forget about religion; hence the doctrine, in the end, would be sterile except among the victims of its secularized form. In an ecumenical age, Weber's doctrines are not popular. To the early twentieth-century world, they were simply commonsense.

Weber frequently alluded to Jews, but it was Werner Sombart (1910) and to a lesser extent Ernst Troeltsch who looked seriously at the Jewish side. Sombart's polymathic *Geschichte des Kapitalismus* was one of the great works of the pre-war era. Weber disliked the book, because Sombart took religious literature too literally in his efforts to identify Jews with the spirit of capitalism. But Sombart, like Weber, had touched seriously on a vital theme of the early twentieth century. He was concerned (like the Austrian economist, Schumpeter) with innovation, the entrepreneur. He looked at modern capitalism which, in the 1890s and 1900s, was very clearly the work of secularized Jews and of secularized (or semi-believing) Protestants, usually Calvinists. He looked back to the seventeenth century, to the origins of 'modern capitalism' as he understood it; he found that, then, the two religions had borrowed quite extensively from each other. In his study of the Jewish element in capitalism he quoted, with approval, articles in the *Jewish Quarterly* in the 1890s, in which the relationship of the two religions was explored; he also quoted with approval Heinrich Heine's disparaging remark about the Scots, who were then arriving in England in droves to fulfil various roles in capitalism, that they were England's equivalent of Jews. In some respects, the Scottish Enlightenment, in the eighteenth century, had been an anticipation of later developments in Vienna: the same desire to systematize, to overthrow outworn structures, to rationalize. The secularization of the Calvinist mind, and the secularization of Jews, gave early twentieth-century intellectual life its characteristic stamp.

BIBLIOGRAPHY

This list of books does not represent my own sources. It is designed as a guide for further reading. I have accordingly been sparing in references to works in languages other than English, and cite them, often enough, to indicate guides to books and articles in other languages.

1. General Histories of Europe in 1878–1919

This subject is gigantic in its complexity; the literature (and other records of the period) to be covered is enormous, and books on the period vary accordingly. A wide and sophisticated coverage is given by James Joll, *Europe since 1870. An International History* (Penguin Books 1980), the chief merit of which is the expounding of leading political ideas. An older book is C.J. Hayes, *A Generation of Materialism* (New York 1941) which efficiently comes to terms with the growth of the lower middle class and with nationalism (it is good on less prominent matters, such as the emergence of Flemish nationalism). J.M. Roberts, *Europe 1880–1945* (London 1967) is a good chronological narrative; the same is true of Gordon Craig, *Europe 1815–1914* (reprinted, New York 1972), though it is more comprehensive on cultural matters. The Cambridge Modern History vol. XII, *The Era of Violence* (Cambridge 1965), can mainly be ignored, but the preceding volume, XI, *Material Progress and World-Wide Problems* (1962), has some good essays, notably that by R. Robinson and J. Gallagher on imperialism. There is a discussion of these and other works by Ann Low-Beer in 'Books and the Teaching of History in Schools', *History* (1974). J.A. Schumpeter, *Capitalism, Socialism and Democracy* (London 1950), has many thoughts, as does P. Drucker, *The End of Economic Man* (London 1938).

2. Economic History

One day it will be possible to write an essay on the disintegration of this subject from its certainties of the 1950s. Basic material is supplied by B.R. Mitchell, *European Historical Statistics* (London 1975) and by the volumes of the *Fontana History of Europe* (ed. Carlo Cipolla, London 1976). The statistics and bibliography are very useful; the essay on German industrialization by Knut Borchardt is especially good. Two old books are still worth reading. J.H. Clapham's *The Economic Development of France and Germany 1815–1914* (Cambridge, 4th edition 1968), though very outdated, is quite easy to read and presents a coherent view. David Landes, *The Unbound Prometheus* (Cambridge 1969) is a classic history of technological growth. The *Cambridge Economic History of Europe* vol. VII (edited by P. Mathias and M.N. Postan) contains some outstanding essays, especially those on Russia by Olga Crisp and M. Kaser, and on Germany by J.J. Lee.

More recent textbooks, each of which has merit, are: A.S. Milward and S.B. Saul, *The Development of the Economics of Continental Europe 1850–1914* (London 1977); Clive Trebilcock, *The Industrialization of the Continental Powers 1890–1914* (London 1981) and Sidney Pollard, *European Economic Integration* (London 1974). In many ways, the economic history of the years up to 1914 makes sense only if put in the context of the inter-war era. D. Aldcroft, *Versailles to Wall Street* (London 1977) and Ingvar Svennilson, *Growth and Stagnation in the European Economy* (Geneva 1954) are convenient, in that they refer to events before 1914. Charles Kindleberger, *The World in Depression* (London 1973) makes demands on the reader, but is especially rewarding for its explanation of monetary factors.

The economic history has to be approached with at least some element of theory. Marxists such as Maurice Dobb (*Papers on Capitalism*, London 1967) and Paul Sweezy (*The Transition from Feudalism to Capitalism*, London 1976) have important things to say. They were challenged by Joseph Schumpeter, whose *Business Cycles* (2 vols., New York 1939) is too technical for most readers, but whose *History of Economic Analysis* (London 1955) is quite approachable. Alexander Gerschenkron, *Economic Backwardness in Historical Perspective* (Cambridge, Mass. 1966) and his *Festschrift* (ed. H. Rosovsky, Cambridge, Mass. 1966) are powerful and learned arguers on the 'neo-liberal' side. S. Kuznets, *Modern Economic Growth* (New Haven 1973) can be read with profit.

On all matters, the *Economic History Review* and the *Journal of Economic History* have many excellent articles. The *Journal of European Economic History* (Rome, since 1972) has attained a very high standard.

Three contentious factors in the process of 'growth' are technology, finance and agriculture. T. Williams (ed.), *The Oxford History of Technology* is (together with Landes's *Prometheus*) a useful compendium of information; S.C. Gilfillan, *The Sociology of Invention* (Cambridge, Mass. 1970) and John Jewkes *et al.*, *The Sources of Invention* (London 1958) are a good beginning for the subject.

In matters of finance, there is much disagreement on monetary lines: both as regards banking, and as regards international finance, or the gold standard. H. Feis, *Europe, the World's Banker* (New Haven 1930) and A.I. Bloomfield, *Short-term Capital Movements under the pre-1914 Gold Standard* (Princeton 1963) were and still are important; both need correction from W.A. Brown, *England and the New Gold Standard* (London 1929) and Marcello de Cecco, *Money and*

Empire. The International Gold Standard 1890–1914 (Oxford 1974, with bibliography).

The place of agriculture in economic growth, and for that matter in politics overall, caused much debate around 1900, not least among socialists. For any discussion of the history of Europe east of the Elbe agrarian questions must take a very large part: there, the problem of 'development economics' was posed. D. Chirot, 'Market and Servile Labour Systems' in *Journal of Social History* vol. 8 no. 1 (1975); R. Redfield, *Peasant Society and Culture* (London 1956); Colin Clark, *The Economics of Subsistence Agriculture* (London 1967); the article on 'Peasantry' in *The Encyclopaedia of the Social Sciences* (1922); Teodor Shanin (ed.), *Peasants and Peasant Societies* (Harmondsworth 1971); D. Warriner, *Economics of Peasant Farming* (London, 2nd edition 1964) and *Land Reform* (Oxford 1969) are, in various ways, good introductions. B. Kerblay edited selected works by the Russian agronomist A.V. Chayanov (New York 1968) and discussed his achievements in *Cahiers du monde russe et soviétique* vol. 5 no. 4 (1964) pp. 411–60. B. Galeski, *Basic Concepts of Rural Sociology* (Manchester 1972); P. Sorokin, *Principles of Rural-Urban Sociology* (New York 1931) and D. Thorner, 'L'économie paysanne' in *Annales ESC* 3 (1964) pp. 417–32 are all useful. So are F. Crouzet (ed.), *Essays in European Economic History 1789–1914* (London 1969) and B. Supple, *The Experience of Economic Growth* (New York 1963).

3. Government and Society

The relationship of economic and political change created many books on 'modernization' and 'revolution', especially in the 1960s. S.P. Huntington, *Political Order in Changing Societies* (New Haven 1968); D. Apter, *The Politics of Modernization* (Chicago 1965); T. Skocpol, *States and Social Revolution* (Cambridge 1979); S.N. Eisenstadt, *Moderniz-*

ation, Protest and Change (New York 1966) were characteristic. A notable work has been Barrington Moore, *The Social Origins of Dictatorship and Democracy* (Harmondsworth 1977).

H. Finer, *The Theory and Practice of Modern Government* (London, 4th edition 1961) and E.N. and P. Anderson, *European Political Institutions and Social Change* (Berkeley 1967) give basic descriptions of the growing bureaucracies. G.V. Rimlinger, *Welfare Policy and Industrialization in Europe, America and Russia* (New York 1971) narrates the growth of public charity.

There are a great many books on towns and cities. Antony Sutcliffe, *Towards the Planned City, 1780–1914* (Oxford 1981) is a very good beginning; it can be supplemented by works on separate cities, of which A. Dyos has been a pioneer in England, and of which Norma Evenson's *Paris: a Century of Change* (London 1979) is a distinguished instance.

Education is a huge subject. It can be approached from C.A. Anderson, *Education and Economic Development* (London 1958); L. Alston, *Education and the State in Tsarist Russia* (Stanford 1979); M. Blaug, *An Introduction to the Economics of Education* (London 1970); John Vaizey et al. (eds.), *The Economics of Education* (London 1966) and *The Political Economy of Education* (London 1972). On France, M. Ozouf, *Nous, les maîtres d'école* (Paris 1972); and on Germany, H.-W. Prahl, *Sozialgeschichte des Hochschulwesens* (Düsseldorf 1968) provide introductions. Carlo Cipolla's *Literacy and Development in the West* (London 1960) is an overall survey of an important subject.

On the place of universities in society in general, G.I. Davies, *The Democratic Intellect* (Edinburgh 1956), though concerned with Scottish universities in a somewhat earlier period, is a brilliant achievement.

The adaptation of religion, and the progress of secularization, have attracted a sizeable literature. The subject was a matter of extreme concern in the later nineteenth century, when it could plausibly be argued that there had been important translations of the various religious mentalities into economic and political affairs. Max Weber's *The Protestant Ethic and the Spirit of Capitalism* (1903; latest edition London 1976) was only one of a great many similar works – e.g. Werner Sombart's multi-volume *The Modern Capitalism* (abridged American edition, 1964) and his *The Jews and Capitalism* (London translation 1913). Ronald Robinson, *The Sociology of Religion* (1976); David Martin, *A General Theory of Secularization* (Oxford 1978); R. Mehl, *Sociology of Protestantism* and F. Boulard, *Introduction to Religious Sociology* (London 1960) can be read with profit. A German view is: R. Marbach, *Säkularisierung und sozialer Wandel im 19 Jahrhundert*. M.P. Fogarty, *Christian Democracy in Western Europe 1820–1953* (London 1957) may soon be supplemented by a much more serious Irish work on European political Catholicism. There is an extremely efficient brief survey of the subject in Hugh McLeod, *Religion and the People of Western Europe* (Oxford 1981), with a good bibliography.

The other mass movement in politics, socialism, has attracted an enormous amount of literature, now of every level, including detailed investigations of factories throughout the continent. A very brave attempt to survey it all is Dick Geary, *European Labour Protest 1848–1939* (London 1981). P.N. Stearns has written extensively: *European Society in Upheaval. Social History since 1750* (New York 1975), *Workers and Protest: the European Labour Movement* (Illinois 1971) and *Lives of Labour* (London 1975). Charles Tilly *et al.*, *The Rebellious Century 1830–1930* (London 1975); R. Bezucha, *Modern European Social History* (Lexington, Mass. 1972) and Clive Emsley (ed.), *Conflict and Stability in Europe* (London 1979) all concentrate on rebellious labour. E. Kaelble, 'Konjunktur und Streik' in *Zeitschrift für Wirtschafts- und Sozialwissenschaft* 1972/92 makes sensible points. George Lichtheim's *A Short History of Socialism* (1970; latest impression London 1983) is a classic. James Joll, *The Second International* (London 1975) and Leszek Kolakowski's three-volume *Main Currents in Marxism* (London 1978) provide strong coverage of the 'ideologues', and Edmund Wilson's *To the Finland Station* (New York 1940) is essential. See also H. McLeod, *Class and Religion in the Late Victorian City* (London 1974); A.R. Vidler, *A Century of Social Catholicism, 1820–1920* (London 1964); E. Halévy, *Histoire du socialisme européen* (Paris 1948) and W. Conze, 'The Effects of Nineteenth-century Agrarian Reform on Social Structure in Central Europe' in F. Crouzet *et al.* (eds.), *Essays in Economic History* (London 1969).

4. *Nationalism, Imperialism and War*

The growth of nationalism in this era has been extensively studied. Hans Kohn, *The Age of Nationalism* (New York 1968); C.J. Hayes, *The Historical Evolution of Modern Nationalism* (New York 1935) and E. Kedourie, *Nationalism* (3rd edition, London 1966) supply various perspectives. D.K. Fieldhouse, *Economics and Empire* (London 1973) examines various cases of imperialism and emerges with a very English answer. The 'feel' of empire is well communicated in J.A. Gallagher and R. Robinson, *Africa and the Victorians* (1958), now a classic; see also his *Lectures*, ed. A. Seal (1982). J. Schumpeter, *Imperialism and Social Classes* (Oxford 1951) is worth reading.

The course of diplomatic exchanges in this complicated era is described by A.J.P. Taylor, *The Struggle for Mastery in Europe 1848–1918* (Oxford 1951, latest edition 1979). Its judgements stand up very well to later research. Paul Kennedy, *The Rise of the Anglo-German Antagonism 1860–1914* (London 1980); Zara Steiner, *Great Britain and the Origins of the First World War* (London 1978); D.C.B. Lieven's forthcoming *Russia and the Origins of the First World War*; V. Berghahn's *Germany and the Approach of War in 1914* (London 1973); F.R. Bridge's authoritative *From Sadowa to Sarajevo: the Foreign Policy of Austria-Hungary 1866–1914* (London 1972) and R.J. Bosworth, *Italy, the Least of the Great Powers* (Cambridge 1979) outline (and more than outline) important subjects. Richard Langhorne: *The Breakdown of the Concert of Europe* (London 1981) is a good summary. Economic aspects of the war's origins have been recently covered by Raymond Poidevin, *Les relations économiques et financières entre la France et l'Allemagne de 1898 à 1914* (Paris 1969) and by René Girault, *Emprunts russes et investissements français en Russie 1887–1914* (Paris 1973). The facts of the arms race are spelled out in Norman Stone, *The Eastern Front 1914–1917* (London 1978) chs. 1 and 2; cf. for the naval side Paul Kennedy, *The Rise and Fall of British Naval Mastery* (London 1976). Foreign policies are often dealt with in the separate national histories (see below).

On the outbreak of war in 1914, Fritz Fischer's *War of Illusions* (London 1975) is in a place on its own. I. Geiss, *July 1914: the Outbreak of the First World War* (New York 1974), an edited collection of documents, takes the story further. G. Barraclough, *From Agadir to Armageddon* (London 1982) is a hard-hitting essay on the failure of 'deterrence'; older works by L.C.F. Turner, *Origins of the First World War* (1970) and L. Lafore, *The Long Fuse* (1966) are still of interest. L.L. Farrar, *The Short-War Illusion* has an important point. W.J. Mommsen, 'Domestic factors in German foreign policy before 1914' in *Central European History* VI (1973) pp. 3–43 talks sense. For a discussion of the strategic thinking of 1913–14, see David French, *British Economic and Strategic Planning 1905–1915* (London 1982). L. Brion-Guerry, *L'année 1913* (3 vols., Paris 1971) and J.-J. Becker, *Comment les français sont entrés dans la guerre* (Paris 1977) discuss the explosion of public opinion. V. Dedijer, *The Road to Sarajevo* (London 1967) concerns the assassination of the archduke.

The two best short accounts of the war are A.J.P. Taylor, *The First World War* (Oxford, latest edition 1979) and Marc Ferro, *The Great War* (London 1963), both paperbacks and regularly reprinted. Much sense was talked by B.H. Liddell Hart, *History of the First World War* (London 1972). In German, W. Schieder, *Der Erste Weltkrieg* (Cologne 1969) also has a good bibliography. Denis Winter, *Death's Men*

(Harmondsworth 1979) discusses the attitudes of soldiers to war. There are many classic accounts of various battles: John Keegan, *The Face of Battle* (Harmondsworth 1979), Alastair Horne, *The Price of Glory* (London 1975), Leon Wolf, *In Flanders Fields* (Harmondsworth 1981) or Robert Rhodes-James, *Gallipoli* (London 1970) for instance. W.S. Churchill, *The World Crisis* (London 1928) and David Lloyd George, *War Memoirs* (2 vols., London 1938) are classics, without continental rivals. A great debate developed around questions of compromise peace and war aims. Fritz Fischer, *Germany's Aims in the First World War* (London 1967) began the process. Other historians have subsequently discovered that their own countries' war aims were not as idealistic as was made out at the time. V.H. Rothwell, *British War Aims and Peace Diplomacy* (Oxford 1971); C.M. Andrew and A.S. Kánya-Forstner, *France Overseas* (London 1981); K.J. Calder, *Britain and the Origins of the New Europe* (Cambridge 1976); R.E. Bunselmeyer, *The Cost of the War 1914–1919. British Economic War Aims and the Origins of Reparation* (Hamden, Conn. 1975) display this, in various ways. War finance, and related social problems, emerge in A.C. Pigou, *The Political Economy of War* (London 1940) and André Bouton, *La fin des rentiers* (1931). N. Timasheff, *The Great Retreat* (New York 1946) resumes many of the arguments; C.S. Meier, *Reconstructing Bourgeois Europe* (1977) is an important survey of the background to 'the peace-makers' in 1919 and subsequent years. Arno J. Mayer, *The Politics of Peace-making* (1967) states the importance of social themes in 1919 and 1920. From this list I have, with regret, omitted a number of excellent books.

5. *Separate Countries*

A. GERMANY

A good introduction for the English-speaking reader is Michael Balfour, *The Kaiser and His Times* (Harmondsworth 1975). The most comprehensive textbook is Gordon Craig, *German History 1867–1945* (Oxford 1981) with a good bibliography. Other good ones are W. Carr, *A History of Germany* (London 1972) and A.J. Ryder, *The German Revolution of 1918* (Cambridge 1967). Martin Kitchen, *The Political Economy of Germany 1815–1945* (London 1978) usefully summarizes recent German work. A number of good German textbooks (*Handbücher*) deserve mention. E. Huber, *Deutsche Verfassungsgeschichte* (latest edition, 1973 in several volumes) gives detailed accounts of political life. The two-volume *Territorien-Ploetz* (1976) covers separate states exhaustively and often entertainingly. The *Handbuch der deutschen Wirtschafts- und Sozialgeschichte* ed. H. Aubin and W. Zorn (Stuttgart 1976) vol. 2, the *Handbuch der deutschen Militärgeschichte* ed. H. Meier-Welcker (Freiburg im Breisgau 1967) and the *Handbuch der bayerischen Geschichte* ed. K. Bosl (Munich 1976) vol. 4 cover everything.

Important German interpretations are those of H.-U. Wehler, *Moderne deutsche Sozialgeschichte* (Köln 1968); Michael Stürmer (ed.), *Das Deutsche Kaiserreich* (Düsseldorf 1970) and I. Geiss *et al.*, *Deutschland in der Welt Politik des 19. und 20. Jahrhunderte* (Düsseldorf 1973) which all contain many lively essays. Wehler's *Krisenherde des Kaiserreichs* (Göttingen 1970) has some very valuable pieces, especially on the Polish issue. Of older books, Arthur Rosenberg's *Imperial Germany* (London 1931) is still valuable. See also R. Dahrendorf, *Society and Democracy in Germany* (London 1968).

For the right in politics, a good start is L.W. Muncy, *The Junker in the Prussian Administration* (Rhode Island 1944); J.J. Sheehan, *German Liberalism in the Nineteenth Century* (1974); two essays by J.C. Hunt, 'Peasants, Grain Tariffs and Meat Quotas' in *Central European History* VII no. 4 (1974) and 'The Bourgeois Middle in German Politics 1871–1933' in *ibid* XI no. 1 (1978); P.G.J. Pulzer, *The Rise of Political Anti-Semitism in Germany and Austria* (New York 1964); G. Eley, *Reshaping the German Right* (London 1980) (with a bibliography, in which the author's own articles should be noted), and an older book, Alexander Gerschenkron, *Bread and Democracy in Germany* (Berkeley 1943). David Blackbourn has examined political Catholicism with great penetration in various places. His book, *Class, Religion and Local Politics in Wilhelmine Germany* (Yale 1980) follows a number of important articles, listed in his bibliography. Two essay collections deserve mention: R.J. Evans (ed.), *Society and Politics in Wilhelmine Germany* (1978) and J.J.Sheehan (ed.), *Politics in Wilhelmine Germany* (1978).

The left has been extensively covered. C.F. Schorske's *Great Schism: German Social Democracy 1905–1917* is now old (1955) but still useful. Dieter Groh, *Negative Integration oder revolutionärer Attentismus* (Frankfurt/Main 1973) and Helga Grebing, *The German Labour Movement* (English translation 1969) have many things to say. Other works are by G. Roth and A.J. Berlau. Events later than 1917 are surveyed in F.L. Carsten, *Revolution in Central Europe* (London 1972); D.W. Morgan, *The Socialist Left and the German Revolution* (New York 1975) and A.J. Ryder, *The German Revolution of November 1918* (Cambridge 1967). D. Halperin, *Germany Tried Democracy* (1960) is a very good survey of the early years of the Weimar Republic. John Moses, *The German Trade Unions* (2 vols., 1982) is a useful start for this essential subject. D. Crew, *Town in the Ruhr* (New York 1979) is a monograph on Bochum. Other monographs are R. Comfort, *Revolutionary Hamburg* (Stanford, Calif. 1966) and Allan Mitchell, *Revolution in Bavaria* (Princeton 1966). There is a good East German work on Berlin: Annemarie Lange, *Das wilhelminische Berlin* (East Berlin 1976). A further East German work is a long exercise in black humour: Dieter Fricke, *Die bürgerlichen Parteien in Deutschland* (2 vols., Leipzig 1968). Further bibliography may be found in D. Geary's *Labour and Protest* (London 1980), including his own articles. H. Pogge von Strandmann, 'Domestic Origins of Germany's Colonial Expansion under Bismarck' in *Past and Present* 42 (1969); H.-U. Wehler, 'Bismarck's Imperialism 1862–1890' in *Past and Present* 48 (1970); J.P. Nettl, 'The German Social Democratic Party, 1890–1914' in *Past and Present* 30 (1965).

Useful articles on German history may be found in the *Journal of Modern History*, the *American Historical Review*, occasionally in *Past and Present*, and in *Central European History*.

B. RUSSIA

J.N. Westwood, *Endurance and Endeavour* (Oxford 1981) has been revised (1981) with a bibliography. It should be read in conjunction with Hugh Seton-Watson's *The Russian Empire* (Oxford 1967); Cyril Black's *Transformation of Russian Society* (1960) and, for economic matters, the *Cambridge Economic History of Europe* vols. VI and VII. There is a good Soviet account: *Akademiya Nauk SSSR: istoricheski institut: Istoriya Rossii* ed. B.A. Rybakov *et. al.*, 1st series, vol. VI: *Rossiya v period imperializma 1900–1917* ed. A.L. Sidorov and K.N. Tarnovski (1968). Vol. V, on the post-emancipation era, is also very useful.

Russia's economic development before 1917 is a contentious matter, since it affects many large political questions as well as 'development economics'. P.R. Gregory discusses some of the issues in *Soviet Studies* 23 (1972/3) pp. 418–34 and in *Jahrbücher für die Geschichte Osteuropas* neue Folge II, no. 25 (1977) pp. 200 ff. (in English). The works of A. Gerschenkron are indispensable; see also the *Journal of Economic History* 1967 (Kahan), 1973 (Barkai) and 1976 (Gregory, Drummond) for various aspects, not least monetary. Olga Crisp's *Studies in the Russian Economy before 1914* (London 1976) are essential. New work in the subject is being undertaken by P.W. Gatrell, 'Industrial Expansion in tsarist Russia 1908–1914' in *Economic History Review* vol. 35 no. 1 (1982) and 'The Impact of War on Russian Development' in *World Development* vol. 9 no. 8 (1981). The overall work of Clive Trebilcock has a good bibliography.

Agrarian Russia presents innumerable problems, the more so as Soviet historians themselves seem to be in some disarray as to its complexities and its relevance to contemporary difficulties. D. Field discusses *The End of Serfdom* (Cambridge, Mass. 1976) with a good sense of the intertwining of

administrative and economic issues. L. Volin, G.V. Pavlov-
ski and G.T. Robinson's works, though now very much out
of date, should still be used as starting-points: their essential
arguments amounted to statements that the tsarist government must be blamed. An extremely thoughtful view of the
peasant question is Teodor Shanin, *The Awkward Class*
(1972) which adapts Chayanov. P.W. Gatrell in *Past and
Present* 1983 will discuss the adaptation of Russians' own
appreciation of their agrarian problems to the understanding
of the English medieval past. K. Fitzlyon, *Before the
Revolution. A View of Russia under the Last Tsar* (London
1977) has excellent photographs and outstanding introduction.

On political matters, there are good essays in N. Stavrou,
Russia under the Last Tsar (Minneapolis 1969); cf. *Russia
enters the Twentieth Century* ed. G. Katkov (1972). G.
Hosking, *Russia's Constitutional Experiment* (Cambridge
1973) complements B. Pares's ancient work. George Fischer
and W.S. Rosenberg discuss Russian liberalism; Jürgen
Nötzold, *Wirtschaftspolitische Alternativen Russlands* (Wies-
baden 1968) is a good, gloomy view of the tasks facing the
revived autocracy after 1905. The socialist revolutionaries
are covered in Oliver Radkey (1958 and 1962), M. Perrin
(1978) and latterly by Manfred Hildermaier, *Die Sozialrevol-
utionäre Partei Russlands 1900–1914* (Cologne 1978). Norman Stone, *The Eastern Front 1914–1917* (London 1978)
reviews the complex of administrative, economic and political issues that confronted the government once it attempted
to face and fight a war. Chapter I concerns military
development before 1914, but overstates its case.

The left, and the Russian revolution, have received vast
attention. A good bibliography may be found in Marc Ferro,
The Russian revolution of February 1917 (London 1972: the
bibliography may be found only in the British translation and
the original French, not in the American version) and *October
1917* (London 1979). The most coherent narrative account
of the Revolution is still W.H. Chamberlin's (1935, two
vols.). The 'notes' to E.H. Carr's three-volume work are

worth reading. Adam Ulam, *Russia's Failed Revolutions* (1981) and his earlier *Lenin and the Bolsheviks* (1968) may be used together with L. Shapiro, *Lenin* (1967) and V. Daniels, *Red October* (1968). A. Rabinowitch has written two good books on the July Days and October. A very good book is J.H. Bater, *St Petersburg* (1973). There are some excellent articles, in *Soviet Studies* and the *Cahiers du monde russe et soviétique*.

C. ITALY

D. Mack Smith, *Italy* (revised edition, London 1969) and C. Seton-Watson, *Italy from Liberalism to Fascism* (London 1972) are informative general studies. Giuliano Procacci, *History of the Italian People* (London 1970) presents a view from the left. E. Neufeld and S.B. Clough should be used for economic matters (in English). There are some distinguished essays in J.A. Davis, *Gramsci and Italy's Passive Revolution* (New York 1979) though they are not about Gramsci. M. Clark, *Antonio Gramsci and the Revolution that Failed* (London 1977), is.

In Italian, there are many excellent works on this period. Indro Montanelli's volumes of his general history, *L'Italia dei notabili* (Milan 1974) and *L'Italia di Giolitti* (Milan 1975) are a good read, even with defective Italian. A. Storti Abate, *L'età giolittiana* (Palermo 1978) is an efficient, short textbook which gives good space to cultural themes. Works which may be compared to the Germans' *Handbücher* are: G. Candeloro, *Storia dell'Italia moderna* vol. 7 'La crisi di fini secolo e l'età giolittiana' (Milan 1974); E. Ragionieri, *Storia d'Italia* vol. 3 'La storia politica e sociale' (Turin 1976); V. Castronovo, *Storia d'Italia* vol. 1 'La storia economica' (Turin 1975). G. Candeloro discusses *Il movimento cattolico in Italia* (Rome 1972) as does G. de Rosa (Bari 1966). Mario Isnenghi and Brunello Vigezzi discuss aspects of Italy's intervention in the war in 1915. See also J.B. Cohen, 'Financing Industrialization in Italy, 1894–1914' in *Journal of Economic History* vol. 27 (1967).

D. FRANCE

In English, there is an efficient survey of the Third Republic by R.D. Anderson (1978), with a good bibliography. The first volume of T. Zeldin, *France 1848–1945* (Oxford 1973) is especially useful, though weak on economic factors. The *Nouvelle histoire de la France contemporaine (Editions du Seuil)* has two distinguished volumes, of wholly manageable size and style, in J.-M. Mayeur, *Les débuts de la troisième République* (Paris 1973) and M. Rebérioux, *La République radicale?* (Paris 1975 and 1976). Both have excellent bibliographies which to some extent excuse me for omitting many outstandingly good historical works produced in France in the last two decades. French historians have sometimes seemed to me, in writing this book, to be the only ones in Europe who are not deeply depressing, though some of them try.

P. Sorlin, *La société française* (Paris 1969) and G. Dupeux, *French Society 1789–1970* (in translation, London 1976) should be read together with E. Weber, *Peasants into Frenchmen* (London 1976). There are many solid works on economic matters. R.H. Cameron, *Essays in French Economic History* (Homewood, Ill. 1970) and C. Kindleberger, *Economic Growth in France and Great Britain* (Cambridge, Mass. 1964) are contemptuous of 'backwardness'. Greater sophistication is shown by F. Crouzet, 'Essai de construction d'un indice de la production industrielle française au XIXe. siècle' in *Annales ESC* Jan.–Feb. 1970 and by writers on France in the *Fontana Economic History of Europe* and the *Cambridge Economic History of Europe*. M. Faure, *Les paysans dans la société française* (Paris 1969); G. Walther *et al.*, *Histoire des paysans* and M. Agulhon *et al.*, *Histoire de la France rurale* vol. 3 (1789–1914) (1976) show, especially the last, French historians at their best.

The French left, on the other hand, frequently displays them, and not only them, at their worst. J. Droz, *Le socialisme democratique* (Paris 1966) is sound; it may be supplemented by C. Willard, *Le mouvement socialiste en France 1893–1905* (Paris 1965) and M. Perrot, *Les ouvriers en grève* (Paris 1974). H. Dubiel, *Le syndicalisme révolutionnaire* (1969) makes much of this subject.

The radicals are well discussed in J. Kayser, *Les grandes batailles du radicalisme* (Paris 1962); D.R. Watson, *Clemenceau* (London 1974); M. Agulhon, *La République au village* (Paris 1970) and M. Ozouf, *Nous, les maîtres d'école* (Paris 1973). J.-M. Mayeur, *La séparation de l'Église et de l'État*, (Paris 1966); E.G. Léonard, *Le Protestant français* (Paris 1953); J. McManners, *Church and State in France 1870–1914* (London 1972). T. Zeldin (ed.), *Conflicts in French History* (London 1970) has good discussions of radicalism.

For the right, R. Rémond, *The Right in France* (Philadelphia 1969) is still valuable. R. Girardet, *La société militaire dans la France contemporaine* (Paris 1953) and more recently D. Porch, *The March to the Marne: the French Army 1870–1914* (Cambridge 1981) mark a good beginning to military subjects. Douglas Johnson, *The Dreyfus Affair* (London 1966) is an excellent brief account; M. Ozouf, *L'École, l'Église et la République* (Paris 1962) goes some way to explaining the failure of political Catholicism as does A. Sedgwick, *The Ralliement in French Politics* (Cambridge, Mass. 1965).

Ph. Bernard, *La fin d'un monde 1914–1929* (Paris 1975) surveys the war, and its social changes. Stephen Schuker, *The End of French Predominance in Europe* (Chapel Hill 1976) is an eminently penetrating discussion of the mind of French statesmen after Versailles. See also M. Larkin, *Church and State after the Dreyfus Affair* (London 1974). The spirit of the Third Republic in its declining years is best communicated by L.-F. Céline, *Voyage au bout de la nuit* (Paris 1931).

E. THE HABSBURG MONARCHY

Perhaps the history of this empire cannot be written: it is a vast subject, with hopelessly intertangled contours. Old books are still, easily, the best introduction to it. R.W. Seton-Watson wrote several good books, notably *The South Slav Question* (London 1911) and *Racial Problems in Hungary* (London 1908). Louis Eisenmann's *Compromis austro-hongrois de 1867* (1904) is a wonderful book. A.J.P. Taylor, *The Habsburg Monarchy 1815–1918* (1948, several times reprinted) is also a wonderful book, with a good bibliography. H.W. Steed, *The Habsburg Empire* (1913) is excellent. There is an 'official' Austrian history, gradually seeing the light of day: *Die Habsburgermonarchie 1848–1919*. To date, three vast volumes have appeared – one on economic affairs, one on administration, and the third, in two parts, on the Nationalities. Most of the essays in these are quite unreadable, redeemed only by their bibliographies. In the main, it is the Hungarian historians who have kept some sense as to what the subject involves. G. Ránki writes penetratingly on economic questions. An enormous history of Hungary is also appearing: *Magyarország története* ed. Zs. Pach; vol. 7, edited by P. Hanák, concerns the years 1890–1918. An earlier version is Hanák and T. Erényi, *Magyarország története 1849–1918*. The Czech lands are ably surveyed in Karl Bosl (ed.), *Handbuch der Geschichte der böhmischen Länder* vol. 3 (1848–1919) (Stuttgart 1968). Of recent monographs, G. Lewis, 'The Peasantry, Rural Change and Conservative Agrarianism in Lower Austria' in *Past and Present* 81 (1978); B.M. Garver, *The Young Czech 1874–1901* (London 1978) and J. Cohn, *The Evolution of a National Community* (the Germans in Prague) (1981) deserve mention.

See also N. Stone, 'Army and Society in the Habsburg Monarchy, 1900–14' in *Past and Present* 33 (1966); J. Freudenberger, 'State Intervention as an Obstacle to Economic Growth in the Habsburg Monarchy' in *Journal of Economic History* vol. 27 (1967); D. Good, 'Stagnation and Take-off in Austria, 1873–1913', in *Economic History Review* vol. 27; I.T. Berend, *Underdevelopment and Economic Growth: Studies in Hungarian Economic and Social History* (Budapest 1979); C.A. Macartney, *The Habsburg Empire, 1790–1918* (London 1969).

F. OTHER COUNTRIES
There are no serious books in English on the modern history of the Scandinavian countries except, in part, Finland. W.

Kossmann, *The Low Countries* (1978) is very sound and helpful for both the Netherlands and Belgium. Raymond Carr, *Spain 1808–1939* (second edition, 1982) is outstandingly good; and there is a compression of it, with a very efficient bibliography, in the same author's *Modern Spain 1870–1970* (1980). There are some interesting books on peasant questions in the Balkans: e.g. H.H. Stahl, *Traditional Romanian Peasant Communities* (1980) and P. Eidelberg, *The Great Romanian Peasant Revolt of 1907* (1974). Poland has recently (Oxford 1982) received an excellent two-volume history by Norman Davies.

7. *Cultural History*

The most approachable overall survey is H. Stuart Hughes, *Consciousness and Society* (Harvester Press 1979). A German work, the *Handbuch der Kulturgeschichte* (Düsseldorf 1978) is an excellent list, which is, perhaps, all that this subject can attempt to be. The *Encyclopaedia of Science* and *Encyclopaedia of the History of Ideas* both published by C. Scribner and Sons (New York 1973) contain some distinguished essays. Edmund Wilson's *Axel's Castle* (New York 1931) and George Orwell's *Collected Essays, Journalism and Letters* (London 1968) contain inspired essays on many modern writers.

A great part of the background to this subject is mathematical and scientific. A good approach to mathematics can be made from M. Klein, *Mathematics* (London 1979); of older books, A. Hadamard, *The Psychology of Invention in Mathematics* (New York 1945) and G. Hardy, *A Mathematician's Apologia* (Cambridge 1964) are essential. A. Ehrenzweig, *A Study in the Psychology of Artistic Imagination* (London 1967) is an important essay. Scientific applications of this may be judged through N. Calder, *Einstein's Universe* (London 1979), R.W. Clark's *Einstein* or – mathematically more demanding – Hermann Bondi, *Einstein and Common Sense* (New York 1980). Henri Poincaré's *La science et l'hypothèse* (Paris 1902) was a landmark in the reshaping of twentieth-century physics.

A great deal of this reshaping occurred in central Europe, particularly in Vienna; and Vienna occupies an essential place in other subjects as well. There is no single book that comes to terms with this: perhaps the task is too demanding. The most recent effort, a series of essays, is Carl Schorske, *Fin-de-Siècle Vienna* (London 1980). W. Johnson, *The Austrian Mind* (Chicago 1972) starts off boldly (with a good bibliography of works on the Jewish side) and becomes a list. Frank Field, *Karl Kraus and his Vienna* (London 1967) and A. Janik and Stephen Toulmin, *Wittgenstein's Vienna* (New York 1973) are ambitious and successful. The artistic component is well surveyed by Nicholas Powell, *The Sacred Spring* (London 1978) and by P. Vergo, *Art in Vienna 1898–1918* (London 1975).

Works on various cultural subjects make up an enormous list. A few of these works are: L. Mumford, *Art and Technics* (New York 1952) which investigates the relationship of architecture and aesthetics (Mumford wrote penetratingly elsewhere on the development of the City). N. Pevsner, *Pioneers of the Modern Movement* (London 1936) can be usefully complemented by J. Joedicke, *A History of Modern Architecture* (London 1959) and by C. Jencks, *Modern Movements in Architecture* (Penguin 1977).

Changes in art are chronicled in J. Rewald, *The History of Impressionism* (London 1946); N. Lynton, *The Story of Modern Art* (London 1980); H. Read, *A Concise History of Modern Painting* (London 1959); G. Howard Hamilton, *Painting and Sculpture in Europe 1880–1940* (Harmondsworth 1967) and Bob Hughes, *The Shock of the New* (London 1980). The catalogue of the National Gallery's *Post-Impressionism* (1980) was very valuable. W. Hofmann, *Turning-Points in Twentieth-Century Art 1890–1917* is important; so is J. Golding, *Cubism. A History and an Analysis* (London 1959). There have been many studies of the Russian aspect of this. It is splendidly outlined by Camilla Gray, *The Russian Experiment in Art 1863–1922* (London 1962).

Of countless works on modern music (of which the new Grove and the *Oxford History of Music* give lists) two 'turning-points' have recently been surveyed in P. Burbridge and R. Sutton (eds.), *The Wagner Companion* (London 1979) with the authoritative new biography by C. von Westernhagen, *Wagner* (Cambridge 1978); cf. E.W. White, *Stravinsky: the Composer and his Works* (London 1979); to be read together with Stravinsky's own *Autobiography* (London 1975). C. Rosen, *Schönberg* (London 1976) updates E. Wellesz's *Arnold Schönberg*, published in Vienna in 1925, but translated (London 1972).

Important works of literature are far too numerous to be listed here. The twentieth-century approach, at least in central Europe, is surveyed very ably by M. Jay, *The Dialectical Imagination* (London 1973). The Fontana and Oxford 'Modern Masters' and 'Past Masters' series are performing a very useful translation. Two books, above all, make up an important background: Thomas Mann's *Magic Mountain* states the dilemmas of the age; Marcel Proust's *Remembrance of Things Past*, excellently retranslated by Terence Kilmartin (London 1981) states the impossibility of doing anything about them.

INDEX

This index does not include most proper names cited only once in the text.